Transformational Relationships

Transformational Relationships

DECIPHERING THE SOCIAL MATRIX IN PSYCHOTHERAPY

Dan
Short

ZEIG, TUCKER & THEISEN
Phoenix   Arizona

Library of Congress Cataloging-in-Publication Data

Transformational relationships: deciphering the social matrix in psychotherapy.
/ Dan Short. — 1st edition.

p.   cm.

Includes bibliographic references and index.
ISBN   978-1-934442-40-1 (alk. paper)
1. Counseling— mental health   2. Family—Psychological aspects.
I. Short, Dan   II. Title

RC480.55.B77. 2010
616.89'14—dc21

Published by

ZEIG, TUCKER & THEISEN, INC.
3618 North 24th Street
Phoenix, AZ 85016

Manufactured in the United States of America

This book is dedicated to all those willing to step into the life of another as a caring companion during life's journey.

I would also like to express special appreciation to Roxanna Erickson Klein, who provided invaluable feedback on earlier versions of my writing.

CONTENTS

Preface .... *ix*

Introduction
*Science and History Have Taught that Relationships Are at the Core
of Healing and Transformation* *1*

PART I
PRINCIPLES OF COMPATIBILITY:
Flexibility in Unspoken Elements of Relating
Is Necessary for Professional Care

Chapter 1/Verification:
*Verification of Personal Understandings, on Critical Issues, Makes
Interactions Less Threatening* 27

Chapter 2/Affect Attunement:
*Affect Attunement Helps Increase the Felt Connection With
One's Self and Others* 65

Chapter 3/Reciprocity:
Sustainable Relationships Require Equanimity 85

Chapter 4/Attachment:
Having a Safe Haven in Times of Stress Helps Increase Coping 97

Chapter 5/Structure:
Social Hierarchies Act as Conduits for the Flow of Shared Resources 147

PART II
STANDARDS OF THERAPEUTIC RELATING:
Therapeutic Relationships Are Defined by Supportive Experiences Not Readily Available (or Recognizable) in Childhood or General Society

Chapter 6/
Transformational Relationships Promote Awareness of Internal Experiences and Needs 209

Chapter 7/
Transformational Relationships Encourage a Stable and Generally Positive Self-Concept 225

Chapter 8/
Transformational Relationships Foster Autonomy Rather Than Dependence 281

Conclusion:
Psychotherapy Is Primarily a Relationship Between Two People 302

Appendix A 313

Appendix B 314

Appendix C 315

List of Case Examples 316

References 319

Index 361

PREFACE

Having witnessed up close the destructive power of unhealthy relationships, I grew up wondering, "What do you do so that others are better off for having known you?" Answering this question is the impetus behind my desire to understand the interpersonal dynamics of health and happiness and the reason I wrote this book for therapists and other professional care providers. My in-depth study of this topic has, in many ways, transformed my experience of others and myself. I wish no less for you, the reader.

Because a central premise of the book is that relationships facilitate growth and learning, I have decided to share my formational life experiences in as open and transparent a manner as possible. Intertwined within my story are hundreds of factual events that occurred in the lives of others, the majority of these narratives coming from my casework.[1] Offering more than an interesting read, these stories help us to see beyond the confines of our own biases and established ideologies. As has been demonstrated throughout history, stories are an important part of any teaching endeavor, because their lessons, emotional meaning, and inspiration are timeless. I hope that while browsing the pages of this book, the reader will catch glimpses of his or her own life experience. This type of reflective association enables one to transcend ordinary experience by observing, as an outsider, familiar thoughts and actions.

Because it is important to distinguish general truth from coincidence and personal fiction, the main points presented in this book have been derived from multiple independent sources of information. These ideas were further scrutinized by reviewing the modern science of relationships, with evidence drawn from an extensive gathering of journal articles, as well as books in clinical psychology, cultural anthropology, social psychology, and history. This synthesis of diverse bodies of study helps address the extraordinarily complex experience of human relations, while making a strong ar-

---

[1] Because confidentiality is essential to clinical practice, all names and identifying information have been omitted.

gument for the transformational power of relationships. As mentioned above, this large body of academic knowledge is combined with my own experiences with clients and significant others. It is these first-hand accounts that illuminate the fundamental principles outlined in this book. For the few minor points that I felt worthy of consideration, but which I could not substantiate with published research, I have qualified the information with statements such as, "My experience has been . . ." In this way, the reader is able to separate well-established models of thought from speculation based on one person's interpretation of events.

While seeking to avoid the use of complex technical jargon or restrictive theoretical frameworks, I found it difficult to eliminate all theorizing. Without the use of any intellectual constructs, there would be nothing more than a disorganized collection of narratives from which the reader would be forced to draw all of his or her own conclusions. Rather than taking this sort of Zen approach, I have attempted to integrate multiple academic perspectives, weaving them together to create an organized view of relationships in healing. As Goldfried (1999) argues, psychotherapy integration encourages clinicians to not place limits on their thought processes or applied work by ascribing to only one theoretical orientation. Accordingly, this text reviews the key contributions of individuals across multiple schools of thought and relevant research produced through a variety of disciplines. Lazarus (1977) eloquently characterized this type of approach when he wrote, "I am opposed to the advancement of psychoanalysis, to the advancement of Gestalt therapy, to the advancement of existential therapy, to the advancement of behavior therapy, or to the advancement of any delimited school of thought. I would like to see an advancement in psychological knowledge, an advancement in the understanding of human interaction, in the alleviation of suffering, in the knowledge of therapeutic intervention" (p. 553).

For these reasons, this book does not seek to indoctrinate the reader with yet another school of therapy. Similarly, the book does not offer an in-depth study of psychodiagnostics. While I have no argument against the classification of disease, the practice of grouping certain distressed individuals so that they can be linked with a particular form of psychological treatment does not fit with the aim of this book. Instead, the book's content has been structured according to scientifically developed categories of social experience, which account for a large portion of human relations. This structure provides an organized examination of specific interpersonal dynamics that yield predictable emotional and behavioral phenomena. The shortcoming of my approach is that it does not fully account for behaviors seen in individuals whose biological systems are radically altered, such as those with autism or brain trauma. However, that limitation does not make the material found in this book any less relevant for work with such persons, since even the most disordered individual still remains more human than not.

Through the medium of print, one can experience a powerful connection to the thoughts and feelings of others. Reading is also a creative task with multiple possibilities for expanding one's worldview. My personal preference for reading informative material is to keep a pen in hand so that I can jot down notes in the margins as I explore the unfolding associations racing through my mind. I believe reading should be an interactive experience. Therefore, it is important to recognize that this text can be read in different ways and for different purposes.

While seeking to bridge the science-practice gap, I found that two individual books were emerging: one that was emotionally stimulating and fun to read, and a second that was much more scholarly, but a slow and tedious exercise. After spending much time trying to combine these styles, I decided that, like oil and water, they just would not blend smoothly. For that reason, the main body of the text is dedicated to narration, exposition, and analogy, while the science underlying these ideas is more fully documented in the footnotes. The result is a multilayered nest of information.

A good first step for readers is to read swiftly through the main body of the text, allowing oneself to become absorbed in the narrative while more or less ignoring subtitles and footnotes. After this initial reading, greater intellectual stimulation can be achieved by skimming through the main text while more carefully studying the footnotes. In this way, the subtle nuances and complexities of the information are better appreciated. Then, when the reader is ready to return for a review, the chapter titles and subtitles can be studied alone. Each title is designed to fully represent the central theme of the subsequent text, thereby chunking all of the information so that it can be considered as a gestalt (similar to studying a city from a mountaintop, as opposed to standing in its streets). The book's content has been arranged using traditional literary methods, in which major points are deconstructed in increasingly finer detail. However, the information also spirals such that concepts in Part I are revisited in Part II while framed from a slightly different angle. This arrangement is meant to help the reader absorb the ideas at a deeper level of abstraction, thereby increasing retention and recall, as well as readiness for general application.

Following years of careful research review, in vivo experimentation, and deep self-reflection, I have attempted to condense my most valuable discoveries into a relatively small package. Much of my life has been dedicated to better understanding the special type of connection that occurs with one person at a time. Therefore, if I succeed in sharing with a single reader the transformational insights that come from an appreciation of one's own relational needs and the needs of those who pass through his or her life, then I will feel deeply gratified.

As stated in the ancient writings of the Tao Te Ching, "To understand others is wisdom. To understand one's self is enlightenment." My hope is that the reader achieves both while exploring the pages of this book.

INTRODUCTION

Science and History Have Taught that Relationships Are at the Core of Healing and Transformation

Psychotherapy is primarily a relationship between two people.
—Thomas Szasz, 2005

For every occupation, there are certain trade secrets a professional must know in order to work competently. In the field of psychotherapy, it is the secret of transformational relationships that separates the novice from the expert. However, since profound learning tends to follow on the heels of uncertainty, this book begins in a place of disequilibrium, with a troublesome question that set the path for my own professional development.

I was a 19-year-old, far from home and descending a cold, concrete stairway in the depths of the London underground. It was late at night, and the dimly lit tunnel seemed strangely deserted. Hearing a noise, I glanced over my shoulder to see a woman struggling with a large baby carriage. She looked exhausted as she strained against the drop of each step, trying to keep the baby from waking. Observing the length of the stairway, I thought to myself, "At this rate it's going to take her forever to get to the bottom of the stairs." However, my friend who was traveling with me saw her and rushed back up the stairs to offer his assistance. A look of relief swept over her face, and together they carried the large buggy down, leaving me standing on what felt like the outer edges of humanity.

I was stupefied by a single question, "Why did it not occur to me to offer this woman help?"

It was not the first time I had felt horribly disconnected from others, but because I would remain riveted by the question, it marked the beginning of a special journey. The meaning and significance of distress endured by others became a point of reference as I sought to find my way into adulthood.

I had stopped attending college classes after only three semesters because I lacked a vision for what I would do with the rest of my life. My best friend of nearly ten years was equally undecided about his future, so he agreed to quit classes as well and travel with me across Europe. A few days after the event in the subway, I became separated from my friend and spent the next two months traveling alone, without a guidebook and with hardly any money. Ironically, it was a series of unfortunate events that allowed me to discover something very important about people and the formation of relationships. By the end of the three-month odyssey, I knew without a doubt that I wanted to return to college and pursue a career as a psychologist.

Looking back, I view this journey as my rite of passage during which I decided to dedicate my life to helping others. I believe that the desire to alleviate suffering in others is the essence of humanity. Failure to act during a moment of human tragedy can haunt a person. Before my transformational process, it was as if I were an apparition drifting among a world of heroes and heroines, none of which I could touch. Then I had my insight, "There are small things that I can do that really do matter to others." The general relevance of this belief will be explained in greater detail throughout the pages of this book. Right now it is important to recognize that while a desire to help others is a natural behavior,[2] individuals sometimes fail to act simply because they do not know what to do or what to say. *As soon as a person learns the secrets of relationships and the relative ease by which another person's life can be transformed, acts of altruism are no more difficult than the performance of any other valued skill.*

In a little over 100 years of practice and scientific development, the concept of providing psychological care has grown into an immense body of knowledge with thousands of diverse theories about what to do while seeking to help others. In order to make sense of it all, it is helpful to take a step back and recognize the evolutionary trend seen across all theories of therapeutic change. At this time, it is difficult to find a school of psychotherapy that has not developed an increasing appreciation for the role of relationship in transforming individuals. Starting with Sigmund Freud, there has been a recognition of the importance of early childhood relationships in healthy functioning as adults. In early writings, Freud (1913) described the importance of cooperative engagement between client and therapist in terms of "positive transference."[3] However, it was Carl Rogers (1942) who popularized the idea that the client-therapist relationship

---

[2] A number of studies have demonstrated that children as young as 18 months of age show innate tendencies towards altruistic behavior (e.g., Warneken, Chen, & Tomasello, 2006; Warneken & Tomasello, 2007).

[3] The concept of therapeutic alliance has since been elaborated on by generations of analytic theorists who believe a sense of therapist–client collaboration is fundamental to progress (e.g., Bordin, 1979; Greenson, 1965).

played a central role in producing change. Rogers (1951) believed that the therapist's stances of empathy, positive regard, and genuineness toward the patient were the essential therapeutic conditions for change.

Roger's writings lead to a shift across the field. Cognitive behaviorists began to recognize the importance of a good client-therapist relationship in order to implement technical interventions,[4] and psychoanalysts began to view immediate relational factors as a core component in the therapeutic process.[5] However, it was Milton Erickson (1934) who led the way in demonstrating the importance of flexible, collaborative relationships that are strategically tailored to the needs of the individual client. While describing his work, Erickson put it this way:

> I don't attempt to structure my psychotherapy except in a vague, general way. And in that vague, general way, the patient structures it . . . in accordance with his own needs. . . . The first consideration in dealing with patients is to realize that each of them is an individual. . . . So in dealing with people, you try not to fit them into your concept of what they should be. . . . You should try to discover what their concept of themselves happens to be. . . . It isn't the amount of time. It isn't the theory of therapy. It's how you reach the personality . . . .[6]

In other words, the appropriate response for a given situation is not found in the pages of a technical manual or in the mind of the therapist, but rather, it resides in the ever-evolving relational context.

Among researchers, there is little doubt that the quality of the relationship between therapist and client is the major determinant of psychotherapeutic effectiveness.[7] A strong working alliance between therapist and client yields both short-term and long-term benefits[8] and might even serve as a primary motivation for continued therapy.[9] After all, some form of in-

---

[4] Aaron Beck (1995) was a particularly strong voice in this movement.

[5] Mitchell and Aron (1999) describe the shift in the analytic perspective.

[6] To achieve this type of flexibility, Erickson argued that one should not plan in advance what sort of thinking he or she will do. Rather, he believed it was important to trust fluid, unconscious processes of reason and observation (Zeig, 1985, p. 120).

[7] This remains the case even when controlling for technique, theoretical perspective, and client population (Ackerman et. al., 2001; Constantino et al., 2002; Henry, 1998; Horvath & Greenberg, 1994; Horvath & Luborsky, 1993; Saunders et. al, 1989).

[8] A positive therapeutic alliance contributes to symptom reduction and positive treatment outcomes (Horvath & Greenberg, 1986; Horvath & Symonds, 1991).

[9] A weakened alliance greatly increases the probability of unilateral termination by the client (Muran et al., 1995; Safran & Wallner, 1991; Samstag et al., 1998; Tyron & Kane, 1990, 1993, 1995).

terpersonal connection is necessary for all types of therapy.[10] However, because improvement occurs regardless of technique or school of therapy, it seems that the therapy relationship is more than a staging ground for therapeutic technique.[11] Relationship appears to be the primary factor in successful psychotherapy.[12]

Another important consideration for those who want to learn how to provide psychological care is the futility that emerges when one becomes overly fixated on the application of theory and technique. Unfortunately, this sort of tunnel vision is often demanded of students during a typical graduate education. Many will identify with my story of graduate training because I have heard it repeated by numerous students from a variety of universities.

Halfway through my first graduate program, I was told to pick a theory of psychotherapy and make an exhaustive study of its particular set of techniques. Other students warned me that if I wanted to make a good grade, I would need to pick the Adlerian approach, because the faculty believed it was the approach that was most respectful of individual equality and right to choice. However, I choose the "eclectic" approach, so that I could have the freedom to use all that I had studied in textbooks and all that I had experienced during a lifetime of learning. My choice was rejected, and I was told to choose something that represented a unified theory of change. So next, I choose the Ericksonian approach, again because of the flexibility it offered. However, my instructors did not like this choice either, and I was again told to select something else. Frustrated with what I interpreted as hypocrisy, my resistance hardened. Following a private meeting during which the lead professor explained all of the reasons why he would like to see me select the Adlerian model of therapy, I chose Gestalt therapy. Although I had previously received A's in all of my classes, in all subsequent practicum work, I would not receive a grade higher than a B.

External validation is nice, but it should never supersede foundational ideas about oneself and how the world operates, unless it is coupled with *very* compelling evidence. Because this graduate training program did not

---

[10] It has been argued that it is through this connection that therapy techniques exert their influence (Lambert & Barely, 2001; Saunders et. al., 1989).

[11] Meta-analytic studies have repeatedly shown that the working alliance is itself therapeutic, with a median effect size of .25, which means that the quality of the alliance accounts for a little over half of the beneficial effects of psychotherapy (Horvath, 2001; Martin, Garske, & Davis, 2000).

[12] Although researchers and other clinical experts do not yet fully agree on how or why this special type of relationship helps improve physical and emotional health, it is clear that it forms the foundation of the effort to provide psychological care for others (Bordin, 1979; Lambert & Barely, 2001; Whipple et. al., 2003).

produce that type of evidence, I continued my nonorthodox[13] approach to therapy. During my first year as a young professional, while attending a conference, I was approached by an accomplished psychologist who had been impressed by my demonstration of skills during role-play exercises. She wanted to know what model of therapy I was working from, to which I replied, "My own." She asked what I meant, and I explained, "I try to use everything I have learned. I try to do whatever seems to work at the moment." She commented that my approach was unusual, but later offered me the opportunity to interview for a position at the state hospital, working with the criminally insane. I could envision myself fitting well in that environment, but decided to continue my work at a domestic-violence agency. This agency gave me the freedom to work independently, and it enabled me to conduct outcome studies from my work with violent and abusive males.[14]

It is from this background that my refusal to commit to a single doctrine of change emerged and helped me remain open to the possibility that jargon and technique are not the defining elements of psychological care.[15] Unfortunately, it took another six years before I collected the literature I needed to argue my point convincingly. By contrast, in an incredibly insightful paper, Rosenzweig (1936) explained three-quarters of a century ago why among different therapies there will continue to be an overall equivalence of outcome. Rosenzweig characterized this phenomenon using a line from *Alice in Wonderland*, "At the last, the Dodo said, 'Everybody has won, and all must have prizes'" (p. 412). This view has been supported by modern research.[16] The futility of arguing for the superiority of a particular theory or technique has since come to be known as the "dodo verdict."[17]

---

[13] The reason why I use the term "nonorthodox," rather than "unorthodox," will be explained in the introduction to Section II.

[14] A system of data collection was set up so that I had outcome data from clients and their partners, collected by a third party. This feedback helped me know when my work was successful and when it was not.

[15] Accordingly, research has shown that the therapist's gender, type of academic degree, years of training, and theoretical orientation do not appear related to therapy outcomes (Berman & Norton, 1985; Okiishi et al., 2003; Okiishi et al., 2006).

[16] Since 1936, the failure of one or more therapies to produce superior results has routinely been found in meta-analytic studies and well-designed psychotherapy studies (Bergin & Lambert, 1978; Elkin et al., 1989; Lipsey & Wilson, 1993; Sloane et al., 1975; Smith, Glass, & Miller, 1980; Stiles, Shapiro, & Elliott, 1986; Wampold et al., 1997). Though a very small number of studies has demonstrated the superiority of one approach over another, the difference is no more than would be expected by chance occurrence (Wampold, 1997).

[17] If you have ever been called a dodo after arguing that your doctrine of change is superior to others, you now know why. It has been used as shorthand for the equivalence of outcomes since 1986, when the phrase first appeared in a paper by Stiles, Shapiro, & Elliott.

Although some therapists are clearly more skilled than others,[18] the differences in skill are not connected to theoretical orientation. Instead, as therapists become more experienced and proficient, greater similarity begins to appear in members of different therapeutic schools. In other words, with increased experience, a greater degree of commonality begins to emerge as jargon and technique give way to universal relational skills.

Like weeds obscuring the view of a garden, the number of psychotherapeutic approaches currently available through systematized programs of training continues to grow.[19] However, when considering the pivotal role of relationships, it might be more accurate to state that there are as many individual approaches to therapy as there are people willing to enter into a caring relationship. For this reason, it is important to approach clients with a curious mind rather than a mind closed off by protocols and therapeutic doctrine. There should be a readiness to allow clients to show the therapist what is needed to help them. Otherwise, the therapist will appear to be out of touch with the clients' strongly felt subjective needs, thus decreasing the clients' respect for the therapist and weakening the relationship. Along these same lines, researchers found that when therapists applied empirically validated techniques to meet manual requirements, there was an overall negative effect on clients. Strict adherence to techniques was unrelated to measures of competence.[20] Even broad facilitative formulas, such as those purposed by Carl Rogers, can be too limiting, as are any invariant set of fixed relationship conditions.[21]

---

[16] Since 1936, the failure of one or more therapies to produce superior results has routinely been found in meta-analytic studies and well-designed psychotherapy studies (Bergin & Lambert, 1978; Elkin et al., 1989; Lipsey & Wilson, 1993; Sloane et al., 1975; Smith, Glass, & Miller, 1980; Stiles, Shapiro, & Elliott, 1986; Wampold et al., 1997). Though a very small number of studies has demonstrated the superiority of one approach over another, the difference is no more than would be expected by chance occurrence (Wampold, 1997).

[17] If you have ever been called a dodo after arguing that your doctrine of change is superior to others, you now know why. It has been used as shorthand for the equivalence of outcomes since 1986, when the phrase first appeared in a paper by Stiles, Shapiro, & Elliott.

[18] The differences in skill can be seen in general outcomes and within the context of specialized work with a specific clientele (Lambert & Bergin, 1994; Lambert & Okiishi, 1997; Orlinsky & Howard, 1980).

[19] Since the 1960s, the number of recorded psychotherapy approaches has increased by approximately 600% (Miller et al., 1997).

[20] By contrast, therapists who deviated from manual guidelines in attempts to accommodate more difficult clients were rated as more proficient (Rounsaville et al., 1988).

[21] The idea that one can determine what is supportive and then provide this to at-risk individuals is too simplistic. Research suggest that supportiveness is much more complex, since the same individuals and behaviors are viewed differently by different persons (Lakey et al., 1996).

Academic theories of change, that lead to a one-size-fits-all therapy relationship, are not as useful as approaches that integrate information from a variety of sources leading to a therapy tailored to fit the client's unique needs and response capacity.[22] As argued by Frank and Frank (1991), therapists should be proficient with a wide variety of techniques and, therefore, able to select for each client the therapy that agrees with the client's personal characteristics and view of the problem. When one is able to set aside rigid ideas informed by orthodox theories of change, there is greater freedom for collaborative exploration with the client. When therapists do not feel they must function within a specific school of thought, their flexibility and ability to pursue different goals by varying means increases, thereby increasing the probability of providing the type of intervention that best suits the client.[23]

The first problem to address is how this type of approach can be taught in a systematic manner to students. And, of more immediate importance, how can this book offer new information without creating yet another academic theory of change? One of my favorite textbooks, from a college philosophy class, is titled *This Book Needs No Title*. It is an exploration of paradoxes. Although I do not wish to devise yet another doctrine of change, I recognize that reason demands explanation, whether constructed at an implicit or explicit level of awareness.[24] So rather than avoiding the question of why relationships are fundamental to change, I will sum up my theoretical position as a simple recognition of the human need for social connectedness.

Those who have fallen outside the sphere of human connectedness cease to thrive, sometimes resulting in tragic consequences, until they encounter someone who has a willingness and sufficient level of skill to reestablish the connection. The importance of relationships in all human affairs was eloquently described by Berscheid (1999), who said, "Relationships with other humans are both the foundation and the theme of the human condition: We are born into relationships, we live our lives in relationships with others, and when we die, the effects of our relationships survive in the lives of the living, reverberating throughout the tissue of their relationships. Relationships thus are the context in which most human behavior occurs, and so understanding and predicting that behavior is difficult, if not impossible, if that context is ignored" (p. 264).

Because people in every society on earth belong to small primary groups that involve face-to-face, personal interactions,[25] it makes little

---

[24] In other words, if you embrace a theory of therapy that argues against having a theory of change, at some level you are still constructing a theory of change.

[25] The grouping of individuals is considered to be an instinctual rather than cultural phenomenon (Mann, 1980).

sense to conceptualize psychological care as anything other than an interpersonal endeavor. Unfortunately, the ideology used to conceptualize the fundamental processes of psychotherapy have traditionally been based on mechanistic tasks performed on inanimate objects, such as a release of dammed-up libido energy (Freud, 1914), peeling an onion (Perls, 1970), or reprogramming thoughts (Ellis, 2000). The reductionistic nature of mechanistic models of change impedes interpersonal understandings. Ideally, organic models should be used to expand our grasp of key elements of human relations, such as a satisfied marriage or the bond connecting parent and child. Though these relationships are not identical to what occurs in therapy, they do serve as useful analogies that help us construct a multifaceted and systematic view of the relational dynamics found in transformational relationships.

Rather than focusing on how to perform a set of techniques, this book will describe how to develop a transformational relationship with clients. My goal is to share what I have come to recognize as my most important insights, all of which have been measured up against research produced by the scientific study of relationships in general and therapy outcomes in particular. These scientifically tested ideas will be used in conjunction with case examples to outline the core components of strong, stable therapy relationships. Since an increased understanding and appreciation for the uniqueness of others is a cornerstone of human relations, it would be counterproductive to recommend a step-by-step protocol for developing quality relationships. Rather, the aim of this book is to equip care providers with the knowledge needed to engage each client in a way that is different from all others before him or her. For a therapist to provide maximum benefit to a wide range of clients, he or she must be capable of fostering strong compatibility while working with many different types of people. This shift in emphasis, from the mastery of replicated techniques to an increased awareness of interpersonal dynamics, cultivates the type of spontaneity and flexibility needed for vibrant relationships with a variety of clients.

PART I

PRINCIPLES OF COMPATIBILITY

Flexibility in Unspoken Elements of Relating is Necessary for Professional Care

Everyone thinks of changing the world, but no one thinks
of changing himself.
—Leo Tolstoy[26]

When I was a teenager traveling across Europe, my first life lesson was that people who speak only one language have a more limited range of territory in which they can function than those who are multilingual. This point was brought home to me by a five-year-old French girl, who looked at me as if I were the stupidest person on earth because I could not understand even the smallest of French words. A Frenchman had been trying to help me as I did my best to mime a train leaving a train station, but he did not speak English. Fortunately, this bilingual child stepped in to help, giving me instructions to the train station using short, simple English terms. She seemed amused by the fact that two grown men could not solve a simple problem.

The same type of confusion can occur in therapy if the interpersonal dynamics of the therapist and client do not match. A good therapeutic relationship requires a strategic match in interpersonal dynamics, so that when the therapist intends to communicate caring, the client feels cared about; when the therapist empathizes with the client, the client feels understood; or when the therapist accepts the client, the client feels accepted.[27] Because

---

[26] Leo Nikolayevich Tolstoy (1828–1910) was a Russian moral thinker, novelist, and philosopher known for his influence on Russian literature and politics.

[27] This point has been argued by others (Goldfried, 2004).

the client is not expected to have the skill needed to adapt to the therapist's style of interaction, the therapist is the one who must be most flexible while building the relationship. *Therefore, the therapist should be the first to change during therapy.*

Relationships grow from more than words. Therefore, it is not only what is said, but also the unspoken elements of relating that are calibrated against the needs of the client.[28] Complex social interactions are built on numerous subtle events that communicate information about the nature of the relationship. At the start of the relationship, important decisions are made about voice tonality, posture, emotionality, who will speak first, and the ownership of material space. And unlike a marriage partner, who has to learn only one interpersonal style, a therapist must be prepared to engage in pluralistic styles with a multitude of different clients.

In summary, an advanced helping relationship is primarily character-ized by complex, contextually defined interactions. For example, if the therapist were to invite new clients to sit wherever they would like within the office, that invitation sets into play a certain situational dynamic. If the client responded by insisting that the therapist leave his or her chair at the desk so that the client can have that space, then a new dynamic would be set into motion. At that point, the therapist could accept the client's re-sponse, reject it, ignore it, analyze it asking a series of questions, and on and on. Each of these responses will have predictable consequences for the de-veloping relationship. In order to respond to these spoken and unspoken elements in a constructive manner, the therapist must be fluent in multiple styles of interpersonal interaction.

Professional Relationships Require Sensitivity to Interpersonal Differences and Flexibility in Responding to These Differences

Clients come to therapy with a limited set of interpersonal abilities and with different degrees of tolerance. A style of relating that is perfectly acceptable for one client may not be for another. Therefore, transforma-tional relationships require sensitivity to differences in clients and flexibil-ity in responding to those differences.[29] While most relationships formed within the general community can rely on standard social protocol (i.e.,

---

[28] Research has shown that even slight movements of an interaction partner's arm or of a facial muscle affect people's views of those partners (Argyle, 1988; DePaulo & Friedman, 1998).

[29] An individually responsive relationship is associated with positive outcomes in therapy (Ackerman et. al., 2001).

good manners), relationships in therapy require greater discernment. In choosing their actions, therapists need to be able to predict which responses to expect from the client, so that core personality traits and prominent situational factors can be used as building blocks upon which the therapy is constructed.

In step with Erickson's pioneering work, contemporary researchers now argue that the improvement of psychotherapy depends in large part on increasing one's ability to relate to clients and on tailoring the therapy relationship to individual clients.[30] Tailoring the relationship to each client demands a greater amount of flexibility on the part of the therapist and a willingness to change one's approach to fit the client's values, beliefs, and perceptions of what is most helpful, thereby creating a collaborative and dynamic interpersonal context.[31] This type of strategic relating is defined by the uniqueness of each encounter. From the beginning to the end of the encounter, the therapist carefully monitors the client's reactions to what is said or done. By contrast, someone who conducts therapy by following a scripted manual, or by routinely asking the same questions and giving the same answers, is not developing a dynamic or collaborative relationship.[32]

Skillful Assessment Is at the Core of the Individualized Approach

Skillful assessment is at the core of the individualized approach. The more that is known about a client, the better equipped the therapist is for the encounter. Each client brings to therapy a unique set of goals, abilities, and social needs,[33] all of which must be determined as quickly as possible. Yet this split-second assessment is not something to be completed during the first visit; rather, it remains an ongoing process in which feedback is obtained following every interaction. Those who do not routinely collect feedback are less likely to understand cause-and-effect dynamics operating

---

[30] When conditions of relating are adapted (or tailored) to specific client needs and characteristics, a positive therapeutic alliance is more likely to form, thus enhancing therapeutic outcomes (Ackerman et. al., 2001; Lambert & Barely, 2001).

[31] Numerous studies have shown that clients are most likely to experience a strong alliance with therapists who conduct themselves with openness and flexibility (e.g., Mohl et al., 1991; Priebe & Gruyters, 1993; Rounsaville et al., 1987; Tyrrell et al., 1999).

[32] Arguments for step-by-step protocols and manulized treatments seem to be based on the myth that clients labeled with a certain diagnostic criteria will all have uniform needs and uniform capabilities (Kiesler, 1966).

[33] This knowledge is important because individuals tend to construct relationships consistent with their psychological goals, cognitive abilities, and current social demands (Laursen & Bukowski, 1997, p. 748).

within the relationship.[34]

Furthermore, each experience with a client can serve as an opportunity for learning more about therapeutic relationships in general. This learning can be accomplished by simply asking questions such as, "What was the most helpful part of this session?" and "What was the most difficult part of this session?"[35] Thus, a fully individuated, attribute-by-attribute consideration of another person is essential to dynamic relations. It should be noted that this method of developing an individual awareness for each client is different than the more common practice of category-based diagnostic labeling, which comes with all of the hazards of stereotyping.[36]

Providers of professional care cannot create rich and dynamic relationships by relying on labels to determine the course of treatment.[37] It is not that categorical groupings, such as those found in the DSM, have no value. However, a special type of reasoning is needed for this tool to help therapists form an understanding of the individual. Rather than moving exclusively from specific behaviors to generalized understandings (i.e., using deductive reasoning to move from recognition of a symptom to a category of disorder), an individuated assessment moves in the opposite direction, from broad understandings and assumptions down to a recognition of the uniqueness of the individual (i.e., inductive reasoning).

Consider, for example, my case of a 17-year-old female who reluctantly entered therapy at the insistence of her parents. Collecting her history, I learned that at home she would argue explosively with her father over her boyfriend (who was serving time in prison for violent behavior), her sexual activities with older men, and her desire to smoke cigarettes. The adolescent's chief concern was that she did not want authority figures telling her what to do. This brings to mind the stereotype of someone who has an oppositional defiant disorder (ODD), and there are certain expectations that subtly influence the treatment of such a person.

---

[34] Researchers have concluded that a major source of poor clinical judgment comes from a lack of feedback, which makes it difficult for clinicians to learn from experience (Dawes, 1989; Garb & Schramke, 1996).

[35] I collect this information at the end of every appointment using a written sentence-stem technique. The exploratory exercise often produces insight because it tends to tap into preconscious knowledge. During the last five minutes of a meeting, as I do my notes, the client completes his or her notes. This qualitative feedback, along with numerical data on overall satisfaction, allows me to better understand the client's subjective experiences and the impact of my behavior. For a copy of the end of session form, see Appendix B.

[36] Problems with stereotyping include the inclusion of subtle prejudices and unsubstantiated assumptions based on group membership (Fiske & Neuberg, 1990).

[37] Evidence suggests that having the same diagnostic label is a poor indicator of how similar or different clients are from one another, especially when predicting the effects of treatment (Beutler & Malik, 2002).

However, more significant to the construction of my response to her was the fact that on the second visit, she was sitting in the waiting room with an energy drink tightly griped in her hand. Once inside the office, she sat the drink down on the floor, halfway hidden behind her purse. Midway into the session, she expressed her honest desire to do the right thing. I agreed with her and demonstrated my appreciation for her sincerity by congratulating her on having quit smoking. She stared at me momentarily with a look of disbelief and suspicion. She had not told me or anyone else about her decision to quit smoking. She then spontaneously began asking my advice on a series of important questions about her relationship with her incarcerated boyfriend. It was not until the very end of the session that she hesitatingly asked, "How did you know that I quit smoking?" to which I replied, "I assumed that the energy drink was a replacement for the nicotine." I further explained that the use of energy drinks was probably only a temporary measure, and she did not want to continue drinking them due to the effect it would have on her health. (I guessed the second part by the way she unconsciously hid the drink behind her purse.) With a look of amazement, she acknowledged that my assessment of her was correct. She left the encounter not only feeling affirmed in her accomplishments, but also certain that her therapist was taking careful note of who she was and what she was currently striving to accomplish.[38]

Merely assigning the DSM label of ODD[39] would not have led me to any of these understandings; however, it did help me know where we were starting and how my clients' general expectations of others might be characterized. Thus, relationally skilled therapists are poised to give clients permission to overcome their challenges in a way that best suits the clients' existing personality and skills. With this approach, clinical decision-making is guided more by an understanding of the client as a total person than by diagnostic labels.

While carefully studying an individual and then considering what has come to attention and why, one can have an impressive ability to make sense of nuance. For the casual observer, who does not recognize the logic

---

[38] As a matter of follow up, this adolescent returned for seven more sessions. Her parents were included in three of these and were then seen over a dozen times separately for consultation in how to repair their relationship with their daughter. She was successful in her attempt to quit smoking. She stopped sneaking out of her house during the night, and there were no more screaming matches between her and her father. Once her boyfriend was released from prison, she dated him for two months, but then decided he was not right for her. She chose to attend a college, and at this time, her grades are good. There have been no further complaints by her parents.

[39] This girl had a MMPI-A: 9-5 code type, which is consistent with the other data collected.

behind this method of assessment, it is as if some form of mind reading has taken place. Instead, this knowledge is really the product of skillful observation and carefully tested predictions.

For example, as a graduate student eager to sharpen my assessment skills, I decided to make some predictions while shopping at the mall. During a transaction at a clothing store, I looked carefully at the girl who was running the cash register and said, "You are a college student, aren't you?" She acknowledged that she was and went on with her work, unimpressed. After all, many college students work part time in retail. Both her age and choice of clothing (her clothing was a different style than that sold by the store, and she did not look as if she belonged there) suggested this was a temporary job and not her career. Next, I asked if she attended a particular university. Its location was near, and again my guess was correct.

However, it was the next question that startled her. I asked if she was majoring in chemistry. With a look of alarm and suspicion, she asked how I knew her major. I explained that it was the way she processed my credit card. She held the card perfectly horizontal both before and after the swipe. The positioning of her wrist above her fingers was the same used by chemists who have been trained not to tip test tubes while moving them around. I remembered being taught the method while taking chemistry in high school.

This is an example of deductive reasoning in which an individual was correctly categorized.[40] Had this girl been a client seeking therapy, the next step would have been to apply inductive reasoning to determine what sets her apart from any other female college student at this university. When using this reverse method (i.e., moving from group properties to individual traits), broad generalizations act as a backdrop against which personal experience is ferreted out. It is at this point of human uniqueness that the process of transformation really progresses. A relational perspective celebrates the uniqueness of each individual, rather than relying on a mechanistic, pigeonhole approach to therapy.

While studying individuals, all ideas about a particular person should be treated as working hypotheses to be tested and either confirmed or thrown out. If a key behavior, such as passive-aggressive hostility, seems evident, then the therapist should provide an opportunity for a passive-aggressive response and see if that response is given. To ensure an even higher standard of nonbiased conclusions, one should apply the rule of three: If a behavior occurs once, it means nothing. If it occurs twice, it could

---

[40] There have been many instances during my learning in which my initial hypotheses proved incorrect. That is why it is important to test these types of assumptions.

be a coincidence. However, if it occurs three times, then there is reason to suspect a psychological pattern.

A Changing Social Environment Requires Dynamic and Flexible Relating

Because the client's social environment is often in a state of transition, sensitivity to individual differences and flexibility of response remains an ongoing task.[41] This means that the relationship between client and therapist will not be the same from session to session, perhaps changing within the space of a single encounter. Relationships are dynamic in terms of not only the activity conducted within, but also changes in the nature of the relationship. Flexibility is, therefore, required not just from person to person, but also from moment to moment.

Individuals are so strongly influenced by interpersonal dynamics that emotional, cognitive, and behavioral systems can alter with the changing social environment. In contrast to trait theory, transformational reasoning does not attribute behaviors and emotions to unchanging personality factors. Not only is this reasoning self-contradictory (i.e., how are you going to use relationship to transform individuals if you believe their behavior is determined primarily by unchanging traits?), but science has also shown that this way of viewing behavior is more often wrong than right. Social scientists Miller and Norman (1975) were the first to call attention to what is now commonly accepted as the "fundamental attribution error." This is the tendency of people to underestimate the situational causes of another's behavior and overestimate the extent to which that behavior reflects personality factors.

When interpersonal interactions do not go well, the tendency is to blame the personality of the other individual.[42] For example, an unhappy spouse might claim his or her partner is too selfish, while an unhappy therapist might claim that the client is too resistant. Few bother to analyze the relationship as a set of evolving dynamics in which nonproductive interaction strategies can be replaced by other more successful strategies.

As stated above, a person's relational needs can change from moment to moment. A client who needs to feel dominant during the first few moments of therapy may not have the same need later in the same session. This

---

[41] In contrast to the physical world, which remains relatively constant and predictable, the social environment is far more ambiguous, fluid, and unpredictable (Reis, Collins & Berscheid, 2000).

[42] This type of distortion in the attribution process has been found to impact clinical judgment (Ross, 1977).

fluctuation can be compared to the need to consume food before and after a large steak dinner. The meal obviously has an impact on the innate drive to consume food. And the same is true for each of the interpersonal operations described in this text.

So if the requirements of the helping relationship vary not only from person to person but also with time and circumstance, then determining how to relate remains an ongoing task. Much like a skillful dancer, the therapist takes the lead in moving to accommodate the relational style of the client and, with a watchful eye, maneuvers the pair around any obstacles to the collaborative relationship. For outpatient therapy, the relationship is voluntary, and, therefore, its sustainability depends on the capacity of one or both individuals to adapt to the evolving interpersonal matrix.

Complementarity Is a Key to Sustainable Relationships

In the early part of the twentieth century, the celebrated anthropologist Gregory Bateson (1936–1958) introduced the concept of complementarity in his studies on the interaction patterns of various cultures. He believed status, or authority, was a defining variable in human interaction and postulated two types of interactions: complementary and symmetrical. Complementary interactions occurred under conditions of unequal status, and symmetrical interactions occurred between individuals of equal status. Bateson believed both leaders and followers are required to maintain functional interactions, thereby making complementarity the basis of an orderly and productive society. Since that time, complementarity has been used to describe the agreement between individuals on how each is to act with respect to each other.[43] As such, complementarity is a key concept in understanding sustainable relationships.

To better understand complementarity, one must recognize that all communication between individuals carries information to be understood at the content level (i.e., what is said) and at the relational level (i.e., how the other is to respond). For a relationship to form there must be some evidence of mutual understanding at the relational level.[44] In fact, people are more comfortable and like one another more when their relationships are characterized by complementarity.[45] These interactions not only create a

---

[43] Or more formally defined as the fit of sequential behaviors at the relational level of communication (Tracey, 1993).

[44] It is complementary interactions that provide partners with felt evidence of a relational fit (Dryer & Horowitz, 1997; Tracey, 1993; Tracey, Ryan, & Jaschik-Herman, 2001).

[45] This is in contrast to symmetrical interactions in which both participants seek to use parallel postures (Dryer & Horowitz, 1997; Tiedens & Fragale, 2003).

more comfortable fit between individuals but also shape the behavior of the participants in predictable ways. For example, submissive actions provoke dominant responses, and dominant actions provoke submissive responses.[46]

As long as two individuals are trying to determine how to feel comfortable with each other, relationship negotiation remains a continuing, covert process.[47] The ease by which mutually affirming roles are negotiated greatly influences the longevity of relationships.[48] With complementary interactions there is agreement and, therefore, greater relationship harmony and confirmation of self-other concepts.[49] By contrast, noncomplementary interactions are more likely to interfere with the flow of interpersonal resources.[50]

Applying this study to therapy relationships helps illuminate subtle processes that ultimately determine the success of the relationship.[51] For example, a mother contacted me by phone to request that I work with her 18-year-old daughter. The girl had been diagnosed bipolar following three years of violent acting out mixed with severe depressive episodes, the last resulting in a frightening and bloody suicide attempt. After I agreed to see her daughter, the mother further explained that her daughter did not want to come to therapy. She had told her mother that her intention was to sit in the therapy office without speaking. I assured the mother this arrangement would work fine with my therapy approach.

When the unhappy girl arrived at my office, I pointed to a large chair and told her to make herself comfortable, which she did by sprawling out with her arms and legs set at perpendicular angles. She had pierced jewelry embedded into her forearm and long fringe dangling from her hippy-style leather boots. She fixed her gaze on me and proclaimed that she had no desire to talk to a therapist. I told her that her mother had already explained this to me and that because I honestly enjoy listening to myself talk, I was

---

[46] The theory of complementarity is now backed by a substantial body of research (Dryer & Horowitz, 1997; Estroff & Nowicki, 1992; Horowitz et al., 1991; Markey, Funder, & Ozer, 2003; Sadler & Woody, 2003; Strong et al., 1988; Tiedens & Fragale, 2003; Tracey, 1994).

[47] The comfort and satisfaction produced by complementary interactions leads individuals to automatically and often inadvertently seek complementary responses from others (Andrews, 1990; Carson, 1969; Kiesler, 1983; Sullivan, 1953; Tracey, 1993; Wiggins, 1982).

[48] The importance of a comfortable fit at the beginning stages of therapy is outlined in the interpersonal stage model of the therapeutic process (Tracey, 1993).

[49] This has proved to be relevant for traditional therapies, such as cognitive–behavioral therapy, in addition to therapies based on a relational model (Tracey, Sherry & Albright, 1999).

[50] Noncomplementary interactions tend to impede joint productivity and produce dissatisfaction with interactions (Estroff & Nowicki, 1992; Horowitz et al., 1991; Kiesler, 1983; Sullivan, 1953.

[51] Complementarity focuses on the "how" of the relationship, not the "what" of therapy (Tracey, Sherry & Albright, 1999).

happy to do all the talking. I then positioned my chair next to hers, facing the same direction, so that my voice did not come *at* her but instead emanated from a position *alongside* her. (I did not want to remain in the spot where she was expecting her "enemy" to be.) I explained that this new position would allow me to speak more softly and that she could listen with her eyes open or closed. As I softened my voice and talked about the goodness of her mind and the goodness of meditation and rest for the soul, she responded by closing her eyes and listening in a relaxed state for approximately 30 minutes. The fact that she did not wish to speak coupled with the fact that I was happy to speak (while she sat and listened) is obviously complementary.

However, the more subtle fit was her rebellious, but submissive, posture coupled with my accepting, but dominant posture. She put herself in a position of listening without comment, which is a submissive behavior. She was also sitting in a chair that I had selected for her to sit in. I responded to her compliance by telling her how to think about her mind and body, which is of course a dominant behavior. Following this ego-strengthening exercise, she asked my advice on some issues, and I gave her my opinion. For the therapy to begin and end well, I had to be the first to change as I sought to negotiate a complementary relationship.[52]

Complementarity Should Be Established Within the First Few Moments of Contact

Complementarity, a felt harmony with the client, should be established within the first few moments of contact. While it has been shown that people develop favorable views for those with whom they voluntarily spend time,[53] such a voluntary commitment to therapy is less likely if the client is unsatisfied with the initial contact.[54] The first moments of contact are crucial, because this is when the client is most intensely conducting his own assessment of the therapist. This instinctual sizing up of others occurs without intention and even without the conscious perception of what is being evaluated.[55] Clients need to answer the basic question; "Will this person provide the help I

---

[52] Complementarity of behavior in therapy has been repeatedly demonstrated to impact therapeutic outcomes (Carson, 1969; Kiesler, 1996; Tracey, 2002).

[53] This is true even if these others were previously disliked (Wilder & Thompson, 1980).

[54] Research indicates that satisfaction with the intake interview is the best predictor of return for more counseling (Kokotovic & Tracey, 1987; Larsen et. al., 1979).

[55] Conscious deliberation is not necessary for clients to quickly and effortlessly appraise the therapist for signs of potential threat and benefit (Bargh, Chaiken, Govender, & Pratto, 1992; Fazio, 1989; 2001; Greenwald, McGhee, & Schwarz, 1998; Roskos-Ewoldsen & Fazio, 1992).

need?" while also determining the safety of the total situation. Threats associated with therapy include the possibility that the therapist might be rejecting or somehow make the client feel worse about him- or herself, or the threat of exploitive manipulation once the client has dropped his or her defenses. More than just being aware of the client's appraisal, a skillful therapist increases the familiarity by which the relationship is experienced. This allows clients to develop trust rapidly. When it has been achieved, the goodness of the fit is often reflected in comments made by clients, such as, "It is as if I have known you all my life" or "I can't believe how comfortable I feel talking to you."

When meeting others, people seek familiar reactions to their behavior and use this social feedback to confirm their ideas of their self[56] and others. This confirmation unconsciously informs them of what to expect from the relationship.[57] When the initial level of complementarity is high, there is a rapid establishment of rapport.[58] This rapport will sometimes arise easily and automatically, when there is a natural fit between the therapist and client's interpersonal style. In other instances, it is the therapist's adaptation to the client's relational model that yields a high level of complementarity. Without this type of adaptive skill on the part of the therapist, the relationship is less likely to develop and move forward.[59]

As much as one may wish to believe in second chances, when dealing with fragile or otherwise wounded individuals, it is imperative to get the relationship right from the start.[60] It is the beginning point that determines the pattern or rhythm associated with an ongoing relationship. Moreover, it is during the first few minutes of the first therapy session that roles are defined and relational dynamics are catalyzed. Once established, these patterns of interaction become self-reinforcing and are, therefore, difficult to alter.[61] As folk wisdom teaches that the first impression is most important, research has shown that client expectancies for the relationship are the best predictor of therapeutic alliance after the first session.[62]

---

[56] The term "self" is used to describe a reflexive awareness of one's own behavior, thoughts, and feelings (Wolfe, 2003).

[57] Evidence for this is found in the literature on self-verification (Swann, 1983, 1987).

[58] On average, it can be expected that during a skillful exchange complementarity will clearly emerge within the first twenty minutes of the first encounter (Sadler & Woody, 2003).

[59] Outcome research has shown that the failure to achieve initial high levels of complementarity is related to the premature termination of therapy (Tracey, 1986).

[60] Research suggests that a therapeutic alliance, as experienced by the client, must be established early in treatment to obtain a successful psychotherapeutic outcome (Gelso & Carter, 1985).

[61] Complementarity has been shown to act as a stabilizing force on interaction patterns (Tiedens & Jimenez, 2003).

[62] This has been found to be true over and above therapist variables, client adjustment, and type of symptoms (Rizvi, Reynolds, Comtois, & Linehan, 2000).

Clients Typically Lack Interpersonal Flexibility

It is reasonable for new clients to be concerned about what will occur in therapy and how each person is to act. For reasonably well-adjusted individuals, much of this initial negotiation is governed by social norms, and the client easily follows the constraints of polite behavior. Well-adjusted individuals are responsive to both the demands of social situations and the latent interpersonal demands of those with whom they are interacting. However, this type of individual is also less likely to require help from a therapist.[63]

In fact, most of those seeking help from a therapist lack important social competencies, including the ability to exercise flexibility while relating to others. In some cases, the individual may react negatively as the therapist seeks to perform his duties and responsibilities.[64] As an example of how violent the response can be, I was put in the position of needing to conduct an IQ test with a seven-year-old boy who was highly intolerant of pressure to perform. After entering my office and being told by his father to sit down, the boy approached my desk and used both arms to swipe all of the testing materials to the ground. So I sat back in my chair and watched as his father verbally scolded him, again demanding that he cooperate with the testing. The boy responded by throwing one of my computer speakers against the wall, and then he switched to pulling books from my shelf to the ground. Still sitting in a relaxed position in my chair, I motioned to the father, indicating that it was his responsibility to take charge of the child. Thus, it was the father that was bit on the leg, spit upon, and hit in the face. This gave me some time to determine how to adapt the clinical process in a way that suited this client's needs. Though interpersonal inflexibility is common with individuals who come to therapy,[65] it is rarely taken into account when defining the processes and procedures of therapy.

When dealing with moderately maladjusted individuals, there should be an understanding that clients may not be able to adjust their behavior to fit the interpersonal style of the therapist. Therefore, it is the therapist who

---

[63] There is a positive relationship between interpersonal flexibility and overall adjustment (Paulhus & Martin, 1988).

[64] While more adaptive people are capable of defining themselves as submissive in some contexts and dominant in others, less adjusted individuals emotionally overreact to behavioral constraints communicated by others (Gurtman, 1992).

[65] Pathological inflexibility is most likely to be encountered when dealing who those who have histories of severe family dysfunction or sexual abuse (Hadley, Holloway, & Mallinckrodt, 1993; Mallinckrodt, McCreary, & Robertson, 1995).

makes these adjustments. When dealing with severely disturbed individuals, one should expect beliefs and behavior that are at odds with the norms set by general society. Therefore, it is the therapist who crosses over into the client's worldview, rather than expecting such flexibility from the client. For a therapist to form a working alliance, he or she needs to possess above-average interpersonal skills. With enough flexibility, the therapist will be able to form a connection with individuals with whom others find it impossible to start a relationship. To finish the story I started, I was able to conduct the testing I needed with the child described above. Once he had exhausted much of his energy on his father, I engaged him in a makeshift game that he enjoyed (i.e., tossing my business cards, one at a time, across the room). During the game, he was required to wait for my signals and to toss the card in the direction that I indicated. Once I had him used to following my lead, I introduced new "games" using items from the test kit.[66]

Providers of psychological care need to encourage clients to communicate and bond in the way the clients know, regardless of how deficient their social skills are. Following an in-depth study of Milton Erickson's relational strategies, I learned to take pressure off clients by explaining that it is up to me to figure out how to work with their handicaps. I would say to them, "It is perfectly alright for you to communicate with me in the way you know how." As one learns to attend to latent, individual styles of communication, it becomes easier to identify the client's personality resources while remaining sensitive to areas of intense vulnerability. Interacting with a severely disturbed individual can be like walking in a minefield. In order to avoid igniting unnecessary resistance and breaks in the relationship it is important to identify areas of intense sensitivity rapidly.

Relations Break Down When You Venture Too Far from the Client's Existing Relational Schema

As suggested earlier, complementarity is most essential for relations with interpersonally rigid individuals. These individuals require explicit confirmation of self-perceived personality traits. For example, an overly punitive and angry father might view himself foremost as a loving father. So efforts to address his behavior would need to confirm this important self-view. A comment such as, "As a loving father, I am certain that you are going to want to discuss the effects of your anger on the children. Isn't that right?" is both affirming and challenging. While the statement fits with the

---

[66] Though the administration was not fully standardized, I scored his responses and was able to include in my report a rough estimate of his nonverbal IQ.

client's need to maintain a dominant posture (by ending with a request for verification rather than a command), it also forces him to address a specific problem (his anger). I have found that even the most closed-off, domineering individuals have difficulty refusing this type of carefully tailored persuasion. In contrast, a disconfirming statement, such as, "A loving father would not do the brutal things you are doing," risks a failed relationship.[67]

In the same way that each client comes to therapy with a set idea of who he or she is as an individual, there are also firmly established ideas about who others are and what to expect from them. For example, some people have an automatic expectation that if they depend on others, they will be supported, whereas others expect to be rejected if they show any evidence of failure.[68] The first set of individuals would obviously have relatively little difficulty during the first therapy session, whereas the second set might understandably resist a discussion about their shortcomings. These trusted ideas about other people are often so longstanding and pervasive that they escape conscious awareness. Yet it is one's fundamental expectation of others that ultimately guides the development and continuation of relationships.

The sooner these expectations are brought into conscious awareness, the easier it is for the therapist to respond sympathetically to the client's behavior and for the client to begin the process of questioning previously unquestioned ideas. My experience has been that it is helpful to have the client closely scrutinize his or her lifetime of relational learning in order to recognize exceptions to generalized expectations.

For example, a 40-year-old male with a remote history of alcohol addiction came to therapy in a state of deep shame and remorse. Prior to his visit, I collected enough information from his extended family to deduce that he had become addicted to oxycodone HCl, which was prescribed for back pain from a herniated disc. He had a father who was terminally ill and who was prescribed oxycodone. I knew the father's pills had come up short every month.

On this client's first visit, he was unable to verbalize the details of his problem. Stealing medication from a dying parent would be difficult for anyone to confess, but for this individual the intense shame made it impossible. So rather than forcing the information out of him, I let him know that

---

[67] When others do not respond in a complementary manner, interpersonal conflict, discouragement, and dissatisfaction with the relationship threaten its continuation (O'Connor & Dyce, 1997; Tracey, 1994).

[68] Cognitive researchers refer to these expectations as "relational schemas," which have been shown to produce if-then contingencies about the way in which the self interacts with another person (Anderson & Chen, 2002; Baldwin, 1992).

I had a good understanding of the problem. Once this was established, he was guided into an intense and deep, inward focus on the emotions occurring within him. Feelings of fear emerged and were traced back to the horrible pain of rejection he had experienced when his former wife had decided to leave him. For the first time, he consciously realized that her abandonment had come shortly after he quit drinking. He now had a deep fear that his current partner would also abandon him if he admitted to the current addiction. After I asked him questions designed to elicit effortful thought[69] about the personality and character of his current girlfriend, he came to the conclusion that she would probably respond with care rather than rejection, and it would be helpful if he elicited her support. Following this insight, he became more honest with his girlfriend, which deepened their relationship. He once again started attending Alcoholics Anonymous (AA) and turned to hypnosis rather than medication to help him manage his back pain. According to his self-report and information from his mother and girlfriend a year later, there were no further problems with drug abuse, and rather than leaving him, his girlfriend decided to marry him.

Before having the client engage in the type of effortful thought described above, it is necessary to establish a complementary relationship that is characterized by an unambiguous show of support.[70] The client should not be left wondering what type of person the therapist is or what sort of intentions he or she has. Because attentional resources are a finite resource,[71] it is important to have the interaction between client and therapist consume as few attentional resources as possible. So when complementarity is established, there is less need to analyze and make sense of the dynamics of the immediate relationship; thus, more attentional resources are left available for greater introspection and deeper emotional involvement.

Complementary Responses Are Mutually Encouraging

In therapy, complementarity exists as a series of matched connections. For example, when the client seeks support, the therapist communicates caring, and as a result, the client feels supported. If the client seeks guid-

---

[70] Support attempts may be ambiguous either because support providers are unskilled at providing effective support—because their behavior contains a mixture of helpful and unhelpful responses—or because they misunderstand the type (or amount) of support that is wanted or needed by the support recipient (Coyne, Wortman, & Lehman, 1988; Dakof & Taylor, 1990; Dunkel-Schetter, Blasband, Feinstein, & Herbert, 1992; Lehman & Hemphill, 1990).

[71] This has been demonstrated by creating situations in which cognitive overload leads to decreasing performance (Gilbert & Osborne, 1989).

ance, the therapist provides direction, and as a result, the client feels more confident. Or if the client risks self-disclosure, the therapist empathizes with the client, and as a result, the client feels understood. Each interpersonal act reduces the threat of chaos by inviting reactions that are familiar and predictable, and, therefore, security enhancing. This type of harmonizing is essential to both social integration and a sense of individual empowerment.

It is not difficult to see that friendliness invites and encourages friendliness, and hostility invites and reinforces hostility. These interactions are horizontal, and both participants use homogenous behaviors. However, complementarity can also exist along a vertical plane, when participants invite responses that are polar opposites yet still connected and harmonious. For example, advice-giving invites deference, and sulking invites scolding.[72] As the behavior of one individual begins to influence the other and as each becomes mutually reinforcing, there is a movement toward increased complementarity and increasingly predictable patterns of interaction.

Although the eliciting power of behavior can have a substantial effect on others, it does not determine the other person's reaction. In theory, every client behavior carries information about how the therapist is to respond. Words and actions are selected to serve as invitations or requests for a particular class of responses or complementary behavior.[73]

Obviously, the more rigid the client's patterns of relational behavior, the more difficult it will be for the therapist to modify the interpersonal experience. Some interpersonal expectations are so strong that clients respond according to an internally constructed reality rather than what is happening in the outside world. For instance, the client may arrive to the session 30 minutes late, saying, "I know I am stupid for taking away time from therapy by always arriving late." This self-critical statement invites dominance and criticism. The therapist may choose a noncomplementary behavior and seek to respond instead with supportive acceptance, "Your arrival is perfectly welcome. The fact that you are willing to come to therapy represents a worthy achievement." However, the client may continue to search for the expected complementary response: "I am not able to believe that. You know my behavior is probably passive-aggressive. The therapist I

---

[72] These differences have been depicted using the circumplex model of interacting (O'Connor & Dyce, 1997).

[73] Accordingly, as the client acts, the therapist will experience complementary emotional responses similar to those experienced by other persons in the client's life (Dryer & Horowitz, 1997; Sadler & Woody, 2003; Tracey, 1994).

saw before you eventually had to let me go because of it." Well-rehearsed interpersonal styles tend to be self-perpetuating.[74] It is under such circumstances that skillful interpersonal maneuvering is required. However, if the therapist is not aware of the client's ability to elicit an expected response, such as rejection in the form of a referral to the next therapist, then he or she is less prepared to select a fitting response, such as, "I am sorry to hear how much trouble your passive-aggressive behavior has caused. Fortunately, I like working with this type of problem."

Summary:
Several Dimensions Are Critical to the Formation and Maintenance of Relationships

For those who embrace contemporary egalitarian values, it might seem crucial that the therapist strive to form a relationship with clients based on equality and mutual understanding. Equality and mutual understanding are appropriate for marriage, close friendships, or other long-term relationships among a group of peers. However, in psychotherapy, the client enters the relationship in a disadvantaged position and often needs help with an immediate problem. This help is provided within the context of a highly influential relationship strictly limited to the professional context. Therefore, the primary task for the therapist during the initial encounter is to develop a therapeutic alliance with the individual for whom care is to be provided.

By analyzing interpersonal dynamics in terms of broad domains, there is greater opportunity for conscious deliberation on the dynamic nature of relationships rather than on the attributes of people. In fact, research suggests that during everyday interactions, socially sophisticated individuals are processing events primarily in terms of relational experiences.[75] Beginning with the work of Leary (1957), interpersonal theorists have attempted to encapsulate all social interchange using a two-dimensional schema, with dominance and submission as one dimension and love versus hate as the other. The basic assumption is that all interpersonal behavior represents blends of two basic motivations: the need for control (dominance) and the need for love (affiliation). While a two-dimensional scheme is parsimonious, experience indicates that individuals who are in crisis and seeking the

---

[74] This is because as people form interpersonal self-conceptions, they tend to develop a confirmatory bias, in which they dismiss or ignore distinctions that would challenge their expectations (Sadler & Woody, 2003).

[75] Rather than being oriented toward the particulars of the individual they are interacting with, these people seem to be subconsciously preoccupied with the character of the relationship (Fiske et. al., 1991).

support of a therapist interact in a more complex manner.[76]

In the following chapters, five broad social domains will be used to illuminate strategic responses relevant to therapy. Formed in response to basic, universal challenges,[77] these domains include: (a) *verification*, which concerns the process of defining oneself and the outside world; (b) *affect attunement* which involves the experience of being emotionally connected to others; (c) *reciprocity*, which concerns the negotiation of matched benefits among equals; (d) *attachment*, which concerns the maintenance of a protective relationship; and (e) *structure*, which concerns the use and recognition of social hierarchy. These dynamics are presented individually for the sake of clarity. However, it should be recognized that these theoretical descriptors are a dissection of complex interpersonal behaviors that, in practice, are more likely to manifest themselves as a kaleidoscope of overlapping needs and objectives.

In summary, this book will highlight central avenues of social connection. As will be seen, the process of providing for the client's interpersonal needs involves both similarity and differentiation. While clients and therapists vary in their ability to form and cultivate a working alliance, it is the therapist who is responsible for understanding how to manage the relational experience for the well-being of the client. The act of using relationship, to help many different types of people, requires understanding and flexibility. When a therapist meets a client for the first time, it is possible to recognize small clues that point to a specific course of action. When the social domains described in this book are used, it becomes easier to identify a comment or gesture and place it within a broader class of actions that serve a particular function. This understanding of general domains of human interaction enables the therapist to reason quickly, so he or she can decide on a course of action that promotes continuation of the supportive relationship until the client's needs are met. Even more importantly, by becoming a student of each individual relationship, the care provider undergoes his or her own personal transformation, on a case-by-case basis. In the words of Scott Peck (1978):"*It is impossible to truly understand another without making room for that person within yourself. This making room...requires an extension of and therefore a changing of the self*" (p. 149).

---

[76] Although reluctant to abandon the two-dimensional "circumplex" model, social scientists have begun to recognize that these two dimensions (dominance and affiliation) do not provide sufficient conceptual basis for a client's fundamental interpersonal orientation. Instead, the conceptual basis must also include consideration of patterns of adult attachment, verification, and reciprocity (Horowitz et al., 1993).

[77] The domains described in this section were inspired by a relational model developed by Bugental (2000).

CHAPTER 1

VERIFICATION

Verification of Personal Understandings, on Critical Issues, Makes Interactions Less Threatening

My thoughts of others, as persons, are mainly filled up with myself.
—James M. Baldwin, 1902

An adage closely associated with successful customer relations, "The customer is always right," is seldom stated by providers of psychological care. This directive is more likely to be given serious consideration by a highly motivated sales staff. Skillful merchants will not risk the loss of clients due to unproductive bickering. Therefore, they become skilled at taking the customer's perspective and working within that subjective framework. Accordingly, this chapter will examine the many advantages of verification and why it should be understood by those who wish to build a strong relationship with therapy clients.

The concept of verification helps shed light on interpersonal dynamics that regulate *belonging* versus *aloneness*. The need to feel both understood and connected through common belief is tremendously important in therapy and can mean the difference between a successful alliance or a failed relationship.

It is common knowledge that beliefs that define one's identity, such as religion or politics, have great importance in the maintenance of relationships. Just as importantly, the degree of value that is associated with the self or others can determine the long-term viability of a relationship.[78] As an example, those who have an overall negative self-concept tend to marry

---

[78] Studies in social science have shown that an individual is strongly motivated to develop relationships that are consistent with his or her working models of self and in which the expressed views of others are in accord with these self-perceptions (Sroufe & Fleeson, 1986; Swann & Hill, 1982; Swann & Read, 1981).

partners who have an equally negative view of them.[79] Furthermore, the need for verification seems to increase with the closeness of the relationship, such that deep relationships are more comfortably formed when a person's core assessment of self is not challenged.[80] The need for self-confirmatory feedback can also be even greater for those meeting with a person in a position of authority.[81]

Verification of one's self-view fosters the experience of being generally understood, and it is the experience of feeling understood that mitigates the amount of satisfaction associated with the relationship.[82] In fact, the subjective perception of being understood provides the basis for feeling validated and cared for by a partner. People seek out those whom they assume to be a kindred spirit so that they may interact more freely and without fear of reproach.[83] This would partially explain the preference of those in addiction programs for working with therapists who are also in recovery. When a therapist in this setting introduces himself saying, "Hi, I'm John, and I'm an alcoholic," then the client's first impressions are that the therapist is a kindred spirit. When applying this relational dynamic to psychotherapy in general, it seems that a client's willingness to develop a relationship with the therapist is based in part on the extent to which the professional's stated impression of the client is congruent with existing core self-perceptions.

Coincidental Similarity on Critical Issues Produces Automatic Mutual Verification, While Perceived Similarity Produces Strategic Verification

It seems to be generally true that people relate best under conditions of mutual understanding. Such understanding is facilitated automatically by familiarity. For instance, when a therapist seeks to establish a relationship with someone who grew up in the same culture, with the same family values, and with the same religious and political ideology, then mutual veri-

---

[79] Those with a negative self-view will often seek out positive dating partners, but will eventually abandon these partners in favor of a marriage partner who verifies the individual's negative self-concept (Swann, De La Ronde, & Hixon, 1994).

[80] People paired with those who perceive them more or less favorably than they perceive themselves report less satisfaction with their relationships than people who receive verifying feedback (De La Ronde & Swann, 1993; Ritts & Stein, 1995; Swann, De La Ronde & Hixon, 1994).

[81] Research has shown that the need for verification is even stronger if the evaluator is highly credible (Hixon & Swann, 1993).

[82] Romantic partners report greater satisfaction when they experience mutual understanding and report less frequent conflicts (Murray et al., 2002).

[83] The positive effects associated with the assumption that one is understood still occur even when other's perceptions are not accurate (Reis & Shaver, 1988).

fication is not difficult to obtain. It will occur spontaneously, without effort. However, if a professional were to rely entirely on spontaneous processes of verification, it would mean limiting one's practice to clients who share the same demographic, physical, and attitudinal characteristics, as well as the same major life experiences.

It has been argued that similarity attracts and that this social attraction is due in large part to the gratification that comes from the validation and verification of one's self-concept.[84] This would explain why relationships with similar others are more satisfying than relationships with others who are dissimilar.[85] It also explains why people congregate in groups that emphasize some core self-understanding as a condition for belonging to the group, such as fraternities, political parties, religions, and ethnic groups. The assumption of shared self-understandings can be an important determinant of intimacy, as the vulnerability associated with self-disclosure is more acceptable when value and acceptance are almost guaranteed.[86] Although it is not realistic to expect this level of similarity in an open and diverse society, the concept will be explored in detail to expose dynamics relevant to verification in therapy.

There is very little doubt that people are more likely to seek out close relationships with others who seem more similar to themselves than different.[87] But more significantly, it is the core beliefs used to guide and define self-identity that are most important for the initial stages of building close relationships.[88] As mentioned before, subjective perception seems to play a more important role than objective fact during the formation of relationships. Therefore, the subjective experience of speaking to someone who is perceived as "like minded" matters more than the partner's actual characteristics.[89]

In addition to initial attraction, there is evidence that perceived similarity also increases satisfaction with a relationship, thus impacting the long-

---

[84] This is referred to in the research literature as the similarity-attraction hypothesis (Byrne, 1971; Clore & Byrne, 1974).

[85] Research has shown that similarity in sex roles is related to satisfaction in marriage (Antill, 1983; Eysenck & Wakefield, 1981).

[86] These variables will predict the outcome of relationships far into the future (Swann, De La Ronde, & Hixon, 1994; Weisz & Wood, 2005).

[87] Studies have shown that in both romantic relationships and friendships, people are attracted to and like similar others more than dissimilar others (Byrne, 1971; Byrne & Griffitt, 1969; Clore & Byrne, 1974; Klohnen & Luo, 2003).

[88] Research indicates that perceiving a romantic partner as similar to one's ideal self-standards is likely to play an important role in the initial attraction process (Klohnen & Luo, 2003).

[89] In a study of perceptual self-similarity, regression analyses showed that perceptual similarity largely mediated the link between actual similarity and attraction (Klohnen & Luo, 2003).

term sustainability of the relationship. In the context of marriage, satisfied spouses tend to believe that their partners possess traits, values, and day-to-day feelings that mirror their own. Less-satisfied spouses, by contrast, see little of themselves or their experiences in their partners.[90] The benefit of these assumptions is a more satisfying and stable relationship in which there are fewer disagreements, less conflict, and a greater sense of safety.[91]

What this means for therapy is if a client were to suddenly say to a therapist, "I get the strong feeling that you and I are a lot alike," the therapist questioning that idea would likely weaken the client's desire to develop the relationship. A better response would be, "Tell me how that is. What similarities do you see that are most important for you?" If the client generally likes the therapist, there is a good possibility that the client's attention will automatically shift to perceived similarities.[92] While it is not wise for professionals to misrepresent themselves to clients, there does seem to be an important function served by one's willingness to act as a placeholder for the client's idealized self.

The Client's Appreciation of Self Can Be Enhanced by the Perception of Similarity in Others

I witnessed the importance of this dynamic early in my career. In 1993, I was working as a counselor at a community mental-health clinic when the courts assigned to my care a 45-year-old male who had acted violently in response to delusions of persecution. He was paranoid and schizophrenic, but refused to take antipsychotic medication. He had employment at a metal shop, where he sat and talked with the workers as they completed their tasks. His employer kept him fed and gave him some spending money. In the context of our weekly meetings, I helped him feel safe and dispelled the paranoid delusions he would develop about his employer and others. Following the mildest confrontation, he would come to my office exceedingly fearful.

On one such occasion, as his eyes wildly searched about the room and his head ducked down low, he whispered, "Are you the man?" This idea

---

[90] The same researchers also report that dating relationships were most likely to persist when women saw themselves in their partners, even though such perceptions were not warranted by their actual similarities (Murray et. al., 2002).

[91] These findings have been observed by different groups of researchers, such as Byrne, 1971; Klohnen & Luo, 2003; and Swann, De La Ronde, & Hixon, 1994.

[92] It has been demonstrated experimentally that liking will lead to perceived similarity, rather than similarity leading to liking (Dryer & Horowitz, 1997).

seemed important, so I assured him I was. He responded by sitting with his back more erect, and his gaze became more confident. He went on to say that the man is "indistinct" and that only he and I knew what that actually meant. As I remember, I nodded in agreement. He explained the immediate peril he faced without "backup." He insisted that a large amount of money was involved and that his life could be taken at any moment. Then he asked, "Do you have my back?" I assured him that I did, to which he responded with obvious relief. Although this interaction happened many years ago, I still remember seeing his body and facial muscles relax.

After he had convinced himself that I was who he imagined me to be, the conversation moved on to a coherent discussion of the upcoming week and the tasks he needed to complete. On another occasion, he called my office in a terrible state of panic, "I am being chased by an army of Martians, and Jesus Christ is their leader! You've got to help me!" I drove immediately to where he was. With the added security of my presence, he was able to make a rational assessment of the situation, which, in turn, caused him to feel embarrassed. He apologized for having to call me, saying, "I don't want you to think I am crazy." I explained that I too sometimes need support and that I was certain he would have my back if and when it was needed. It was this sort of interaction that kept him relatively stable, without the benefit of medication, for the years I served as his counselor and safe haven.

For those not planning to work with individuals who are psychotic, it is important to recognize that many clients come to therapy searching for someone who seems to have what they need. Those who want marriage counseling will be most comfortable with a therapist whom they imagine to be in a happy marriage. Those who want to overcome addiction will be most comfortable with a specialist whom they imagine has been successful in his own recovery. Consider the disappointment if, at the very beginning of the relationship, the person you have chosen to place your confidence in insists on replacing your idealism with a more realistic assessment of his or her shortcomings. Unfortunately, since it seemed like the honorable thing to do, I have tried this reality-based approach. In most instances, the new clients responded by not coming back. This lesson helped me better understand why the importance of verifying a false perception of similarity to a client's ideal self has been argued since the conception of psychotherapy. It was Freud (1914) who originally theorized that the rapid-forming attachment of patient to analyst grew out of an opportunity to interact with one's idealized self.[93]

While verification of an idealized self is important, there is another side to the coin. In some instances, clients need a relationship with some-

---

[93] Reik (1944) later expanded this notion and identified it as a core component of therapy.

one whom they perceive to have the same faults they do. Often people will seek out relationships with those who perceive themselves having the same problematic characteristics.[94] While conducting group psychotherapy, I frequently observed clients commenting, "I am so relieved to learn that I am not the only person with this problem!" Early in my career, I learned to carry the comforting effect over into individual psychotherapy by telling clients about others who have had similar struggles and prevailed in the end. This way, an element of hope is added to the important endeavor of better understanding one's own problems. After all, it is not only our strengths that we need to make sense of, but our weaknesses as well.

Objectivity is added when clients are able to view their faults as outside observers. This ability provides verification of the "flawed self." Milton Erickson seemed to be able to take this type of verification even further. Having had the opportunity to speak with several of Erickson's former clients, I have been amazed by the differences in perception of who he was. Beyond random chance, the clients I met were convinced they could see their problems in him. Someone with paranoid schizophrenia told me that no one else knew Erickson as well as he did because he was the only one to recognize that Erickson was secretly schizophrenic. A different client, who struggled with extreme anxiety issues before meeting Erickson, told me that Erickson was secretly obsessive-compulsive. Yet another confidently said that Erickson was a kind narcissist. It seems Erickson's ego did not stand in the way of clients who needed to develop a favorable view of their own flawed aspects of self, while gaining a better appreciation for the idealized self they wished to become.

The Assumption of Similarity Is Typically Automatic

Here an important point needs to be made, especially for those who are asking themselves, "How do I make clients respond this way?" Verification is not a deceptive strategy designed to *make* clients project an "idealized self" or "flawed self" onto the therapist. Verification is instead a spontaneously occurring relational dynamic that serves as a starting point for relationships.

This was something I learned while still a young graduate student. Eager to expand my skills, I joined a professional society for group psychotherapy. During a training event, four experts from four different schools of thought were brought on stage, one at a time, to demonstrate their therapeu-

---

[94] For example, social scientists have observed that depressed people prefer other depressed partners to nondepressed partners (Locke & Horowitz, 1990).

tic model. When the psychodynamic approach was demonstrated, I volunteered to serve as a group member. This was my first exposure to this therapeutic method, so I was uncertain of what to expect. Once on stage, the leader sat motionless, with his fingers loosely folded and a perfectly neutral expression on his face. It was as if I were staring at the Mona Lisa. Anyone who attempted to ask him a question, such as, "What are we supposed to do?" received a brief, neutral, uninformative reply. Members of the group soon became visibly agitated. I had read about the blank-screen technique in class, but did not know how unpleasant it was to be at the receiving end. Unhappy with the experience, I moved my chair away from the circle to face a different direction.[95] To my surprise, the rest of the group followed suit, leaving the group leader on the outside of a newly formed circle. He now had no one to engage. The newly formed group began its own conversation, which was filled with laughter and mutual appreciation. After a while, I looked over my shoulder to see what he was doing. He still had fifteen minutes of demonstration to go. While his body and general expression remained in the same neutral pose as before, the color of his face was reddened, and I could see beads of perspiration running down the sides of his face.

This expert later argued that his technique had accomplished its intended purpose. However, I noticed that no one approached him afterward to find out how to perform his technique in their own practice. My feeling was that he failed to create an alliance with the group because he had been trying too hard to make the group members project their own ideas, beliefs, feelings, or characteristics onto him for interpretation. In other words, he was trying to force a response (by means of the blank-screen technique) that would have been a naturally occurring phenomenon in a complementary relationship.

In the absence of other strong ideas about who someone is, the readily accessible self-concept acts as a default bank of understanding. If people cannot tell what others are like, they will naturally assume the others have ideas, beliefs, feelings, or characteristics that are similar to their own. The use of one's own self-understandings helps produce a provisional map for navigating unexplored interpersonal terrain and prevents one from becoming lost in a fragmented and confusing social landscape.[96] For example, a person who uses deceit will automatically question the honesty of others'

---

[95] My id wanted to get up and leave the stage, but my superego blocked that action, so this seemed like a reasonable compromise between my personal needs and the demands of the situation.

[96] This is known by researchers as self-referent processing (Markus, Smith & Moreland, 1985).

statements, whereas someone who strives to be a person of honesty and integrity may not think to question the veracity of others' remarks. This was a difficult lesson I had to learn during my first days and weeks as a counselor for compulsory clients. My natural response was to believe everything I was told. As soon as I discovered how dishonest some clients could be, I had to reconfigure my interpersonal map and communication style, but without becoming overly cynical or dismissive of those who might be telling the truth.

It is important to note that there are certain circumstances in which self-understandings are most likely to be used for understanding others. Many of these conditions normally occur in therapy. For instance, self-referent processing is likely to occur when a person meets someone new or when a person is put in a situation that causes one to become inwardly focused or self-conscious. In addition, this provisional map is used if the behavior of the other individual is ambiguous or if quick thinking is required.[97] Because these conditions are often part of the early stages of a therapy relationship, the client's perception of the therapist will naturally be driven by the client's own self-concept, unless the therapist seeks to make it otherwise.

Given the benefits of perceived similarity, in most instances it would be counterproductive for the therapist to force recognition of his or her individuality. Yet this is exactly what happens if the therapist begins the relationship by using behavior that is strange or unfamiliar to the client, or if the therapist seeks to indoctrinate the client, thus making his or her own ideas the focus of conversation. A more subtle mistake is to correct clients when they falsely attribute their own behaviors or ideas to the therapist. Even with standard social etiquette, we are taught that it is rude to correct someone for this sort of mistake.[98] When it is necessary to correct faulty inferences or attributions, one should take into account the strain it places on the relationship. Because people are happiest in their relationships when they believe they have found someone who understands and shares their experiences, it is important for the professional, whose craft depends in great part on the strength of the therapeutic alliance, to appreciate the importance of perceived similarity.

---

[97] Self-referent processing is less likely to occur when the actions of others are remarkably different from one's own and/or the circumstances allow or encourage a thorough consideration of the other person (Markus, Smith & Moreland, 1985).

[98] On occasion, some correction may be unavoidable. For instance, during the second visit of my very first therapy client, the client said to me, "I told my girlfriend what you said last week—that I was right and that it was her fault I hit her." I had made no such remark and recognized this idea to be a dangerous one that required correction.

It Is Risky to Challenge Foundational Elements of the Client's Belief System

To expand this line of reasoning, it should be noted that in most instances it is counterproductive to fight with the client's belief system. Many individuals doggedly defend their beliefs as if these beliefs were their most prized possession or some other important part of self.[99] Try to take away people's beliefs, and they will automatically recoil as if you were seeking to inflict injury. Under these circumstances, continued struggle is futile. The tendency to protect one's beliefs can result in total denial of any evidence to the contrary.[100]

It should be emphasized that efforts to protect one's belief system or worldview is not pathological behavior. Human beings are constant meaning-makers. They are involved in a continuous process of acquiring and organizing beliefs about the self, others, and the world. As a result, certain core ideas will become deeply held.[101] When ideas at the center of a web of beliefs are threatened, the alarmed reaction, or "resistance," is an effort to maintain rationale continuity, thereby making sense of one's experiences. For individuals to maintain a sense of reality, there must be an intact system of beliefs.[102] This is not to imply that a person can never be challenged or experience a change in perspective. However, the sudden destruction of one or more foundational beliefs is, in itself, a traumatic experience.

When experiencing a crisis, individuals will often turn to long-held beliefs for a sense of comfort and certainty.[103] This tendency to become more confident in traditional ideas not only explains why conservative-leaning politicians find political advantage in keeping their constituency focused on threats to national security, but it also explains why skillful therapists do not challenge clients' core beliefs. When deeply established beliefs are affirmed by a trusted other, the affirmation helps take one's mind

---

[99] Beliefs can share many of the psychological properties of favorite material possessions, and certain beliefs even act as a symbol of self (Abelson & Prentice, 1989).

[100] This is because many aspects of social perception are guided by top-down, theory-driven processes in which the client's existing goals, schemas, and expectations shape the way in which new information is viewed (Baldwin, 1992; Holmes, 2002; Olson, Roese, & Zanna, 1996; Taylor, 1998).

[101] Such core beliefs also tend to be emotion laden (Wolfe, 2003).

[102] A general sense of reality includes meaning derived through self-identity, personal values, and recognition of personal agency (Mahoney, 1991).

[103] Research has shown that when people are merely reminded of their mortality, they begin judging more favorably those who share their worldview, and they develop a more negative view of those who threaten their worldview (Greenberg et al., 1997).

off the threat.[104] This would explain why emotional benefit may be derived from a therapist's willingness to build a consensus with the client, especially a defensively proud client, on value-laden issues.

Complementarity with a diverse clientele requires a readiness to set aside, temporarily, one's biases, personal values, and normal frames of reference. Those in a state of turmoil are dependent on their existing system of beliefs, and it is within this space that they will be able to reason and expand their experiential reality. Therefore, accomplished therapists do not impose their worldview on those who have come for psychological care, but they instead meet all clients inside the space from which the clients view the world.

I first recognized the importance of this dynamic during a summer job when I was a young adolescent. I'd been hired to go door to door to collect personal information for a commercial directory. My task was to convince individuals to divulge personal information to a stranger standing at the threshold of their homes (good training for someone who would later become a therapist). In one such instance, an unhappy woman answered the door, her hair in curlers and a chain locked across the door. She told me in no uncertain terms that she would not give me any information about herself and that it was wrong of me to ask this of her. I agreed with her that it was an awful thing to ask of someone, and then I commented on "how difficult it is these days to know who to trust." She responded with a discussion about the pitfalls of modern society. I listened, occasionally nodding my head and remarking on ideas I had not previously considered. Having already drifted outside her door, she commented that I seemed like a nice enough individual and spontaneously offered all the information needed for the directory. Although I had not yet had any formal training in therapy, I recognized that my willingness to agree with her position and to acknowledge the value of some of her fundamental beliefs caused her to relax considerably and to act more trustingly toward me.

Later, as a novice counselor meeting with a man twice my age, I again found verification to be very helpful. This man had been court-ordered to therapy as a result of violent behavior toward his wife. He was very angry at the injustice that he believed had been done to him. His wife had left him and filed for divorce. When he was a child, his father had beaten him. Moreover, he felt that white supervisors had kept him from advancing at

---

[104] Research has shown that individuals who have experienced a threat to their well-being will spontaneously exaggerate their conviction and sense of clarity about value-laden issues, and when presented with value-affirming ideas, they are more likely to decrease rumination about threats (McGregor et. al., 2005).

work. To express his displeasure, he pounded on my desk and declared that as a "white man" I had no way of understanding his experiences as a "black man." The look in his eyes was like that of a trapped animal, which made his eventual softening all the more remarkable.

As soon as he paused for a breath, I matched his energy and began my own diatribe about how pathetic it is that some of our nation's greatest heroes have gone unrecognized for their contributions just because their skin was black.[105] After naming several respected black leaders, I lectured on how Martin Luther King, Jr.'s philosophy of nonviolence enabled him to accomplish things that would have been impossible otherwise. This lecture naturally transitioned into a discussion about the client's life and any behavior that he felt needed to be corrected. After having completed the counseling program, this client volunteered to be interviewed on video. While describing his experiences for prospective new clients, he remarked, "You come in to counseling thinking that you do not want to be there and that you have nothing to say. But then Dan has this way of getting you to open up, and the next thing you know you are talking about things that you realize really need to be discussed." Without the strategic use of verification, I doubt he would have returned for a second visit.

Threats to a Firmly Held Self-Concept May Drive the Client Away

As mentioned earlier, it is especially important that therapists avoid threatening a client's core self-concept because that self-concept acts as the nucleus for an entire web of beliefs. In practical terms, avoiding such threats means therapists will accept, without correction, self-derogatory comments made by clients with a negative self-concept, as well as boastful remarks made by those who have a very favorable self-view.[106] During the first few moments of meeting new clients, I have observed clients physically recoil if my greeting was more positive or negative than they judged themselves worthy of receiving.[107] Verification of the client's self-concept is most important for those who have a high need for self-certainty and less crucial for clients who are uncertain how to think of themselves or for

---

[105] The reasons for matching and even escalating the client's emotional energy is explained on page 70.

[106] Social scientists have demonstrated that people with positive self-views prefer to interact with individuals who view them favorably, and those with negative self-views prefer to interact with those who communicate an unfavorable view of them (Swann, Stein-Seroussi, & Giesler, 1992).

[107] In some instances, a friendship will be cut short and replaced by another who is more willing to support the existing self-concept (Weisz & Wood, 2005).

those who are open to exploring new ideas.[108] An observant therapist will quickly recognize strongly held self-views, because clients with a low tolerance for uncertainty about the self-concept typically describe themselves in such a way as to elicit verifying feedback from the therapist. For example, a client with a negative self-conceptualization will start a conversation by saying, "You are going to think I am ridiculous for what I am about to tell you . . ."

When complementarity is not achieved, and instead people encounter repeated doses of feedback challenging their self-view, they will actively seek to remedy the situation. If they are still interested in building a relationship with a disconfirming person, they will strive to make that person recognize them as the type of person they believe themselves to be.[109] Therefore, it is necessary, at the start of a relationship, to accept and validate the subjective reality of clients' ideas and feelings about self. Otherwise, there is the risk of insulting and potentially alienating the client. In refusing to accept the subjective reality of the client's self-concept, there is the increased chance that the client will, at best, feel miserably misunderstood and, at worst, feel unable to continue the relationship.[110]

This dynamic is so influential that it is possible for clients to recognize they have benefited from the first couple of sessions, yet refuse to return to therapy if the therapist does not verify a firmly held self-concept. This phenomenon is especially common for those who convert psychological distress into somatic symptoms (e.g., gastrointestinal distress or migraine headaches) while insisting that they are a person with physical disabilities rather than psychological problems.[111] These clients are notorious for refusing to return to a therapist if he or she tries to convince them that their somatic symptoms are psychological in nature. For this reason, I typically do *not* argue about the etiology of the somatic complaints. Instead, I talk about the abundance of research showing that most people recover better from disease or injury when they have good, solid support from others.

In a similar manner, some clients seek to justify chronic anxiety by

---

[108] Social scientists have demonstrated that individuals tend to form relationships with those who support their social identity and withdraw from those who do not (Pinel & Constantino, 2003; Sorrentino & Short, 1986).

[109] For example, research subjects who had been accused of being more (or less) aggressive than they believed themselves to be reacted by presenting themselves in a less (or more) aggressive manner (Swann & Hill, 1982; Swann, Wenzlaff, & Tafarodi, 1992).

[110] When individuals who are seeking verifying feedback come up empty-handed, they often turn to a different relationship partner for compensatory verification (Swann & Predmore, 1985).

[111] The associated DSM-IV diagnosis is Somatization Disorder. The MMPI-II profile is 13/31 code type.

searching for an external explanation. Unfortunately, this type of focus precludes a search for internal solutions. In one such case, I met with a woman, aged 60, who had previously spent four years in therapy with a female therapist whom she described as highly "demanding." While my client worked with this therapist, all of her symptoms had become decidedly worse. The former therapist had told my client that she had an environmental illness that caused her shortness of breath, a racing heartbeat, and problems with concentration—symptoms commonly associated with panic attack. Convinced that she was allergic to her surroundings, my client had sold her beloved home in California and was living in Phoenix, essentially as a homeless person. By this time, the alleged allergic reactions were occurring daily. Wanting to believe the problem was outside of her, she was constantly moving between potential rentals, hoping to find one in which she did not feel she would die during the night. She was absolutely terrified. During her last session with the therapist in California, the therapist had told her, "You are the very worst case of environmental illness I have ever seen . . . After leaving me, you will continue to get worse and worse!"

By my fourth session with her, I was able to get my client to agree to some behavioral and psychological goals. She agreed to stop drinking alcohol and return to her AA meetings (which she felt had been helpful in the past); she also agreed that she would like to decrease her anxiety and put an end to the panic attacks. This goal represented an important shift in her focus of attention so that internal gains might be achieved. She then asked my opinion on her experiences with the previous therapist.

I knew it was a bad idea to make any negative remarks about this trusted authority figure. So I spent as much time as possible seeking to prepare her for the shock of what needed to be realized, while simultaneously seeking to strengthen our therapeutic alliance. However, by the sixth visit, my client's desperation was overwhelming. She demanded that I intervene with hypnosis immediately, otherwise she felt that she would go insane. Although I had been using an indirect approach to hypnotic suggestion since the first session, my influence was not powerful enough to overcome the suggestion she had received from the previous therapist ("After leaving me you will continue to get worse and worse!"). This coercive therapist in California did not need to use hypnosis to convey a very punitive and highly destructive expectation.

Knowing that the former therapist had ordered my client to call her on a routine basis and tell her everything that she was doing, I suggested that my client did not have to share the contents of this session with her nor did my client have to allow this woman to dominate her, as her mother had done during childhood.[112] My concern was that if the therapist in California learned about my comments, she would undo everything I was seeking to achieve. Finally, using the context of a formal hypnotic trance, I suggested that once I began reducing her anxiety, her physical suffering would also be reduced. Following this exchange, the client no longer seemed interested in talking with me. Although she told me she would call back to reschedule, I neither saw nor heard from her again.

I believe the challenge to her thinking was too much, despite the fact that she had reported in previous sessions that therapy was helping her. On the fourth visit, she had rated her satisfaction with therapy as a 9 on a 10-point scale. Looking back, I imagine it was necessary for her to believe that all of the time, money, and trust she had invested in the therapist in California was worthwhile, that she herself was a strong female in comparison to other women, and that her symptoms were caused by a physical condition rather than an emotional disturbance. The therapist before me, who seemed to be highly critical and controlling, was able to verify key self-perceptions learned in childhood, whereas I had failed to do so. I attempted to gratify my client's wish for a rapid intervention, but did not know how to communicate what I thought she needed to hear while verifying her core beliefs.

As bewildering as it may seem, people with very low self-esteem are more likely to feel at ease with unfavorable feedback than with praise alone.[113] It has been found that people with negative self-views prefer partners who evaluate them unfavorably, are more inclined to seek unfavorable feedback, and tend to elicit evaluations that confirm their negative self-views. Finally, as would be expected, given the importance of verification, satisfaction with the relationship may, in some instances, require the therapist to abstain from the liberal use of praise.[114]

While simultaneously striving to respect negative self-views and still have a positive influence, I have found that it is possible to embed encouraging statements within a comment that verifies some self-defined negative attribute. For example, with a low self-esteem client who insisted that she

---

[112] My client was clearly resentful of her mother's past and present behavior, which involved a great deal of hostile dominance, criticism, and highly controlling behavior.

[113] For example, in this type of study, when low-esteem subjects are given a choice between a roommate who likes them and one who does not, those with extremely low self-esteem will choose the one who does not like them; or after an important performance, low-esteem subjects show a greater readiness to listen to negative rather than positive evaluations of their work (Swann, Pelham, & Krull, 1989; Swann, Wenzlaff, Krull, & Pelham, 1992; Swann, Wenzlaff, & Tafarodi, 1992).

[114] Accordingly, it has been found that those with negative self-views whose spouse is critical of their abilities report greater marital satisfaction and closeness than individuals with negative self-views who are praised by their spouse (Swann, De La Ronde, & Hixon, 1994).

was "air headed," I responded with a chuckle, "Yes, that was an air-headed thing to do; however, your recovery was quick and impressive." My indirect use of praise still caused the client to blush with an embarrassed grin, but it was not as hazardous as using direct praise alone. Although it might seem that it was my use of the word "air-headed" that made the client blush, the end-of-session evaluation indicated that my client found the most difficult part of the session to be my suggestion that she had impressive abilities.

It is important to recognize that noncomplementary positive evaluations might indirectly harm the therapeutic relationship with low self-esteem clients.[115] Regardless of the theoretical explanation, given the tendency of those with low self-esteem to dismiss positive evaluations as inaccurate, a therapist seeking to build credibility with such a client must first demonstrate a readiness to verify ideas that are important to the client. When attempting to help the client develop a more positive view of self, the therapist will need to tread lightly, keeping in mind that the universal need to feel good about one's self is met only if the new more positive ideas do not threaten people's sense of knowing themselves. In other words, therapy must not intrude upon clients' confidence in their perceptions and readiness to trust themselves. Verification promotes the idea that "I am right," which then contributes to a positive sense of self, even when the verified idea was negative.

Another way of understanding the need (of low self-esteem individuals) for verifying negative feedback or criticism is that a certain sense of safety is experienced after making the decision not to need praise or approval. The lower the self-image, the more difficult it is for anyone else to knock it down. I have had numerous teenagers who grew up under conditions of constant criticism say that it is safer and easier to hate themselves than to try and defend themselves. A similar type of self-deprecation is built into the religious activities of some strict fundamentalists. At first, it is hard to understand why someone would eagerly sing about their own wretchedness and unworthiness; however, within the context of a highly critical social environment, explicit self-degradation preempts all attacks. While speaking in a Bible study group to a very religious young woman (with strong expectations of criticism from dominant males), I asked what she liked best about herself. After blushing and stammering for words, she replied that she had never thought about this. She then anxiously indicated that it felt sinful to her to answer such a question. Recognizing her obvious

---

[115] One explanation is that those with negative self-views find self-confirming feedback more gratifying than interactions that challenge fundamental ideas about self (Pinel & Constantino, 2003).

discomfort, I switched my approach, criticizing her for not being willing to acknowledge the magnificent work God had done while making her into a beautiful woman and loving wife.[116] She responded with a look of relief and agreed with the comment, as did her husband.

Accepting a negative self-view does not mean that any time a client is self-critical, the therapist should respond with negative feedback.[117] On the contrary, the therapist should constantly strive to meet peoples' need for positive feedback.[118] Even those with low self-esteem continue to desire self-enhancing feedback. Any time a client is feeling uncertain of how to perceive her- or himself, the therapist should emphasize the goodness of the client's mind, body, and spirit in a way that the client finds meaningful. However, when focusing on confidently held self-views, people tend to respond better to feedback that verifies these views.[119]

As mentioned earlier, one way to verify a strongly held negative self-view while still offering self-enhancing input is to acknowledge a defect and then attach an acceptable compliment—for example, "Yes, you are shaky, but sharp." I said this to a 67-year-old client who had just stated how disgusted he was with the obvious tremor in his hands. He had also just caught a typo on a worksheet I had given him. The fact that he was a retired school teacher made my acknowledgment of his "sharp" proofreading ability especially gratifying to him. As a second example, a woman who grew up during the Great Depression insisted she was beyond help, to which I responded, "You certainly had a disturbing childhood. You must be a very strong person to have survived it." During childhood, she had been made to believe she was a horrible burden to her parents. Her mother made it clear she did not love her. When she was five years old, she spilled some water on the dinner table, to which her alcoholic father responded by packing her suitcase and driving her to a children's home as part of a terrifying, experientially based threat. As an aged woman, she knew she was inadequately equipped for healthy living. She was deeply disturbed and knew it. I verified that understanding, while still seeking to emphasize a positive quality I knew she would accept.[120]

---

[116] Encouraging clients to utilize their religious beliefs and practices inspires hope and fortifies their efforts to maximize their health (Miller, 1983).

[117] This idea will be explained in greater depth in chapter 6.

[118] The problem seems to be that these individuals find it difficult or impossible to accept the self-enhancing feedback (Shrauger, 1975).

[119] Again, these self-views may be in either a positive or a negative direction (Pelham, 1991).

[120] While describing herself, she made frequent reference to amazing displays of physical strength, especially for a woman her age. She really wanted me to recognize how heavy the objects were that she was lifting. So it was safe to assume that she was at least toying with the idea that her physical strength was an important quality. I then expanded the idea to include psychological strength.

It is absolutely essential not to misunderstand the point that is being made. Just because a person has low self-esteem does not mean that he or she is immune to the damaging effects of criticism. In the same way that a surgeon would never cut randomly at a patient's body with a scalpel, the therapist should not make a critical remark unless there is evidence that the client requires the comment in order to feel verified. It would be devastating to tell people with low self-esteem that they are not so smart, when perhaps intelligence was the one positive quality they were willing to attribute to themselves. The therapist's comments must always be guided by the client's. So if the client complained about his or her looks, saying, "At least I can be brave enough to admit my flaws," the therapist wishing to respond with verification can simply say, "Yes, this is true." This brief acknowledgement helps the client feel understood and encouraged.

On the other side of verification, it is easy to see why those with highly narcissistic belief systems are naturally repelled by anyone seeking to focus on their deficiencies.[121] As would be expected, high-self-esteem individuals have a tendency to judge positive feedback to be more accurate than negative feedback.[122] Furthermore, people with positive self-views spend more time looking at evaluations they expect will confirm their self-views than at evaluations that threaten their self-views. The information that confirms their positive self-view is recalled with greater ease than those statements that are inconsistent with the narcissist's positive view of self.[123]

Back during my first year as a therapist, I attempted what I foolishly believed to be a brilliant maneuver with a highly narcissistic, 22 year-old male. He had been court-ordered to counseling for violence against his female partner, yet during the assessment interview, he kept himself barricaded behind a wall of infallibility. He could not bring himself to admit to any type of character flaw, no matter how small. Sensing that he wanted nothing more than to get out of the client seat, I suggested that we literally trade chairs. I told him he could sit in the therapist chair and do all the questioning, and I would be the client. In other words, I was allowing him to change roles with me. Not seeing the ambush, he gladly switched chairs and, with a smile on his face, asked me what sort of help I needed. While speaking in the first person, I systematically exposed his weaknesses, insecurities, and hidden defenses. He sat motionless as I spoke. He could not

---

[121] As a general rule, offering positive feedback will enhance the therapists' credibility (Chang, 1994).

[122] There is some speculation that this strategy contributes to the maintenance of high self-esteem (Jacobs, 1974; Kivlighan, 1985).

[123] Again, this is believed to be a means by which positive self-conceptions are sustained (Swann & Read, 1981).

stop my dialogue because he was the one who had asked the question, and, without recognizing what he was doing, he had agreed to allow me to pretend to be him. By the time I finished, his face looked as if he were in a state of shock. Of course, he did not return for any more therapy, despite the fact that he risked going to jail for failure to comply with the terms of his probation. With the benefit of time and reflection, I came to realize that I had decisively won a battle, but at the expense of the therapy alliance.

Since my days as a novice, I have increased my skill and changed my approach towards narcissistic clients. When possible, I use comments such as, "This type of counseling is extraordinarily difficult. Very rarely do I see people who have enough courage to do this voluntarily. My experience has been that only one in two hundred are capable of doing what you are doing right now" (i.e., a narcissist admitting that there might be personal flaws to work on in therapy). I recently received a phone call from the wife of one such client. She remarked that I was the first therapist in 10 years that her husband had been willing to listen to. She then asked, "Is it true that he is only one in two hundred who have the ability to do what he is doing in counseling? He keeps quoting that statistic to me."

A Treatment Strategy That Does Not Fit the Client's Paradigm of Change May be Rejected

When we are seeking to communicate ideas that fit with the client's understandings, it naturally follows that discussions about treatment should be framed within the client's paradigm of change. Because clients enter therapy with differing rationales for change, verification at the cognitive level requires individualized treatment planning that has been tailored to the client's expectation for what should be accomplished. When the rationale for change is complementary to the client's belief system, there is increased opportunity for a collaborative alliance to form.[124] In order to achieve this match, it is the therapist who needs to exercise flexibility. For example, the therapist may adopt the client's ideas as the treatment plan is formed, or the therapist may use the client's statements as a starting point and then progress to other ideas during treatment planning.[125]

During any conversation about a problem situation, clients will give small clues that gradually illuminate the paradigm of change they hold. For

---

[124] When there are similarities in client-therapist perspectives and expectations toward therapy, there is a greater probability of positive treatment outcomes (Reis & Brown, 1999).

[125] These methods have been associated with strengthening the therapeutic alliance (Horvath, 2001).

instance, when describing the problem of physical pain, one client might say, "My hand hurt so bad I could hardly look at it." A different client might explain, "My hand hurt so bad I couldn't stop staring at it." Each sentence suggests some underlying strategy for how to deal with pain. The first client is seeking to change the experience of pain through distraction. Therefore, this client is more likely to understand treatment plans that incorporate the clinical strategy of distraction. The second client is seeking to use sensory input, so this person should be more responsive to clinical strategies that emphasize self-monitoring. Accordingly, research indicates that strategies for pain relief, such as distraction, are more effective if the individual spontaneously copes with pain by looking away.[126]

As another example, one client might say, "I need someone to tell me the answer [to this problem] so that I will know what to do." A different client might explain, "I want to hear my options so I can start experimenting with doing things differently." The first client has constructed a statement derived from categorical, black-and-white thinking and, therefore, is probably ready to place total trust in a treatment plan, *if it is devoid of uncertainty*. The second client is speaking in a manner that is more uncertainty oriented and, therefore, is likely to readily accommodate new information. In response, the first client should be told exactly what to do: "Each time you have an anxious or obsessive thought, write it down on a piece of paper. Keep paper and pen available at all times. Next week, when you return for your next session, bring the list with you." Whereas the second client is given a list of options, with varying probabilities for success and known risks associated with each option. The therapist might even add, "If you do not like any of the options I have given you, then feel free to come up with your own during the week. My suggestions are intended to get you started in your thinking. You are certainly free to come up with your own ideas." The two different treatment plans will be judged as reasonable or unreasonable depending on the client's understanding of what therapy should offer.

While seeking to better understand the client's paradigm of change, I have found that some clients (including those who are psychotic) respond well to direct questions about what will be most helpful, whereas others struggle to articulate any reply at all. Direct questioning seems especially difficult for people who are new to therapy or those who have been trained to sit passively as the doctor acts on them. A third group of clients will answer questions about what they need from therapy by reciting advice given

---

[126] For a partial research review see Short, 1999, p. 306.

[127] Uncertainty-oriented individuals have been found to be skeptical of ready-made solutions (Sorrentino, Hewitt & Raso-Knott, 1992).

to them by a doctor or friend. For example, this client might say, "I was told that I need EMDR." The therapist might respond, "Do you know what EMDR is about?" And the client may answer, "No, I have no idea."

With careful probing, it becomes evident that all clients come to therapy with some base expectation for what it will take to cause them to act differently. For example, the client who is searching for external guidance might eventually admit, "I am so critical of myself. I just want someone who will tell me the right thing to do." For such clients, verification of their thinking is inherently therapeutic, whereas a lecture on how people change—saying, for example, "You have to find your answers from within yourself"—would be received as further evidence of their personal inadequacy. "I'm so dumb for not realizing that!" they might respond.

Regardless of the clients' belief system, the most crucial idea to communicate to them is the significance of their self-understandings and your sincere desire to honor these: "If there is something I seem to be failing to understand, please speak up and tell me so that I can correct my thinking." As long as there is no risk of harm,[128] a therapist can be most effective by respecting the client's assumptions about personal control and responsibility, aligning with his or her view of the problem and the anticipated solution.

In some instances, it may seem that the client's demands for therapy are unreasonable. However, after careful consideration, the therapist may be able to devise a way to work within the client's paradigm of change. On one such *occasion,* while working at the Milton H. Erickson Foundation, I encountered a man who was in a psychotic state and urgently insisting that the receptionist help him find Erickson (who had been dead for twenty years). Both the delusional man and the receptionist were relieved when I offered to take him back into my office and help him find Erickson. At the age of 14, the man had allegedly received life-changing therapy from Erickson during the context of a single visit. Since then, he had subsisted as a starving artist. He showed me a three-inch-high stack of photos, all of which depicted schizophrenic artwork, with Erickson's likeness located in every piece. The evidence of his obsessional fixation on Erickson was surreal. He had spent countless hours painting these murals, some of which were six feet in width. He explained that he had been driving all night in his van, that he was "being chased by federal police who might arrive at any moment," and that he was contemplating ending his life unless he could find Erickson.

---

[128] When working with destructive behavior that is supported by externalizing blame, such as with domestic violence and addiction, it may be harmful or even dangerous to accept the client's attribution of blame for the problem.

I responded by telling him that if he would close his eyes he would hear Erickson's voice speaking to him as a boy. The man's affect and demeanor changed instantly as he began to recall in great detail his experiences at a pivotal moment in his life. The more he remembered about the session with Erickson, the more animated and joyful he became. In an excited and enthusiastic tone of voice, he said, "Do you know what Erickson told me? He said, 'I bet you have never seen your name before.' So I thought to myself, 'Who the fuck is this to tell me that I have never seen my name?' So he took out a sheet of white paper and wrote my name, then he took a small mirror and flashed it up at me!" At this point, the man jumped up from his chair and, with bulging eyes, said, "It was my name, but it was *backwards! It was so fucking backwards!*" After recounting a few more memories from his session with Erickson, the man began to sing a contemporary religious hymn. The song had a chorus that contained the lyrics, "I needed the message not the messenger. Jesus brings us the message. Yeah, yeah, yeah!" He wanted me to sing with him, so I joined in on the fun. It was only after we finished singing that I realized the parallel. In a highly symbolic way, he had let me know that he was content with the message alone (i.e., the therapy experience) and did not actually have to have contact with the original source of the message (Milton Erickson).

Once again, he had received what he needed within the context of a single meeting. In just under 90 minutes, I watched his thinking transform from a wildly delusional state to a focused, rational state in which we could discuss his future plan of action. My advice was for him to return to his hometown and find a therapist he felt he could trust. He agreed to go first to meet with a priest who had helped him with food and shelter in the past. A year later, I was approached by his new therapist while I was presenting at a large conference. He said that his client had wanted me to know that he was doing well.

Verification of the Client's Motivation for Change
Forms the Essence of a Relationally Oriented Treatment Plan
and of the Overall Therapeutic Alliance

The last major topic on the subject of verification is motivation for change. Since the early days of psychoanalysis, lack of proper motivation has been used to explain many treatment failures. The traditional perspective has been to blame poorly developed motivation on the client, attributing it to internal factors such as resistance, denial, or personality traits. However, this view ignores the impact of relational dynamics and impedes clinical responsiveness by implying that client motivation cannot be influenced. In contrast, Milton Erickson (1959) viewed client motivation as the fulcrum around which all technique revolves. In his words, "The best technique is to have a worthy purpose." In other words, when the therapist's efforts are perceived by clients as verification of their own purposes, the probability of success is greatly increased.

When individuals recognize that things are no longer working for them, and they decide that change is needed, powerful emotional energy is generated.[129] This motivational energy is then channeled whenever deeply held desires are translated into concrete goals. So while it is tempting for therapists to impose academically derived goals (e.g., goals listed in a treatment manual or goals that fit the doctrine of change from a school of therapy), therapists are less likely to facilitate therapeutic progress if they do not possess a good understanding of what the client hopes to accomplish. Client motivation is better cultivated through the process of verification. In other words, it is the perceived purpose behind the technique and the technique's fit with the client's objectives that will ultimately determine the outcome.

Important information about client motivation is commonly derived from a clinical assessment designed to highlight the identified problem and treatment goals. However, the potential for action is not activated unless the identified problem resonates with clients' theories about the nature of their distress. *The treatment goals should fully encapsulate the client's subjective desires.*[130] When the therapist is willing to conduct an exhaustive review of the clients' position on these matters, then appreciation for their personal needs is powerfully conveyed.[131]

Careful review of the client's stated problems and/or goals can have a tremendous impact, even before therapy is formally begun. For example, a 27-year-old female client, calling to set up her first appointment, asked me if she could fax me a list of her problems. The long list included divorce, bankruptcy, eating disorders, major depression, panic attacks, and "hanging out with a bad crowd." After reading this list, I decided that the amount of energy she'd put into stating her problems was a clue to what she needed from

---

[128] When working with destructive behavior that is supported by externalizing blame, such as with domestic violence and addiction, it may be harmful or even dangerous to accept the client's attribution of blame for the problem.

[129] Whether or not this energy is acted on will depend in part on the anticipation of goal attainment (Atkinson, 1983).

[130] Goal consensus has been linked to successful collaboration (Shick & Greta, 2001).

[131] Accordingly, research indicates that therapy sessions with greater client-therapist discussion of goals and expectations are rated as "good" by clients (Hoyt et. al., 1983), and goal-related discussions are associated with patients viewing therapy as helpful (Goldstein et. al., 1988).

therapy. Therefore on the first appointment, I acknowledged her list as being a helpful tool and then read it aloud, item by item, while she carefully listened. During this encounter, she was exceedingly critical of herself and of her comments. Yet she remarked that hearing her problems read in my voice gave her an entirely different perspective. By the end of the session, she said, "These are things I have never said to anyone else. I did not think I would tell you so much." She seemed convinced that something significant had taken place. On her second visit, a week later, I conducted more traditional therapy. I did not see her again for two years, after which she sent an email that read, "Okay, [in] the past two years, since the whole big breakup and depression, I have really turned my life around." She was no longer losing herself to abusive relationships with men. Aside from whatever therapeutic events may have taken place outside the office, the most important component of our therapy seems to have occurred on the first visit, when she had the reality of her problems verified by an external voice.

Relational dynamics are just as important for goal setting. I have had more than one client respond to a standard procedure for outlining immediate, short-term, and long-term goals[132] with comments such as, "Wow, this helps. I feel like I just made more progress right now than all my therapy with the last therapist," or, "This helps give me hope, now that I know what we are going to do." Though difficult to illustrate with a single case example, my experience has been that, in many instances, what is done to the client is not nearly as important as the way in which it is done. Ironically, these clients are responding with surprise to the exposure and verification of their own motivational processes, variables that exist outside the therapist's range of control.

In addition to general objectives, there should be some sense of what the client is trying to accomplish on a *moment-by-moment* basis. The therapist should demonstrate this understanding through words and actions that address the needs of the client, as the client perceives them. For example, is the client most interested in finding a place to sit? Is the client most interested in making a good impression? Or is the person just trying to get through the session without crying? Is it the client's goal to share a disturbing childhood experience, or is he or she wishing to prove that there is no need for therapy? It is not helpful for therapists to focus all of their energy on assessing long-term therapy goals while failing to clarify what the client wishes to have happen in the immediate moment. It would be disastrous for a therapist to insist on hearing the faults of someone who is

---

[132] The form used to guide this interview can be found in Appendix C.

seeking to make a good first impression.[133] In order to receive a favorable evaluation by the client, the therapist must demonstrate an understanding of that person's immediate motivational concerns.[134] Using the example from above, the therapist would need to verify the importance of making a good first impression and then let the client know that his or her efforts to make such an impression have succeeded. The skillful practitioner is then able to take the resolution of immediate goals and translate it into progress toward long-term objectives.

Some Clients Are Primarily Interested in Preventing Distress

While therapists are seeking to understand client objectives, whether short-term or long-term, the fundamental starting point is investigation of the distressing experience that the client is seeking to prevent. Clients are often drawn to therapy with the goal of solving problems linked to emotional pain and distress.[135] So most clients will evaluate the therapist's actions relative to their intent to ameliorate distress.[136]

This type of motivation is especially likely to characterize those with attachment anxiety,[137] as they are chronically concerned with negative outcomes.[138] This motivational perspective can create a major dilemma for clients who perceive the therapy encounter as a set of performance demands to be feared and avoided. Under these circumstances, it is the therapy itself that can become the immediate source of distress.

As an example, a young female client sought to explain her fear of failing in therapy by relating her experiences with an anxious father. She did not recall any instances of abuse or severe mistreatment during childhood; however, her father's obsession with preventing failure robbed her of almost all opportunities for building confidence in her abilities. He did her homework for her. He arranged her bedroom. He picked out her wardrobe.

---

[133] The frustration created by a misinterpretation of immediate goals is likely to result in a premature disruption of the relationship (Dryer & Horowitz, 1997).

[134] Automatic liking is linked to the pursuit of shared goals (Ferguson & Bargh, 2004).

[135] I pinpoint the greatest area of distress before every session by asking the client to complete a subjective rating scale while sitting in the waiting room. This scale increases the precision of my initial inquiry and primes the client's introspective reasoning. For a copy of the presession form, see Appendix A.

[136] In regard to motivational impact, the client's interpretation of the therapist's intentions is more important than the therapist's private understanding of his intentions (Horvath, Marx, & Kamann, 1990).

[137] This concept is further explained in Chapter 2.

[138] These individuals commonly seek to prevent negative outcomes through the use of avoidance goals in achievement settings (Elliot & Reis, 2003; Smith et al., 1999).

His chronic overprotection kept her encapsulated in a world of fear and caused her to grow up feeling utterly incapable in almost all areas of thinking and doing. The life philosophy repetitiously embedded in her psyche was, "Be careful, and don't take chances!" Because she had learned to fear nebulous, unspoken catastrophes, it was exceedingly difficult for this individual to pursue new opportunities. She was blocked by an overarching need to prevent negative outcomes.[139]

This type of orientation can result in great resistance to or greater compliance with therapy, depending on the therapist's response. Because verification is vital to relational ties, individuals experiencing this type of distress are most likely to bond with a care provider who is willing to make a proactive attempt to prevent negative outcomes, saying such things as, "I will not ask you to do anything that would set you up for failure. Rather, I want to acknowledge how much you have already achieved just by being here today. I am impressed by your courage."

This type of careful attention to the client's needs can be accomplished in a manner that is both subtle and highly efficient. Although the total number of experiences feared and avoided by the client may seem unending, the greatest portion is often related to a single threatening idea. For example, fear of physical harm is a common concern for those who have been abused. This general threat can quickly become paramount to all other issues. While speaking to a client who is primarily interested in the prevention of bodily harm, a therapist should emphasize the physical safety associated with the therapist's office: "Nothing can harm you here. You are perfectly safe here in my office." After only one or two such comments, I have found that clients with this particular concern will often remark that they can hardly wait to return to my office because of the safety they experienced there. By contrast, if the client were not concerned with preventing bodily harm, this sort of comment would seem silly or insulting.

Fear of failure is a common concern for those who were punished as children in relation to their achievements (or lack of).[140] I have had many such clients explain, "It never mattered how well I did on my schoolwork. My father always found fault." Therefore, while speaking to this type of client, the therapist should place emphasis on the apparent success associ-

---

[139] This type of avoidance has been researched in terms of prevention motivation (Higgins, Shah, & Friedman, 1997).

[140] Mothers of high-fear-of-failure children expected independence and achievement behaviors earlier than mothers of low-fear-of-failure children, and those subjects whose mothers gave neutral responses following satisfactory behavior and punished them following unsatisfactory behavior had higher fear-of-failure motivation than those whose mothers rewarded and were neutral, respectively (Teevan & McGhee, 1972).

ated with each therapeutic activity: "You are doing really nice work. Keep elaborating on that point. I think you are really getting to the heart of the matter!" This type of comment will resonate with such individuals because it compliments their intense effort to avoid shame associated with failure.[141] Another helpful strategy is to set goals that are focused on the accumulation of numerous small successes.[142] When objectives are broken down into a series of small steps, there is an implied reduction in the risk of absolute failure, which thereby verifies the client's need to avoid failure.

Surprisingly, in other instances, an individual may avoid opportunities for achievement not out of fear of failure, but out of fear of success. With newfound success comes changes in identity, increased expectation from others, and increases in responsibility, any of which may seem overwhelming. Ironically, individuals in this state of mind experience verification when the therapist says regretfully that progress in therapy is going to be slow and that they should not expect to see any changes in the near future.

I learned the importance of this dynamic the hard way, while working with a 35-year-old male who, after each major psychological breakthrough, would relapse into a deep depression, during which he would stay in bed for weeks at a time.[143] Finally, I recognized his tremendous fear of success and adjusted my comments so that his retreat into depression was not necessary. With some additional instruction on how to deal with comments from family members (who also seemed uncomfortable with him achieving success), my client was able to make further personal and social progress while stilling avoiding major markers of success. (For example, though he was happily dating and had accumulated a large network of friends, he still was not *married*. And although his reckless and irresponsible spending habits had been replaced by volunteer fundraising for charities, he still had not achieved *financial independence*, instead living off a trust created by his father.) After having left therapy, the client contacted me to let me know that I was an outstanding therapist and he was feeling good, but he and his father agreed that, unfortunately, the therapy was not a success.

There is no single response or technique that is suitable for all clients. Even praise or positive reinforcement can create resistance if it requires the client to operate outside the parameters of his or her current motivational system. As an example, a woman was referred to me for outpatient therapy following her hospitalization for suicidal behavior. She was a young mother, age 35, who had stood at her kitchen window watching her two small boys playing in the backyard as she held a butcher knife to her bare

---

[142] This is one of several core strategies used by Milton Erickson (Short, Erickson & Erickson, 2006).

[143] For more information on this client see page 82.

ribs. Prior to this incident, she had attempted to hang herself. This woman felt herself to be exceedingly vile and was convinced that her boys, whom she loved dearly, would be better off with any other mother.

In the therapy room, her fragile state was apparent from the tremble in her voice and the shaking of her hands. During our discussions, she wrapped her arms around her chest as if she were naked and horribly vulnerable. Her self-esteem was exceedingly low; she said, "I hate my body and all this fat. I cannot look at it. I have to shower in the dark."[144] Later, she expressed a fear of progress, saying, "I get nervous whenever I start to make progress. After losing a lot of weight, I will suddenly binge on food." So at the end of the first appointment, I carefully told her she was doing good enough at this time,[145] and she was to force herself to make progress *slowly*. I suggested she visualize an internal meter and stop her progress before feeling that she might return to self-destructive behaviors. The advice pleased her. During the second session, she commented, "While talking to a friend about my therapy, I told her what a relief it was to hear that I did not have to make progress right away." By the third session, she reported that she had maintained a healthy diet throughout the week, saying, "This is something I have not been able to do for a really long time!" During this session, she confessed to having been sexually molested as a child, something she said she had never admitted to a therapist before. She also admitted to having a problem with alcohol abuse, adding, "This is something I have never admitted to *myself* before."[146]

She viewed her increased insight and self-disclosure as evidence that the therapy relationship was helping her. This was a hopeful idea, which further decreased the intensity of the depression.[147] Five weeks after starting therapy, she reported that her drinking had decreased significantly, that she had gone out with her husband and the boys to the movies for the first time in two years, that she had begun talking to the other mothers at her son's school, and that she and her husband had made love for the first time in a long while. Yet the development she seemed most delighted by was her newfound excitement about Christmas. She said that she had dreaded Christmas ever since she was a child. (It seems that at age seven, she was sexually assaulted under a Christmas tree.) This year she was excited about

---

[144] It has been found that individuals who were incestuously abused often view their bodies as an enemy and engage in self-mutilation and self-destructive behavior (Johnson, 2002, p. 56).

[145] She had already eliminated the suicidal impulses.

[146] Having been raised as a Catholic Hispanic, the act of confession had special meaning for this individual.

[147] Hope has been described as the antidote for depression and the reason why the placebo effect is so high for antidepressant medication (Kirsch, 1990).

putting up lights and a tree and about going out to buy gifts. After hearing her progress, I was ecstatic with joy. I carelessly told her how amazing her progress was—"and in such a brief period of time!" Immediately, I saw her body sink into the couch. Although I tried to correct my mistake, the damage was already done.

That evening, at 7 p.m., she called in a complete state of panic. Problems had developed shortly after she had left the therapy session. While waiting for her son to get out of school, she "began to fall a part." The statement she kept repeating on the phone was that she couldn't handle it all. She choked on her words as she explained that she was reacting to the praise in therapy. She expressed the intense pressure it created for her saying that if she did not make perfect and immediate progress her husband would leave her. As part of her downward spiral, she had consumed an entire bottle of vodka and was now waiting for her husband to return from work and discover her sad state. Despite my urging, she refused to schedule another appointment.

Fortunately, I had already acquired written permission to communicate with members of the family, so five days later, with help and encouragement from her mother and sister, she decided to call and schedule another appointment. During the next visit, I apologized for my mistake and promised to be more careful. I assured her that, the next time I noticed her making progress, I would refrain from commenting. During the following months, she remained free from depression even after discontinuing antidepressant medication. She started playing tennis (something she had really enjoyed during college), quit drinking, and got a part-time job in a department store. After a total of 15 sessions (spread across 12 months), she opened her own small business doing furniture restoration. A year later, in a follow-up session, she reported no further trouble. The point to be recognized is that brief remarks can make a big impact.

By contrast, during a training event, I listened to a colleague tell a group of interns to relax and not worry so much about what they say to clients. He assured the trainees, "You are not going to destroy the therapeutic relationship with a single comment." He then turned to me to ask if I agreed. I told him that my experience did not support his statement and that I have found small comments can have a really big impact. As irony would have it, following that exchange he no longer spoke to me. While communicating in any relationship of significance, it is important to measure the anticipated effect of one's words carefully before speaking.

This last example brings us to fear of rejection, another strong motivator. The mere possibility of rejection can result in strong resistance to self-disclosure (a dynamic that will stall therapies that base their entire doctrine of change on self-disclosure). Although clients are not likely to directly announce their fear of being rejected by the therapist (because it is a topic they are trying to avoid), this fear is easy to recognize. In many instances, the individuals will be working too hard to convince the therapist/authority figure of their competencies or likeability. It is as if they have come to a job interview rather than therapy.

For example, one such individual, a male, 38 years of age, began his therapy by requesting advice for his interactions with colleagues at work. He spent the first quarter of the session elaborating on how expertly he handled challenging situations at work. This facade of self-assuredness did not match his presenting problem. So after listening politely, I asked, "Why do you want therapy around this?" The implication of my question was that he was handling things at work just fine. With that verification, he transitioned to deeper matters, "Well . . . uh . . . there are actually other issues going on too . . . with my partner. I am gay." This very competent professional person had gotten himself involved with a romantic partner who was addicted to crystallized methylamphetamine and who was engaging in high-risk sexual encounters with strangers. Later, it became apparent that this client feared being rejected by male authority figures, a fear that was exacerbated by his status as a short, homosexual male from an ethnic minority group.

If I had begun by offering him advice on the presenting problem, there is a great probability that he would have felt misunderstood and unfairly judged. While seeking to make sense of the client's subjective experiences it is important to remember that sometimes the apparent trouble is not really the problem. Skillful relating requires some patience and careful investigation into why the client thinks the problem is a problem.

In most instances, *success in therapy will be evaluated against the client's subjective understanding of the problem.*[148] This makes perfect sense if the client's motivation for seeking therapy is to stop or prevent the experience of personal distress. While seeking to understand why clients are distressed by their problem, the therapist should encourage elaboration of detail: "What do you think makes this so distressing?" When the client lists several different areas of distress, the therapist should encourage discernment: "Which of these is causing the most trouble for you?" or "If we were only able to address one of your problems in here, which one would be

---

[148] The results of a comprehensive review of over 2,000 process-outcome studies since 1950 indicate that the ability to accurately focus on the client's problems is highly related to successful treatment (Orlinsky, Grave & Parks, 1994).

most important to resolve?" The answers to these questions help equip the care provider with content for discussion that conveys a thorough understanding of the client's needs.

When a client with low introspective capacity externalizes the problem—saying, for example, "My main problem is that no-good teenage son of mine"—then verification takes place not by means of agreement, but by the therapist's willingness to take these concerns seriously and explore them further. The therapist might respond, for example, "When did you first stop liking your son?" or "What did you, as his parent, intend to accomplish by this point in his life?" If the client is willing to admit to some mistakes, then attention can be shifted inward by explaining, "In order to help you prevent further trouble between you and your son, we need to identify which of your mistakes had the biggest impact on your son's behavior." As can be seen, the line of questioning gradually leads the frustrated parent to a position of greater personal agency without encouraging more self-infuriating blame. I have had clients respond well to this approach when their motivation to prevent further trouble outweighs the need to protect pride by assigning blame. If that motivation is not there, then an entirely different approach may be needed. For example, the therapist might meet in private with the person who is in the disadvantaged position and, therefore, more highly motivated to take advantage of a supportive relationship. In this case, the use of verification would be very direct: "Based on what you are telling me, I think it would be better for me to meet with your son rather than with you."

Some Clients Are Primarily Interested in Increasing Future Rewards

While not as common, there are clients less interested in preventing distress and more interested in increasing future rewards.[149] I have had individuals come to therapy without evidence of psychological pain. Rather, they are excited about some new opportunity: "I have met a man that I love and he wants to marry me. But before making this big of a decision, I would like to talk about my thoughts and feelings with someone who is completely unbiased." The client who made this statement was a confident, emotionally healthy woman with great poise and strong self-esteem. Her primary motivation was to maximize her achievement and success in a fundamentally important area of her life. Rather than feeling uncomfortable with comments

---

[149] This second type of motivational system is known as promotion motivation, which focuses on the attainment of positive outcomes rather than the prevention of negative outcomes (Higgins, 1998).

about their successes, clients with this type of motivation are likely to bene-fit from formal recognition of their accomplishments. Furthermore, they are more likely to feel verified by relationships that create space for personal achievement.[150] These individuals are likely to have high self-esteem and some degree of eagerness to actualize their capacity for achievement. Thus, a primarily nondirective approach is indicated for clients who enter therapy confidently oriented toward specific achievements. The use of a hands-off approach is less insulting, and it creates greater opportunity for satisfaction as these clients display their ability to help themselves.[151]

When highly achievement-oriented clients require redirection or ad-vice, it is helpful to frame their struggle as something that does not need to affect their pride.[152] This type of framing is done in order to maintain a com-plementary interaction. When help or advice is given to those who cannot allow themselves to feel they need it, the relationship bond breaks down.[153] However, if the task that has been failed is carefully set a part from the col-lection of abilities that the clients use to define themselves then there is less risk of insult. For example, while giving needed marital advice to an ambi-tious businessman, the therapist might comment, "If this were a business decision, you would not need my advice. You know what you are doing while in the office, and you have plenty of success to prove it. However, your wife has some needs that are different from the needs of a company. And there are some things that you would not be expected to know unless you had been trained as a psychologist, as I am. Do you want my advice?" Similarly, it is often difficult for teachers who pride themselves on the effec-tiveness of their behavior management in the classroom to come to therapy and admit that they need help managing their own children's behavior. And it is just as difficult for therapists who have pride in their clinical accom-plishments to go to another provider and seek psychological care. In order to care for such individuals, it will be necessary to first validate those com-petencies upon which their self-esteem depends.

---

[150] Researchers report that individuals with a high need for achievement fare better in work settings when they set their own goals, whereas low-achievement individuals function better when goals are set for them (Locke et al., 1981).

[151] These individuals react to being helped with negative affect and negative self-evaluation if task performance reflects on important self-attributes and if the helper is similar to or has a close relationship with the recipient (Fisher et al., 1982).

[152] For problem-solving situations that require a change in behavior, advice is one of the most efficient interventions available; however, when it fails to produce immediate results, fur-ther exhortation is not likely to increase compliance (Burnum, 1974; Edwards et al., 1977).

[153] Research has shown that individuals with high self-esteem are less likely to seek help if the area in which they are seeking help is believed to reflect negatively on important self-attributes (Tessler & Schwartz, 1972).

Another important dynamic to recognize with achievement motivation is that it enables individuals to accept risks in order to achieve success. While operating from this mind-set, the client can be openly challenged and confronted with the tasks that are before them, as long as a positive outcome is more probable than not.[154] For example, a therapist might say, "The type of care and attention that your teenage daughter needs from you right now [18 months after the death of the father] will not be easy, because there is a part of you that wants to be supported and shielded from loneliness [i.e., to be out dating men]. But if you are willing to be there for her as a fully dedicated mom, then the rewards are certain to last a lifetime. Once she is a full-grown adult, she will recognize your sacrifices and appreciate them." For those who are motivated by achievement, this type of statement acts as a strong incentive.[155]

Although less common, some clients come to therapy already curious and introspective and strongly oriented toward their own intellectual achievements. Such individuals are involved in a process of questioning and self-analysis both inside and outside the therapy office.[156] Rather than being spoon-fed directions or advice from the therapist, clients in this state of mind are more likely to experience verification when challenged to outline their beliefs and to test them in order to see what can be learned. This can even be accomplished when using techniques that are typically associated with highly directive therapies. For example, while working with a client who studied philosophers, monitored her internal dialogue, and psychologically analyzed her interactions with others, I was asked to use hypnosis to help her increase her self-care. After the trance ended, upon opening her eyes, she declared, "That was brilliant, absolutely brilliant!" When I asked what it was that she appreciated so much, the client explained, "It was the way you worded your suggestions. You told me that I could modify them any way I needed in order to achieve my goals." In this way, I honored her

---

[154] Research has shown that those with achievement orientation have higher tolerance for risks and will choose a task that is likely to maximize their sense of achievement as long as the probability of success approaches 50/50 (Atkinson, 1957).

[155] By contrast, those who are more so motivated to avoid failure need help finding a path to escape failure, such as, "You and your child have suffered a great deal already, and I do not want anything else bad to happen to you. Therefore, you must put enough time and effort into supporting your child so that neither of you have to face this tragedy on your own. But without your support, the situation with your child will get much worse. She has not started using street drugs yet or other more self-destructive behaviors, but we do not want to wait around for this to happen." If there is a patient whose motivational system is difficult to determine, then it is possible to make one's case using both angles of approach.

[156] With individuals classified as uncertainty oriented, there is a greater willingness to engage in hypothesis testing, to test and evaluate beliefs against new evidence, and to think about expectancy-incongruent information (Driscoll et al., 1991; Sorrentino & Roney, 1990).

request while also leaving space for her to use her own intellect to determine what goals to pursue.[157]

Verification Is Sometimes Delivered in the Form of Confrontation

Because human interaction can be so complex, verification requires
more than simply agreeing with everything the client has to say. That type
of superficiality does not take into account the possibility of ambivalence,
nor does it lend itself to the formation of deep relationships. What if the
client does not believe what he or she is saying? What if the client's actions
are contradictory to deeply held values and beliefs? Even if the client's
statements are perfectly congruent, most find it insulting to discover that
others are simply saying whatever they imagine you want to hear. Emotional pandering is especially disappointing for those who seek input from
a third party with the hope of obtaining objective feedback. At the moment
clients decide that they are only being told what they want to hear, trust
and respect are forfeited. While seemingly paradoxical, disagreement can
sometimes serve as a component of verification.

As stated at the beginning of the chapter, it is not necessary to agree
with every statement a client might utter. In some instances, verification is
better facilitated by means of confrontation. This is most likely to be the
case when the behavior that is being confronted is contrary to the client's
deeply held values. For example, a therapist might insist, "I have known
you for a longtime, and the arguments you have used to justify this behavior
just do not fit with who you have claimed to be."

A skillful use of confrontation is typically grounded in the values belonging to the individual who is being confronted. While engaged in domestic-violence work, I had a client brag, "I don't take shit from nobody.
On the way here, some son of a bitch tried to pull in front of me on
[Highway] 635, so I ran his ass off into a ditch!" Although the possibility of
one of my clients experiencing road rage while on the way to anger-
management counseling made perfect sense, the revelation was still unsettling for me. I imagined how terrified the other driver must have been, perhaps not even knowing why my client had decided to run him off the road.
However, the person sitting in front of me did not think in those same
terms. He still believed that his violent tendencies served an important role
in defining and establishing himself among others. In addition, his thinking
was very concrete. So in a casual tone, I asked, "What does your car look

---

[157] Researchers have found that personal-goal-directed approach motives are associated with
greater happiness and meaning in life (Urry et al., 2004).

like? Did it get scratched up?" With his head sinking down to his chest, the client replied, "Yeah. . . it's kind of fucked up the passenger's side." Having established this fact, I framed my confrontation within the context of his value system: "Don't you think it would have been better not to mess up your own car? Can you see why this is a problem? Do you understand why you need to learn more self-control?" The rest of the session was spent in what seemed to be productive dialogue. The client responded to me as someone who had a good understanding of him. What I verified and affirmed was his right to arrive at his intended destination without something bad happening to him. At the same time, my comments were structured in such a way as to encourage greater responsibility for his actions.

In addition to verifying some of the client's foundational values, it is also important to validate the client's decision to seek input on important issues. This too can be achieved by means of confrontation. On more than one occasion I have had a client say, "I am asking you about this because I know that you will be honest with me, even if it is something I do not want to hear."

One of my favorite examples of this dynamic was told to me by an old friend from college. After I'd met Stephanie at the airport, she described the status of her marriage by saying that she was much happier now that she had a newfound appreciation for her husband and for other people she felt blessed to have in her life. When I asked her to explain, she responded, "It began with my grade school friend griping me out. She told me, 'After I say this to you Stephanie, you may hate me forever. However, I don't care, because as someone who loves you, I can't just standby and watch you wreck your marriage. Your husband is trying his best to make things better, but you do nothing but criticize him day and night. You are the one making things miserable for the two of you! And if the marriage does fall apart, you are going to have no one to blame but yourself!'" Stephanie explained to me that after hearing this, she felt horribly angry at her friend and planned to have nothing else to do with her. However, as she explained, "I could not stop thinking about what she had said, and then after a couple of weeks, the anger started to subside. That was when I realized that she was right, I haven't given my husband a fair chance. Then I realized how hard it must have been for her to say that to me and that I was lucky to have her as my best friend. Only a best friend will tell you something you do not want to hear, out of love." This was a person who trusted her friend and for good reason. The marriage had been in bad shape, and this intervention really did make a difference.

An important point about confrontation is that the therapist should be willing to dissect events so that his or her thinking is not reduced to a dichotomy. In other words, rarely is a person's response to a given situation either all right or all wrong. Often it is necessary to confront clients for some part of their thinking or behavior while simultaneously affirming core aspects of their identity.

As an example, there was a 55-year-old woman of Spanish decent who had been hospitalized for suicidal behavior and was coming to me for follow-up therapy on an outpatient basis. After the first dozen visits, she was still spending much of her time contemplating different methods of killing herself. Her husband had betrayed her trust, so she felt the marriage was devoid of love, and her daughter was preparing to leave for college in a matter of months. Because her entire purpose in life had been focused on raising her children, she had no desire to live past the point of her daughter's departure. As she explained to me, "My children do not need me anymore now that they are grown. It will be better off for them if I am gone." Rather than viewing this transition point as a midlife crisis, she viewed it as an end-of-life catastrophe. No matter what I said, she absolutely refused to consider the possibility that killing herself would harm her children.

However, I knew that she had very strong resentment toward her husband for his affair and sorely resented the money he spent on his expensive hobbies. She often described him as being "narcissistic and selfish." So, left with few options, I decided to confront her by declaring that her suicidal ideation was narcissistic and selfish. After casting an angry stare, she did not say anything else about the subject during that session. However, toward the end of her next visit, she commented, "Now I am no longer so depressed, because it was so narcissistic, and I don't want to be that way, like my husband. It was *crazy* to think that way. I have been saying to myself, 'How could I ever do such a thing?' Every day, all day long, I kept saying to myself, 'Narcissistic and selfish! Haaa!' Because that is not who I am. I have devoted my life to caring for my children."

With a smile on her face she continued, "Now I can't believe that I had plans to kill myself, and that if I had done this, my daughter would have been without guidance and help from her mother!" Wanting her to understand my intentions,[158] I commented, "I wanted to put a new idea in your head." With a burst of laughter, she interjected, "And it exploded! I spent many hours planning how I was going to insult you, and I had to make certain I pronounced all of my words correctly, so that I would not get any

---

[158] In an analogue study, Thomas, Polansky, and Kounin (1955) found that client perception of the therapist wanting to help increased clients' commitment to continue treatment and willingness to be influenced (Thomas, Polansky & Kounin, 1955).

disrespect. And that thinking too was very narcissistic!"

The confrontation not only put an end to the suicidal ideation, but also increased this client's flexibility in how she conceptualized her husband and herself. She also became closer to me after confessing to the powerful emotional response she had experienced in relation to something I had said. If I had been unwilling to have her question her behavior, I doubt any of these gains would have been achieved.[159]

Verification of Fundamental Self-Understandings Is Crucial During the Early Development of a Therapeutic Relationship

While in many cases the primary therapeutic objective may be to provide the client with new, more positive self-understandings, it is also the case that all individuals need the comfort and predictability that comes from a sense of knowing one's self. It is by means of a stable self-view that individuals are able to predict and control their world as they organize their ideas about what is real.[160] This self-view is what determines the information people attend to and recall, the social interactions they seek out, how they respond to others, and their interpretations of their experiences. For these reasons, clients are certainly justified in their motivation to verify and maintain a consistent self-image. Of course, to satisfy these verification needs, clients must find someone who is willing to view them the way they view themselves. The emotional payoff is so great that a sense of mutual understanding may contribute more to growth in a relationship than the satisfaction of having found a way to solve the presenting problem.[161] Therefore, it is crucial for therapists to address a client's need for verification during the very beginning stages of therapy. In this way, therapy begins with acceptance and utilization rather than reorientation or education. Such an approach enables the client to feel more comfortable with the change process and more readily trust the therapist's competence.

Unfortunately, verification of the client's core beliefs is most difficult at the time when it is most needed (the beginning stages of therapy). The problem is that these needs tend to be hidden behind social norms and role-governed behavior during the beginning of relationships. For these reasons,

---

[159] It has been demonstrated that inducing doubts about self-characteristics tends to undermine the impact of these qualities on self-esteem and increases the probability of behavioral change (Briñol & Petty, 2003; Swann & Ely, 1984).

[160] The need for self-consistency has long been argued to play a fundamental role in personality functions (Lecky, 1945).

[161] Research in marital relations indicates that the need for mutual understanding most often outweighs the need for problem resolution (Miller et. al. 1986).

it is often beneficial to give clients permission to set aside temporarily normal social etiquette, inviting them instead to interact during therapy in a way that feels natural and spontaneous. In this way, the care provider can develop a more intimate understanding of the idiosyncrasies that characterize the individual.

In more extreme cases—for instance, those who fit the criteria for personality disorder—the discrepancy between one's private experience and the carefully constructed social self may be pervasive and chronic. However, as with any other individual, these clients require verification of latent self-views. Those self-views are more likely to be made manifest when the therapist offers acceptance and validation of the clients' immediate experiences. Ironically, when people are seeking to change their lives, they need reassurance and acceptance more than they need correction.

The final point to be recognized is that verification should be expressed in a number of different ways, and it should be done often. One of the most obvious forms of verification is providing an affirmative verbal reply, such as, "Yes" or "That's right," or even a nonverbal affirmation such as a head nod or leaning forward with a look of approval as the individual is speaking. The result of these small signals of acceptance (and, thus, verification of the other person's action) is a heightened state of interpersonal connection.

More dramatic forms of this type of verification have been used to great effect outside the therapist office—for example, within the context of charismatic Christianity. During a charismatic prayer session, the rest of the group does not remain motionless and silent as someone prays, but instead enthusiastically whispers statements such as, "Yes! Yes! Yes!" "Amen to that!" "Yes, Jesus hear this prayer!" while simultaneously nodding affirmatively and perhaps holding their hands up into the air. The sense of connection created by these actions can be very powerful. While seeking to expand my repertoire of experience, I participated in such a group and had some of my prayer statements verified in this manner. And as would be expected, I felt an instant appreciation and connection to the verifying individual.

As a very different example, there is a similar use of verbal affirmation used by lovers in the bedroom. Some will intensify the shared experience by screaming, "Yes! Yes! Oh God! Yes! Yes!" As a humorous example, while in graduate school, my wife and I lived in a small, first-floor apartment directly under the bedroom of a sexually active female who would repeatedly scream out these exact same statements as her bedframe rocked rhythmically against the wall. Although we initially tried to pretend we did not hear the noise coming down through our ceiling, one night my wife broke the ice with an exasperated comment, "She has got to be faking! No orgasm lasts that long!" I did not want to embarrass our neighbor by asking about the nighttime noise; however, my guess is that her statements were designed to heighten her lover's experience.

In regard to therapy, it can be very helpful to simply nod affirmatively whenever the client makes a statement that you, as a therapist, can at least agree to in part. Another method of nonverbal verification is posture and positioning. While conducting therapy, I noticed that clients delivered more verbal content if I leaned in as they spoke. Impressed with my discovery, I went to share the information with a colleague, who seemed surprised that I had just figured this out. She explained that her discovery of the effect was accidental. One day, while leaning forward to stretch her back, her client suddenly begin to speak with more energy and conviction. Along the same lines, I have had the experience of leaning back in my chair and having the client respond by stopping mid-sentence to ask me if there is something wrong with what she said. Although it is unlikely that every client will respond so dramatically to the positioning of the therapist, it should be recognized that when some form of verification is present, the client will respond with greater levels of intimacy. When verification is absent, the client is more likely to remain guarded or even withdraw from the relationship.

CHAPTER 2
AFFECT ATTUNEMENT
AFFECT ATTUNEMENT HELPS INCREASE THE FELT CONNECTION WITH ONE'S SELF AND OTHERS

No more fiendish punishment could be devised, were such a thing physically possible, than that one should be turned loose in society and remain absolutely unnoticed by all members thereof.
—William James, 1890

Similar to how infants need to see their mother's laughter in order to know how to experience their own joy, adults are best able to regulate affect when experiencing an emotional connectedness with others. Therefore, another foundational interpersonal dynamic that should be familiar to anyone seeking to provide care is affect attunement.[162] Like verification, affect attunement comes from similar, rather than divergent, experiences. In addition to creating a sense of closeness and oneness, which come from sharing and participating in the same internal state, affect attunement provides social evidence of our own psychological subsistence. However, this type of convergence occurs in emotional rather than cognitive domains.[163] So while *verification* is typically used to refer to matching beliefs or attitudes, *affect attunement* is the term used to describe emotional synchronization.[164]

As will be seen, the dynamics of affect attunement are somewhat different from cognition-based complementarity. For example, unlike established beliefs and attitudes, intense emotional states are much more fluid, sometimes shifting during the course of a single conversation. Therefore,

---

[162] Affect attunement has been described as the major process underlying attachment and the formation of close relationships (Hrynchak & Fouts, 1998; Stern, 1985).

[163] Thus, different regions of the brain are activated; verification requires prefrontal activity, and affect attunement elicits the activities of the basal areas, including the brain stem (DiMatteo et al., 1980).

[164] Affect attunement has been defined as an intersubjective relatedness in which there is a match of internal states and a sense of emotional connectedness between individuals (Stern, 1985).

attunement is an ongoing activity.[165] Also, unlike cognitive contagion, emotional contagion is less conscious, more automatic, and relies mainly on
nonverbal communication. In order to understand why affect attunement is
so important to therapy,[166] it is helpful to consider the social function of
emotions.

Though emotional experiencing can certainly occur in a private setting, the cultivation and expression of emotion is primarily a social phenomena.[167] As stated by Zajonc (1998), emotions "are the basis of social interaction, they are the products of social interaction, their origins, and their
currency" (pp. 619–620). Emotional communication often leads to shared
emotional experience,[168] which leads to a deeper understanding of self and
others.[169] This is why attention to the client's feelings, combined with empathetic responding, has come to be an essential component in most psychological therapies.[170]

Now that emotion has been identified as a valuable relational resource,
it is reasonable to consider the economics of different interpersonal transactions. For example, what happens if you invest a lot of emotional energy
in an interaction and then get nothing in return? The eventual result is
bankruptcy.[171] Perhaps this is why the sharing of emotions is so important
to the formation and maintenance of relationships.[172] And while intense

---

[165] During mother-infant interactions, behavioral evidence of attunement occurs once per
minute (Stern, 1974).

[166] Attunement between client and therapist has been shown to promote positive therapeutic outcomes (McCluskey, Roger & Nash, 1997; Stern et al., 1998).

[167] The first systematic study of human emotion was conducted by Charles Darwin (1899),
who emphasized the social communicative function of emotion and its role in the survival
of the species.

[168] This dynamic is referred to as emotional contagion, which is the tendency to take in and
feel emotions that are similar to and influenced by those of others (Hatfield, Cacioppo, &
Rapson, 1994).

[169] Stern (1985) argues that affect attunement is necessary for emotional growth and results
in knowing that feeling states are valid and shareable.

[170] Most approaches to psychotherapy now acknowledge that the experience of emotion is
central to psychological well-being and that its expression and the way it is dealt with in
therapy are closely associated with therapeutic change (Iwakabe, Rogan, & Stalikas,
2000).

[171] Berenbaum and James (1994) found that people who reported having grown up in family
environments in which they were not permitted to openly and directly express their feelings, or otherwise felt emotionally unsafe, showed elevated levels of alexithymia, a diminished ability to identify one's own emotional state.

[172] Moreland (1987) concluded that the development of shared emotions is one of the principal causes of the formation of small groups. Others argue that emotional communication
facilitates coordination of activities for mutual benefit, promotes bonding and group co-
hesion, helps identify potential antagonists, and helps maintain well-regulated social
hierarchies (Reis, Collins, & Berscheid, 2000).

displays of emotion can deepen a relationship,[173] the expression of divergent emotional experiences can just as quickly alienate or break down a relationship. For example, consider the romantic pursuer who, after professing his love to a less passionate partner, suddenly finds himself abandoned. When action is initiated without the benefit of a shared emotional context, there is greater risk of rejection or conflict. This is why in therapy it is important to affirm the existence of a shared emotional link before seeking to problem solve or modify client behavior.[174]

When relational complementarity is used as the guiding principle,[175] it is easy to see why it is so important to respond to the expression of emotion in a manner that both supports and encourages readily accessible affective processes. When a person does not know how to internalize the emotional experiences that drive and motivate the other person, there is less chance of establishing a strong interpersonal influence.[176] As will be explained in greater detail in the chapter on attachment, secure emotional attachments are characterized by a readiness to express sadness in response to others' sadness and joy in response to the accomplishments of others. Or, as noted in a Biblical mandate, "Rejoice with those who rejoice; morn with those who morn" (Romans 12:15). This is, in fact, the essence of affect attunement. However, the application of this powerful dynamic is not limited to these emotions alone.

Anxiety, disgust, and even anger can be crucial for communicating relational fit and thereby increasing attraction to an interaction partner.[177] Of course, when joy is met with joy, the interaction will be both enticing and interpreted as a supportive response. However, when clients enter therapy feeling angry and not prepared for joyful interaction, then a cheerful greeting from the therapist will only serve to alienate them as they seek to confirm their original idea that no one can help them.[178] By contrast, an expres-

---

[173] It has been found that the intensity of emotional experiences and the degree to which emotions are expressed in interaction are positively associated with the degree of relational closeness with the interaction partner (Barrett et al., 1998).

[174] Similarly, Siegel and Hartzell (2003) argue that parents should attune to and express their understanding of the child's emotional experience before seeking to correct or modify his external behaviors.

[175] Carson (1969) defined complementarity as the extent to which the behavior of one participant elicits specific behavior from the other participant and is viewed as necessary for continued interaction.

[176] Harvey and Kelly (1993) argue that without attunement the ability to relate to and learn from one another is seriously compromised.

[177] Similarly, it has been found that the expression of negative emotion in a communal relationship does not reduce attraction for that person (Clark, Pataki, & Carver, 1996).

[178] Research on person perception and social schemata has shown that people develop rich and elaborate schemata about others that include expectations for their future behavior and assumptions about the extent to which a recipient anticipates the other to be a source of social support or conflict (Fiske & Taylor, 1984; Markus & Zajonc, 1985).

sion of emotion that validates the client's immediate emotional experience produces greater opportunity for engagement.[179]

For example, while training as a school psychologist intern, I was assigned a student whom my supervisor identified as "a complete misanthrope." My advisor briefed me on the case, saying, "I have worked with this sophomore since forth grade. He will not let anyone in. He has attacked other children and destroyed protective barriers placed around his desk" [to separate him from others].

As she predicted, the first time I approached him, he turned his head only slightly and from underneath furrowed eyebrows grunted, "God damn it! Do I have to go meet with another shrink?" During the first session, he refused to speak to me or to look in my direction. So after five minutes of awkward silence, I sent him back to his classroom, which was a fully self-contained unit.

After having two weeks to collect my thoughts, I decided this adolescent must be horribly lonely. He operated entirely at the fringes of his social universe. So for my second visit, I was better prepared and had some idea of how to interact with him. After being met in the classroom with the anticipated greeting, "Oh, God damn it! It's you again," I simply motioned with a wave of my hand and led him out of the classroom, in the wrong direction, down the wrong halls, outside the school, around the gym, and back into a hallway close to where we had started. Finally, from close behind me, he called out in irritation, "Where the hell are you taking me!" Spinning around to face him, my reply matched his intensity, "I don't know. Why the hell are you following me?"[180]

This question was one that he needed to consider. I knew he would follow me because he was in desperate need of someone with whom to interact. This was a fact he would slowly come to realize.[181] Shortly after, we arrived at my office (a room that had been intended for use as a janitor's closet and, therefore, had just enough space for a desk, two chairs, and a bookshelf). I began the conversation with a brief tirade, "What kind of lousy room is this that *they* have us meeting in? This desk looks like it belongs in an elementary school! And where is our air conditioning? It's hot in

---

[179] It has been found that when establishing relationships with hostile individuals, complementarity in hostile behavior is more beneficial to the development of therapeutic alliance than friendly behavior (Kiesler & Watkins, 1989; O'Connor & Dyce, 1997).

[180] The hostile tone conveyed in this statement was meant to reinforce the student's immediate behavior. In fact, behaviorally oriented researchers have found that hostile responses are more adequate social reinforcers for hostile individuals than are praise and approval (Brokaw & McLemore, 1983).

[181] Because I did not provide an answer for why he was following me, he was forced to search for an explanation, the only likely one being that he wanted to be with me.

here!" I persisted in my complaints about the room and everything in, above, and around it—long enough for him to wish for an opportunity to speak. I matched his emotional tone so that he felt encouraged and able to relate. However, I never complained about the boy or his behavior.[182]

In a spontaneous and enjoyable manner, we went back and forth, each taking his turn complaining about things. Eventually, he looked over at the bookshelf and saw a chess set. "I guess we could play chess," he said. "But you would probably beat me." Wearing the same frown on my face as his, I responded, "Yeah, I probably will beat you, and that is not going to be much fun. But we might as well go ahead and play the game." After I finished beating him, I sadly protested, "Oh, man! It is already time to go. Now you are not going to have a chance to even the score." By this point, the student's affective tone made a noticeable shift. He said, "I'm free anytime you want to come get me." So, of course, I shared his sentiment, "Well, I would really enjoy meeting with you again. Maybe with enough practice you will be able to get really good at chess."

As it turned out, not only did he get good at chess, but he also began developing friendships and applying himself academically. For the first time in years, he had other children who wanted to sit with him at lunch.[183] By the end of the first semester, he was allowed to attend several mainstream classes and had raised all of his grades to A's and B's. By the end of the year, he was fully mainstreamed, he had formed a new bond with an uncle who played chess with him each week,[184] and he was the only high school student to cry when I said goodbye at the close of my internship. Of course, I felt his sadness and cried with him.[185]

Because emotions serve as a catalyst for behavior, they are sometimes regarded as being potentially dangerous. This is especially the case with negative emotions such as anger. For that reason, many professionals eliminate the expression of negative emotion from their repertoire of tech-

---

[182] This was my method of providing indirect approval. If you use criticism to dispatch almost all of the items in the room, but without commenting on the only remaining item (i.e., the boy), then, by implication, the remaining item is an object you must not dislike.

[183] The three boys who sat with him were also social outcasts; however, with him, they formed a new social group.

[184] Learning to play chess during counseling gave him a tool for engaging his uncle. My guess is that he was then able to acquire support or nurturing that had not been available from his mother and father. Therefore, his dramatic progress should not be attributed entirely to the therapeutic relationship, but rather to the collective events that followed.

[185] We feel other people's feelings by feeling our own internal reactions. Because the feelings in our heart, sensations in our belly, or rhythm of our breathing is an important source of emotional knowledge, people who are more aware of their bodies have been found to be more empathetic (Siegel, 2010).

niques.[186] In the case described above, the client had not been helped by any of his other counselors because the type of emotional relating that he required was outside of the range of traditional therapist behavior. In the absence of a subjectively felt human connection, he resorted to verbal and physical violence. This was the only way to keep from being entirely isolated. It seems that what the young adolescent needed was someone who was willing to resonate with his immediate affective state while simultaneously addressing his needs.[187] Although we still interacted as two distinct individuals, he was no longer in a state of emotional isolation.[188] Similar to moving a goldfish from one tank of water to another, the therapy relationship gradually prepared him for new ways of emotionally experiencing others.[189] Overly abrupt changes produce shock and, therefore, threaten the alliance.

Here it is important to recognize that it is the client's subjective reaction to the relationship that should be used as the standard against which the therapist calibrates his or her interactions.[190] Mirroring emotions expressed by the client (including negative emotions) is not risky as long as the therapist's behavior is in line with professional ethics, and it is interpreted by the client as evidence of understanding[191] and an act of support.[192]

Synchronizing With the Client's *Emotional* Experiences Helps Increase Therapist Care and Client Receptivity

My experience has been that a judgmental mind is a closed mind. Therefore, in order to discover what a client is experiencing, a temporary suspension of judgment is necessary. In regard to affect attunement, sus-

---

[186] Ironically, social science indicates that in less close relationships, people are likely to suppress expression of negative emotion, while in close relationships, partners express more emotion, both positive and negative (Collins, & DiPaula, 1997).

[187] The expression of emotion, including anger and sadness, has been shown to facilitate the building of relationships (Tiedens, 2001).

[188] Resonance requires that client and therapist remain differentiated, knowing they are separate and distinct, while also become linked to each other's internal experiences (Siegel 2010).

[189] People become more similar—in appearance, motivation, and emotion—to their friends and romantic partners over time (Zajonc et al., 1987).

[190] Research findings on therapy outcomes indicate that client-perceived relationship factors, rather than objective raters' perceptions of the relationship, better predict positive results (Lambert & Barely, 2001).

[191] Feeling understood increases client satisfaction with therapy and feelings of safety in the relationship, and makes it easier for clients to self-disclose or to approach difficult personal areas (Greenberg et al., 2001).

[192] It has been widely accepted that it is the client's perception of the relationship that is most crucial to outcome (Gurman, 1977; Lambert, Shapiro, & Bergin, 1986; Orlinsky & Howard, 1986; Patterson, 1984).

pending judgment means that the therapist refrains from placing positive or negative values on the emotional reactions of the client and instead becomes increasingly curious about the needs or situational dynamics underlying the emotions. When affect attunement is established, there is greater probability that the therapist will move from a focus on what the client has to say to an understanding of what the client has experienced.

This subtle shift can produce dramatic results. For example, a 15-year-old boy was brought to my office for a second opinion. Prior to his visit with me, he had seen a psychologist who had diagnosed him with attention deficit/hyperactivity disorder (AD/HD). Following his appointment with me, he was scheduled to go meet with his school counselor for a talk about "attitude problems." Before the interview, I had the boy and his mother complete standardized behavioral checklists. These were scored before the meeting, and the interpretation yielded a profile indicative of AD/HD.

After entering the office, the boy sat slumped with his arms crossed and his eyes looking off in another direction. Soon it became evident that he was angry at his teacher and generally untrusting of adults. He explained that because he was black and an athlete, his teacher just dismissed him as someone who didn't care about academics. I joined him in his anger and commented on how clueless some adults can be (of course, implying that I did not want to be a member of that category). Encouraged by the emotional validation, he went on to complain about how she had yelled at him for sleeping in class when really he was doing his best to pay attention. He talked about how hard it was to focus on her notes. His emotional tone carried a great deal of frustration, so I got him to explain as best he could exactly what was happening.

He responded, "I will be sitting there taking my notes from the overhead, and suddenly, she is no longer talking! When I look at the notes I have copied and at what is up on the overhead, she has already moved on to a different page. Whenever I ask to see the other page, she won't let me. So I have to find other kids after class and get them to let me copy the notes I missed."

My response was one of absolute dismay. "I have worked inside the schools with hundreds of kids who have attention problems. Hardly ever are they trying to reorganize themselves while on the go in between classes. There is something not right here!"

Suddenly narrowing his eyes and looking intently into mine, he used a single word, "Yeah!" to indicate that he finally felt understood. So I continued my probe, "What other weird things have you noticed happening?" He gave a vague reply that indicated general confusion about daily events. So I asked more specific questions, "Do you ever have problems with suddenly falling asleep at your desk, and then when you wake up you find that there is some drool coming out of your mouth?" He threw his hands up with a look of exasperation, "Yeah, and its embarrassing! There I am in class trying to wipe my mouth off before anyone sees me."

I probed again, "Have you ever fallen asleep while in the middle of doing something outside of the classroom?" Again, he said, "Yeah! I was at home reading the paper, then the next thing I know I am waking up covered in sweat. I don't get it, because I was not sleepy, and it was not hot in the room."

Then I asked if he ever had problems remembering something that happened earlier in the day. My curiosity resonated strongly with his recent experiences of confusion, "Yeah! That was weird! I got all mad at my cousins when I found an empty pizza box. I was griping at them for not waking me up to see if I wanted some. However, they told me I had been there eating with them. And my auntie said the same thing. So I did not know what was going on."

Before going any further, I told him I wanted to bring his mother in and ask her some questions. When I used the word "mother" he gave me a funny look. I took note, but did not pursue it. My interview with the boy had been private, so she did not know any of the details he had shared. Now with her and the boy in the room, I asked about the pizza incident, and she described the events exactly as he did. Then I asked, "Have you ever called out to your son, and it looked like he was awake, but he did not respond to you, until you went over to touch him or shake him?"

"Yeah! It happened right before my visit with the last psychologist," she said. "We were in the grocery store. I called his name but he just stared forward, so I walked over to him, 'Baby, what's wrong with you?' When I put my hand on his shoulder, he suddenly snapped out of it. The psychologist told me it was the AD/HD."

Next I asked them both if he had ever fallen to the ground while trying to walk across the room. As I expected, during fifth grade he had gotten in trouble, for "clowning around" after he had collapsed while going to the pencil sharpener. He was still frustrated by the fact that the teacher did not believe him when he said he had not intended to fall to the ground.

After hearing this example, the mother suddenly understood why I was asking questions about reoccurring lapses in consciousness. Her eyes locked onto mine with what seemed to be an expression of horror. Reaching over to grab the boy's hand, she asked him, "Should we tell the doctor the truth?" Not waiting for his reply, I interjected, "Yes! Please do. It will probably make us all feel better."[193] With a deep sigh, she explained, "I am not his mother. I am his aunt. I call myself his mom because I do not want him to have to explain to everyone that his real mom is in prison. She has a severe seizure disorder. And so does my younger sister." With her face full of emotion, she turned to the boy she had risen as a son, "I'm so sorry, baby, I never thought about that. I didn't put it all together."

The major point of this story is that I was not the first care provider to sit and talk with this boy about his problems. He had been taken to see a medical doctor just five days before his interview with me. He had a history of severe asthma, so since the age of one, he had made routine trips to the hospital emergency room and been interviewed by numerous physicians. He had also met with other psychologists. However, no one else had gotten enough information from him. He was a quiet boy who had secrets he did not wish to reveal. It was not until someone began to demonstrate an understanding of his emotional experiences that it became possible for him open up.[194] While I was listening to him, it was not his words that interested me as much as the confusion and frustration that he sought to communicate. Without this level of understanding, I would not have known the right questions to ask.[195]

As follow up, his aunt called two months later to inform me that a diagnosis of absence epilepsy had been made and that the physician felt the boy's life would have been in jeopardy if this disorder had not been caught before he started driving. Although he only came for one visit with me, my guess is that the empathetic exchange that took place during therapy was emotionally beneficial.[196]

Hostility Is Avoided During the Reciprocal Expression of Anger

Because it is almost impossible to overstate the importance of demonstrating positive regard and civility during alliance building, this point will

---

[193] Data from brain research and studies using client surveys indicate that disclosing distressing thoughts to an empathetic listener produces a sense of relief from emotional, as well as physical, tension (Farber, Berano & Capobianco, 2004; Lieberman, et al, 2007; Pennebaker, 1997).

[194] Accurate emotional communication, which usually occurs spontaneously and outside of awareness, appears to be a characteristic of satisfying close relationships (Ickes, 1997), whereas inaccurate decoding of the partner's affective state appears to be one of the hallmarks of distressed relationships (Noller & Ruzzene, 1991).

[195] Those who are more capable of recognizing various types of emotional distress in others are better able to make sense of the behavior of others and are more likely to respond with empathy, kindness, and helping behavior (David Allyn, 2004).

[196] Overall, empathy accounts for more outcome variance than does differences in amount and content of treatment (Greenberg et al., 2001; Miller & Hester, 1980).

be further elaborated on relative to the concept of affect attunement. Since it is in the absence of respect that the seeds of abuse are sown, recognition of the intrinsic value of the client and the central importance of his or her welfare acts as a basis for all forms of intervention. Regardless of the client's emotional state, an escalation of hostility is not helpful in therapy. Therapists who use antagonism, shame, or disparaging comments, under the rhetoric of "therapeutic confrontation," can do more harm than good.[197] Even if legitimate support is provided, therapeutic progress is likely to be undermined by the presence of any hostility.[198]

If this statement seems to contradict information in the previous section, then a closer study of the material is required. It is important to recognize that affect attunement is not equivalent to behavioral acting out. This may seem like an odd statement, because in general society, the expression of emotion is most often followed by affect-driven behaviors. Feeling and doing become mixed, as if they were one in the same. That is why the anger of one family partner will often lead to an escalation of mutually destructive behavior.[199] By contrast, skillful therapists can reciprocate powerful emotional energy without becoming entangled in unproductive behaviors. They can join the client in expressing anger, but without directing hostile behavior toward the individual. This distinction is crucial. A transformational relationship is not likely to develop when clients are made to feel that they must defend themselves from the care provider.[200]

Similarly, it is not necessary to match the client's behavior when there is an expression of sexual energy, nor is there a need to inflict stinging rejection.[201] Instead, the client's emotional energy is gently guided toward more appropriate targets, as the therapist demonstrates his or her passion for boundaries and professional ethics. Thus, a strong and urgent emotion

---

[197] Poor-outcome cases have been linked to a pattern of patient-therapist complementarity (vicious cycles) in which therapists respond to patients' hostile communications with hostile communications of their own (Safran et al., 2001). This dynamic has historically been a problem in recovery programs (Mann, 1950; Selzer, 1957).

[198] Vinokur and van Ryn (1993) showed that social undermining (i.e., conflict, criticism, making life difficult, and inducing feelings of being unwanted) in close relationships produces a negative effect on mental health that is stronger than the effect of social support.

[199] The term negative affect reciprocity is used to describe the expression of negative affect by one spouse, which is then reciprocated by negative affect from the other spouse, leading to the continuance of negative affective states and negative behavior across time (Gottman, 1979).

[200] Accordingly, clients who are more defensive in therapy have shown less improvement at the conclusion of therapy (Piper, DeCarufel, & Szkrumelak, 1985).

[201] Clients are more likely to benefit from therapy when they feel comfortable with the therapy relationship and are not overly concerned about rejection (Eames & Roth, 2000; Kanninen et al., 2000).

is met with strength and urgency. However, the client does not become the target of hostility or exploitation, because a knowledgeable care provider recognizes that these are incompatible with the core objectives of therapy.

While for some it may seem obvious that the therapist should always remain respectful, it is important to recognize that the tendency to reciprocate behavioral hostility is an insidious problem.[202] In some instances, hostility toward the client may be unconscious and unintentional. While most professionals are seeking to create positive interactions by demonstrating an earnest desire to provide help, these gestures are sometimes met with suspicion and resistance,[203] making it difficult to develop a positive feeling toward the client.[204] Furthermore, individuals who are most familiar with negative interaction styles will naturally use hostility in an attempt to influence the behavior of the therapist or to facilitate engagement. When interacting with a client who is hostile, the therapist's "supportive" messages may carry implicit criticisms, or the therapist's interpretations may become less sympathetic and more judgmental.[205] Even if care providers recognize that they should not respond defensively to criticism from clients, there still might be a momentary scowl on the face, which insecure clients will notice and take as evidence of disdain.[206] Furthermore, attempts to use humor to diffuse the situation could inadvertently convey subtle hostility if the humor is characterized by sarcasm or teasing directed at the client's behavior. These are some of the reasons why it is so easy to become caught up in the reciprocal escalation of behavioral hostility before the therapist has time to recognize what is happening.

What is needed is a method for neutralizing behavioral hostility while demonstrating the type of affect attunement that allows the client to take the therapist seriously. This is achieved by directing the expression of negative energy away from the client, thus creating a vacuum, which is then filled with kindness and respect.

For example, after collage, I took a job as a substitute teacher and on

---

[202] Moskowitz (1993) found that men are most likely to overestimate their degree of friendliness.

[203] People who have more psychological symptomology are more likely to expect hostile behavior from others and to engage in negative complementarity with others (Rubin, Abeles, & Muller, 1992; Safran, 1990).

[204] Helpers whose offer of help was rejected expressed more negative expectancy violation, more negative affect, and more unfavorable evaluations of the recipient than did those whose offer was accepted (Rosen, Mickler, & Collins, 1987).

[205] Microanalyses of the interpersonal process revealed that care providers generally responded poorly to hostile patients. These conflicting interpersonal processes remained unidentified by both professional and lay therapists (Strupp, 1993).

[206] Even those transactions that only briefly communicate rejection will still have a negative impact on the alliance (Horvath, 2001).

my first week was sent to a middle school that had difficulty retaining teaching staff. Having found my way through the noise and chaos of the halls to my assigned room, I was greeted at the doorway by one of the coaches. He was much taller than me and had an exceedingly large chest. Putting his hand on my shoulder, he warned, "Hey, you have a Samoan in this class who is a dangerous kid. He has already seriously injured one teacher. Do not try to take him on by yourself. If you have any problems, come next door and get me." I thanked him for his offer and walked into the classroom wondering if I would know which student was "the Samoan."

Shortly after, a very large adolescent came parading into the room, flipping two desks over onto their sides as he walked down the aisle. After he sank into a desk, a girl called out, "Hey! That's my desk!" Then both of them looked over at me—her with an irritated expression and him with a glib smile. I smiled back to him and kindly requested that the girl find another seat for the time being, saying, "You will get your desk back, eventually." Fortunately, other students stepped in to upright the over turned desks so I did not have to react to that provocation.[207]

Then, after the tardy bell rang, I walked to the front of the class and made a stern announcement: "Your teacher has left a test for you all to take. There are no options about doing this. And to make certain everyone behaves, I am going to have one of your classmates come up to the front of the room and tell the class how it is going to be!" Then I looked at "the Samoan" (who was still sitting in the wrong desk) and motioned for him to come to the front of the room.

Stunned, he point at his chest. "Me?"

After I motioned again with a welcoming smile and a wave of my hand, he came to the front of the room. Then I repeated the instructions. "Now, you turn to face the class and tell everyone the rules for taking this test."

With a sudden loss of confidence, he replied, "I don't want to."

So I softened up as well. "You do not have to, but if you are not going to tell the class the rules for taking the test, then I need you to go sit in that desk right there [a desk set by the teacher's desk] and listen quietly as I tell the class the rules for taking the test."

Without protest, he took his seat in the assigned spot. Forty minutes went by with no further trouble from him. After turning in his test, he asked me for a bathroom pass. He had been very cooperative with me

---

[207] Some tolerance, allowing people to express their hostility openly, is needed for those who have never been allowed to defy an authority figure. Such individuals have a lifetime of pent up resentments, but have never been allowed to have a voice and express their anger; they are never allowed to win.

throughout the test period and had completed his work, so I decided to cooperate and give him his pass (so he could wander the halls briefly before taking on his next teacher). This single interaction was not enough to form a trusting relationship. However, with repeated exposure to that type of acceptance, combined with the expression of positive feelings, I would have succeeded in building a strong connection with an otherwise alienated individual.

In this example, it is important to recognize that I did communicate subtle hostility, but it was not directed toward the student. He was prepared for me to lash out at him verbally. He might have even been prepared for an attempt at a physical takedown. However, he was not prepared for me to direct my stern comments away from him and toward the class. It was "they" who needed to be told what to do during the test and how to act. Even more so, I was giving him the opportunity to exercise the authority, if he was willing to accept the responsibility.[208] He knew that I was engaging him, but because there was nothing for him to retaliate against, he stopped initiating hostile behavior. That was the vacuum into which I poured small amounts of kindness (by smiling at him and being sympathetic to his wishes when he said he did not want to announce the rules to the class).

In therapy, there are numerous options for where to deflect hostile energy during the process of affect attunement. One of my favorites is to get mad at the disease.[209] Though this alliance-building technique (i.e., treating the disease as a common enemy) may seem novel, it has been used for centuries, as evidenced in a quote by an unnamed physician from around 1200 CE: "Know that I and thou and the disease are three factors mutually antagonistic. If thou wilt side with me, not neglecting what I enjoin on thee and refraining from such things as I shall forbid thee, then we shall be two against one and will overcome the disease."

Similarly, American philosopher and psychologist William James (1906) also recognized the importance of directing hostile energy toward a common enemy, but one that is not a member of humanity, such as disease, natural catastrophes, and poverty.[210] Any human experience can be externalized and treated as an entity used to contain the expression of negative emotion. "We are not going to let this thing beat us!"

---

[208] Because no single student is "the class," there was no risk of hurting the feelings of a particular individual.

[209] Of course, if the client were feeling sad, then I would feel sad about the disease rather than mad.

[210] William James is considered to be the father of American psychology. These comments are found in his famous essay *The Moral Equivalent of War.*

In addition to getting mad about an addiction that has destroyed a client's life or a childhood that was horribly brutal, it is also possible to direct negative energy toward innocuous objects. For example, I have made the clock on the wall into a common enemy—"I cannot believe how little time that clock is giving us for our meeting!" This allows clients to know that I share their frustration that the session did not last longer.

Having described the alliance boost that comes by directing hostile energy away from members of the dyad and toward a common enemy, it is important to note that an experienced therapist will not use estranged friends or family members as the common enemy. Anyone who has worked with unhappy married people knows that it is common for one spouse to come to the therapist searching for someone to be sympathetic to his or her cause. Such a client will often seek to spend the majority of the session complaining about the spouse. Joining in with this type of hostility (e.g., "Your wife sounds terrible!") is typically a *poor* choice. If the client has an anger-management problem, then any vilification of the spouse could actually put the couple at greater risk for domestic violence. Even if that were not the case, this type of response certainly would not help the marriage and does not help the client gain any insight into his or her own behavior. It is similarly unwise to direct negative comments towards the client's parents or other significant people in his or her life. Instead, it is better to reciprocate the emotional energy by directing negative feelings toward nameless individuals who do not have any real presence in the client's life. "If you and your wife decide to get a divorce, I just hope that no unethical lawyers get involved. I can't stand it when I hear about a greedy, attack-dog attorney making twenty thousand off of a nasty divorce that he helped prolong in the courts!"

Positive Emotional Experiences Are a Crucial Component of the Client-Therapist Relationship

Because negative feelings spread more easily than positive ones,[211] it could be argued that the communication and joint experiencing of positive emotional states requires a greater amount of interpersonal skill. After the problems created by an escalation of hostile feelings have been recognized, it is important to consider the role of positive feelings protecting and main-

---

[211] Negative events tend to elicit stronger and quicker emotional, behavioral, and cognitive responses than neutral or positive events. Thus, unpleasant emotions are more likely to lead to emotional contagion than pleasant emotions are.

taining relationships.[212]

While it does not work well to engage joyfully a person who is feeling miserable, there are moments that follow the validation of a negative state in which it is possible to shift rapidly to a positive state. If therapists are watching the client close enough, they will see when the client is ready to shift into a different emotional frame of reference.[213] At that time, the emotional exchange can cycle into another negative topic or to a positive experience, such as a humorous remark or deep, affirming gaze, which then can trigger a cascade of positive emotions.

For example, one day I found myself sitting across from a 12-year-old boy who had been secretly moved to Arizona by his mother so that his exceedingly violent and heavily armed father would not find and kill them. The father had received a dishonorable discharge from the military and was on a list of FBI suspects for a series of sniper attacks on the East Coast highways. The boy had witnessed his father's violent behavior and knew about the man's threats to kill his mother. The boy did not feel that he could spend another night in their one-room shelter because his infant twin sisters were crying throughout the night, so he could not get any rest. Unfortunately, he decided that any anger he felt toward his mother or sisters was evidence that he would turn out to be just like his father. To make matters worse, he had talked about his situation with the children at his new school and, as a result, was being mocked for having a "crazy dad." During the schoolyard teasing, he was pushed to the ground, tearing the knees out of his only pair of jeans, which he knew his mother did not have money to replace.

So there he sat in front of me, his bent glasses sitting crossways on his red, corkscrewed face. His breath came in short gasps as tears rolled down his cheeks and as he rocked back and fourth, rubbing his hands down the top of his thighs, just above his scraped up knees. Shaking his head back and forth, he rhythmically chanted, "I just can take it any more, I can't take it any more, I can't take it any more." I had been sharing his sadness and his fear.[214]

But after awhile, his hands became still, and he shifted his gaze up toward me. So I took the opportunity to surprise him with an unexpected

---

[212] A stable relationship seems to require that there is more than double the amount of positive versus negative feeling expressed (Gottman, 1994).

[213] If someone suddenly shifts a larger part of the body, such as readjusting the pelvis or uncrossing the legs, then a meaningful psychological shift has most likely occurred, and the individual will be more likely seek to pursue a new topic or explore a new attitude (Frey, Jorns & Daw, 1980).

[214] His situation was honestly a sad one, and I was sincerely afraid. The mother had warned me that the father might know where they were hiding and that if the father were following her, he would certainly seek to abduct his son from my office.

question, "What is it that you *really* cannot take any more?"

His response was, "Talking to my dad on the phone."

Now I was surprised. "You call him?"

He explained that he secretly went to a pay phone once a week, but that he would never tell his father where they were hiding. I asked how long his phone calls lasted, and he responded that they were only a few minutes in duration.

Seeking to obtain a commitment, I asked, "So this time on the phone is what you really cannot stand?"

With a new expression on his face, he noted, "It's really not that much time."

Then I asked another odd question, "How long do you think your father will live?" When he did not have an answer, I went on to explain the differences in life expectancy for those who had a destructive and hostile personality type as compared to those who are good at giving and receiving care. I also pointed out that his use of humor matched that of people who live to be over a hundred. Throughout all of these exchanges, my movements were highly animated, and my energy level was high.[215]

By this point, he was smiling, and we spent the rest of the session making funny remarks and discussing exactly how he was going to use his natural sense of humor to make one or two friends at his new school.[216] Because he was capable of confronting a father that terrified most adults, I pointed out that he did not need to be bothered if one or two playground bullies remained unwilling to like him. All of these ideas made perfect sense to him and fit with the emotional context that had been created.

A day later, when I had an opportunity to see his mother, she commented on noticeable changes in her son. "I do not know how you guys do it! After his first visit with you, he came home joking and laughing. It is the first time I have seen that child laugh in over five years." Following his involvement with me, the boy started to feel more positive about himself and his future, despite the fact that I was unable to do anything to change the horrendous circumstances with which he was faced.[217]

A final crucial point, which is likely obvious to most anyone who has

---

[215] Because higher energy causes more attention to the emotional expression, the energy level at which emotion is displayed will influence the likelihood of emotional contagion (Barsade, 2002).

[216] Numerous studies have found that positive affective experiences increase attraction and solidify social bonds (Clark & Watson, 1988; Gouaux, 1971; May & Hamilton, 1980; Veitch & Griffitt, 1976).

[217] Similarly, research suggests that positive interpersonal involvements increase feelings of self-worth, contribute to a sense of personal control, and foster generalized positive affect (Cassel, 1976; Hammer, 1981; Thoits, 1983).

not yet been exposed to years of training in psychotherapy techniques, is that casual conversation is important to building intimacy. People want to be treated as human beings rather than objects to be examined or manipulated. While problem identification and goal setting are important activities, most people want to be known in terms of their recent experiences, casual interests, or idiosyncrasies that set them a part from others. And it is during these moments, when you engage in casual conversation, that the potential for a positive reciprocal interaction spiral is greatest. When given permission to relax and engage in lighthearted conversation, clients learn that their symptoms and problems are not the sole ingredient for important interpersonal experiences. In this way, a new emotional experience is created.[218]

The Imitation of Posture and Movement Helps Communicate Attunement

The importance of seeing one's own behavior or words mirrored in others is not a new concept. Nearly four decades ago, Heinz Kohut (1971) coined the term *disintegration anxiety* to depict the feeling of threat to self resulting from the failure to be mirrored by others. Kohut (1984) argued that all individuals have a need for "accurate mirroring," and if this need is unmet, it results in a state of distress characterized by emptiness, incoherence, or feelings of worthlessness. Out on the street, when we wave to someone, we want to see the person wave back. It is not only the acknowledgement of the greeting that is important, but also the manner in which it is imitated. Waving to a person, who returns the greeting with the nod of the head, typically does not produce as much satisfaction as a matched wave. One of the quickest means of communicating acceptance of another person's state of being is to incorporate that person's observable behavior into our responses. In regard to therapy, mirroring small movements and verbally tracking client behaviors has long been viewed as a means of increasing rapport.[219]

When therapists are using verbal tracking, it is natural to synchronize this behavior with a description of client behavior. For instance, clients are made aware of the significance of their adjustments as the therapist focuses on breathing, saying, for example, "I can see that your breathing has slowed. And that you are taking in air with easy, relaxed movements." While one is

---

[218] Similarly, the practice of altering rigid relational patterns through exposure to positive interpersonal experiences with the therapist is a core tenant of short-term psychodynamic models of therapy. This practice is referred to as a "corrective emotional experience" (Teyber, 2000).

[219] For example, Charny (1966) observed that when postures assumed by the patient and therapist become congruent, the dialogue becomes more positive, interpersonal, specific, and bound to the therapeutic situation.

saying this, it would be natural to synchronize one's breathing with the client's or also match his or her posture. When this type of attunement occurs, clients are provided with palpable evidence of their existential reality and, thus, greater motivation to improve their existence.[220]

Interestingly, it seems that most individuals mimic others' behavior without intending to and without realizing that they have done so.[221] Functioning as an act of communication and belonging, motor mimicry is heightened in relationships where there is a close bond or strong alliance.

As an example, I had a 35-year-old *client* who doubted his ability to benefit from therapy. He openly expressed his appreciation for me as a therapist and my efforts to assist him, but was not certain I could help him overcome two decades of highly dysfunctional behavior, which numerous psychiatrists had diagnosed as bipolar disorder and which he believed to be a physiological problem rather than a psychological one. As he was reaching the end of his explanation, I slowly lifted my left arm into the air while still looking deep into his eyes. He noticed the movement of my left arm and stopped talking. I slowly shifted my gaze to my arm, and then I looked directly at his right arm, which was now frozen up in midair. When the client turned his head and discovered that his own arm was up in the air, he shouted, "Oh shit!" and waved his hand around as if something frightening had landed on it. He then turned to me with delight and eagerly asked, "How did you do that?" I responded by pointing out that the therapy may be having an influence on him at deeper levels than he might initially recognize.

Three years later, when this individual had turned his life around from chronic unemployment and unhealthy dependency on his family to starting his own business, he asked me, "Are you going to include me as one of the success stories in your next book?" I assured him that I would. By this time, his confidence had shifted more inwardly, so that he no longer needed to believe that only powerful drugs or powerful doctors could save him. In reality, my demonstration with his spontaneous arm movement was not that extraordinary, though its impact was spectacular.

At that time, he knew we had a shared goal (i.e., his well-being), he liked me as a person, and he wanted me to like him. These are the same conditions that research has shown to be necessary for automatic motor

---

[220] Research has demonstrated that if individuals' momentary awareness of self is heightened by including in the environment a stimulus that is self-symbolic in some way (a sort of mirror), individuals typically engage in more self-evaluation and increase efforts to regulate their behavior (Wicklund, 1982).

[221] This phenomenon is referred to as "the chameleon effect" (Chartrand & Bargh, 1999).

mimicry.[222] As he was talking, I moved my left leg forward and noticed that he automatically moved his right leg forward. So next, I moved that leg back and moved my right leg forward; accordingly, he mimicked the behavior without conscious awareness. So when I raised my arm in the air, his responses had already been tested. I knew he would imitate the behavior, and I simply used the shifting of my gaze as a means of drawing attention to what he was doing. I find that this happens often with clients with whom I have developed a strong rapport. When I lean to the left, they lean to the left. If I cross my legs, they cross their legs. In most instances it is not necessary to point out the spontaneous behavior to the client, but rather to simply take note of the fact that a strong rapport has been formed and can be further nourished by the therapist's willingness to mimic the client's movements and posture as an act of attunement and validation.

---

[222] Motor mimicry is most likely to occur when people perceive themselves as similar (Cappella & Palmer, 1990), when they have shared goals (Lanzetta & Englis, 1989) or shared attitudes (McHugo, Lanzetta & Bush, 1991), if they like the person they are responding to (Bernieri & Rosenthal, 1991) or wish for this person to have a liking toward them (Bavelas et al., 1986).

Chapter 3

RECIPROCITY
Sustainable Relationships Require Equanimity

*Someday, and that day may never come, I'll call upon you
to do a service for me. But until that day, accept this justice
as a gift on my daughter's wedding.*
—Don Corleone, *The Godfather*, 1972

The concept of reciprocity has ancient origins that can be traced back to numerous world cultures, as expressed in both religion and philosophy. An awareness of the human tendency toward reciprocity has been promoted by influential leaders to avert conflict, as demonstrated by the moral imperative of *Muhammad,* "Hurt no one, so that no one may hurt you,"[223] and the wisdom of *Confucius,* "Never impose on others what you would not choose for yourself."[224] The ethic of reciprocity has also been used to elevate the quality of interaction among members of society, such as in the teachings of Jesus Christ, "Whatever you want people to do for you, do the same for them,"[225] and in Greek philosophy, "What you wish your neighbors to be to you, such be also to them."[226] Then there are also universal notions of reciprocity expressed in the Buddhist philosophy of Karma; the divine justice of Judaism, "an eye for an eye"[227]; and the vernacular of modern times, "What goes around comes around." While the ethic of reciprocity serves is a basis for the modern concept of human rights and social

---

[223] This statement was made during The Farewell Sermon, delivered before Muhammad's death, on the ninth day of Dhu al-Hijjah, 10 A.H. (632 C.E.).

[224] Cited in the Analects XV.24, translation by David Hinton.

[225] From the Gospel of Luke 6:31, the International Standard Version.

[226] A Pythagorean maxim found in The Sentences of Sextus the Pythagorean, 406 B.C., rendered by Thomas Taylor, 1818.

[227] Obadiah Shoher argues that the literal reading of Exodus 21:23–25, the first occurrence of the phrase "an eye for an eye," applies the punishment only for harming pregnant women, whereas Exodus 21:18–19 prescribes only reimbursement of medical costs and work income for the harm done to men.

justice, it is also the one-on-one process of continually reconciling our actions against the actions of others that determines the sustainability of any
given relationship.

More than a cultural trend, religious tradition, or tool of economics,
the need for reciprocity seems to emanate from psychological and even biological processes. Core sociopsychological experiences, such as obligation,
cooperation, duty, sympathy, and anger over injustice, all involve behavioral
accounting relative to the action and experience of others. The presence of
oxytocin in the brain has been linked to the mirroring of emotion that
makes this type of social orientation possible.[228] Outside the world of human relating, examples of reciprocity can be found in the grooming habits
of primates, the cooperative work of rats,[229] and in the collaborative efforts
of lower ranking baboons as they compete with the alpha male for repro-
ductive females.[230]

As will become evident in this chapter, reciprocity serves as one of the
clearest examples of horizontal complementarity. Relationships characterized by reciprocity become deeply interconnected, as the actions of one individual both justifies and compels the other to respond with behaviors
that likewise justify and reinforce the behavior of the original actor. The
only way to escape this spiraling loop is to refuse any favors and ignore any
insults from those with whom you do not wish to become involved (thus
the ominous quote from Don Corleone).

It Is Within the Context of Cooperative Endeavors
That Equanimity Will Flourish

The concept of justice is a powerful component of emotional coping.
When people perceive that an injustice has occurred, they are likely to respond with anger or outrage. If the accused is later "brought to justice" and
suffers a punishment equal to the crime, then the emotional tension is alle-
viated. However, justice is impossible to conceive of without an underlying
assumption of equality. The idea that everyone is accountable to the law or

---

[228] Pfaff's theory (2007) is built on recent findings showing that human beings have neural
mechanisms that literally create the sensation of another's pain in our own brains. In
stressful or conflictual environments, these mechanisms are inhibited, leading to isolation,
selfishness, and immorality.

[229] The cooperative behavior of female rats is influenced by prior receipt of help, such that
they work harder for an unknown partner if they were previously helped by that partner
(Rutte & Taborsky, 2007).

[230] Amongst a group of wild baboons (Papio c. Cynocephalus), coalitions were formed during conflicts against a high-ranking male and in contests for consorts (Noë, 1990).

that everyone has equal rights is essential for any exercise of justice.

When thinking about the verbal interchange between client and therapist, it may be less common to think about justice; however, the twin concept of fairness is obliviously relevant. No person wants to be treated unfairly, and most do not want to consider themselves as having acted unfairly toward others. Therefore, this universal social accounting system needs to be taken into consideration during all interpersonal exchanges.

While perfect equality is more of a guiding principle than social reality, general equanimity, by contrast, seems to be a requirement of sustainable relationships. The difference between equality and equanimity is one of social domains; the former pertaining more so to social structure, while the later is associated with social accounting. As should be clear by now, healthy relationships do not require the absence of social organization (i.e., dominant and submissive roles), but rather the management of reciprocal obligations and benefits so that individual resources are not depleted. In other words, person A cannot continually give energy and resources to person B, unless B gives something back *before* A is depleted. When equanimity is established, there is a sharing of experience and joining of behavior that tends to strengthen both participants.

In relationships characterized by reciprocity, when people initiate a pattern of behavior, such as providing corrective feedback, they are open to becoming the recipient of that same behavior. This dynamic stands in stark contrast to the unilateralism imposed in abusive or controlling relationships. The terse phrase "Do as I say, not as I do" sets the stage for cruelty. Neither individual is likely to grow or find increased strength from the relationship. By contrast, reciprocity acts as a safeguard—"I am not going to do that to you because I would not want it done to me." Similarly, the old adage "If you can dish it out, then you better be able to take it in" also speaks to the principle of reciprocity.

While reciprocity certainly contains elements of verification, it goes beyond mere acceptance by creating a shared constellation of costs and payback. In other words, I cooperate with you so that you will cooperate with me. If you show a strong emotion, you can expect that I will demonstrate strong emotion as well. If I help you with something important, then I should be willing to receive help back from you. In this way, both individuals share in the same set of benefits. It is at this point that the application of reciprocity to therapy gets tricky, since it threatens the unilateralism of a traditionally defined helper-helpee relationship. However, within the context of a relational model, therapy is viewed more as a bilateral agreement in which the two participants share joint responsibility for the final outcome.[231]

In contrast to involuntary relations, which are governed by power and control, voluntary affiliations depend on collaboration and shared risks and benefits. The implication for therapy is that the therapist-client relationship will need to develop as a cooperative endeavor in which both individuals are free contributors.[232] It also means that if therapists wish to be helpful to clients, they should allow clients to return the favor in some way. Furthermore, if therapists wish to disagree with certain client behaviors, then therapists should be willing to accept equal risk, thus allowing clients to disagree with the therapists' behavior in return.

While reciprocity can be strategically employed to drive sequences of interaction that would otherwise fail to occur, it does not threaten freedom of will. For example, after listening to an angry client elaborate in great detail all the reasons why the failed marriage is entirely his wife's fault, I will sometimes respond, "I have sat for twenty minutes and listened carefully to everything you had to say. Now will you likewise sit and listen to my feedback?"[233] After listening, the client is entirely free to point out problems with my statements. And in this way, a reciprocal process of listening to one another is begun. Therefore, while creating a collaborative alliance, it is not control that is sought, but rather a spirit of voluntary cooperation.[235]

Once the unilateral approach to helper-helpee relations is rejected, it no longer makes sense to dictate a treatment plan for the client. Rather, the therapy plan needs to be negotiated between client and therapist.[236] From this perspective, there is a readiness to learn about the client's preferences and to discuss concessions to be made by the client and by the therapist. The seeking of mutual consent initiates an interaction sequence that ulti-

---

[231] Sequential analyses of dyadic interactions revealed that help seekers and help providers influence one another's behaviors during support interactions such that no one person is solely responsible for the outcome of an interaction (Barbee, 1990; Cutrona, 1996).

[232] Accordingly, cooperation in therapy has been linked to reductions in somatic complaints and paranoid symptoms (Kolb, Beutler, Davis, Crago, & Shanfield, 1985).

[233] I have heard professional negotiators say, "Whoever talks most during negotiation loses." Similarly, the therapist should never seek to outtalk an emotional client. A 20-minute diatribe by the client is best met with no more than five minutes of feedback from the therapist.

[234] It has been pointed out that this type of sequence makes both parties simultaneously givers and receivers of feedback (Claiborn, Goodyear & Horner, 2001).

[235] It has been argued that the therapist should contract with the client so that the client expects to participate, rather than merely cooperate, in order to achieve positive outcomes (Schulman, 1979).

[236] When therapists and patients achieve consensus about a treatment plan, and when therapists explain the rationale for the plan and how it works, patients are more satisfied with the initial session (Eisenthal, Koopman & Lazare, 1983).

mately increases the probability of acceptance. In other words, if I ask your permission before I act, then it is less likely that you will reject my action. Because the seeking of consent is reciprocal, the benefits of increased acceptance are also enjoyed by both participants.

Healthy Collaborations Balance Giving and Receiving, Which Results in Mutual Involvement and Mutual Benefit

A therapeutic relationship is one in which the well-being of the other matters. While the client and therapist do not share equal roles, there is reason for the interest in each other's well-being to be a shared concern.[237] As most care providers know, supporting others provides meaning and a special type of satisfaction.[238] Perhaps that is why clients who are able to help their therapists in some way experience an emotional boost and are more appreciative of the relationship.[239]

The ecology produced by a positive reciprocal-interaction spiral spreads beyond the capabilities of just one individual. Rather than viewing the therapist as the principal agent of change, the relationship itself can be seen as fertilizer within which both the client and therapist grow. In a positive reciprocal-interaction spiral, both individuals are happy to contribute to the well-being of the other, and both enjoy various rewards. These rewards might be psychological, such as mutual respect and affirmation, as well as material, such as clients experiencing a reduction in physical distress and therapists receiving financial remuneration. Certainly, when the relationship is functioning at optimum levels, each encounter will produce some growth or learning for both the client and the therapist.

Typically, clients are content with the fee they pay as being the reciprocal benefit for the services they receive. However, there are occasions in therapy when something is said by the therapist that the client perceives as extraordinarily beneficial. And it is after such instances that clients might feel compelled to offer some additional reward for the therapist. For instance, having recognized that my children are important to me, my clients have recommended outings that the children are certain to enjoy or offered some small token for the children, such as a pen or party favor. When this occurs, the gesture can typically be traced to a moment when the client felt

---

[237] Researchers argue that support-seeking and caregiving behaviors are highly interdependent and meshed in complementary ways (Collins & Feeney, 2000).

[238] Research has shown that acts of kindness can boost happiness. Students who performed five acts of kindness during a single day experienced a significant increase in well-being (Lyubomirsky, et. al., 2005).

[239] People prefer relationships in which both parties give and receive care (Hays, 1985).

especially grateful for something I did. In one such instance, I had a woman, who identified herself as a "typical Jewish mother," bring me a large meal from a kosher bakery. With a smile and motherly undertones, she commented, "You are too skinny, you need more meat on your bones." Her method of showing love was to feed people. During the previous session, she had experienced a major emotional breakthrough and apparently felt a need to offer something in return.

When considering the needs of the client and the importance of reciprocity, one realizes that attempts to establish equanimity should not be rejected. If reasonable acts of reciprocity are refused, it places the other individual in a position of shame and diminishes the experience of interdependence that would have otherwise strengthened the relationship.[240]

The exception occurs when the gift is too extraordinary to count as a fair exchange. If a copious gift or act of gratitude is offered—one that cannot possibly be reciprocated—then action needs to be taken to prevent a capsizing of the relationship. If clients begin therapy by suggesting that they are prepared to offer large sums of money to a cause favored by the therapist,[241] or if clients come to therapy wearing provocative clothing and make seductive advances, then the therapist will need to redirect the interaction. Unfortunately, there are instances in which the clients' sense of personal value is so exceedingly low that they cannot imagine anyone having a serious interest in them without the provision of some highly enticing bribe. These individuals tend to be exceedingly vulnerable and highly submissive. Therefore, their miscalculation should be handled in a way that is gentle and does not cause unnecessary humiliation. This can be accomplished by changing the subject to a topic that creates a different emotional focus or by simply explaining how healthy relationships develop.

Such a client recently sat cross-legged and with her feet on my couch, describing her love of casual sex. During the discussion, she pulled her legs up to partially reveal her underwear and leaned forward to emphasize the full extent of her cleavage. By simply averting my gaze to a point off to the side of her and mentioning the importance of a girl protecting herself by using good boundaries, her energy was dramatically altered. With a sudden blank stare on her face, she placed both of her feet on the ground, pulled the edge of her dress down over her knees, and began to tell me of a frightening

---

[240] Studies compared people who received love without giving it and people who gave love without receiving it, finding that the lack of reciprocity was aversive even for those in the benefited position (Baumeister & Wotman, 1992; Baumeister, Wotman, & Stillwell, 1993).

[241] I had one client seductively reveal that she had donated two million dollars to the institute to which her previous therapist belonged.

experience with a man who attempted to violently rape her. Her self-esteem was exceedingly fragile; therefore, I handled the redirection with care. From that point forward, the client acted in a less provocative manner. When she indicated that the help I was giving was worth more than what I was paid, I let her know that it made me feel good to see her making progress toward stronger boundaries. And so, in that way, the social accounting system was made even.

When low self-esteem individuals fail to find someone who will reciprocate their positive gestures, problems with self-concept are made worse. This is particularly true for clients who are unable to assert their needs and, therefore, do for others that which they wish to receive. Such an individual is likely to be liberal with praise and emotionally moved if it is reciprocated. For most social settings, when a person shares a compliment, it is enough to respond with a warm "thank you." This response can serve as a reciprocal reaction by affirming that the other's opinion is something of importance. However, in therapy, when the client compliments the therapist, more explicit forms of reciprocal recognition may be indicated. Though the entire interaction, from start to finish, may be casual and brief, the effect can run much deeper. For instance, a client who had spent most of her childhood trying to prove her intelligence to a highly critical mother, responded to my dialogue with kind approval, saying "That last *reframe* you used was very helpful." I responded with a look of surprise and delight in my voice: "Not many of my clients know the names of the therapy techniques I am using. I am very impressed." My acknowledgement seemed to catch her off guard. However, the smile that appeared on her face suggested that the compliment was meaningful.

Following the maturation of a transformational relationship,[242] there are some clients who may become intensely interested in the idea that, in some small way, they have been able to contribute something of value to the care provider. If the individual feels indebted, it is helpful to respond to an expression of gratitude by pointing out the client's contributions to the care provider's well-being. Under these circumstances, I tend to emphasize what the client has helped me, as a professional, learn about the dynamics of human interaction. This is always a sincere statement because I do learn something from every person with whom I work. This type of reciprocal gratitude helps clients feel more comfortable with their own acknowledgement of what they have received. Furthermore, in any gathering of individuals, all group members should have the opportunity to feel that they have

---

[242] Strong and Claiborn (1982) noted that it is toward the end of the therapy experience that clients become more interested in the therapist as a person and a mutual participant in the relationship.

participated as valued contributors.

Relational Comfort Is Increased With Reciprocal Disclosure

Beginning with Freud's (1913) insistence that the patient must disclose to the therapist everything that comes to mind, the concept of self-disclosure has become an essential component in most psychological therapies.[243] This activity helps strengthen the therapeutic relationship when the client's self-disclosure is met with understanding and acceptance.[244] While self-disclosure by the therapist was initially discouraged, the contemporary trend is toward greater openness on the part of the therapist.[245] Because responsiveness is an important determinant of intimacy,[246] and because enduring relationships are more often characterized by mutual self-disclosure,[247] it is hard to imagine how a strong relationship would develop in the absence of reciprocal self-disclosure. If one accepts the idea that intimacy is a defining characteristic of close relationships,[248] then the importance of mutual self-disclosure is very apparent.[249]

Rather than weakening the position of the therapist, reciprocal self-disclosure builds trust while increasing the relevancy of therapeutic feedback: "You have been honest and direct with me, and I appreciate it. Now I will be just as open and honest in my response to you."[250] After I make such a statement, most clients will thank me for my candor. Research has shown that clients have a greater liking for therapists who offer reciprocal self-disclosure.[251]

---

[243] Beginning in the 1960s, researchers began to recognize that more successful patients show more self-exploration and self-disclosure during psychotherapy (Truax, Tomlinson & van der Veen, 1961/1965).

[244] People are happiest in their relationships when they believe their partners know their true selves, yet accept them nonetheless (Swann, Hixon, & De La Ronde, 1992).

[245] The trend in current therapeutic practice is for clinicians to be more disclosing (Strkker & Fisher, 1991).

[246] Perceived partner responsiveness has been associated with intimacy in interpersonal exchanges (Laurenceau, Barrett, & Pietromonaco, 1998).

[247] Reciprocity of self-disclosure does not necessarily occur within the same interaction episode (Derlega, Wilson, & Chaikin, 1976).

[248] It is interesting to note that loneliness comes from of a lack of intimate interactions rather than of a lack of social contact (Reis, 1990; Wheeler, Reis, & Nezlek, 1983).

[249] Intimacy has been closely linked to reciprocal self-disclosure (Derlega, Wilson & Chaikin, 1976).

[250] Negative feedback is generally more acceptable when it is immediately preceded by positive feedback (Stockton & Morran, 1981), that is why I like to compliment clients for being honest and direct before offering constructive criticism.

[251] Specifically, clients who received therapist self-disclosures that were similar to their own self-disclosures liked their therapists more and had less symptom distress after treatment (Barrett & Berman, 2001).

While concepts such as the "transparent therapist" date back to the existential movement of the 1960s,[252] the type of self-disclosure described here is not driven by the Rogerian philosophy of self-congruence (i.e., an intrapsychic process), but rather by an appreciation for the role of reciprocity in bringing balance to relationships (i.e., an interpersonal process). In other words, as the client makes him or herself more open and vulnerable, the therapist develops a tailored response that in some way matches or compliments the client's behavior. This type of reciprocity helps the client feel accepted and understood[253] while also strengthening the relational bond.[254]

For example, the client might confess, "I was feeling anxious before coming here. I did not know what I would say." This self-disclosure could be reciprocated by the therapist at the emotional level, "I also get a little anxious when I am about to do something that is really important," or at the situational level, "I did not know what I would say either—not until now." Both comments reveal something about the therapist. The first response is geared more toward emotional exploration. The latter is aimed more at intellectual understandings. While both are beneficial, they will achieve slightly different results.[255]

Of course, reciprocal behavior does not always need to be immediate. There may be one session that is devoted entirely to the client's exploration of important childhood memories, and it may not be until the following week that the therapist uses an example from his or her own childhood to communicate some idea to the client. Although the client rarely makes the connection at the conscious level, my experience has been that following these types of reciprocal disclosures clients are openly appreciative of how "real" the interactions feel to them.[256]

---

[252] Early research indicated a significant relationship between therapist transparency or self-congruence and the patient's level of self-disclosure or self-exploration (Truax & Carkhuff, 1965).

[253] This type of therapeutic self-disclosure, tailored to reflect the client's feelings, opinions, wishes, values, or beliefs, has been described elsewhere in terms of active listening and empathic feedback (Crowell et al., 2002).

[254] Knox et al. (1997) found that therapist self-disclosures led to client insight and made the therapist seem more real and human, which, in turn, improved the therapeutic relationship and helped clients feel reassured and normal. Similarly, meta-analytic studies indicate that people like others as a result of those others disclosing something of importance to them (Collins & Miller, 1994).

[255] It has been argued that it is important to distinguish self-disclosures that reveal feelings (immediacy statements) from those that are information focused (Hill & Knox, 2001).

[256] Similarly, Hill et al. (1988) found that clients gave the highest ratings of helpfulness and had the highest subsequent experiencing levels (i.e., involvement with their feelings) when exposed to therapist self-disclosures.

It is also important to note that when therapists are able to discuss openly their own strengths and weaknesses,[257] they serve as a model for clients searching for ways to communicate their own strengths and weaknesses. My experience has been that personal disclosures help most clients feel that the person they are working with is honest and, therefore, someone to be trusted. While there are some client groups with whom it is not advisable to confess mistakes,[258] in general, people tend to respond favorably to the admission of weakness.[259] This is especially true when clients are struggling to reveal their own weaknesses.

On the flip side, therapists' willingness to discuss their own strengths and accomplishments will likely enhance the relationship if it is a reciprocal activity located within the context of the clients' exploration of their personal strengths and abilities. This type of response will provide a little deeper connection between client and therapist, but this response should only take place after the client's recognition of personal strength has been fully verified. In other words, the clients remain the topic of conversation as their strengths are verified by the therapist. Then later on, when the clients need a break from talking about themselves, the therapist can reflect on important skills he or she has learned.

As can be seen, the benefits of therapist self-disclosure are well documented; however, too much of anything can be harmful. Clients typically seek help from someone whom they assume will sit and listen to *their* problems. Therefore, therapist self-disclosure should be kept brief.[260] Rather than therapists pursuing a policy of absolute transparency, there are some concerns or feelings of distain that therapists should keep to themselves.[261] I have had clients come in and tell stories of having their genitals mutilated by parents or of being forced to drink a sibling's urine as a punishment. While listening to these types of stories, it is possible to have internal reactions that do not need to be disclosed. Under these conditions, intimacy is best fostered by responding in a way that helps the client feel understood,

---

[257] A survey of former clients who had received at least six sessions of treatment found that clients rated therapists' sharing of personal information as having a beneficial effect on therapy (Ramsdell & Ramsdell, 1993).

[258] See the comments about individuals with a personality disorder, page 190.

[259] People who are open about their flaws tend to be viewed as likeable, worthy of assistance, and deserving of forgiveness (Allyn, 2004).

[260] It has also been argued that therapist self-disclosure should be infrequent (Hill & Knox, 2001).

[261] Hill, Mahalik, and Thompson (1989) found that reassuring disclosures were viewed as more helpful than challenging disclosures in terms of both client and therapist helpfulness ratings and subsequent client experiencing levels (Hill, Mahalik, & Thompson, 1989).

validated, and supported,[262] rather than dirty, damaged, or ostracized.

In contrast, it seems that therapists who are not prepared to deal with this sort of unpleasant information often respond in a way that signals clients to avoid further intimate self-disclosure. When this happens, clients hold the information in a shameful state of secrecy ("Not even my therapist wants to know about this"). While colleagues have commented that I have a strange knack for getting clients with the most bizarre personal histories, my suspicion is that I get average clients who share information that would otherwise be kept from those who do not seem ready to hear it. As one client recently commented, "I like talking with you better than with my last therapist. Somehow it seems more real. I guess because you are not afraid to say things about yourself." What my clients do not know is that my self-disclosures are strategically tailored to be brief (so that attention is not taken away from the client's internal focus) and affirming (so that the client feels understood and validated).

Finally, excessive therapist self-disclosure can go so far as to compromise the role of therapist. While prohibitions against duel relationships are commonly aimed at sexual misconduct, any instance in which the roles of the client and therapist become confused can be equally problematic. Therefore, the professional care provider should never self-disclose so much personal information that it becomes unclear who is the therapist and who is the client.[263] Because the therapy session should be focused on the needs of the client, it is unnecessary for the client to develop an intimate understanding of the therapist's needs or private experiences.[264] Similarly, therapists should not make reference to their own private bodily functions, nor should they disclose information about their sexual experiences.[265] Such comments are not likely to produce therapeutic benefit, but rather to create suspicion of the clinician's intentions or disgust over what most would perceive as inappropriate behavior.

---

[262] This type of response is crucial for developing intimacy, because it indicates awareness of central aspects of the self, which include goal attainment, positive affects, and the personally relevant activities that foster them (Reis & Shaver, 1988).

[263] It is commonly agreed that therapists should avoid using disclosures that are for their own needs, that remove the focus from the client, that interfere with the flow of the session, or that burden or over stimulate the client (Edwards & Murdock, 1994; Simon, 1990).

[264] In a review of analogue literature, Watkins (1990) concluded that therapists who self-disclosed in a moderate or nonintimate way have been viewed more favorably and have elicited more client self-disclosure than therapists who did not disclose at all, who disclosed a lot, or who disclosed very intimate material.

[265] It has been argued that the most appropriate topic for therapist self-disclosure involves professional background, whereas the least appropriate topics include sexual practices and beliefs (Hill & Knox, 2001).

Chapter 4

ATTACHMENT

Having a Safe Haven in Times of Stress Helps Increase Coping

All of us, from the cradle to the grave, are happiest
when life is organized as a series of excursions,
long or short, from the secure base
provided by our attachment figure(s).
—John Bowlby, 1988

After working at the London Child Guidance Clinic, starting in 1936, John Bowlby formulated attachment theory to explain the problems that developed when young children were removed from their parents and placed in the care of unfamiliar caregivers in strange surroundings. His theory centers on the universal need to form and maintain secure relationships. This innate tendency to seek closeness and maintain an affectional bond is elicited most powerfully at times of physical or emotional distress.[266] When in danger, children naturally seek support from and increase proximity to their parents.[267] Similarly, after a crisis or seemingly threatening situation, it is not uncommon for adults who are typically self-reliant to resist being left alone. Thus, emotional attachment (or bonding[268]) is most likely to occur when the distress of a dependent is matched with the support of a caregiver. Throughout our life span, our most intense emotional experiences tend to occur during the formation, disruption, and renewal of relationships (e.g., at occasions such as weddings and funerals, or in places such as hospital waiting rooms and divorce court). Therefore, the question of complementarity between client and therapist should take into account the

---

[266] Some have even suggested that the overall goal of psychotherapy should be to enhance clients' ability to elicit social support in their everyday lives (Brehm, 1987).

[267] Children as old as eight to ten years continue to view their parents as a primary basis of all types of emotional support (Shaver & Hazan, 1993).

[268] A therapeutic bond is conceptualized as a positive interpersonal attachment characterized by mutual trust, confidence, and acceptance (Hatcher & Barends, 1996; Safran & Wallner, 1991).

client's need for separation and connectedness, a need that can vary from encounter to encounter.

The Need for Attachment Security Is Common to Therapy

At the start of life, there is a coordinated relationship between parent and infant in which the infant's signals of distress trigger the parent to increase proximity and offer comforting strokes. In older children, a coordinated attachment relationship is still crucial; however, it is psychological availability or parental attention that the child seeks to maintain. The parent who understands the child's attachment needs will respond to distress signals by increasing the ease by which the child can relate to the parent or the parent to the child (e.g., participating in a shared activity or reflecting on parent-child similarities rather than differences). As one mother would say to her young daughter when the girl started to act cranky, "You seem to be suffering from lack-o-lovitis," which the mother followed up with a hug and a few moments of sitting and talking with her daughter. The mom claimed that this response often produced a dramatic change in her daughter's mood and behavior. Of course, the need for psychological closeness and affection does not disappear in adulthood.

During therapy, it is important that the therapist recognize the client's distress signals and respond in a way that will be interpreted as care or protection. As will be explained later in greater detail, the simple act of reflecting on the client's earlier experiences with a capable attachment figure can have a beneficial effect. In some instances, I have helped new clients come out of a state of intense distress (including psychotic episodes) by simply having the client share with me the most important memories from his or her work with an earlier therapist who successfully created a secure attachment. In instances such as these, the threat to the client's well-being, as well as the provision of a safe haven, may occur at preconscious levels. Often, clients will respond with statements such as, "I do not know why, but when I am in your office I start to feel more safe. There is just something about being here in this room." With adults and older children, protection is often accomplished psychologically, and the therapist does not have to physically hold or move closer to the client. Although, when clients sheepishly confess, "I don't know why, but for some reason I feel like I really need a hug," I consider the attachment system to have been healthily activated and, thus, respond with compassion.

Because the attachment system is activated most strongly during times of adversity, and it is during times of adversity that people seek therapy, the provision of attachment security is almost always complimentary, especially at the start of therapy. When there is a reliable source of secure attachment in the home, outside support is less important. However, those coming to therapy tend to have weaker or more insecure attachments in general.[269] Those who do not feel that they have someone to turn to for love and protection are less likely to have well-developed ego strength[270] or self-care skills[271] and, therefore, suffer from a variety of emotional issues.[272] For these reasons, therapists who are prepared to serve as a secure base tend to be a good fit for insecurely attached individuals.

Developing a strong therapeutic alliance with individuals who have not had the benefits of secure attachment does not come without challenges.[273] For example, even the slightest offense can be interpreted as evidence of impending rejection and result in a wide range of defensive behaviors, including (but not limited to) a reduction in self-disclosure, withdrawal into silence, lashing out with critical remarks, denial, emotional suppression or projection, erecting a superficial wall of conformity, or premature termination of the therapy relationship.[274] With these clients, the probability of misunderstanding remains high, as does the possibility of uncomfortable social interactions.[275] Thus, responding to a person's attachment needs is more complex than simply being emotionally warm and affirming. Skillful psychological care requires an appreciation for the amount of support and emotional closeness that is needed at any given moment.[276]

---

[269] Individuals with insecure adult attachment styles are overrepresented in clinical samples (Dolan et al., 1993; Mickelson, Kessler, & Shaver, 1997), and it is a troubled relationship, especially a distressed marital or family relationship, that is the most common presenting problem of those seeking psychotherapy (Berscheid & Reis, 1998).

[270] The correlates of insecure adult attachment include lower levels of self-esteem and poor emotional adjustment (Cooper et al., 1998; Collins, 1996; Pietromonaco & Barrett, 1997; Rice et al., 1995; Rice & Whaley, 1994).

[271] Eating disorders have been associated with severe separation and attachment difficulties during childhood (Armstrong & Roth, 1989; Sours, 1974).

[272] Negative emotional states associated with insecure attachment include anxiety, depression, paranoia, loneliness, shame proneness, anger, and resentment (Cooper et al., 1998; Robert, Gotlib, & Kassel, 1996; Simpson, 1990; Simpson, Rholes, & Phillips, 1996).

[273] Insecure attachment is closely related to significant interpersonal problems (Brennan & Shaver, 1998; Horowitz, Rosenberg, & Bartholomew, 1993).

[274] By contrast, persons with a secure attachment style possess greater self-confidence, psychological well-being, and greater capacity for functioning in the social world (Diehl et al., 1998).

[275] A comprehensive review of research indicates that individuals with insecure attachment are more likely to misperceive a partner's interest, loyalty, and responsiveness; to have either a heightened or suppressed emotional response to perceived threats; and to manage stress by means of excessive clinginess or withdrawal (Lopez & Brennan, 2000).

[276] Theoretical models have been created to specify the type of social support that is most effective in preventing deleterious physical or mental consequences following different kinds of stressful life events (Cutrona, 1990; Lehman & Hemphill, 1990).

Another important reason for therapists to be versatile in their handling of attachment dynamics is that many of those coming to therapy have their own, unique ideas about what constitutes social support. Consequently, insecurely attached adults report less available support, less benefit from the support they receive, and a larger gap between what they say they need and what they say they receive. Since these individuals are less likely seek support from others,[277] the lay support available from neighbors and coworkers is not likely to reach the threshold needed to alter long-standing negative expectancies. By contrast, skillful care providers understand that supportive statements, which are ambiguous, have a tendency to activate negative rather than positive expectations about the intentions of others. Once activated, these doubts and vulnerabilities place the insecurely attached adult at risk for the types of interpersonal difficulties listed above. As demonstrated in research, this problem is less likely when the support message is specific and tailored to the client's understanding of what constitutes genuine concern.[278]

For an insecurely attached person, everyday experiences, such as having someone disagree with one's comment, can seriously challenge the weak sense of self and the already pervasive mistrust of others. Unfortunately, individuals with this type of heightened need for support are more likely to elicit negative responses from others, including their therapists. For instance, I have had clients start the therapy session by lashing out in an angry tone, telling me that my textbook smarts are not going to help their situation, or some clients spend much of the first visit describing all of the reasons why they do not need help. In one instance, an extremely nervous client spent the entire hour speaking so rapidly that I was never allowed a chance to respond. In such cases, my experience has been that, if handled correctly, a client who begins the relationship by attacking the therapist will eventually shift into a position of tremendous gratitude. Someone who blocks the therapist from commenting will, once a safe connection is formed, listen with focused attention and bated breath. While a fearful client is likely to struggle for control of external factors, the skillful therapist avoids control battles, instead focusing on the development of attachment (i.e., uncovering strongly felt emotional needs and responding with care and protection).

Another experience that can be emotionally traumatic for those who

---

[277] Insecure attachment has been associated with pessimistic beliefs about the risks, costs, and futility of seeking help from others (Lakey & Cassady, 1990; Wallace & Vaux, 1993).

[278] Insecure individuals are more likely to appraise their support experiences in ways that are consistent with a negative model of attachment when the support message is ambiguous (Collins & Feeney, 2004).

are insecurely attached is day-to-day separation from an attachment figure. Due to a weak sense of connection, leaving to go to school, to work, or on a short trip out of town can generate tremendous emotional upheaval. Both children and adults can become so agitated by routine separations that they lapse into crying, fighting, or vomiting. With controlling, hostile individuals, there can be paranoid fits of jealously, threatening accusations, and stalking behavior. Of course, if the therapist is viewed by the client as a significant care provider, then any threat of separation can elicit a strong reaction from the client.

Depending on the level of insecurity in the client, the threat of separation can be very subtle, or even symbolic, and still elicit a strong reaction. For instance, the client might experience stressful separation during a pause in the conversation, when the therapist leans back in his or her chair, at the beginning and ending of a session, or during a discussion about the future possibility of concluding therapy. I have witnessed instances in which each of these triggered great emotional turmoil. In once such case, a patient had her boyfriend write me a letter explaining that she would no longer meet with me because of the way I ended the sessions. This was a person who started each session as giddy as a small child, eagerly seeking as much positive attention as possible. However, when it came time for the sessions to end, she would become increasingly agitated. During the final five minutes, she would start a line of conversation that she felt was imperative to explore fully. Upon hearing that she had only five minutes to speak, she would respond with intense rage, typically storming out of the room and, on her last visit, slamming the door behind her.

The most intense reaction to separation that I have seen occurred when I traveled to Europe for three weeks. A client who had be doing remarkably well in therapy, and who had evidently formed a strong emotional attachment, responded to my trip by leaving a voice-mail message telling me he now realized it was useless to try any more and that he no longer wished to live. I called his number repeatedly, seeking to reestablish the connection, but he would not accept any incoming calls. The message on his voice mail indicated that he no longer wished to live and instead hoped that the serial killer who had made the news would come to his house. For the next 11 months, he spent most of his time in bed, taking enough psychotropic medication to maintain a semicomatose state. During this period, he would phone me during the late hours of the night, leaving 5 - to 15-minute monologues. I would respond by leaving *short,* encouraging messages.

Eventually, he returned to therapy, and the session was very positive and upbeat, until the end, when I suggested that at some point in the future we should talk some about his father. This man's father had died when the man was still young. After that comment, my client's face flushed, and I have not seen him face-to-face since (though he continues to keep in touch through email).

For those who do not understand the dynamics of attachment, these behaviors can seem unreasonable and arbitrary. However when viewed through the lens of attachment, problems with connecting and separating are more easily understood.

In contrast to those who are insecurely attached, securely attached individuals have little difficulty seeking support and accepting help when needed.[279] They are likely to be a pleasure to work with in therapy as their relationships tend to be characterized by positive feelings about themselves and others.[280] These individuals are likely to feel comfortable in care settings, easily establishing an emotional connection to the therapist.[281] Because they readily interpret other's attempts at support as meaningful, secure individuals are more likely to find comfort in the goodwill of others.[282] Of course, because securely attached individuals tend to be self-confident, socially skilled, and open to supportive relationships, they are not as likely to be in a position requiring professional care.[283] Because secure individuals respond more capably to life's challenges, they constitute a small percentage of a therapist's typical caseload.[284]

Recognition of Attachment Strategies Increases Understanding of Emotional and Behavioral Functioning

The recognition of individual differences in attachment security leads to a better understanding of how people deal with stress and distress. This

---

[279] Ironically, this finding suggests that securely attached individuals will create larger pools of social support and, therefore, have less need for paid support (Butzel & Ryan, 1997; Florian, Mikulincer, & Bucholtz, 1995; Shaver & Hazan, 1993).

[280] Social interactions are influenced by two types of internal working models: a model of the self and a model of others, either of which can be primarily positive or negative (Bartholomew & Horowitz, 1991; Hazan & Shaver, 1987; Simpson, 1990).

[281] Individuals in this category are characterized by greater trust, commitment, and satisfaction with the support they receive (Collins & Feeney, 2004; Collins & Read, 1990; Mikulincer, 1998a; Shaver & Hazan, 1993; Simpson, 1990).

[282] Relative to insecure individuals, secure individuals appear to be predisposed to make more generous support appraisals (Collins & Feeney, 2004).

[283] Accordingly, research has shown that individuals classified as securely attached have less emotional distress and negative affect (Simpson, 1990), fewer physical symptoms (Hazan & Shaver, 1990), and lower fear of death (Mikulincer, Florian, & Tolmacz, 1990).

[284] The benefits of attachment security among adults are so numerous that some consider it a general resilience factor across the life span (Mikulincer & Florian, 1998).

understanding can then translate into a more skillful handling of the therapy relationship, as dynamics of care and closeness versus autonomy and separation are orchestrated.

Perhaps the simplest way to recognize these general differences is in terms of interpersonal space or physical boundaries. If therapists are not flexible with the space between themselves and their clients, there will be some individuals whom they frighten. These individuals will feel the therapist has invaded their interpersonal space. Then there will be others who feel rejected or uncared for because the therapist maintained too much distance. Both the timing and the intensity of these movements are important.

The same is also true in terms of emotional boundaries. There are some clients who, during the first visit, need to tell their therapist everything there is to know, including how often they masturbate and the quality and consistency of their bowel movements. Then there are others who need the first session to be limited to generally superficial conversation, and they give only vague hints of distress or indirect reference to the problem. These two extremes are typical of individuals with insecure attachment.

In contrast, securely attached individuals find it relatively easy to get close to others, are comfortable giving and receiving support, and don't worry about being abandoned or about someone becoming too emotionally close to them.[285] Because less skill is needed while relating to securely attached individuals, this chapter will focus more closely on the different manifestations of insecure attachment and the discernment needed for the provision of care.[286]

Insecure Attachment Is Associated with Two Major Dimensions: Anxious and Avoidant

To understand the nature of the difficulties that arise with attachment, there are only two major dimensions that need to be understood: attachment anxiety and attachment avoidance.[287] The first dimension, attachment anxiety, reflects the degree to which a person worries that a care provider will not be available in times of need. The second dimension, attachment avoidance, reflects the extent to which a person distrusts a care provider's good-

---

[285] Those who exhibit insecure styles—particularly highly avoidant people—tend to have romantic relationships defined by the opposite set of features (Mikulincer et al., 2005; Simpson, 1990).

[286] It is helpful for the therapist to know the various forms insecurity can take and how it may hamper the creation of trust and the creation of healing relationships (Johnson & Whiffen, 1999).

[287] These two dimensions can intersect, thus yielding a four category model (Bartholomew & Horowitz, 1991).

will, resulting in an increased need to maintain high self-sufficiency and low emotional dependency.

Depending on how high or low a person is on one or both of these dimensions, certain individual behaviors, emotional coping strategies, and interpersonal strategies can be reliably predicted. For example, those who tend toward an anxious attachment style are likely to be hyperalert to separations, overwhelmed and angry when left, and preoccupied with the drama surrounding family or romantic relations at the expense of moving out into the larger world. By contrast, those who tend toward an avoidant style are likely to constrict or suppress intolerable feelings and memories, thereby failing to recognize that a separation is having an impact on them.[288]

During *Attachment Anxiety,* There Is Heightened Involvement in Self-Insecurity

The first dimension, attachment anxiety, is believed to result from a person's underlying negative image of self.[289] When a basic liking or acceptance of self is lacking, emotional and behavioral functioning tend to destabilize.[290] Because a certain amount of self-liking is needed for emotional well-being, those with attachment anxiety experience chronic emotional distress.[291] This emotional distress is often pervasive, due to the fact that the individual has become hyperattentive to distressing stimuli, thus creating a subjective world of constant danger and disaster.[292] This heightened emotional drama serves the strategic purpose of soliciting the attention of those from whom the insecure individual wishes to receive love and support.[293]

In addition to being hypervigilant, those with an anxious attachment style tend to overgeneralize painful experiences, which leads to anxious

---

[288] These behaviors that are first apparent in childhood later translate into adult interactions (Goldberg, 1997; Karen, 1994).

[289] Early attachment experiences have led these individuals to view themselves as essentially unlovable (Brennan, Clark & Shaver, 1998).

[290] Accordingly, researchers have found that attachment anxiety is significantly related to low self-esteem and a tendency to criticize oneself (Bartholomew & Horowitz, 1991; Murphy & Bates, 1997; Roberts et al., 1996).

[291] Attachment anxiety has been consistently associated not only with anxiety, but also with depression and other negative emotional states, such as grief and loneliness (Hazan & Shaver, 1987; Mickelson, Kessler, & Shaver, 1997; Wayment & Vierthaler, 2002).

[292] Attachment anxiety is organized by rules that direct attention toward distress cues, thereby inhibiting the development of a sense of safety and self-confidence (Kobak & Sceery, 1988; Mikulincer & Florian, 1998).

[293] Target attachment figures are anxiously and continuously monitored for signs of impending abandonment (Fraley, Davis & Shaver, 1998).

rumination. As a result, they tend to be overwhelmed by negative affect during and after stressful events.[294] In some instances, I have observed such individuals become overwhelmed simply by hearing about others' negative experiences.[295] Similarly, those with an anxious-attachment style have difficulty suppressing painful thoughts and are less able to contain the spread of negative affect when recalling their own painful experiences.[296] This decreased ability to contain the spread of negative affect can lead to what some have described as emotional bleed. When asked to describe an experience that is emotionally painful, the client can "bleed out," breaking down emotionally faster than the therapist can repair the damage. When these difficulties of emotional containment are paired with an attachment strategy of exaggerating displays of distress in order to solicit care, then the results can be dramatic; clients might claim they can no longer breathe or that it is impossible for them to stop crying, or in some cases, they might drop to the ground in a fit of emotion.

In one such case, a 49-year-old female traced her current feelings of guilt and shame to an incestuous relationship that began between her and her older brother when she was eight years old. As she spoke, she began to sob in a very emotional manner, her body slowly curling inward. During this emotional release, she managed to position herself at the edge of her chair, leaning forward so that she eventually fell to the floor. Once she was on the floor, her crying continued, uninterrupted, with her face buried in the carpet.

As I sat in my chair, trying to decide on an appropriate response, I became concerned that her behavior might turn into cause for further shame and humiliation. I knew I could kneel down and help her back into her chair but that would have required physical contact, which did not seem wise with someone who was unable to distinguish sexual from nonsexual touch.[297] I could have offered words of encouragement, but that would have only further highlighted her neediness and dependency on external reassurance.

---

[294] In this regard, the cognitive patterns lead to predictable emotional events (Mikulincer & Florian, 1998).

[295] Similarly, researchers have found that persons who hold a global anxious attachment style may become emotionally overwhelmed while witnessing other's plight (Mikulincer et al., 2001a).

[296] Problems with hypervigilance, exaggeration, and rumination consume working memory while heightening the individual's subjective appraisal of internal and external threats (Mikulincer & Shaver, 2003, p. 74).

[297] Outlining ethical and clinical guidelines for the use of touch in therapy, Durana (1998) stressed the importance of understanding client issues such as client readiness, appropriateness of physical contact for the client, the client's interpretation of physical touch, and the potential for misinterpretation by the client and others.

When she eventually stopped crying and looked up at me, I explained, in a positive and optimistic tone of voice, that she had probably experienced a transformational moment and that she would feel entirely different on the inside once she got herself off the floor.

With a curious expression, the woman moved back to her chair and asked me what I meant.

I responded, "This very deep and thorough cry you just had is an act of cleansing. It is clear evidence of the strong and good conscience you have."

During her life experiences, which included epileptic seizures that often occurred in public, this woman had lost all sense of personal dignity. She had been excessively dependent on her husband (though not emotionally bonded) and, now at nearly 50 years of age, she was trying to determine whether she was capable of taking care of herself. Therefore, in therapy, she needed the experience of being able to *pick herself up off the ground.* Fortunately, she responded positively to my confidence in her. Later, I was able to get her husband to join the therapy so that he could serve as the attachment figure. My preferred strategy is helping clients connect with an attachment figure inside their social network, rather than seeking to make myself the sole target of emotional bonding (especially when clients have problems establishing clear boundaries).

A third factor often associated with attachment anxiety is perfectionism. A tendency toward maladaptive perfectionism can develop for a variety of reasons, including excessive criticism, overly protective parenting, or an exceedingly demanding environment. It has been my observation that parents who are themselves perfectionists tend to have a compulsive need to correct their children, and this compulsion leads to excessively controlling behaviors.[298] This style of interaction is most likely to have a damaging effect if the amount of positive affection received by the child is low and the parent's need for control is excessive and chronic.

When individuals have not learned to feel good about themselves, they are likely to do anything they can to minimize the possibility of regret or failure.[299] Unfortunately, when perfection is used as a strategy to counter these feelings, the result is constant and harsh self-scrutiny, dissatisfaction with one's performance, and constant concerns about the evaluations of others.[300] Such a person comes to believe that even the most minor of mistakes

---

[298] Researchers have speculated that a love withdrawal style of discipline, involving threats to withhold affection, may cause children to pursue perfection in order to gain their parents' love and acceptance (Mallinckrodt & Wei, 2003).

[299] Minimizing this possibility is necessary in order to protect an already fragile self-esteem (Josephs et. al., 1991).

[300] These responses tend to occur even when the individual is successful (Davis, 1997; Dunkley, Zuroff & Blankstein, 2003).

will lead to devastating outcomes. Unfortunately, the use of perfectionism as a coping strategy only perpetuates the cycle of negative feelings.[301]

With clients who struggle with maladaptive perfectionism, it is sometimes helpful for therapists to join with the client by admitting to their own flaws, at a strategic moment, and then model healthy self-acceptance. Sometimes, the client's perfectionism is difficult to recognize because it has been hidden behind unrealistic demands and criticism of others. The clue to this tremendous internal conflict emerges when clients complain that "everyone" is pressuring them to be perfect. Upon further questioning, it becomes evident that it is the clients who are their own worst critics. Clients need to be aware of this self-criticism, because once the internal pressures are resolved, it is easier modify their aggression toward others.

For example, a 51-year-old male, with a history of violent behavior, came to the session in a state of intense frustration and anger. Two days earlier, he had received disappointing business news, which he responded to by declaring to his wife, in a convincing manner, that he no longer wished to live. As he explained to me, "When I heard the bad news, I said something really stupid." But his behavior had been so disturbing to his wife, especially given his history of unstable behavior, that she had stopped speaking to him entirely.

As I sat and listened to him explain his trouble at home, the client became increasingly agitated. His neediness prevented him from understanding the impact his behavior had on others. Instead, his fear of rejection only increased his resentment as he argued that he is never allowed to make any mistakes. He believed that he was being forced by his wife into an unfair and impossible situation. As his face became increasingly red and his hands began to tremble, it became clear that he was caught in a spiral of escalating distress, possibly leading to renewed threats of suicide. Any use of confrontation or correction, at this moment, would have been interpreted by the client as yet another person demanding perfection from him.

However, this emotional escalation needed to be stopped. So when he paused for a breath, I interjected, "I need to apologize to you, because I also made a mistake." This statement temporarily distracted him from his own thoughts, allowing space for me to continue. "I almost always prepare clients for worst case scenarios," I said. "I could have prepared you for how to react and how to deal with your emotions should you receive this bad news. I just was so confident that it would not happen this way. I should not have allowed myself to get overly confident."

---

[301] More specifically, perfectionism is associated with chronic feelings of depression and anxiety (Grzegorek, et al., 2004; Wei et al., 2004; Suddarth & Slaney, 2001).

After I finished speaking, the client sat up straight and, with much less evidence of anxiety, he transitioned to a discussion of how he wants to take a more proactive role in his marriage. The reduction of tension in the room following my comment was extraordinary. Because the client was essentially overwhelmed by a long-held belief that he had to be perfect, I needed some mechanism for reducing that internal pressure. I accomplished this by demonstrating acceptance of my own minor flaws. This intervention rested on the strength of my own ego and modeled, in a very immediate way, the type of behavior that would be most helpful to the client.

Another defining characteristic of those with an anxious attachment style is excessive dependence on others. It can be seen in children who are constantly seeking to control and cling to their mother or in adolescents who seem addicted to attention from others (even negative attention). Or it can be seen in adults who fall in love at first sight and then become enmeshed in unhealthy ways. Many of these individuals learned to be suspect of their own capabilities at a young age.[302] Then, when they are adults, deep-seated feelings of personal inadequacy compel them to search for validation and reassurance from others.[303]

Along with this excessive dependence comes a tendency to seek extreme closeness to over-idealized others. Individuals in this state of mind can become possessive of a target attachment figure in a way that not even they themselves find rational. In therapy, I have had clients describe their attachment anxiety to me with statements such as, "I know this sounds absurd, but it sort of bothers me to think of you meeting with other clients. There is a part of me that wants to think of you as being here for me alone." Of course, this sort of dependency leaves the individual vulnerable to extreme distress, especially when intimacy needs are not met.

For instance, a young male client once complained, "I am afraid to say no to my wife when she wants sex. The last time I did, she became completely hysterical, as if I had just told her I wanted a divorce."[304] Prior to marriage, this man had taken pride in his highly active sexual life; however, his wife's unyielding need for verification by means of physical intimacy had altered his libido.

"Don't get me wrong," he said. "You've seen my wife. She is a beautiful woman. And I love her. But I never get a break. She can have sex three to

---

[302] In other words, their parent's caregiving strategies promoted dependency (George & Solomon, 1999).

[303] This feeling of personal inadequacy has been associated with not only strong feelings of anxiety, but depression as well (Wei et al., 2005).

[304] When others are reluctant to get as close as they would like, anxiously attached individuals tend to worry that their partner does not love them and will, therefore, abandon them (Simpson, 1990).

four times a day and still want more—and she wants it every single day. I don't know how much more I can take. I suppose most any other guy would be envious, but I find myself wanting to hide. I just need a little time to build back my desire for sex."[305]

As was happening with this couple, it is not uncommon for excessive demands to be met with a desire to withdraw. Since any form of withdrawal increases the desire for pursuit, an unfortunate cycle is created.

This self-perpetuating insecurity can lead to disastrous consequences. For example, one newly married couple found themselves in a horrible mess when the anxiously attached wife misinterpreted a lack of attention from her husband as evidence he no longer loved her. Because in the past she had been with uncaring males, who had all cheated on her, she became thoroughly convinced that her new husband would eventually leave her for another woman. She had previously considered him to be the ideal male and did not think she could survive losing him to another woman. So in an effort to decrease the pain of the inevitable, she initiated an affair with a handyman. The reality of the matter was that her new husband loved her deeply and was hoping she would be the first female to remain faithful to him (two previous wives had each abandoned him after having affairs). It was the husband who called to set up the appointment. He said to me, "Dr. Short, my wife has gotten herself into a situation where I think she is going to need some help." His tone was entirely sympathetic. In therapy, she went into a visible state of shock when she recognized the legitimacy of his continued desire to be with her, despite her infidelity. Her strong impulse was still to leave him due to unbearable feelings of shame and remorse;[306] however, she eventually recognized her need for a man such as him. And he truly did not want to lose her. So with just one visit, a reconciliation was worked out.[307]

Another important point to recognize is that due to an underdeveloped sense of self, some clients may try to change themselves into what they imagine the therapist wishes them to be. However, this type of relationship does not promote a healthy transformation of self. Because the emphasis is placed on self-abandonment rather than personal growth, the changes that occur require a dissociation from one's own identity and de-

---

[305] Although they do not always seek out sex, anxiously attached individuals often wish for more intimacy than they receive (Hazan & Shaver, 1987).

[306] Although these individuals initially engage in herculean attempts to attain greater proximity, support, and love, in the long run they lack the confidence that the connection can be sustained (Mikulincer & Shaver, 2003).

[307] At the time of this writing, two years since that visit, the man returned for individual therapy and informed me that he has been diagnosed with cancer. His wife is still with him, wanting to provide love and support, and he is grateful for her presence.

tachment from one's own hopes and dreams, which, of course, does not help the client build self-confidence. The dilemma for these individuals is that they often feel forced to choose between perpetual loneliness or self-abandonment. They feel this way because they are operating under the faulty assumption that being one's self and being in a relationship are mutually exclusive. Therefore, during therapy, rather than have the uniqueness of the client disappear; it is important to encourage him or her to bring the full self into the office, including the parts of self that have become marked with distrust and shame.

As mentioned earlier, separation anxiety is another byproduct of excessive dependency. People who feel that they must rely primarily on others, instead of themselves, for validation are easily threatened by any separation from the attachment figure.[308] In children, the behavior usually surfaces when attendance at school becomes mandatory. For adults, even routine separations can result in a frantic search for evidence of support, making the insecure individual seem clingy, demanding, and reluctant to develop friendships outside the romantic attachment. For instance, one frustrated husband complained to me, "There is a fight almost every morning when I try to leave for work. She will not let me out of the door. She gets mad at me for leaving, but I have to work!" Turning all attention inward to a single intense relationship, these individuals tend to become over involved with minor issues and continually rehash past conflicts.[309] Because they can be highly sensitive, these individuals have difficulty developing trust and have difficulty enjoying their relationships.[310]

Conflict occurring within the relationship is only exacerbated when the needy individual perceives the possibility of competition for affection.[311] Between mother and child, the mother's insecurity might be expressed as displeasure at the child's enjoyment of other adults. For example, "What's the matter with my cooking? How come you spend all of your time bragging about the food your friend's parents cook?" Between romantic partners, the jealousy can result in distressed reactions to behaviors that have not even occurred. As a bewildered client explained, "If my fiancée sees an attractive woman with blonde hair, she automatically becomes furious and

---

[308] Any attempt by the attachment figure to facilitate a temporary separation is perceived by the insecure individual as an absolute loss of supportiveness (Wei et al., 2005).

[309] Becoming over involved in minor issues and continually rehashing conflicts can create what feels like an emotional roller coaster, in which the ups and downs can occur daily or even multiple times within the day (Sable, 1997).

[310] Rather than focusing on positive interactions, these individuals tend to maintain constant vigilance for signs that the relationship is threatened (Tidwell, Reis & Shaver, 1996).

[311] Rather than appreciating their partner's loyalty, insecure individuals are likely to respond with varying levels of jealousy (Simpson, 1990).

starts to yell at me. It does not matter that I have not even looked at the female. She yells at me anyway, insisting that she knows that I want to look at this other woman." The more intense the attachment anxiety, the more likely it is that the other partner will have to restrict his or her social contacts to maintain peace in the relationship.[312] In extreme cases, contact with one's own extended family or with a therapist is strictly prohibited. My experience has been that whenever this type of control is being exercised, the relationship also tends to be characterized by domestic violence.

For individuals who do not yet recognize the possibility of receiving support from multiple sources, it is exceedingly important to introduce the idea into their thinking. While speaking to an anxious client, I will gently suggest, "This person may not always be available to provide the support you are seeking, so we should talk some about the possibility of having others who can help you out when you need it." I used a similar tactic while seeking to help a 68-year-old woman who knew her husband would be dying soon. She was exceedingly dependent on him and horribly anxious. "Dr. Short, I do not know what I am going to do if [he] dies," she said. "I just can't live without him. I can't take it. I won't be able to stand it!"

This woman had responded to the death of her mother, two years prior, by becoming suicidal with some psychotic symptomology. After leaving the hospital, she had laid in her bedroom for months, essentially unable to function. Although it was exceedingly difficult to get her to leave the house, her husband eventually convinced her to come to therapy. Fortunately, we were able to fit in 30 sessions before his death. During that time, I conducted a couple of mock therapy sessions, in the pretend future, as it might be following his death (at this point, her husband was still alive). These measures, along with some basic ego strengthening, helped her develop a greater awareness of her capacity for self-sufficiency. Following his death, she did not go crazy, nor did she develop a catastrophic depression. She was sad and tearful, some days crying for hours at a time. But throughout the ordeal, she remained functional and even helped care for others in the extended family. Eventually she got past her first holiday season as a widow, and after that point, her grief slowly started to give way to more lengthy periods of joy and greater self-confidence.

Another consequence of being overly dependent on others is an insatiable need for reassurance and external validation. Those with adult attachment anxiety depend greatly on the approval of others in order to counterbalance fears of interpersonal rejection, abandonment, and loss of

---

[312] Research has shown that the higher the attachment anxiety, the more likely the insecure individual is to respond negatively to any person outside a small circle of close relationships (Mikulincer & Shaver, 2001).

love. Unfortunately, these individuals often perceive rejection or disapproval even in its absence. After becoming angry at others for perceived rejection, they often look for fault within themselves, thereby increasing their insecurities.[313]

For some who grew up in critical environments, with parents who used guilt to control or who blamed the child for their own inability to form a close relationship, there is a tendency to be blind to faults in others. Such individuals become so preoccupied with self-criticism that they are not able to develop a skeptical or discerning view of the target of their affection. My experience with these clients is that they are easily manipulated by others who are seeking to take advantage of them. When desperate for external approval, a person will be willing to do almost anything for the one who dangles verbal praise like a carrot: "If you will only do this, then I will know that you are truly amazing." They also struggle to defend themselves against people who use guilt to manipulate or threats of abandonment: "You do not appreciate all that I have gone through because of you. No other man would be willing to put up with this."

Unfortunately, someone who feels unworthy of care and who fears abandonment is not likely to see through these types of manipulative strategies. As a result, they are easily taken advantage of. When therapy is conducted with this type of individual, it is important to determine if he or she is in an abusive relationship, at home or at work. Others may be exploiting them for financial gain, sex, or for other selfish interests. If the client is being exploited, then it is often useful to reflect out loud about what has been happening, using a skeptical analysis. In response, one such client commented, "I never looked at it that way. I always felt so guilty because my mother always blamed me for her problems, and so did my sister! But now I can see that I have a right to take care of myself." Because these clients are already prone toward self-devaluation—"I feel so stupid for not seeing it earlier"—the therapist should take great care to speak in a way that is affirming, rather than condescending.

Then there are those whose anxiety results in a failure to accurately observe and understand others, leading to a breakdown in sympathy or compassion. This is more likely to occur with individuals who have assumed a dominant position in a relationship. In these cases, the anxiously attached adult can become overly demanding or overtly hostile, without recognizing that others must cope with their own fears and insecurities and that they might be experiencing extreme distress during intense inter-

---

[313] This pattern results in an escalation of the negative internal dialogue (Bartholomew & Horowitz, 1991).

actions.[314] It is important that the therapist spell out, in concrete terms, interpersonal information that needs to be recognized. For example, "Your words and actions may matter more to your wife than you realize. Your opinion of her probably means a great deal."

In this particular session of couples counseling where I spoke these words, the husband responded by negating my statements, as I expected he would. However, his wife's eyes began to fill with tears, and without speaking, she vigorously shook her head, affirming my statement. The client took a second look at his wife and seemed baffled, "You really do care that much about what I think?" He had spent the past ten years of marriage absolutely convinced that his thoughts and actions held no real significance to her. Therefore, when he had become angry, he had lashed out with a false sense of impunity. Once this misperception was corrected, he responded with greater care and protection of his wife's feelings. He also made several symbolic gestures that communicated her importance to him. Soon after, the marriage became much warmer, and mutual affection was shared more freely.

A third defining characteristic of those with an anxious attachment style is the controlling behaviors that occur while seeking to eliminate personal distress.[315] The private logic behind the attempts to control are characterized by desperation: "I have to make you notice me" or "I have to make you love me." Such a person is likely to approach the task of forming and maintaining a relationship as if it were a battle. Strategically speaking, the individual's experience of chronic distress doubles as a secret weapon, as he or she uses tears and other dramatic displays of emotion to capture and hold captive the attention and care of the target attachment figure.[316] Unfortunately, in addition to creating fatigue, this relational strategy takes away time and energy that could have been used for developing a deeper understanding of self and others, a more positive connection through humor and play, or personal confidence through risk taking and self-reliance. Because these individuals are stuck in a seemingly unending state of distress and dependency, their emotional growth and maturity become impeded.

Whenever a person experiences a strong need to control others, feelings of anger and disappointment are certain to follow.[317] While such indi-

---

[314] Accordingly, researchers have found that adults who have higher attachment-related anxiety are less skilled at decoding nonverbal messages and less likely to show signs of responsive listening (Feeney, Noller, & Callan, 1994; Mikulincer & Nachshon, 1991).

[315] As there is a great deal of dependency on others for self-esteem needs, there is an equally strong need to control the object of this intense desire (Bartholomew & Horowitz, 1991).

[316] This behavior is based on the premise that others can be forced to offer care when the need is great enough (Kobak et al., 1993; Lopez, Mauricio, Gormley, Simko, & Berger, 2001).

[317] Ironically, those with attachment anxiety are often angry at the very same individuals from whom they desire sympathetic attention (Feeney & Noller, 1990; Rholes, Simpson, & Orina, 1999).

viduals see themselves as painfully under benefitted, anxiously attached individuals view their over idealized partners as intentionally withholding the intimacy they so desperately desire.[318] In therapy, I often hear these individuals bitterly complain, "What point is there in going to couples counseling with someone who does not love you?" To which the partner is likely to retort, "I do love you and try to show it, but nothing I do is ever good enough for you!"

In one such case, after this sort of exchange had taken place, the anxiously attached female turned to me and, with tears in her eyes, asked, "How can a man claim to love you and then buy you hand cream for Christmas!" Blushing, the husband tried to explain, "It was just a place holder. I did not know what to buy and wanted to let you pick out a better gift later." Interrupting him, she wailed, "You humiliated me in front of my entire family!" The more he sought to defend his action, the angrier and more belligerent she became. Her face flushed red and her voice filled with fury.

The only way to halt the rapidly deteriorating interaction was for me to stop her husband from responding so that I could verbally engage his wife and redirect her attention inward.[319] Once I was able to get her to acknowledge that these terrible feelings of inadequacy had been with her before she met him, the hostility vanished. Using a traditional model of psychotherapy, I had her recall some painful memories from childhood. This exercise left her crumpled in her chair and sobbing heavily.

Having greatly increased her emotional vulnerability, I brought the husband back into the interaction. He needed to learn how to act as a secure attachment figure. So I said to him, "Why don't you take her a tissue, and see if she will let you hold her hand." He then went to his wife, and, embracing her in a hug, he whispered supportive affectionate statements, such as, "I am here for you."

The effect was immediate and profound. Now feeling loved, she related to me the story of how they initially met and how safe he had made her feel. After this moment of emotional bonding, there was no more conflict during sessions and much less tension at home. Before therapy, her anger from the past had been extinguishing all the warm feelings she had been hoping to find in marriage. The therapy was not difficult with this couple because the man truly cared for his wife. However, as is common with anxious attachment, she was overemphasizing his failure to provide adequate care, and as

---

[318] This perceived injustice can result in chronic feelings of anger and resentment (Grau & Doll, 2003).

[319] My experience has been that self-evaluation or self-consciousness is the antidote to belligerence.

a consequence, she was making herself more and more hostile.[320]

When they are not busy seeking out care, those with anxious attachment tend to be compulsive and controlling *caregivers*. Operating from a position of fear and distress, they often have difficulty accepting the idea that the needs of their child or spouse may differ from their own.[321] This perception can make their attempts to care for others seem intrusive. As one client explained to me, "It is not that my mother did not love me. She loved me *too much*. She was always saying, 'Be careful, you might get hurt!' And always acting as if I were at the edge of disaster, when all I wanted to do was go play with my friends. That is why I think I am such a nervous wreck now." The same type of anxious, controlling support often mixes doomsday predictions with blame and guilt: "You do not know how much I have sacrificed for you. Because of what you have done, all is now lost."[322]

This type of support (or domestic tyranny) finds its way into all areas of living. Invasive care can be exercised in areas such as food (what a person eats or how much one weighs), money (how much a person spends or what one buys), speech (certain topics are off limits), contact with others (which people are or are not considered appropriate friends), proximity (where one is allowed to go), sex (what a person is allowed to do with his or her own body, or who a person is allowed to marry), and personal belief systems (especially religious ideology). More bizarre fixations include attempts to control another person's breathing (one client was repeatedly told by her mother, "Stop breathing my air!"), state of consciousness (another client remembered as a young child seeing his mother wrap sleeping pills inside his baloney), and attempts to control bodily functions, such as the frequency of urination (by withholding water) or bowel movements (by administering unnecessary enemas). Ultimately, the fundamental goal of these controlling behaviors is to capture the heart and mind of the object of attachment. In other words, there is an overriding need to control what the person thinks and feels about the anxious individual.

It is important to recognize that stopping a child from running out in front of a speeding vehicle, or screaming at an adult partner to slam on the breaks before hitting another vehicle, is not automatically a sign of anxious attachment. Some amount of interpersonal influence is needed for crisis

---

[320] Accordingly, when the different types of insecure attachment have been compared, it has been found that the anxious partner is the more likely perpetrator of violence (Roberts & Noller, 1998).

[321] Individuals who are preoccupied with their own worries tend to be selfishly motivated in their caregiving, acting without regard for their partner's actual needs (Collins & Feeney, 2000; Feeney & Collins, 2001).

[322] The caregiving of such individuals tends to be more negative than positive (Feeney & Collins, 2001).

prevention and social order. However, in cases that involve insecure attachment, the efforts to control are guided primarily by a need to eliminate personal distress while paying little or no attention to the distress experienced by others. This self-oriented perspective does not promote altruism, but instead leads to a deficit in compassionate or helpful responses.[323] The implication for therapy is that sometimes what seems obvious to everyone else may not always be recognized by the client and, therefore, needs to be spelled out in concrete detail. I have found that it is important to describe not only the distress that others might be experiencing, but also the likely consequences if there is a failure to act.[324]

The cases that tend to be most disheartening are those in which parents are failing to meet the needs of their children due to an anxious attachment to a romantic interest. After the death of a spouse or after a divorce, it is not uncommon to see anxious individuals desperately seeking an new adult attachment. Their desire to go out on dates or leave town with a new lover seem exceedingly selfish to those who recognize that the deserted children are already traumatized by the loss of the first parent. However, for these anxious parents, the fear, loneliness, and feelings of abandonment experienced by the children do not enter into their conscious awareness. In therapy, it is sometimes possible to explain the children's probable distress so that the children's needs are no longer out of mind. However, in other cases, anxious individuals may be given all the information they need, but fail to act on behalf of the children and then refuse to return for further therapy.

I was involved in one case that illustrates some of the difficulty in focusing the parent's problem-solving efforts in the right direction. My son had just made friends with a little girl who was very sweet. She and her mother had participated at our church in a family class I taught on personal boundaries. Her mother seemed nice, though overly dependent. The father, I did not trust. I had seen the man sit in a chair at someone's house, carelessly tossing aside a book that had been sitting in the chair and placing his feet up as if he owned the home and everything in it. Seeing this, I remarked to my wife that he had some sort of serious boundary problem. My wife correctly pointed out that I did not have much evidence.

However, two weeks later, I got a call from a colleague who was supervising care for the family. As a matter of coincidence, a graduate intern had

---

[323] The higher the level of attachment anxiety, the lower the quality of caregiving and the greater the tendency toward negative or hostile behavior (Collins & Read, 1994; Mikulincer et al., 2005).

[324] Research shows that when the partner's needs are made clear to the anxiously attached individual, the level of support will dramatically increase (Collins & Feeney, 2000).

just completed an intake session with the girl's father. Though I was not the direct supervisor for this intern, I was codirector of the training program. Therefore, I was included in the problem-solving process. The situation was urgent because during the counseling intake, the father had confessed to having fantasies of sexually molesting his daughter. We agreed that, as the direct supervisor, my colleague would take charge of the case, which would begin with an immediate call to the girl's mother, to see what she knew.

Upon questioning, the mother confessed that her daughter had recently remarked that her father was making her feel uncomfortable when he watched her bathe and helped her dry off. The daughter did not think he was respecting her boundaries. However, the mother had dismissed her daughter's concerns as a childish misunderstanding of the material the girl learned in class. I asked the therapist if he had told the mother that Child Protective Services would need to be involved. My advice was that the girl must not be left alone with her father under any circumstances, that she be bathed by her mother, and that either the mother or two younger brothers sleep with the girl in her bedroom at night. The therapist said that he thought the mother understood not to leave the girl alone, but that he would call her back to make certain she knew that under no circumstances could the child be left alone with her father.

When the supervising therapist contacted the mother a second time, he informed her of the seriousness of the situation and that Child Protective Services would be contacting her. She was unhappy with this level of interference and felt that her husband was a victim of misunderstanding. She had no interest in moving anyone into the girl's bedroom. She informed her husband that a social worker was coming to the house to interview their daughter. She wanted to leave for work by 9 a.m., and the social worker would not arrive until 11 p.m., so she asked him to watch their daughter until the social worker arrived.

The next morning, after she left the house, the man dragged his daughter, screaming, into her bedroom and locked the door. Both of her younger brothers tried to come to her defense. They beat on the door and begged him to stop. However, there was nothing they could do to prevent him from brutally raping their sister. Shortly after, he was taken into police custody.[325]

At first, the mother was reluctant to accept the reality of what had happened. However, after the denial passed, her desire to preserve the marriage relationship, at any cost, vanished. Although the tragedy should have been prevented, the children's mother eventually recognized their distress

---

[325] From this incident, I learned not to warn the nonoffending parent of impending investigations. Not doing so is also important for the sake of preserving evidence.

and switched from defending the father to seeking protection and care for her children.

During Attachment Avoidance, There Is Detachment From Self and Others

Now that the key characteristics of attachment anxiety have been described, we turn to the second major category of insecure attachment, which is known as *avoidant attachment* style. As with the other attachment styles, the learned behaviors of this style serve the strategic purpose of maintaining bonds with a care provider, even if the care provider is unreliable, unstable, or sometimes dangerous. However, unlike those with attachment anxiety, individuals who are avoidant tend to distance themselves from care providers and from their own emotional experiences during moments of distress. Rather than seeking external support, they strive to maintain a sense of self-reliance.[326]

The excessive self-reliance and independence exercised by these individuals often dates back to childhood. As a result of the parents' nonresponsiveness or inconsistent caregiving, the child fails to develop a sense of being cared for and protected. Problems with parenting might occur because the parent is excessively angry, emotionally absent due to mental illness, or withdrawn due to the death of a child. Parents who have an avoidant attachment style are likely to be preoccupied with something other than their children, such as work or alcohol consumption. Or these parents might be preoccupied with another sibling, such as in cases where one child is overidealized and used as a surrogate spouse (thus effectively blocking deep or meaningful relationships with any of the other family members, including the emotionally exploited child).

Regardless of the exact cause of their parent's unresponsiveness, experience has taught the children that open expression of strong emotion will cause the parent to become more distant and rejecting. Children who openly confess their needs might be mocked for acting childish or have their complaints about physical discomfort dismissed as manipulation. Therefore, at an early age, these children learn to suppress feelings of pain, anger, or fear. They convince themselves that they have very little need for love or affection, and they are, therefore, not likely to show affection toward their parents or seek sympathy when injured.

One client tried to explain to me the extent of his emotional emptiness by sharing an event from childhood. His voice was entirely flat as he recounted, "When I was little, we lived on a farm. There was a barn, and one

---

[326] The need to maintain a strong sense of self-reliance is a defining characteristic of this attachment style (Kobak, Cole, Ferenz, & Fleming, 1993).

day my father called me into it. He was standing there in boots, and he pointed to a cute little mouse that was running around his feet. As I watched it, he suddenly stomped his foot down, crushing the mouse under his heel. He then looked me straight in the eye and said, 'That is you, if you ever cross me!' I was only six years old." What this man learned from his father was not to express anger, fear, or disappointment and not to come to his parents for help.

On another occasion, while playing with kerosene as a child, this same man accidentally set his leg on fire. Rather than going to tell his mother or father, he wrapped the inflamed sores with socks and masking tape. He then wore long pants each day, in the heat of summer, and tried to walk as if there were no pain so that his parents would not discover the injury. Because it is during childhood that individuals learn how to relate to others, this man did not know how to seek out love or affection from others.

Parents who, for one reason or another, are not inclined to nurture or spend time with their children find it useful to promote extreme independence: "This kid is unique. He barely needs me. He's been doing fine on his own ever since the younger siblings came along." Even with parents who are not as angry and hostile, as in the example above, the emotional abandonment experienced by the child is likely to result in a deep sense of inadequacy: "What is so wrong with me that my own parents do not want to be with me?" These thoughts can sometimes be countered with extreme notions of self-reliance: "I don't need anybody!" However, suppression is still needed so that emotional experiences that the parent would not respond to positively—such as fear, anger associated with abandonment, and loneliness—are kept a deeply buried secret.

When avoidant individuals are faced with problems, their default solution is to try to handle the stress alone.[327] The possibility of asking for help simply does not register. If the thought of asking for help does enter into conscious awareness, it is experienced as an uncomfortable possibility.

I can think of an example from my own childhood that illustrates this need for extreme self-reliance. As an eighth grader working on a project in woodshop class, I noticed something that seemed odd. Everyone else in the room was working in pairs, and some were in groups of three or four. Most of them were working on small projects, such as breadboxes or birdhouses. My project was by far the most complex. I was building a coffee table with cabriole legs that I had designed from my own pencil sketches. Looking

---

[327] By defensively denying the value of close relationships and extolling self-reliance, these individuals are able to downplay their fear of interpersonal dependence (Bartholomew & Horowitz, 1991; Brennan, Clark & Shaver, 1998; Collins & Feeney, 2004; Klohnen & Luo, 2003; Wei et al., 2004).

down at the unfinished project, I took note of how many clamps I had used to hold a variety of boards in place so that I would not have to ask anyone for help while I was nailing the boards. I recognized that my method was much slower and more tedious than it would have been if I had asked for assistance. However, it just felt too strange to ask someone to come to my aid. Similarly, I did not have a natural impulse to offer help to others or the ability to discern when someone was in a state of distress or need. This was the deficiency that became obvious and caused me so much distress as I stood in the London underground watching my friend help the young mother down the stairs (see page 1).

Rather than seeking support during moments of hardship, avoidant individuals turn inward to search for the resources needed to address the problematic situation.[328] This default response may occur with or without conscious awareness. Those who are higher in avoidance are less likely to seek support in response to stress.[329] Even when avoidant individuals find a partner who cares deeply and works hard on the relationship, they often are unable to make use of their partner's attempts at support.[330] Avoidant adults are not likely to express strong need for their adult partners,[331] and in some cases, I have seen parents who even fail to grieve the death of a child. Because of their lack of emotional connection to others, extremely avoidant individuals can seem somewhat inhuman. However, in most cases, the display of strength is illusionary.

Faced with the task of resolving life's challenges without support, extremely avoidant individuals feel compelled to maintain a sense of invincibility.[332] Although the inflation of self enhances the sense of personal strength and self-worth, it is not easy to maintain.[333] In an attempt to protect their fragile self-esteem, these individuals often turn a blind eye to

---

[328] To maintain a readiness to deal with life's daily challenges, these individuals require strong evidence of individual achievement and a capacity for self-reinforcement (Lopez, et al., 1997; Sable, 1997; Wei et al., 2005).

[329] When these individuals do seek support, they are more likely to request help indirectly by hinting or sulking (Collins & Feeney, 2000).

[330] This is due in part to the fear or discomfort associated with needing others (Grau & Doll, 2003).

[331] As would be expected, highly avoidant men tend to experience lower levels of distress following relationship termination (Simpson, 1990).

[332] Accordingly, children with avoidant attachment tend to describe themselves as perfect (Cassidy & Kobak, 1988) and as adults, they inflate positive self-appraisals in reaction to threatening events, viewing themselves as invulnerable to negative feelings (Collins & Feeney, 2004; Mikulincer, 1998a).

[333] The resulting self-concept is "brittle" and "defensively maintained" (Bartholomew & Horowitz, 1991; Brennan & Morris, 1997; Cooper, Shaver, & Collins, 1998; Fraley et al., 1998).

their own negative traits.[334] While this strategy allows the individual to maintain a facade of being self-sufficient, it also requires considerable mental effort.[335] The individual's readiness to function at home, school, or work is further diminished by the need to avoid certain conversations and performance opportunities, or even to avoid certain people all together.[336] As one client explained to me, "When someone tries to tell me something I do not want to hear, that's it, there are no second chances. It is as if they no longer exist in my universe."

Another means of keeping distressing thoughts suppressed while maintaining involvement with others is to keep oneself perpetually distracted. I have had several clients explain their reluctance to turn off the television as a fear of the thoughts that would otherwise flood into their awareness. Because the noise of a low interest distracter must be ever present, individuals who use the TV for distraction will not enter into a room or go to bed without the TV playing.[337]

Another method for dealing with personal inadequacy is to project it onto others.[338] The broad spectrum of negative behaviors that can be projected onto others ranges all the way from criticizing a partner for being overly critical to an obsession with the idea that one's partner is having an affair when, in fact, the exact opposite is true. The more drama that is created by the accusations, the more effective the distraction and, thus, the greater the likelihood it will continue to be used. When this externalization occurs in therapy, it is easily recognized, because clients come across as being far more interested in the actions of others than in their own functioning. Although cathartic monologues focused on others' behavior can be highly dramatic, they do not help increase the client's ability to relate to others. Therefore, my preference is to redirect the client to the reality of the immediate relationship, saying, for example, "What is it that you want from talking with me? Is there something you would like me to understand about you as an individual?" For an avoidant individual, this type of question can be very unsettling. This type of client is seeking to avoid intimacy,

---

[334] This is accomplished by suppressing thoughts about personal weaknesses and imperfections (Mikulincer, 1995; Mikulincer, Dolev & Shaver, 2004).

[335] This mental effort leaves less energy available for fundamental social tasks, such as critical thinking, analysis of people and events, and empathy for others (Mikulincer & Shaver, 2003).

[336] When others attempt to make avoidant individuals aware of their use of defensive strategies, they may respond by becoming angry or by ending the relationship (Simpson, 1990).

[337] When the distraction is something that is really absorbing and can hold the attention, its effectiveness is increased (Wegner, 1992).

[338] The projection of one's negative traits onto others is common among highly avoidant individuals (Mikulincer & Horesh, 1999).

so any reminder of the need for self-disclosure and openness to receiving care is potentially disturbing. Therefore, such reminders should be given with great care and at a slow pace.

As mentioned earlier, clients who are avoidant tend to distance themselves from a felt need for care and have difficulty identifying their feelings. If an immediate need for comfort or support were acknowledged, it might lead to an unwanted reactivation of previously suppressed thoughts about unmet needs for nurturing and security. Therefore, during moments of hardship, a psychological barrier is erected and maintained in a variety of ways.[339] Although avoidant individuals show adequate levels of well-being and functioning in daily life, when they are confronted with severe and persistent stressors, they become less able to block unwanted thoughts and feelings. This inability will sometimes result in a collapse of defense systems, followed by emotional breakdown.[340]

I have seen many instances of fiercely independent individuals being so shocked by an unexpected emotional breakdown that they temporarily set aside their mistrust of care providers and seek help. In one such case, I met a 26-year-old man who had grown up as an only child with parents who were stiff and emotionally distant. During his childhood, he was no more successful at forming attachments at school, where he felt he was a stranger among other children. The day before calling to schedule an appointment, he experienced a frightening emotional breakdown while in the presence of his first girlfriend. He had been operating admirably under the pressure of her demands for attention, a highly competitive graduate program, financial issues, and the stress of a two-hour commute to her house. However, eventually the wall of emotional suppression collapsed. While at her house, he became flooded with a lifetime of loneliness and pain. This caused him to cry uncontrollably for approximately three hours. The behavior was not in line with his cool demeanor, and, therefore, the incident really frightened him and his girlfriend. The first therapy session was arranged only four days after the incident, but already his girlfriend was acting differently toward him. He was deeply concerned he might lose her.

Yet an even greater concern was his mother's subsequent revelation that his grandmother had been hysterical and crazy and that his mother

---

[339] More specifically, it is maintained by shifting attention away from attachment-related threats or minimizing the appraised magnitude of threats; by suppressing thoughts related to the possibility of rejection, separation, and loss; and by repressing painful memories (Fraley & Shaver, 1997; Fraley, Garner, & Shaver, 2000; Lussier, Sabourin, & Turgeon, 1997; Mikulincer, Florian, & Weller, 1993; Mikulincer & Orbach, 1995).

[340] Relative to other attachment styles, avoidants show greater signs of distress and maladjustment during conditions of cognitive overload (Mikulincer, Horesh, Eilati, & Kotler, 1999; Mikulincer & Shaver, 2004).

had spent her life depressed and secretly overwhelmed with fits of tearful-ness while sitting alone in her bedroom. He was very concerned that this condition was genetic and that he was doomed to a lifetime of the same type of chronic dysfunction. I responded by pointing out that neither his mother nor his grandmother had received the therapy they needed.[341] I ex-plained to him that he did seem to have an avoidant attachment style, but that by coming in for therapy and being willing to explore his emotions, he would most likely be cured of this problem. To address any skepticism he might have, I explained that the therapy would enable him to deal with fu-ture challenges without risk of being flooded by suppressed feelings.[342]

The client was cautiously optimistic. I then added that, ironically, one of the best things that could happen would be for his girlfriend to break up with him, even if just temporarily. My explanation was that this breakup would provide a perfect test of whether or not the therapy had worked. If he were able to endure this sort of experience without a complete emo-tional breakdown, yet still be able to feel some sadness and discuss it in therapy, then we would know that he was cured and that he would not have the same troubles as his mother and grandmother. I made this state-ment because after hearing about the men his girlfriend had dated prior him (most of them physically abusive), I did not think she would be prepared for the level of vulnerability he had suddenly displayed. I wanted to prepare him for a separation, but in such a way as to counteract the possibility of depression.

Three weeks later, he proudly announced that he and his girlfriend had broken up. "She was saying that things were not working-out," he told me. "She had a party she was going to, but she did not invite me, even though I had just spent two hours driving over to see her. I did not want to ruin her evening, so I just left a note on her bed saying that we needed time apart. I did not cry one bit. Driving home, I actually felt a sense of relief."

Two weeks later, he and this girl were talking again, but more so as friends. She reported a new level of respect for him that she had never felt toward a man before. During this same session, he told me that he felt much more confident about himself and did not feel a need for any more therapy.

In contrast to those with adult attachment anxiety, those with attach-

---

[341] His mother was currently taking antidepressant medication, but this clearly was not suf-ficient treatment.

[342] Research has shown that the tendency of avoidants to suppress distressing thoughts leaves them vulnerable to a rebound of this material whenever environmental demands draw cognitive resources away from thought suppression. When they are given the op-portunity to integrate distressing experiences more completely with other thoughts and memories, the danger of being overwhelmed by this material under conditions of high cognitive and emotional load is reduced (Mikulincer, Dolev & Shaver, 2004).

ment avoidance are not as uncomfortable with themselves as they are with others.[343] Having spent much of their life feeling uncomfortable with closeness and avoiding self-disclosure, avoidant adults are likely to lack the relational skills needed for successful long-term relationships. A lack of training and preparation for intimacy within the child's home tends to snowball, as the child or adolescent also avoids intimate relationships outside of the home, further depriving him or herself of social learning opportunities.[344]

One of the crucial skills these individuals lack is the readiness to turn to others during times of great hardship or distress. Rather than communicating their distress to a parent, spouse, or therapist, avoidants are more likely to use coping strategies that contain the distress without involving others.[345] As one client related to me, "As a child I would go into the bathroom and find mom sitting in the bathtub, with no water, in dry cloths. When I asked her what was wrong, she would say, 'Nothing at all.' A little bit later she would be cooking dinner as if nothing happened. For my family, this was normal, but there is something wrong with that behavior!" In order to help this woman better understand her mother, I explained avoidant coping styles and added that in some instances an avoidant parent may actually get in her car and be gone for days at a time. Hearing this, the same client exclaimed, "Yes! Mom did that too!" In other words, when the therapist knows how this (or any other) interpersonal dynamic operates, then he or she is able to hear the "bizarre," fragmented pieces of a client's life and respond with the type of coherent understanding needed for constructing effective therapy goals.

Another common result of avoidance is bitter loneliness and unresolved distress, as well as chronic displeasure with others.[346] Given these dynamics, the avoidant individual is likely to be critical rather than accepting of his or her partner.[347] Due to a need for conflict avoidance, communication with the avoidant individual is often blocked by defensive maneuvering.[348] Rather

---

[343] While attachment anxiety results from viewing one's self as essentially unlovable, attachment avoidance is believed to result from a view of others as essentially untrustworthy or threatening (Brennan, Clark & Shaver, 1998).

[344] As well as being disinclined toward involvement in long-term romantic relationships, avoidant adults are more often inhibited and less socially skilled (Cooper et al., 1998).

[345] These strategies might include drinking "to cope or eating for emotional comfort (Brennan & Shaver, 1995).

[346] This unhappy attitude is felt most acutely in relation to romantic partners, who were initially expected to provide the comfort and relief denied since childhood (Mikulincer, Dolev & Shaver, 2004; Tidwell, Reis & Shaver, 1996).

[347] Thus, these relationships are characterized by significantly lower levels of intimacy, less enjoyment, and less positive emotion (Hazan & Shaver, 1987; Tidwell, Reis & Shaver, 1996).

[348] These defenses include the use of minimalization, a failure to state a position on issues, denial of problems or of unhappy feelings, and excessive defensiveness (Miller et al., 1986).

than enjoying a general ease and comfort with intimacy, avoidantly attached individuals become nervous or agitated when anyone gets too close.[349] The desire is not to avoid relationships all together, but rather to keep others at an emotionally safe distance. This is accomplished by avoiding conversations or physical interactions that demand emotional involvement, interdependence, and closeness.[350] While suffering from a lack of emotional connectedness,[351] such clients will naturally approach the therapeutic relationship with reluctance, perhaps even dread, especially if they expect that therapy will require greater intimacy than they can tolerate.[352]

Because it is helpful for the care provider to know what is troubling the person seeking help, therapy often starts with a request for self-disclosure, such as, "What can I help you with? What are you unhappy about?" However, avoidant individuals seek to avoid self-disclosure.[353]

In my practice, I have discovered that when highly avoidant individuals are asked to rate their subjective distress using a scale from 0 to 10, across multiple categories, the scores that come back often range from 0 to 1, thus implying that the individuals have come to therapy with absolutely nothing bothering them. Rather than the therapist labeling these clients as resistant, it is more helpful to understand that these individuals tend not to acknowledge their distress. Therapy can be adapted to the capabilities of this type of client by using questions that do not require as much emotional disclosure, such as, "Tell me what happened that caused you to decide to come to therapy?" In order to get a little more information about what clients might be feeling, it can be helpful to allow them to externalize their feelings, but without the use of projection or blame. For example, "You said that your wife is worried and that she thinks you need counseling. If she were here in the office, what would she say you are struggling with?" Providing just a little distance between these clients and their feelings decreases their need to withdraw from intolerable demands for intimacy.

Unfortunately, while witnessing other's plight, avoidant individuals are likely to respond in a way that is emotionally detached or even angry

---

[349] Avoidant individuals often experience conflict with those who demand greater intimacy (Grau & Doll, 2003).

[350] Classic avoidant traits include keeping thoughts and feelings to one's self; being shy, reserved, suspicious, and distrustful of others; and making social contacts slowly (Brennan & Shaver, 1995; Collins & Read, 1990; Cooper et al, 1998; Feeney & Noller, 1990).

[351] Avoidant individuals have been found to be at risk for a variety of mental and physical health problems associated with low intimacy (Tidwell, Reis & Shaver, 1996).

[352] Accordingly, research has found that these individuals are less likely to seek therapeutic assistance and more likely to distrust therapists (Mallinckrodt, King & Coble, 1998).

[353] This is especially true if the self-disclosure requires acknowledgement of personal vulnerability (Dozier, 1990; Horowitz et al., 1993).

and cynical.[354] This detached attitude is in line with habitual emotional coping strategies (i.e., to distance from sources of threat and suffering). When avoidant individuals do attempt to provide care for others, their approach is likely to be more task oriented than empathetic or comforting.[355] Because empathy requires an awareness of one's own experiences with suffering, those seeking to repress painful memories or suppress distressing thoughts are threatened by situations that evoke compassion.[356] As would be expected, those with an avoidant style are more likely to identify with others when the other people show signs of feeling good.[357]

This dynamic is especially important to understand when working with couples who are avoidant or a family with an avoidant parent. An important part of the therapy process will be to help the avoidant individual develop a greater capacity for empathy. The temptation is to struggle against the client's defense system while trying to make the avoidant partner recognize the suffering of others in the family. However, much less resistance is created when the therapist instead seeks to have clients recognize the joy that others have experienced in relationship to them.

For example, while speaking to a father who was having difficulty recognizing his son's suffering, I interrupted an unhappy exchange, saying, "I know that you are upset with your son right now because of his grades, but tell me about a time when you knew that he was really happy to be with you." The father began describing how it felt to come home to his son when he was younger. "You were always standing there at the window watching for me, you would come up to hug me. Nothing in the world made me feel better than that." After speaking these words, the father buried his face in his arm, and while turned toward the wall, he wept for a period of ten minutes, occasionally apologizing for the emotional breakdown, "I'm sorry, I'm sorry." During this time, the angry adolescent, who had become extremely distant and disengaged from the family, also began to tear up. Although the boy would not speak, the muscles in his face showed signs of intense internal work. At that moment, a powerful connection between father and son was reestablished, without the use of words.

Similarly, while working with men who have become angry and violent toward their partners, I have gotten surprising results after asking the

---

[354] This finding has been documented in numerous studies (Bartholomew & Horowitz, 1991; Collins & Read, 1994; Mikulincer & Florian, 2001; Simpson, Rholes & Nelligan, 1992).

[355] Unfortunately, these individuals provide the least emotional support when their partners need it the most (Feeney & Collins, 2001).

[356] That might be because people who are suffering act as a vicarious source of painful thoughts, memories, and emotions (Mikulincer et al, 2001a).

[357] In the absence of distress, the attachment system is deactivated, which then permits other more casual forms of relating (Mikulincer, Orbach & Iavnieli, 1998).

question, "What would it feel like for your spouse to be able to greet you at the door and feel happy that you have returned home? What type of thoughts would be going through her head if she could truly feel this way?" It is with this type of careful questioning that the client begins to recognize how much of his own loneliness and fear he has suppressed.

Fearful Attachment Produces Chaotic Relationships

Many researchers have suggested that there is a third type of insecure attachment, which represents a combination of anxious and avoidant styles. This third type is known as *fearful attachment*. Individuals in this category have very serious impairments in their ability to form relationships and, as a group, are some of the most difficult to reach and the most difficult with which to form a working alliance.[358]

The loneliness, anger, and fear that reverberates within these individuals often dates back to their earliest days. As a result of a frightening and traumatic childhood, which may have included acts of emotional, physical, and sexual abuse, the individual's ability to piece together a fluid and coherent picture of the past is severely compromised.[359] The result is strong feelings of ambivalence about all intimate relationships. While there may be an unconscious longing for affection, there is also deep resentment about what was inflicted or denied during childhood. Having difficulty making sense of their own emotional reactions, these individuals tend to blame their troubles on their partner while engaging in desperate attempts to maintain what is essentially a love-hate relationship.

These individuals are likely to come to therapy with a great deal of need.[360] At the same time, and unlike those with an anxious attachment style, individuals with a fearful style have great difficulty accepting support from others. Although they lack the self-sufficiency needed to handle problems on their own, these individuals tend to resist the formation of close supportive relationships for fear of the pain of potential loss or rejection.[361]

In order to make sense of the confusing and contradictory behavior

---

[358] Comparisons have been made between this group and the diagnostic category of Borderline Personality Disorder (Eames & Roth, 2000).

[359] Accordingly, affectional feelings and memories are more extensively excluded from a fearfully attached individual's awareness than they are from the awareness of those individuals with anxious or avoidant attachment styles (Sable, 1997).

[360] Individuals with a fearful orientation usually report a great deal of emotional distress and are highly symptomatic (Carnelley et al., 1994; Feeney & Ryan, 1994; Kemp & Neimeyer, 1999; Lopez et al., 1998).

[361] Ironically, these individuals tend to be highly dependent on others for the validation of their self-worth (Klohnen & Luo, 2003).

common with fearful attachment, one should recognize these individuals' intense ambivalence about emotional closeness. Because of low self-regard and excessive self-criticalness, those with fearful attachment are highly dependent on others for decision-making and security. Yet because of low regard for others and fear of rejection, there simultaneously exists an intense discomfort with intimacy and avoidance of close relationships. This ambivalence is likely to cause great confusion in relationships and is likely to carry over into the therapy relationship.

If this type of client feels pushed into an intimate, trusting relationship, the benefits that such a relationship is intended to produce will not be realized. On the contrary, the client can quickly decide that the relationship is more threatening than supportive and, thus, have a strong negative reaction.[362]

An even more risky tactic is to instruct this type of client to reflect on past experiences with primary caregivers. Although this technique has long served as a foundation for traditional psychotherapy, the clients described in this section have typically experienced profound distortions in the child-parent attachment experience. Inducing the client to revisualize these experiences will only intensify feelings of vulnerability, fear, and pain. As these feelings intensify, it is possible for the client to lose track of whose behavior is causing these feelings.[363] If the client is feeling rejected, shamed, or even hated during interactions with the care provider, then the therapy relationship will, of course, feel threatening.[364] Although these clients may initially seem to be rather helpless,[365] my experience has been that they tend to overreact to perceived injustices, unleashing a great deal of fury. Even when handled with extraordinary care during the session, these clients may still use the time in between visits to consider all the possible ways that the therapist might be failing them.

In one such instance, a client entered my office and took control of the conversation before I had any time to speak. "Fuck you!" he said. After pausing to glare into my eyes, he further clarified his position. "Fuck you,

---

[362] These individuals have a tendency to become severely anxious, depressed, and angry during close relations (Collins & Feeney, 2004; Mallinckrodt, King & Coble, 1998; Sable, 1997; Zuroff & Fitzpatrick, 1995).

[363] This response is referred to as transference in psychodynamic therapy. Paradoxically, psychodynamic therapies utilize transference as a primary strategy for treating psychological problems (Alexander, 1963).

[364] For persons scoring high in anxiety and avoidance, the visualization of past interactions may contextually activate their negatively valued interpersonal expectations of self and others (Mikulincer et al., 2001b).

[365] Individuals in this category tend to describe themselves as overly inhibited and unassertive (Bartholomew & Horowitz, 1991).

Dan! Fuck you, fuck you, fuck you!" This man was having to deal with the fact that his wife was going to divorce him and there was nothing he could do to stop it. In between sessions, he had decided that I was not doing enough to help him save his marriage.

The most crucial skill for the therapist to exercise with this type of client is maintaining enduring patience and a gentle demeanor while implementing clear and consistent boundaries for relating. If a protective environment is established, the client will respond with gratitude. In the specific instance mentioned above, the man requested an additional hour of therapy. When he left, he shook my hand and sincerely thanked me for being there to help him through this difficult time. This change in behavior did not occur in response to a single statement from me, but rather, after two hours of patient, gentle responding.

Collecting Attachment History Helps Identify
the Default Attachment Strategy

Now that the different categories of attachment have been reviewed, it is useful to know how to assess quickly which general category may fit a given client. Although several different paper-and-pencil instruments have been researched and developed for this purpose, this level of scientific rigor is not necessary for applied care. When therapists are seeking to provide a transformational relationship, the formation of a productive alliance is more important than assigning the client a diagnostic label. That having been said, it is helpful to have a general idea of an individual's propensities as the interpersonal dynamics unfold and a highly individualized relationship is developed.

In regard to emotional attachment, the first distinction to be made is whether clients are securely or insecurely attached. This is quickly determined by asking clients to provide some information about their childhood.[366] Those who are securely attached convincingly and coherently describe diverse childhood experiences in which warmth and attachment to care providers clearly play a central role. For example, "My most important childhood memory is our family campouts. Everyone pitched in together and helped each other out. And it was the same way at home, my parents were always there for you when you needed them."[367] The implication for

---

[366] Knowledge of family history can also function as a clinically useful index of psychological well-being and prognosis (Duke, Lazarus & Fivush, 2008).

[367] In general, securely attached individuals possess greater access to memories of early childhood events, especially those events associated with strong emotion (Hesse, 1999; Main, Kaplan, & Cassidy, 1985).

therapy is that those who can readily describe positive experiences that occurred during childhood probably have less need for the formation of an attachment bond to the therapist. In addition to having supportive family members, these individuals also tend to have established additional support networks that can be utilized as a vital resource during therapy.

By contrast, clients who have been negatively impacted by childhood care providers are more likely to focus on negative experiences, or they may offer general descriptions of childhood that are void of meaningful content, such as, "I had a fairly normal childhood. My parents were not worse than any other parent." When asked about childhood, these clients may become emotionally unsettled or respond with disinterest: "I don't remember much from my childhood. Just a few memories here and there." In some cases, childhood memories may be entirely repressed. When clients are able to relate various experiences, there is a disconnect between these memories and their understanding of what these experiences meant to them.[368] For example, the client might defensively say, "I had good parents and a decent childhood. I knew my parents loved me, even though they didn't really say so. My father was busy with work, but he did his best. He busted my butt sometimes, but I deserved it. I was a happy kid." Another useful question to ask is what the clients learned from their parents about supportive relationships or how the parent responded to their childhood needs.[369]

When there is evidence of insecure attachment, the distinction between attachment anxiety and attachment avoidance is fairly straightforward. An anxious individual will obviously be seeking support, while avoidant individuals are reluctant to depend on others for care.[370] More specifically, those with an anxious style are likely to describe themselves as having problems,[371] whereas avoidant individuals tend to withhold information about the challenges they face. Finally, while those with an anxious orientation have greater memory for negative childhood events and can describe the confusion or anger created by the relationship with their parents, those with an avoidant orientation do not easily recall negative events.[372] When the client's response to the therapist vacillates rapidly between

---

[368] Insecurely attached individuals are more likely to seem somewhat incoherent as they relate various childhood experiences (Crowell et al., 2002).

[369] Since individuals tend to have the same attachment style as their parents, it may be helpful to analyze the parents' attachment behavior (van IJzendoorn, 1995).

[370] Those with an anxious style tend to self-disclose freely and indiscriminately, whereas avoidant individuals are clearly uncomfortable with self-disclosure (Mikulincer & Nachshon, 1991).

[371] Individuals with insecure attachment tend to readily display distress and report higher levels of intrusive psychological symptoms (Kemp & Neimeyer, 1999).

[372] Avoidant individuals also tend to idealize their childhood while denying or devaluing the impact of early attachment relationships (Crowell, 2002; Hesse, 1999; Main et al., 1985).

overidealization and sudden victimization, then a fearful attachment style might explain the seemingly contradictory behavior.

Attachment Security Is an Interpersonal Phenomenon Rather Than a Fixed Trait

Following an encounter with a 16-year-old female that was both fascinating and sad, I developed a new appreciation for the relevance of attachment dynamics to therapy. In addition to being emotionally disturbed, this unhappy adolescent was really detached from her adoptive parents. She did not have any apparent desire for dependency or emotional closeness to anyone. Upon mention of her adoptive mother, the girl would respond explosively, "She is a fucking bitch, and I hate her! I don't need help from anyone, not you, and especially not from that fucking bitch!" The woman who had adopted her was a kind, quiet woman and unrelenting in her efforts to win her daughter's love. However, as the surrogate mother, she was a likely target for the hate and fury this girl felt for the abandonment by her biological mother.

As an adolescent, the girl frequently ran away from home and had no interest in submitting to authority figures or complying with school rules. She attended class when it suited her. When she felt unhappy with one of her teachers, she would unleash a string of profanity and then simply leave the classroom and the campus. Placing her in a fully self-contained classroom and on a level system did not improve the situation. As the school psychologist, I met with her occasionally, but our counseling sessions did not result in any recognizable gains.

Then an unexpected event produced some dramatic changes. She became ill and was so weak that she could hardly lift herself up in bed. During this time, her mother was able to care for her daughter in the way that she had always wished, spoon-feeding her soup and offering warm sympathy for her misery. After a couple of weeks of this care, the girl returned to school a different person. She attended class, handed in work, and participated appropriately in classroom discussions.

When I met with her, she had a softened look on her face. She told me about her mother caring for her during her illness. As I remember, I commented, "You know, your mother really does love you." Hearing this, the girl began to cry. I asked if she loved her mother as well, and she nodded through her tears. The sad part of the story is that the mother did not know how to maintain the attachment bond once her daughter returned to full health, and at the time I did not possess the knowledge needed to coach her. Within two weeks, the girl's former attachment style returned, and with it came a new onslaught of antisocial conduct and involvement with the criminal justice system. Before the end of the year, she was ordered by a judge to be placed in a psychiatric unit at the state hospital. Her mother was heartbroken. She confided to me that she felt like a failure as a mother. She was exceedingly anxious about her daughter's immediate circumstances and yet had no means available to protect her daughter.

An interesting question to ask about this case is whether the mother was anxious because of her daughter's behavior and placement in an institution (which would make perfect sense), or was she anxious because that was her security orientation, one that over the years had continued to weaken the mother-daughter attachment?[373] In other words, if the mother was insecure in her attachment to a newly adopted daughter and responded with attachment anxiety, then the neediness and overprotectiveness of an anxious style would exacerbate avoidant behavior in a child who had already experienced the loss of a biological mother. The more her daughter acted out and distanced herself from her mother, the more that behavior would reinforce the mother's expectations that eventually she would lose her daughter to some terrible fate, thus creating an unfortunate spiral. Those who had known the family for years accused the mother of being a "rescuer" and "enabling" the girl's behavior. Others blamed the girl, saying that she had the same genetic makeup as her biological mom, who ended up in prison. Regardless, it is certain that there was a short period when the relational dynamics shifted, and with that shift came the type of behavior and emotional functioning associated with secure attachment.[374] I have since learned that attachment is something that can be built up, torn down, or shifted from one style to another.

While it is true that attachment style depends in large part on early experiences in childhood, there is evidence that relationships in adolescence and adulthood influence attachment behavior.[375] Shifts in attachment -related behaviors can occur relative to those who have the greatest proximity.[376] I have had many adult clients complain, "When I go back home to

---

[373] Within the research literature, this is referred to as a self-reinforcing relationship feedback loop (Downey et al., 1998).

[374] As this case illustrates, attachment security (or lack of) should be conceptualized as an interpersonal phenomenon more so than a fixed personality trait (Kobak, 1994; Lewis, 1994).

[375] The specific characteristics of an immediate adult relationship have been shown to influence attachment security (Owens et al., 1995).

[376] In some cases, even within the same family there will be a substantial amount of variability in people's security of attachments from one relational partner to another (Baldwin et al., 1996; Collins & Read, 1994; Cook, 2000; La Guardia et al., 2000).

visit my family, I become a different person. I feel different on the inside and thoughts come into my head that are normally not there." As an example, a man may be avoidant in relation to his wife and anxiously attached to his mother. The person's relational style may also change based on the setting.[377] For example, a father may be available for emotional connections during vacations, but then be anxious, critical, and controlling while at home. When carefully considering the matter, most everyone can recall examples of this type of variability.[378] Given the dynamic nature of this interpersonal phenomena, it is important to continually reassess which set of circumstances are most conducive to the evolution of a secure attachment during therapeutic relating.

Therapists Operating From a Position of Secure Attachment Are more Likely to Engage in Therapeutic Relating

Anyone who has flown on an airplane knows that in the event of an emergency, you always secure your own oxygen mask before attempting to help a child. However, in therapy, is it necessary to secure one's own emotional attachments before helping others? The answer seems to be yes. There is ample evidence that therapists who have obtained a position of secure attachment are more likely to succeed at therapeutic relating. To begin with, it is generally the case that securely attached individuals offer the best opportunities for forming close, comfortable, emotional attachments.[379] Although it is common to conceptualize therapy as a one-way process in which support travels from the care provider to the care receiver, an individual's ability to provide support is highly related to his or her ability to seek and use support.[380] Furthermore, when there is a genuine interest in forming close relationships with others, that feeling tends to be noticed and reciprocated.[381]

---

[377] It is also possible for a person to relate in a way that is contextually sensitive so that different attachment styles are used with the same set of individuals (Ogilvie & Ashmore, 1991).

[378] When surveyed, 88% of adults will report using two of the three core attachment styles, and 47% report using all three (i.e., secure, avoidant, anxious-ambivalent) (Baldwin et al., 1996).

[379] The ability to form such attachments has a direct impact on interpersonal attraction and partner choice (Klohnen & Luo, 2003; Latty-Mann & Davis, 1996).

[380] Without a strong capacity for intimacy and sense of confidence, it is less likely that a person will be able to provide sensitive care to others (Collins & Feeney, 2000; Crowell et al., 2002).

[381] Research has shown that therapists who experience greater comfort with closeness are more likely to have clients who report a strong, early emotional bond with them (Dunkle & Friedlander, 1996).

In order to understand why secure therapists provide more sensitive and responsive care to others, it is helpful to recognize some of the internal dynamics that are operating.[382] Because they already feel loved, accepted, and cared for by others, secure therapists have fewer personal needs to tend to during the therapy encounter. Because they do not have an emotional vacuum, it becomes easier to develop close emotional connections without becoming confused by feelings of romantic attachment.[383] This level of emotional contentment allows secure therapists to direct their resources more completely to the task of taking the client's perspective so that empathy for suffering and altruistic recognition of needs can emerge.[384] This empathy and altruistic recognition then lead to more positive and accurate interpretations of others' behavior and greater attention to the subjective needs of the individual.[385]

Other advantages include more competent handling of unexpected relationship experiences and an increased capacity to respond with flexibility to relational challenges.[386] As a client who was a skillful special education teacher put it, "I do not respond to a student who is becoming upset by becoming upset myself. As long as there is no need to intervene I just move along. Yesterday, [a student identified as emotionally disturbed] looked up at me and said, 'Yuck! Get away from me. You are old!' I just kept walking down the aisle, and there were no further problems from him." This student probably expected some type of negative reaction from his teacher, or at least a sad face. Instead she showed him how not to be bothered by rude comments from others, which was probably his most important lesson for the day. Similarly, securely attached therapists are more likely to provide experiences that challenge their clients' expectations of the world.[387]

---

[382] This increased capacity for care is a robust finding documented in numerous studies (Carnelley, Pietromonaco, & Jaffe, 1996; Collins & Feeney, 2000; Feeney & Collins, 2001; Feeney, 1999; Fraley & Shaver, 1998; Kunce & Shaver, 1994; Simpson et al., 2003; Simpson et al., 2002; Westmaas & Silver, 2001).

[383] There is evidence that secure people in general tend to differentiate more clearly between romantic and nonromantic opposite-sex partners (Tidwell, Reis & Shaver, 1996).

[384] In contrast, therapists scoring higher on an anxious attachment have been found to respond less empathically, especially with clients who have secure and dismissing attachment styles (Rubino et al., 2000).

[385] Securely attached individuals use problem solving that is more accommodative and collaborative (Feeney, 1998; Kobak & Hazan, 1991; Levy, Blatt, & Shaver, 1998; Lopez, Gover, et al., 1997; Mikulincer, 1998b; Pistole, 1996; Scharfe & Bartholomew, 1995).

[386] These abilities might be due in part to a greater tolerance for ambiguity and a reluctance to make hasty judgments (Feeney, 1998; Mikulincer, 1997; Mikulincer & Arad, 1999).

[387] This is based on the assumption that most clients lack experiences with secure attachment (Dozier, Cue, & Barnett, 1994).

In sum, it appears that the most capable therapists not only have an academic knowledge of technique, but also, more importantly, an emotional readiness to relate from a position of secure attachment. From experience, I can testify to the increased ease and expanded range of therapeutic relating that is possible when a secure attachment style is fully developed.

Priming of Secure Attachment in Therapy
Is an Important Adjunctive Treatment

While reviewing progress in therapy, clients will often remark, "I couldn't have done this on my own," or as one client put it, "I could not have done it without someone else beside me." Although some individuals need occasional guidance and direction, there are many instances when clients already know what needs to be done, but because of limiting beliefs and emotional disequilibrium, they fail to act. An interesting point to consider is whether the mere idea of receiving care and support from others makes clients more capable of dealing with psychological problems and even physical threats.

I spent some time reflecting on this question after a conversation with a friend. She was telling me about one of the most harrowing moments of her life, the delivery of her first and only child. As difficult as birthing can be, this woman had been warned by a doctor that for her it could prove fatal. She was in her late thirties, diabetic, and medically fragile. To make matters worse, she had been talked into foregoing the use of any anesthesia by a midwife, who insisted on natural deliveries. Though my friend was in a hospital, when the pain from the contractions became unbearable, no one was there to help her. The time for anesthesia was already past. This woman's husband stood motionless in the corner of the room, helplessly watching her scream, and the midwife was not even in the room.

Before my friend realized how insufficient her birthing arrangements were, the contractions began to hit with such frequency and violence that she found herself unable to speak or breath. Soon the only thought in her mind was that if she just let go, death would come and put an end to the insufferable pain. At about that moment, the phone rang and was answered by her husband. The caller was a close friend who was also a therapist. When she heard what was happening, she ordered the husband to put the phone to his wife's ear. The therapist then began to repeat a solitary statement, "You are loved. There are people out there who care for you and want you to get through this!" Hearing these words, my friend found strength and a renewed capacity to fight for survival.

After telling me her story, she concluded, "I am confident that the phone call was what kept me alive."[388] While in a position of great distress and insecurity, she found benefit from someone else who was willing to act as a secure base of attachment.[389]

Not only is it possible for a therapist to create a context conducive to secure attachment, but also, by the therapist doing so, the client will be better able to cope with the challenges and demands of therapy. The importance of this benefit should not be underestimated. With a felt sense of secure attachment, the client is less likely to be incapacitated by negative emotions, thus allowing a greater depth of psychological exploration.[390] Secure attachment also makes it less likely that the client will cling to firmly held beliefs and expectations, thus permitting greater flexibility and open-mindedness when exposed to new information.[391] Accordingly, a sense of secure attachment appears to be necessary for the type of introspection and self-reflection used to establish a working alliance.[392] Given these dynamics, it is easy to see why the priming of a secure attachment is likely to play a key role in any transformational relationship.

What is surprising is how easily a secure attachment can be established, even with severely damaged individuals. For example, during my early days as a domestic violence counselor, I was visited by a man who was capable of horrific violence and whose reality testing was disturbed. His girlfriend was also in therapy with a female counselor. During therapy, this girlfriend described a deadly conflict that took place while driving down the road. In a fit of rage, the man kicked open her door and pushed her out of the moving vehicle and into the street. This occurred some distance from their house, so it took her a while to walk home. When she finally arrived, bloody and with

---

[388] In regard to this event, academics would say that there had been a contextual activation of secure attachment.

[389] Accordingly, researchers have found that the sense of having a secure base can be contextually activated by actual or imagined encounters with available and responsive others, even for those who have chronic doubts about their attachments to others (Baldwin, 1992, 1997; Mikulincer et al., 2000b).

[390] Secure attachment has been associated with the arousal of positive affect, which presumably counters the impact of negative affect (Lopez & Brennan, 2000; Mikulincer & Florian, 2000).

[391] That is why, when compared with individuals with insecure styles, those with a secure style are more capable of recalling (across several distinct situations) information about their relationship partners that is incongruent with their prior expectations of partner behavior (Lopez, 1996; Mikulincer, 1997; Mikulincer & Arad, 1999).

[392] Without this type of psychological availability, it will be difficult for the client to provide a coherent and well-organized developmental history; to make sense of interpersonal relationships, both positive and negative; or to integrate and interpret past experiences (Buchheim & Mergenthaler, 2000; Fonagy et al., 2002).

torn clothing, she found her boyfriend sitting casually on the front porch, whittling a piece of wood. When he saw her, he seemed surprised and asked, "What the fuck happened to you? You look like shit!" She screamed at him for kicking her out of the truck, but he had no memory of the event.

While talking with her counselor, the woman also confessed to violent behavior herself. "During our last fight, I became angry and threw a refrigerator into his back," she said. It was a small refrigerator used to keep drinks cold, so she was able to lift it over her head and hit him hard enough to incapacitate him temporarily.

The fact that they were both so violent made it difficult to get my client to consider the impact of his actions or the importance of creating a more loving environment in the home. The man was very hardened. He had been given a dishonorable discharge from the navy for violent behavior. Most of his childhood was repressed from memory. Although he was young, his face and arms bore the scars of a difficult life.

Struck by his callous demeanor, I decided to probe his memories for evidence of one person who showed him love during his childhood. My client instantly responded that both of his parents hated him, and they let it be known that they wished he had never been born. However, I persisted, asking if there was a grandmother or an aunt, a school teacher, or the parent of a friend—anyone—who had shown some kindness or love toward him. He confessed that he did not have friends as a child and was considered a troublemaker by the teachers at school.

Then, as best I remember, I informed him that it did not have to be a human creature. With that, his face softened, and he told me that though his parents would not allow any pets, he had always wished to have a dog. Then one day, while wondering alone, down a dirt road, he was approached by a large golden dog. The dog licked his hands and ran with him. For the first time, he felt loved.

After telling me the story he sat quietly for some time, and then asked, "Do you think she [his girlfriend] could ever love me?" His question was sincere, his voice trembling as he asked it. It was the first time in therapy he had made himself vulnerable, and it provided a perfect opening for the type of psychological work that needed to be achieved. After this, he was willing to admit to mistakes in his behavior and to practice strategies for avoiding violent confrontations at home.[393] As remarkable as this sudden shift may

---

[393] The transformation in my client's behavior was witnessed by his girlfriend, who told her counselor that his counseling was really making a difference. I expect that the long-term outcome could have been good, but tragically, he was informed by a physician that he had a malignant brain tumor. After coming to tell me that he had only been given a short time to live, he broke off all communication. My hope is that he died with the feeling that he was indeed loved.

sound, the behavior fits entirely with what would be expected after arous-
ing feelings of attachment security connected to his deeply valued experience with a loving animal.[394]

This same type of psychological shift can be achieved by a variety of
means. One method that has proven effective during research investigations
is to suggest the possibility of being in the presence of responsive care providers.[395] More potent images for the priming of attachment security might
be produced from actual memories of a loving parent, a nurturing friend, or
a favorite teacher. I have also seen dramatic results when a client is asked to
reflect on experiences with a former therapist, who provided help and support during a time of great need.[396]

The easiest method I know for priming attachment security is to hang
a picture in the office that depicts an act of loving support. On my wall
there is a commercial photo of a small boy who has fallen asleep on top of
his father while visiting the beach. Often clients will comment on the picture, automatically assuming that the man in the picture is me. Several have
said that they feel good when they look at the picture or that they saw it
and immediately felt safe in my office. Whether or not the reason for this
feeling is consciously realized does not matter.[397] What is most important is
the client's willingness to be open to support.

Researchers have documented the effectiveness of using a photograph
as a means of priming attachment security.[398] In fact, images of symbolic
care providers can be so powerful that the client can react to such a representation in the way one would with an actual partner. For example, one
client informed me, in an angry tone of voice, that he had taken his picture
of the Virgin Mary off the wall and placed it in a drawer. When I asked why
he had done this, he quipped that for many months he had been praying for

---

[394] Research has shown that the priming of memories of attachment security will cause people to perceive others in more positive terms (Cohen, Towbes, & Flocco, 1988) and to
increase openness to belief-discrepant information (Brennan & Bosson, 1998; Mikulincer
& Arad, 1999).

[395] In one such study the participants were told to imagine being surrounded by people who
were sensitive and responsive to their distress, compelled by love to offer assistance, and
willing to set their own activities aside in order to assist with a problem (Mikulincer &
Shaver, 2001).

[396] Similarly, in research studies, a simple request to visualize a secure, avoidant, or anxious-
ambivalent relationship for a few moments served to prime people with that way of relating, leading them to later respond to interpersonal information in different ways (Baldwin
et al., 1996).

[397] Studies have shown that security priming works similarly whether it is induced consciously or unconsciously (Mikulincer et al., 2005).

[398] The images used in the research depicted a same-sex distressed person being helped and
physically comforted by an opposite-sex partner (Mikulincer et al., 2001b).

God to send him a woman so that he could have his sexual needs satisfied. With absolute conviction he declared, "She is not coming out of the drawer until God sends me a woman!" But the removal of this symbol of love and protection, over time, only caused him to feel lonelier, so following the brief exile, the Virgin Mary was reinstated as someone to watch over this lonely individual.

When images associated with love or protection are summoned in therapy, there is an affective softening and an increased readiness to explore new possibilities.[399] Because attachment security provides an important sense of personal safety and comfort with others, even a temporary activation of this sense of security allows chronically insecure people to open themselves to alternative worldviews.[400] This opening, in turn, helps them become more accepting of people who offer alternative ways of seeing and doing things (i.e., their therapist).[401] Thus, the results of providing secure base support, both immediately and over time, are increased self-acceptance and increased readiness to enjoy one's relationships with others.[402]

Therapists Can offer a Reparative Relationship as a Surrogate Attachment Figure

When someone in distress comes to therapy and, as a result, experiences safety and a renewed readiness to deal with challenges in the outside world, then a particular type of complementarity has been achieved. When a sense of security is facilitated by the therapist's responsiveness to the client's expressions of distress and anxiety, then the therapist is acting as a significant attachment figure.[403] By definition, a therapeutic alliance consists of a collaborative effort to achieve therapeutic goals in the context of an af-

---

[399] Research has shown that representations of attachment security act as resilience resources for immediate challenges, helping decrease the amount of avoidance and defensive maneuvering while increasing unimpeded exploration (Elliot & Reis, 2003).

[400] Additionally, activation of attachment security is associated with more realistic self-appraisal (Mikulincer, 1995), adding yet another reason why it is helpful to the therapy process.

[401] This outcome has been observed both inside and outside of the clinical context (Baldwin et al., 1996; Collins & Read, 1990; Hazan & Shaver, 1987; Mikulincer et al., 2005; Mikulincer & Shaver, 2001).

[402] More specifically, research has shown that increases in attachment security lead to higher levels of self-esteem, perceived competency, self-confidence, and self-efficacy; increases in exploratory behavior and goal pursuit; and increases in learning, discovery, and overall happiness and well-being (Feeney, 2004).

[403] Other characteristics that help establish the therapist as a reliable attachment figure include constancy, availability, sensitivity, and genuine concern (Farber, Lippert, & Nevas, 1995).

fective bond or positive attachment.[404] Therefore, when considering the importance of relationship for positive therapy outcomes, the significance of attachment dynamics must not be ignored. In order to serve as an attachment figure for those who have exceeded their ability to cope, the therapist needs to have an obvious desire to help and to be consistently available. Clients need to know with absolute certainty that the care provider is someone they can go to when experiencing distress or uncertain accomplishments.[405] So in addition to having a sincere interest in the well-being of others, those who intend to act as a secure base for distressed individuals should appreciate the significance of proximity-seeking and availability.[406]

In an ideal world, anytime a client (without adequate social support) experienced significant distress, his or her therapist would be available for face-to-face contact. Seeking out support (from a highly trained individual) during moments of isolation and distress is a very useful coping strategy that should be reinforced. However, in a world of limited resources and copious demands, this type of arrangement is impossible. Even worse, when the demand for care exceeds one's ready availability, the natural response is to withdraw. While I always try to communicate empathy for the client's uncertainty about time away from the office, there have been occasions when I found myself wanting to hide from a particularly needy client.

Unfortunately, clients who already struggle with chronic feelings of rejection or abandonment are particularly sensitive; thus, even the slightest degree of emotional withdrawal can trigger intense distress and set into motion an intense and unfortunate cycle of demand and withdrawal.[407] The solution is to view proximity seeking as vital to secure attachment and, therefore, something that should be encouraged within the parameters of healthy boundaries. Exactly what those boundaries may be is something to be determined by each individual therapist. If I have a crisis-oriented client who protests delays in rescheduling or expresses anxiety over my vacation leave, then I will offer to communicate by text message or even conduct an appointment by phone if needed. This type of reassurance not only calms

---

[404] This basic definition has gained acceptance beginning in the early 1990s (Bordin, 1994; Gaston, 1990; Henry & Strupp, 1994; Horvath & Symonds, 1991).

[405] Uncertain accomplishments are those achievement-oriented activities that are novel and not yet integrated into the self-concept. For this reason, some amount of external validation is needed (e.g., "Did I really win?").

[406] This point has been argued by experts in the fields of therapy and attachment relations (Mikulincer et al., 2005).

[407] A similar dynamic has been noted by marriage researchers who have observed a self-reinforcing feedback loop known as the demand-withdraw pattern, in which one partner demands and the other withdraws, prompting more intense demands by the first partner, followed by even greater withdrawal by the second (Christensen & Heavey, 1990; Gray-Little & Burks, 1983; Levenson & Gottman, 1985).

the client, but it also tends to decrease the demand. Very rarely has anyone called me during vacation, but almost always a great deal of appreciation is expressed for my interest in making help available.

By contrast, when separation is forced on a client who is seeking security, cooperation is diminished and resistance increased. For some clients, the threat of separation can potentially become an issue at the end of each session. When this occurs, the client may resist ending the conversation at the appointed time, or the client may even seek to start a quarrel. Even if the client seems unwilling to end the session, there is no need to be alarmed. It is a temporary feeling produced by insecurity that will naturally pass once the attachment bond produces an increase in self-confidence. For the client who still does not wish to leave the office, even though the appointment has ended and the next client is waiting outside, a brief comment can extend the secure attachment: "As you leave my office, you can take my voice with you so that at any moment you need, I can be there speaking to you. And with time that voice can transform into the voice of others who you perceive to have wisdom or strength. And with time the one you hear speaking to you might transform into your own voice. This is a source of security that you have available to you both night and day." In this example, an experiential component was used to create a context within which the client organizes emotional experience and learns to regulate feelings of security.[408]

In addition to seeking out the therapist during times of distress, it is perhaps equally important that the client view the care provider as someone with whom he or she would want to share uncertain successes. I first recognized the importance of this during my doctoral internship, when I met with a 16-year-old male whose face was pierced with metal studs and his hair formed into a purple mohawk. He had been sent to the school nurse on numerous occasions after cutting his arms with pieces of metal or glass. During his initial visit to my office, he insisted that no one could stop him from cutting on himself and that he had a right to do what he wished to his body. As I remember, I verified this fact and then began to ask his opinion on a wide variety of subjects. I spoke with respect recognizing his importance as an individual. I told him he could come back for another visit any time he wished.

Several weeks later, he requested a second visit. The instant he walked into the office, I could see evidence of a transformation. He no longer had metal in his face or tall, purple hair. He still wore heavy silver earrings and had short spiked hair, but his new appearance seemed to reflect pride in

---

[408] In this particular instance, the client responded to my comment by smiling and saying, "Thank you." She then left the office without any evidence of anxiety.

personal style rather than agony over a lack of attention. His posture had softened, and he spoke with the voice of a vulnerable child. When asked how things were going for him, he described with pride how a coach had taken notice of him. With his eyes becoming moist, he related how the coach had insisted on seeing a math test that he had passed with a *B*. The coach had looked him in the eye and said, "I'm proud of you. I know you worked hard for this grade," and then gave the boy a hug. Now looking into my eyes, the boy added, "I think he really cares [about me]." The encounter with his coach had served as a transformational moment. Afterward, he started caring more deeply about his performance at school and enjoyed a newfound pride in his accomplishments. And as would be expected, he lost all interest in self-mutilation.

The coach's therapeutic intervention at first seemed to be all that was needed. After the boy left my office, I humorously thought to myself, "With coaches like that, who needs psychologists?" But a couple weeks later, I stopped to consider why the boy had requested a second appointment with me. It was an interesting question that forced me to recognize the real significance of our last session. Although it was important that he have his academic performance acknowledged and validated, the boy's greater success was in having attained positive recognition from a powerful and respected member of the school community (i.e., the coach). However, the reality of this larger success was still so new and uncertain that the boy needed outside confirmation of the idea that the coach truly cared. So it was my job to let him know that he had a right to his new feeling of being valued by important others.

Unlike most therapy techniques, the dynamics of attachment are often set into motion during the course of casual conversation. It is the small comments or gestures at the beginning or end of the session that can sometimes determine the emotional context under which therapy will be conducted. A brief parting comment, at the end of a visit or phone call, can make a significant difference. For example, the statement "I'm glad that you decided to call me today, even though you were initially concerned about the inconvenience it may cause. I truly want to be there for you when you are in need," communicates the therapist's readiness to serve as a safe haven that will produce demonstrable effects on the client's emotional and cognitive states.[409] For this reason, it is important to for therapists keep in mind what it is that they are seeking to accomplish during all moments of the encounter.

---

[409] This was demonstrated in a controlled study in which a passing comment, "I'll be next door. If you need any help, do not hesitate to ask," was used to achieve a measured increase in self-confidence and cognitive efficacy (Sarason & Sarason, 1986).

The Intensity of Emotional Attachment Should Vary
According to the Client's Attachment Style

The last point to be clearly understood is that the provision of psychological support is not an all-or-nothing phenomena. Whether it involves the giving of advice, the expression of concern, or the amount of self-disclosure that is requested, all caregiving activities can vary in their intensity, frequency, and duration. Therefore, the skillful therapist makes an effort to discern the level of emotional closeness that is right for a particular client on a particular day.

For example, clients experiencing attachment avoidance will naturally be reluctant self-disclose in therapy. Because there is a tendency to mistrust the therapist, these clients should be given an opportunity to show their strength and say what they are doing well, rather than being forced to dwell on their weaknesses. Rather than spending the entire therapy hour discussing their emotional problems, the clients may make only one or two brief statements about emotional distress. These statements can be acknowledged by the therapist, and the rest of the session can focus on concrete planning and problem solving. If the therapist fails to decrease the intensity of the emotional dialogue for someone who is avoidant, it is highly probable that the client will develop strong negative feelings about the therapy.[410] As has been explained in this chapter, individuals who experience avoidant attachment need a sense of independence and, therefore, respond well to permission to exercise their self-sufficiency. In is not only during the context of a single meeting that this occurs, but also when deciding on the frequency of appointments. My experience has been that some clients are better able to tolerate their need for psychological assistance if they are given permission to separate their visits by a period of months rather than days or weeks.

In contrast, clients who are experiencing a strong attachment anxiety may need most of the therapy hour to explain what they are feeling and why they believe they are seriously in need of help. This client may also wish to schedule two to three visits within the same week.[411] For these individuals, a deep exploration of their issues will be highly gratifying. Further relief is added if, after a careful study of the client's history, the thera-

---

[410] Avoidant attachment to one's therapist is also associated with clients' experiencing sessions as both shallow and rough (Mallinckrodt et al., 2005).

[411] Not only do these individuals wish more frequent and intensely personal contact, but some also literally wished to be "at one" with their therapists (Mallinckrodt, Gantt, & Coble, 1995).

pist says that there is some hope and that, with the proper set of goals, the client's situation will be greatly improved.[412] This type of feedback is important because clients with attachment anxiety often seek approval from others in an effort to counterbalance excessive internal criticism.[413] At the start of therapy, it may be necessary to provide frequent and direct reassurance. However, as therapy progresses, there should be an effort to expand the client's capacity for self-approval rather than having the client continue to rely on the therapist for reassurance. In order to help ease the client into this transition, it can be helpful to substitute permissive reassurance for direct reassurance. For example, rather than saying, "You did well with that task," a therapist can say to the client, "You have a right to notice when you have done something well and to congratulate yourself. Would you be willing to do that?" Another procedure that helps with the transition is to educate the client on what needs to be done and why: "In order to diminish that critical voice inside your head, you will need to learn how to recognize the good things that you are doing and give yourself some praise. This will provide longer lasting relief than seeking approval from others." Understanding the reason behind a therapist's actions can help prevent misinterpretation of the therapist's feedback.

In closing, it is important to recognize that throughout human history, emotional bonds have been the favorite subject of poems, drama, and music. Now social science has recognized that individuals are most likely to thrive when there is security in relationships. When a secure base of attachment is missing, individuals have great difficulty functioning in families, at work, or in solitude. Because relationship has been shown to be the primary remedial force in therapy, it is essential for therapists to understand the dynamics of emotional attachment and its practical applications for therapy. When people have a secure attachment base, they are more likely to explore their environment, take risks, and learn new skills. There are numerous approaches the therapist can take to promote secure attachment. The options for intervention range from acting as a surrogate attachment figure to direct coaching for couples and parents so that they can better respond to those seeking their support. Like it or not, any contact with the needy is a trial as they seek to determine the significance of their existence. In the words of Mother Teresa (1995):

---

[412] While it is not difficult to form an emotional bond with this type of client, agreeing on the tasks and goals of therapy may require some guidance (Mallinckrodt, Porter, & Kivlighan, 2005; Meyer & Pilkonis, 2001).

[413] This need for approval can lead to a dynamic in which the client feels that he or she must get the therapist's reassurance in order to maintain self-esteem (Wei, Heppner, & Mallinckrodt, 2003).

The greatest disease in the West today is not TB or leprosy; it is being unwanted, unloved, and uncared for. We can cure physical diseases with medicine, but the only cure for loneliness, despair, and hopelessness is love. There are many in the world who are dying for a piece of bread, but there are many more dying for a little love.

Chapter 5

STRUCTURE
Social Hierarchies Act as Conduits for the Flow of Shared Resources

Submissive behavior directed up the dominance hierarchy
can be readily understood when considered in relation
to the deep-seated need for reassurance contact
experienced by an emotionally or
physically distressed chimpanzee.
—Jane Goodall, 1986

As suggested by Goodall, there is a natural tendency among all organized societies for the needy to seek support from those in a dominant position. In humans, the tendency is to go progressively higher on the dominance hierarchy, depending on the severity of the problem.

For example, consider the difference in status between a surgeon and a physical therapist. A backache is typically not considered to be a terminal condition, so the individual will seek help from a massage therapist or physical therapist. However, if there is something wrong with the heart and that condition is considered life-threatening, the individual will consult a surgeon, someone who is much further up the dominance hierarchy both in terms of financial compensation and behavior. While the physical therapist is socially sanctioned to exercise some dominant behavior during healing, it is not nearly as much as the person who is preparing to cut open his or her patient's chest or skull. When a surgeon starts to intervene, there is very little the patient can do; in most cases the patient has been anesthetized and has forfeited important symbolic boundaries such as clothing. Furthermore, surgeons surround themselves with a team of individuals who act on their command. An interesting question is whether surgeons would be as successful in their healing endeavors if they acted as the patient's servant, in the same manner a waitress or waiter cares for a customer.

Logic indicates that only under unique circumstances would someone who is scared and hurting actively seek out a subordinate in order to receive urgent care and guidance. When the dynamics of attachment are considered, it becomes apparent that the psychotherapeutic relationship fits with Bowlby's (1973) essential notion of attachment as a bond developed with an individual who is perceived as wiser and/or stronger. A person who is in great distress typically does not look down the dominance hierarchy for care and protection, but instead seeks expert care from someone assumed to have greater insight or understanding than they do. Under these circumstances, it is almost by definition that the relationship is structured with the therapist in the dominant position. [414]

In the discussion of dominance and submission, it is common to make references to power and to assume that it is the dominant individual who wields all the power. However, that is not true. As will be explained later, in much greater detail, dominance and submission both serve the purpose of organizing and bringing structure to relationships. Although social scientists commonly refer to this organization as the power domain, I prefer to use the term *structure*, because it does not conjure up images of oppression and battles for control. All relationships have some form or structure. More importantly, this structure can be achieved equally well by means of dominance or submission. In the same way that a trench is a conduit for water when it rains, the organization of a relationship into dominant or submissive roles is a conduit for the flow of shared resources. [415]

While the design of therapy relationships and the need for relational complementarity are examined, [416] it should be understood that clients cannot be bullied into good mental health. If a dominant interpersonal style were all that were needed in therapy, then harsh authoritarianism would have already proven itself sufficient for recovery from behavioral and psychological problems. By contrast, history and social science have shown that most individuals possess an instinctual tendency to resist or oppose anything that unjustly limits their freedom of choice. [417] That is why a therapist

---

[414] Similarly, research into brief therapy has indicated that the therapist's role is inherently powerful, even in the low-alliance cases (Reandeau & Wampold, 1991).

[415] The human species, though relatively weak and vulnerable, has the most complex system of social organization. As a result, its abilities are unmatched by any other living creature.

[416] Complementarity in this chapter refers to interactions in which one person takes a one-up position and the other a one-down position, relinquishing control by agreeing, approving, or complying. By contrast, symmetry refers to interactions in which both speakers vie for control by changing the topic, disagreeing with a statement, or by making a demand (Heatherington & Friedlander, 1990).

[417] Coercive forms of dominant behavior are likely to produce a stronger desire for whatever has been denied (Miller & Rollnick, 2002).

should not take unilateral action against the *client's* symptoms.[418] Even if one's intent is positive, it is not wise to try to force change upon a client.[419]

Although aspirations of equality among client and therapist seem to promise ideal relational strategies and safeguards, when the science of relationships is considered, it will become evident that heterogeneous complementarity (i.e., dominance and submission) will result in stronger relational bonds. Perhaps the greatest problem with absolute equality (besides the fact that it is not possible) is that it does not result in dynamic interaction. During therapy, there will always be one person who leads the attempt to manage both individual and shared resources.[420] These resources include time (how long the encounter will last), communication (who will speak about what), status (who is more healthy and knowledgeable), social attention (who is the focus of attention), intimacy (closeness of contact), and goods (payment for services). Most often, these resources are managed by the therapist, but not always. For example, if the therapist suggests that a client owes a no-show fee for a missed appointment, and the client in return talks the therapist out of collecting the fee, then in the context of that interaction, it is the client who is dominant. Similarly, if the client were to request extra time at the end of the session and, despite the protests of the therapist (who is concerned about the next client in the waiting room), the meeting lasts 15 minutes longer than the scheduled time, then in the context of that interaction, it is again the client who is dominant.[421]

Although it might seem that the therapist should always take the dominant position, a more nuanced approach is required. As a novice therapist, I struggled to achieve strong relational bonds with individuals who were uncomfortable with a submissive position in relationships. At that time, the clientele I worked with consisted of men who had been court-mandated to participate in counseling for violent and abusive behavior. In many instances, their violent behavior had occurred not only at home, but also at work, when these men were confronted by bosses seeking to assert their dominant status. Although I was aware of the clients' chronic need for dominance and control, I was reluctant to take a submissive position, for fear of being exploited. Many of the men were exceedingly hostile and highly skilled at verbal intimidation and tactics of psychological abuse. A

---

[418] There is a strong instinct in humans to resist any unsolicited attempt to take away something that has become associated with the "self." As most parents know, this instinctual behavior can be clearly seen in children as young as two years of age.

[419] Efforts by therapists to control client behaviors have been negatively correlated with alliance (Lichtenberg et al., 1988).

[420] It is the role of the dominant individual to manage shared resources (Cook, 1987).

[421] By academic definition, it is the person who successfully controls resources that is the socially dominant individual (Hawley & Little, 1999; Hawley 2002).

certain amount of guidance was required on my part in order keep the meetings safe and productive for everyone involved. Some individuals responded surprisingly well to my insistence on maintaining a dominant position, while others dropped out of counseling after only one or two visits.

Interestingly, I noticed a unique behavior common to those who were unwilling to accept guidance. These men often sat back in their chairs in a seemingly relaxed posture, their elbows extended and one hand lifted up in the air above their head. This kingly posture caught my attention because my clients would maintain it for an unnaturally long period of time, as if the elevated hand had become cataleptic. On one such occasion, as the client stubbornly resisted my efforts to establish myself as the conversational leader, he not only rested with one hand up in the air, but then also kicked one of his legs up over the arm of his chair, thereby spreading his legs wide apart and tilting his groin slightly toward me. At first, I considered the Freudian idea that the client might have latent homosexual impulses. However, this conclusion did not fit any of the other situational dynamics. By the end of the session, I still did not have a satisfactory explanation for these behaviors, but, as expected, this client also dropped out of therapy prematurely. It was only after studying social psychology and ethnology that I developed a better understanding of the client's instinctual behavior.

Changes in posture are often used to signal differences in dominance. When people expand themselves and take up a lot of space, they are seeking to establish a dominant position within the relationship, whereas when they constrict themselves and take up little space, they are taking a submissive position.[422] The behavior seems to be fairly universal, as it is found in animals as well as humans.[423] Dominant and submissive positions in relationships are sometimes metaphorically represented by different positions in height, as found in the children's game of king of the hill.[424] We use the term *one-up* to describe those who are in the dominant position. Therefore, clients with a high need for dominance might posture themselves with one hand suspended up in the air, or in some cases, they might stand in order to look down on the therapist.

The same type of posturing also has more subtle variations. Even when

---

[422] Postural expansion occurs more frequently among people who have high status and constriction more frequently among people who have low status (Argyle, 1988; Eibl-Eibesfeldt, 1975; Weisfeld & Beresford, 1982).

[423] For example, dominant chimpanzees adopt postures that make them appear as large as possible, while the chimps who observe the display of dominance will constrict themselves, bowing low to the ground with their limbs pulled in (Goodall, 1986; de Waal, 1982).

[424] In most all instances, up signals dominance and down signals submission (Lakoff & Johnson, 1999; Tolaas, 1991).

the body is kept still, the face is still used to signal social status, and dominance is communicated through an upward head tilt and a direct eye gaze. In contrast, a submissive posture is signaled when the eye gaze is averted and the head and shoulders are rounded downward.[425] Concerning the clients mentioned above, I strongly suspect that these men did not wish to assume a submissive position within the context of therapy (or perhaps anywhere else). My experience has been that it is exceedingly difficult to create the type of relational dynamics necessary for clients to feel safe in a position of submission if, as children, those clients were abused or terrified by angry, dominant parents.

Because flexibility on the part of the professional care provider is of paramount importance, skillful therapists assess the client's need for dominance or submission as early in the relationship as possible so that necessary adjustments can be made. Even within the context of day-to-day encounters, untrained individuals quickly determine who is dominant and who is submissive in order to determine who will manage shared resources, who has the power to influence outcomes, and who will evaluate whom.[426] The old adage "You have to know your place in order to make it in the world" speaks to a phenomenon observed among all species that live in groups.[427]

Within the context of a helping relationship, the clues needed to determine the client's customary status are so numerous that they are impossible to miss if one merely considers the question of dominance and submission. For instance, when calling to set up the first appointment, does the client use a voice that suggests authority and a right to attention, or does the client speak in a way that is hesitating and tentative? Does the client tell the therapist when he wishes to come in, or does he ask the therapist to tell him when to come in? On the first day of therapy, does the client ask for permission to sit and then wait for some indication of which chair to sit in, or does the client look for the largest chair in the room and then sit there? Also, does the client ignore interruptions or critical comments from others in the room, or does she almost invite interruption by quickly cutting off her comments whenever she assumes that someone else wants to speak? When the client speaks, does he lock your eyes with his gaze and tilt his head slightly back, or does he cast his gaze to the floor and look out from

---

[425] These behaviors have been observed in the lab as well as in naturalistic settings (Chiao, 2006; Senior et al., 1999).

[426] The process is almost instantaneous, and dominance and submission are detected from facial cues in as little as 33 milliseconds of exposure (Chiao, 2006; Tiedens & Fragale, 2003).

[427] This instinct is so strong that animals have been found to be sensitive to cues about social dominance before sensing the presence of predators (Cheney & Seyfarth, 1985).

under his eyebrows?

The answers to these questions give some indication of the type of therapist response necessary to achieve complementarity. For instance, when the client is most comfortable asking for information, then he or she will naturally form an easy alliance with a therapist who is dominant enough to speak as an authority on certain subjects. By contrast, the client who states one firmly held opinion after another, until eventually ending the conversation by insisting on having the final word, will naturally feel most comfortable with a therapist who is submissive enough to sit and listen.

Keep in mind the general conclusion of outcome research, that it is the quality of the relationship, rather than therapeutic technique that accounts for most of the change that takes place in therapy. Therefore the question "What can I do to create change?" is secondary to the question of how to form a meaningful connection with the client. Because the needs of individuals and the influence of relationships can change on a moment-to-moment basis, it is not enough to assign the therapist the dominant role perpetually and the client the submissive position, or visa versa. Rather, it is important to recognize the *contextual dynamics* of dominance and submission so that both can be strategically employed in the undulating process of a transformational relationship.

Dominance in Therapy Is Expressed as Prosocial Behavior, Rather Than as Aggression or Coercion

Before we go any further, it is important to address misconceptions about the dominant role and to dispel the myth that dominance always leads to the disempowerment of others.[428] To argue otherwise, one would have to assume that Mahatma Gandhi disempowered the people he led or that Martin Luther King, Jr., stole power from the community for whom he dared to dream. Rather, it should be recognized that there are different ways of exercising dominance within a relationship, and these ways can be either helpful or harmful. When one seeks to manage or control shared resources, there are two general approaches that can be taken. The most optimal strategy for a therapeutic alliance is one that fosters cooperative relationships and encourages goodwill. This is the essence of reciprocity, as mutual helping and sharing result in a lasting sense of loyalty and gratitude. Because this strategy considers the needs and desires of others, it is referred

---

[428] There is research indicating that therapists who are aware of the dynamics of power between themselves and their clients are more likely to engage in behaviors that promote the personal power of their clients (Worell, 2001).

to in the research literature as prosocial dominance. By contrast, any strategy that disregards social consequences in favor of the individual gaining immediate access to resources by means of intimidation, punishment, threats, or deceit is referred to as coercive dominance.[429]

To illustrate some interesting differences between prosocial and coercive dominance, I can recall as a college student when I found myself suddenly caught in a contest of resolve. It was late in the evening, and I was cornered by a belligerent individual holding a small handgun. As he vehemently explained, the tires on his BMW had just been slashed, and he wanted to know who did it. The fact that the owner of the gun was a weightlifter who routinely subjected his body to testosterone injections only added to the intensity of his aggression. The fact that the vandal had just confessed her crime to me[430] put me in an awkward, if not dangerous, position. When this angry, gun-wielding individual stepped toward me, demanding information, I responded by moving still closer. Although I cannot remember if I actually placed my hand on his shoulder, I know that I assumed a somewhat dominant posture, saying, "Whoever did this probably wants to see you angry, completely bent out of shape. But how are you going to win by getting yourself thrown in jail? You've got to put that gun away before anyone sees it!" After a few such statements on my part, I was surprised to find that he did not press me any further for the identity of the culprit, but instead put his gun away and left. Because I was speaking as a friend, it was difficult for him to justify any further aggression toward me. While he was seeking to gain my submission through the threat of violence, I had responded in a more dominant manner by insisting on actions that were protective of him and others as well. The point that should be recognized from this illustration is that dominance is not synonymous with aggression.

Not only in civilized society, but in the animal kingdom as well, it is most often the case that prosocial dominance will enjoy more populous support than coercive dominance.[431] Prosocial dominance is, therefore, a crucial aspect of successful leadership in democratic societies and, by extension, an important part of the many relationships that form within the context of a free society. By contrast, coercive leaders have to rely on deceit and violence,

---

[429] Prosocial strategies, for managing resources, promote success in relationships by maintaining friendly ties and attracting positive regard from others; whereas coercive strategies tend to destabilize relationships (Hawley, 1999b; Hawley, Little & Pasupathi, 2002).

[430] It was the weightlifter's girlfriend who had punctured the tires after seeing him engaged in an act of infidelity.

[431] Becoming the dominant animal in a group of monkeys requires good social skills, including control over one's own aggressive behavior (Raleigh et al., 1991).

otherwise they are not respected and are not followed voluntarily.[432]

Another important distinction between the two forms of dominance is that coercive dominance is more often fueled by anger and rage and, therefore, is more likely to yield impulsive behavior detached from careful reason and consideration of long-term consequences. The reckless reaction of the Bush White House to the terrorist attacks on 9/11 serves as an example (i.e., invading a country that had absolutely no involvement in the terrorist attack and killing thousands of civilians in the process). By contrast, prosocial dominance is characterized by an ability to inhibit aggressive behavior and suppress emotional responding.[433]

Within the context of therapy, prosocial dominance will ideally manifest itself as a professionally mandated directive to reduce or eliminate the client's suffering. So the client might be directed toward greater self-examination by means of confrontation: "You might not want to hear me say this, but your greatest enemy at this time is your own destructive anger." Or individuals who have been exploited by others might be given permission to protect themselves by withholding information: "Before you reveal anything more about yourself to me, you can take a moment to make certain you know which experiences you would like to keep private at this time."[434] Each of these statements indicate a dominant, rather than submissive, posture, and just as importantly, they point toward the increased welfare of the client.

Protherapeutic Dominance Is Indicated When the Client's Anger Is Being Used Coercively

While therapists serve in the role of care provider, there are a multitude of culturally sanctioned relational approaches that represent some variation on what is essentially a station of leadership. These approaches are predicated on one's willingness to assume the dominant position in the relationship. For example, when the therapist acts as a teacher, guide, coach, or safe attachment figure, it is most appropriately in response to clients who are seeking help from someone assumed to be stronger or more

---

[432] Typically, people will comply with coercive dominance only as long as the power holder can monitor their behavior and deliver punishments (Blau, 1956).

[433] These differences have been found to correspond with differences in prefrontal versus subcortical activity, in which case the prefrontal cortex plays an important regulatory role (Raine et al., 1998).

[434] Self-preservation requires a determination of where one begins and ends. These boundaries are marked to a great extent by ownership of thought and physical space. The client must not feel forced to submit to uncomfortable physical proximity or excessive self-disclosure. Even in therapy, there is a need for privacy and personal space.

knowledgeable than they are.[435] By contrast, imagine how disconcerting it would be for clients, who have decided to submit themselves to therapists' care, to discover that the therapists are insisting on submitting themselves to the clients' judgment: "What do you want to talk about today?" "How do you feel about it?" "What do you think you should do?" "What do you want me to do?" "Have I done anything to upset you?" There is nothing wrong with any of these questions alone, but strung together, they communicate a lack of substance or opinion on the part of the therapist. In other words, this line of communication would force the client to take the lead position during the encounter, which could be overwhelming for someone who is unprepared for the attention and responsibility that accompanies a position of leadership. Such an arrangement risks violating the fundamental logic that brought this type of client to therapy: "I need help; therefore, I will meet with someone who can tell me what to do." While attention tends to be directed up a social hierarchy, influence tends to travel down.[436] So for someone seeking to be influenced in a meaningful way, the education and status of a socially sanctioned healer are likely to yield a gratifying experience, even before there has been enough time for the process to yield concrete results.[437]

Just as it is important for therapists to know how best to respond when the client makes it obvious that he or she would prefer the therapist be willing to act as a leader, it is also important for therapists to know how to respond to those seeking to challenge or defy their authority. Although it might seem that such a client would respond poorly to anyone assuming a dominant posture, this posture is often what is needed to produce a positive outcome. When an individual is propelled through his or her interpersonal relations by anxiety or rage, the need for testing limits or demonstrating control over others can become exaggerated and chronic. However, much like a dog chasing its tail, these interpersonal strategies do not produce the desired results. If left in the dominant position, these individuals remain as anxious or angry as before, possibly becoming even worse. As explained by Nicolas Cummings (2002) during a personal interview:

Having defeated their parents and conned their teachers, they would

---

[435] Research has shown that when people display dominant nonverbal behavior, others think they are stronger and more competent (Keating, 1985).

[436] In an effort to predict and possibly influence what is going to happen to them, people gather information about those with power (Fiske, 1993).

[437] Those who have studied suggestive therapeutics tend to view the status of the therapist, and his or her willingness to be directive, rather than passive, as important components of psychotherapy (e.g., Frank, 1974).

come to see a therapist and think maybe this is the person who will be there for me. To test this idea, they start to do things to defeat the therapist. They try to frighten, intimidate, or con the therapist. Most of all they try to make him angry. Most therapists try to cover up their anger by becoming nicer and nicer. For these patients, that is a green light to clobber you. "You Goddamn phony! I'm going to kill you." This defeat would result in tremendous hostility toward the therapist for having failed them.

In other words, to submit to such an individual only reinforces problematic patterns of behavior, thus risking further harm to the client and perhaps to others.

Long before my conversation with Cummings, while I was working as a novice counselor in the field of domestic violence, I learned firsthand the importance of maintaining a dominant posture in certain contexts. Initially, I relied on the humanistic principles emphasized in graduate training. My understanding was that I should attempt to win the client's trust gradually through a demonstration of kindness and acceptance. However, during later training by experts in the field of domestic violence, I was told that passively seeking the client's acceptance was the wrong approach.

"During intake, you ask if he has a problem with violence or abuse," I was told. "If he says yes, then you work with him. If he says no, then you refuse him entrance into the domestic violence program." As the trainer explained, "Some of these men are not nearly as interested in self-improvement as they are in finding additional means of controlling their partner. If she has promised that she will not move out as long as he agrees to counseling (and he makes his therapist agree to a set of therapy conditions that presuppose he does not have a problem), then the likely outcome is that she will be further abused and violated, and you will have become complicit in that abuse."

Although I refused to abandon my posture of caring and empathy, I came to realize that in certain instances, unwavering resolve was also required. The kindness and acceptance that I wished to demonstrate eventually served a useful purpose; it just needed to be supplemented with a greater capacity for leadership or dominance. As soon as I implemented my version of the no-tolerance strategy, an interesting thing happened. Compliance seemed to increase. There were very few clients I sent out the door. The rest seemed to respond far better to counseling than they would have if I had began the relationship in a submissive posture. Again, as Cummings (2002) said, when working with a therapist who maintains a dominant position, "these people can become the most devoted and grateful patients. .

. . They are like a four-year-old child who is terrified because he or she cannot find someone strong enough to rely on."

Protherapeutic Dominance Is Indicated When the Client's Anxiety Is Linked to Coercive Behavior

I have seen similar dynamics occurring while I've sought to provide care for clients who present with high levels of anxiety. When the anxiety is pervasive, it can manifest in part as an obsessive desire to control the surrounding environment and all those who inhabit that environment. Similarly, individuals who are experiencing a momentary state of panic can be very controlling, much like people who feel that they are drowning. So in the same way that lifeguards must not allow themselves to come under the control of a panicked swimmer, therapists must exercise caution when submitting to the wishes of a highly controlling individual. If the therapist allows the client to take charge of the relationship, there is the danger that the client will gradually seek to increase the experience of control by dictating where the meetings can be held, where the therapist can sit, what the therapist can say, what color clothing the therapist can wear, and on and on until the therapist is made completely inconsequential. While prosocial dominance is characterized by acceptance, flexibility, and acts of kindness, a therapeutic relationship with such an individual will initially need to be defined as one in which the therapist is in charge.

For example, while working as a school psychologist, I had an anxious foster mother of a sixth-grade girl insist on meeting with me. This mother began the meeting by demanding that I conduct psychological testing on her daughter in order to determine why she was so violent. The mother then expressed her desire to have the girl placed in a more restrictive environment at school. As I remember, her argument was based on the fact that the biological mother drank alcohol during pregnancy, and the foster mother believed the girl, who was a twin, had fetal alcohol syndrome. Before agreeing to these demands, I told her that I would like to get a little more information. So I asked her to give me a narrative account of the problem behavior. The woman dismissed my request, indicating that she had already described the girl's behavior. However, I persisted, asking her, "When was the last time she did something violent?"

"Recently."

Again I sought further clarification. "How recently? How often does it occur?"

Her reply was, "I don't know, it is hard to remember these types of things."

Originally, I wanted her elaborate on the meaning of her words because that is how to conduct a skillful assessment. But now I was suspicious. "If there is a problem that is so severe that it requires testing and special placement at school, then you should be able to recall at least one instance of this behavior," I told her.

With this additional pressure, she began to comply. "Well, there was an episode this week. She was verbally abusive to me when I asked her to do her homework. It was horrible."

Again I sought clarification. "What did she say?"

If I remember correctly, the foster mother continued to stall. "What do you mean?"

I persisted, "What where the words that she said to you?"

Her response was, "She told me that she did not want to do the homework and then marched away!"

I was quiet for a little while so that she could have a moment to reflect on her own words. Then I asked if the homework was eventually completed. The woman confessed that it was. When I asked her if she could think of any other more serious examples of alleged violence, she said that she could not think of any.

I followed up my meeting with the foster mother by unobtrusively observing the child in the classroom. The girl was a bit feisty, with an orphan Annie–type persona, but generally compliant with the teachers. Her grades were average, and she was liked by her friends, though feared by some boys. By contrast, the foster mom seemed to be an overly anxious and controlling person who did not need to be allowed to take control of the dialogue with me or the classroom goals for the child.

Regardless of diagnosis or etiology, when an act of surrender by the client is necessary for the establishment of a productive relationship, it is wrong for the therapist to conform to the structure established by the client. Because individuals identified as having a personality disorder are often influenced by exaggerated amounts of anxiety and anger, it is most likely that therapy for these individuals will need to be delivered by someone who is both ready and able to provide prosocial dominance.[438] Whether the client feels angry, anxious, or beaten down, the well-trained therapist will recognize when an individual needs to feel contained by the interpersonal exchange rather than being allowed to flounder and flail. In the same way that a newborn infant will cry and thrash about until swaddled, fundamen-

---

[438] Bateman and Fonagy (2000) suggested that effective treatments for personality disorder tend to require long-term relationships with a powerful attachment figure who is willing to adopt a relatively active rather than a passive stance.

tally insecure individuals will test the limits and boundaries of each new person they encounter until they discover someone who can counteract their untamed impulses. As soon as this type of client determines that you hold the dominant position and that you are seeking to promote his or her interests, then evidence of appreciation and acceptance will emerge.

Therapeutic Dominance Is Indicated When It Is Complementary to Those Seeking to be Influenced or Protected

To understand what is meant by *contextual dynamics*, it is helpful to consider this statement by de Waal (2001): "Dominance is a social phenomenon that resides in relationships, not individuals" (p. 300). In other words, people will alter their dominance and submissiveness depending on relationship partners and situations in which these partners find themselves.[439] A male from a patriarchal society may be prepared to maintain a dominant position while managing financial resources; however, while sitting at the dinner table he may become surprisingly submissive as the matriarch dictates what food should be eaten and how many servings are required before leaving the table. As soon as roles and boundaries are established for a particular setting, and the dominant position is designated, chaos and conflict are replaced with harmonious interactions. The result can be stunning, such as when a musical director steps out in front of a choir to lead a symphony of voices. In that position, the director will demonstrate dominant behavior. However, if that person is sitting in the cardiologist's office following a heart attack, he or she is likely to behave in a way that is more submissive, asking the doctor what he or she needs to do in order to avoid further problems.

As a fluid component of interpersonal dynamics, dominance and submission both reinforce and elicit behavior that is complementary. Typically operating beneath the level of conscious awareness, dominance automatically invites submissiveness, and submissiveness invites dominance. When a person asks what to do, the easy response is to tell him or her what to do. When a person steps up on a chair and begins to speak, the instinctual response is for members of the crowd to become quiet and turn to listen. When complementary behavior is not forthcoming, the relationship can become strained, possibly resulting in a break off. It is not difficult to imagine why two individuals who insist on being in charge could have difficulty being in the same room, but just as problematic are two individuals who

---

[439]The need for assimilation versus control are important factors influencing dominant or submissive posturing (Tiedens & Jimenez, 2003).

insist on deference to one another. For the relationship to last, eventually someone will need to acquiesce and take the complementary role.[440]

Within the context of therapy, it is reasonable to assume that, in most instances, it will be the therapist who is expected to take the dominant role. The reasons why a client may prefer this type of arrangement are numerous. If the client was raised in home with strong parents who were highly critical, then this individual may need a therapist who can provide supportive messages that carry as much authority as the introjected criticism of the parents. In other words, when fighting a powerful enemy, one will seek out an equally powerful ally. Or, in other instances, the client's opinion of self may be so weakened and the need for assurance so great that a positive dominant voice would be much more welcome than the more obscure voice of a therapist who is operating under egalitarian principles and, therefore, fearful of imposing ideas on another individual. Or for other reasons, the client may simply want a clear answer from someone willing to speak as an expert.[441]

It Is the Dominant Member of a Dyad that Determines What Topics Are to Be Discussed and What Questions Will Be Asked

Now that some of the conditions under which a dominant posture benefits the therapy relationship have been summarized, it is time to explore the most likely manifestations of protherapeutic dominance. Often described as "talk therapy," the process of providing psychological care depends in many ways on the quality of the dialogue that develops during the encounter. The person who successfully manages this vital resource will determine what topics are discussed, which details will be elaborated upon, and what questions should be asked.

Although it might seem that clients should know more about their concerns or immediate needs than the therapist and, therefore, take the lead, it is not uncommon for a distressed individual to sit submissively waiting for the therapist to take the initiative by deciding on the topic of discussion. In one such instance, I sat across from a woman who said she had visited another therapist on the preceding day, but did not think she would return because she did not feel understood. I asked her what she had

---

[440] Research has shown that when people respond to dominance with submissiveness and submissiveness with dominance, there is greater comfort and liking, but when symmetrical responses occur, the interaction is less comfortable (Tiedens & Fragale, 2003).

[441] Studies on persuasion have shown that certainty-oriented individuals will seek input from an expert rather than striving to resolve the issue themselves when the issue is important (Sorrentino et al., 1995).

discussed with the other therapist, and she indicated that he had wanted to know about her feelings. As she explained what should have been a disappointing experience, she seemed strangely detached and indifferent.

Following her brief reply, she sat passively on the couch, gazing at me and politely waiting for her next set of instructions. So I asked her to tell me the worst thing that has happened to her in recent months. Cocking her head to one side, she responded, "Now there is an interesting question. Let me see. I guess it would have to be last week when my husband put a loaded gun to my head."

Although there was no alteration of her mood or change in expression, I recognized that I had stumbled onto something important. So I sought some elaboration, "Did you happen to mention this to the therapist you saw yesterday?"

Again she gave a quizzical turn of the head. "He never asked, and so I guess I just didn't think to bring it up with him."

This client was not prepared to lead the therapeutic discussion, nor was she ready to start an open-ended exploration of her emotions. She needed someone she could trust to gently lead her.

A common scenario is for the client to confess, "I have never done this before, so you are going to need to tell me where to start." This is essentially a request for the therapist to take a dominant position in regard to the conversation that has yet to unfold. Because many clients will assume that their care provider has special knowledge about the problems they face and the means for addressing those problems, it is reasonable to expect such individuals to submit themselves to the clinical interview, answering questions they would never reveal under different circumstances. Along these same lines, clients will generally look to the therapist for guidance on how much or how little to reveal about themselves.[442] After an emotional outpouring, some clients will seek assurances: "I'm sorry for crying like this. I don't know if I am supposed to do this in here." And while discussing topics that are normally off limits for polite social dialogue, many clients will indirectly search for guidance on how much to reveal.

In addition to selecting the questions to be asked, dominance is also exercised when ignoring questions from the client that are counterproductive. Coercive questioning by others typically comes in the form of "why" statements. For example, a client once asked me, "Why do you insist on talking to me as if I am a crazy emotional bitch?" When clients ask this type of question, it is exceedingly important to remember that a therapist does not

---

[442] Jacobson and colleagues argue that intimacy is a commodity and, as such, is often managed by the dominant individual in the relationship (Jacobson, 1989; Jacobson & Gottman, 1998).

have to answer every question that he or she is asked. The image I use to capture this idea is one of a fish that carefully swims past fishhooks without getting hooked. In this particular situation, I wanted to take back control of the conversation, so I chose a response that showed indifference to this client's accusation combined with genuine concern for her subjective distress: "It must be miserable to feel that others have such low regard for you. I doubt this is the first time you have had to endure this experience."

As I hoped, the client responded by giving an honest accounting of her experiences with a verbally abusive mother. Had I responded in a defensive manner, I would have affirmed the client's dominant position as one who is sitting in judgment of the therapist. Because I took the dominant position, I was able to lead the conversation in the direction of a productive outcome (she expressed sadness and pain, and I acted as a surrogate attachment figure, providing sympathy while building a case for her basic goodness as a person).

It is also possible to ignore provocation altogether by simply changing the subject of conversation or by sitting comfortably in a state of unblinking silence. However, this is extremely dominant behavior that could seriously undermine the therapeutic qualities of the relationship if it is not logically and justifiably related to the promotion of the client's well-being.

It Is the Dominant Member of a Dyad That Claims Knowledge of Healing Rituals and the Authority to Tell Others What to Do for the Sake of Their Own Well-being

It is often said that knowledge is power, so it should come as no surprise that the person who claims to have specialized knowledge of relevant healing or problem-solving strategies is likely to take a dominant position when approached by those in distress. The practice of communicating a persuasive etiology and then prescribing a course of treatment to a submissive care receiver is not limited to the practice of medicine and psychotherapy. Since antiquity, primitive cultures around the globe have had healers or shaman provide explanations for the cause of illness and then prescribe healing ceremonies.[443] This type of dominance (i.e., "I know what you should do to solve your problem") counteracts the client's sense of helplessness and hopelessness while producing a meaningful increase in positive

---

[443] Cultures as diverse geographically as the Yanomami of the Amazon, the Walbiri of Australia's Northern Territory, and the Gwi of the Kalahari Bush in Africa expect healers to ascertain the cause and define the treatment of maladies (Bloom, 2005).

expectations.[444] In some instances, the future well-being of the client may depend in large part on whether or not the therapist is able to compete against other coercive forces acting against the client.

As an example, a 27-year-old woman came to me for help with her marriage. Although she did not believe she deserved a man as kind and successful as her husband, she desperately wanted to save the marriage from her own angry outbursts and attention-seeking behavior. Her husband traveled often, and during his absence, she would rendezvous with a hostile male who was seeking to add her to his list of extramarital affairs. Unfortunately, he viewed her repeated refusals as an enticing challenge. This information had come out following many weeks of slow and careful alliance building.

I also learned that this woman's mother was an uneducated immigrant who was exceedingly violent. The last time my client had attempted to argue with her, the mother had kicked in her daughter's bedroom door and grabbed her by the hair while slapping her face. Even worse, I learned that it was the mother who originally set up the romantic encounter with a married man, presumably because she did not like the man her daughter had married. My guess was that, in an effort to have more complete control over her daughter's life, the mother's energies were focused on destroying the marriage. Because neither my client nor her husband knew how to stand up to this woman, the marriage was likely to fail.

After a couple dozen appointments, I attempted to help my client establish boundaries with her mother, such as refusing to listen to her mother complain that her husband was worthless and stupid. In order to deflect some of the mother's inevitable rage, I insisted she tell her mother that it was her psychologist who was making her establish these boundaries. As soon as the mother learned of my involvement, she told her daughter that she also needed therapy and would, therefore, come with her to all of her future counseling sessions. It was a request that my client could not refuse.

My assumption was that the mother wanted to take charge of what was happening in therapy and would accomplish this using a combination of guilt and intimidation, as she had with her daughter. If I did not allow her to join therapy, I was certain she would coerce her daughter into finding a new therapist who had better family values. For these reasons, I felt a showdown between me and the mother was unavoidable.

As expected, the mother began the session by taking control of the conversation. Crying, she spoke of the different ways her daughter failed to

---

[444] Seemingly benign remarks that reflect professional expertise, such as, "What you're concerned about is exactly the kind of thing therapy can help with," have been shown to favorably influence outcome expectancies (Bloom, 2005; Glass, Arnkoff, & Shapiro, 2001).

appreciate her or recognize her needs. After about fifteen minutes, the mother reached her first stopping point. I turned to my client and said, "This is not going work. You are going to have to choose between me or her."

My client looked shocked and bewildered. "What do you mean?"

I explained, "I cannot help you with your mother in here, and I will not continue under these conditions. So you can choose to stay here in my office with her, in which case I will leave the room so that the two of you can talk, or you can choose to stay and talk with me, in which case your mother will need to leave the room."

With a look of fright and desperation, she spoke under her breath, "Please, do not make me do this."

I explained that I was sorry, but there was no other way.

So after a brief moment of consideration, she turned to her mother and asked her to wait outside please. Recognizing that she could not remain dominant in this setting, the mother quietly left the room.[445] Following my client's tremendous act of courage, I congratulated her, but emphasized that finishing her meeting with me was just a tiny success and that her real victory would come from choosing to stay in a healthy marriage with a husband who truly loved her, rather than growing old as a divorcee, living with an abusive mother. The client was very quiet during the rest of the session. Although she scheduled another appointment, she did not show up for the meeting. This did not surprise me. My hope was that the last session would be enough to help her reconsider how powerful she could be when standing up for something she believed in.

However, after fourteen months passed, I heard from her again. During this time, she recognized that she did need her husband and that when she was forced to choose between him or her mother, it was the mother who would have to leave. So she set limits on when her mother could come to her house, and she set limits on what her mother was allowed to say to her. She returned to complete her therapy, sometimes accompanied by her husband, and eventually accomplished all of her goals.

The dominance I used during a critical moment was intense, but no more so than what my client encountered with her mother on a daily basis. Furthermore, the type of dominance I was demonstrating was neither hostile nor coercive. I controlled the resources associated with therapy while leaving plenty of room for her to exercise her own free will.

Given the fact that many clients enter therapy in a submissive posture, awaiting prescriptive injunctions, it is important for the person who is in

---

It was the first and last time I would ever see this client's mother.

the role of care provider to know how to respond with complementary dominance. For some care providers, the use of a dominant posture will go against earlier conditioning and, therefore, feel uncomfortable.[446] However, one should recognize that clients who have submitted themselves to professional care and who are eager to comply with the therapist's recommendations will also be hopeful that some type of direction will be offered. Under these conditions, it is not necessary for therapists to explain the logic behind their statements or to conduct a detailed analysis of their behavior while seeking critical input from clients. Rather, clients who are seeking direction simply need to know what to do next.

It Is the Dominant Member of a Dyad That Defines Progress (or Lack of) and Controls the Formal Written Record

Another behavior that is expected of the dominant member of the dyad is the definition of what constitutes progress. In accord with standard clinical practice, it is the therapist who maintains the written record, and it is the therapist who typically scores and evaluates any formal testing. These customary procedures, which have been adopted from the medical model, tend to position the therapist automatically in the dominant role. The same dynamic occurs in more casual methods of evaluation, as the therapist remarks on whether or not there is evidence of progress. For those clients who have taken a submissive role, this type of feedback[447] is not only expected, but also provides important external validation in response to the base question "Am I doing what I am supposed to be doing?"

Because subordination is natural behavior, found among any group of people, it would be a horrible mistake for the therapist to reject the client's submissive posture, or even worse, to give it a negative label, such as overly passive or dependent.[448] As has been demonstrated in research, role concepts (i.e., leader versus subordinate) help guide social interaction and are also conducive to a sense of well-being.[449] Therefore, it is important for the

---

[446] Influencing agents who have a low need for dominance have been found to be less comfortable interacting with submissive individuals (Cialdini & Mirels, 1976).

[447] Feedback takes many forms and often is called by other names, such as interpretation, praise, reinforcement, immediacy, and confrontation (Claiborn, Goodyear, & Horner, 2001).

[448] What makes this labeling so terrible is that judging a client in this way is dominant behavior that will naturally trigger more submissive behavior. Yet if the client is being criticized for not being assertive enough, then the result for the client is confusion and deep inner turmoil.

[449] In meeting normative role expectations, individuals gain a sense of identity, predictability, and stability; of purpose; and of meaning, belonging, security, and self-worth (Cassel, 1976; Cohen, 1988; Thoits, 1983; Wills, 1985).

professional care provider to recognize that his or her willingness to pro-vide a positive evaluation of client behavior can lay the foundation for much needed feelings of success.

The Exercise of Coercive Dominance Is Likely to Be Harmful

The final and perhaps most crucial point to be made about dominance in therapy is that dominance is not always helpful. There are circumstances in which a display of dominance can be harmful to the client or to the thera-peutic relationship. As one client explained, "I think it was that doctor I saw a year ago that created this problem. He wouldn't listen to me. He just kept telling me what my problems were. He wouldn't back down on anything." Anytime the effect of dominance on the client is negative, then the interac-tion no longer qualifies as prosocial dominance. When dominance is not being used to meet the client's needs, its use should be scrutinized. In gen-eral, one should be suspect of long-term relationships in which the therapist plays the dominant role throughout the length of the clinical relationship.[450] This type of perpetual dominance is likely to be accompanied by controlling behaviors that do not foster increased self-confidence and problem-solving capacities, but instead foster unhealthy dependence on the therapist (a con-cept that will be explored in greater detail in chapter 8).

There are some very painful lessons that have been learned by well-intended care providers who thought they knew exactly what a client must do. The most dramatic example I know of occurred when a physician real-ized that the acute contusions on his patient's body could not have come from falling down the stairs, as she had claimed. After uncovering the vio-lent behavior she had been subjected to at home, the physician insisted she leave her partner and go to a shelter. The woman was not ready to leave the relationship, so the physician had his nurse cancel the rest of his appoint-ments for the day, and he worked to convince her that leaving her relation-ship was the only safe option. Despite her fear, she finally consented and was in the process of leaving the house when the abusive partner discov-ered what she was doing and killed her. Unfortunately, the doctor underes-timated the importance of listening to this woman's opinion of what she felt she could safely do.[451] If he would have been willing to back down and acknowledge her concerns, then she might have been able to plan her es-cape more carefully, perhaps with other professionals who had better train-

---

[450] Chronic low status can have damaging effects on mental and physical health (Stansfield & Marmot, 1992).

[451] This story was related to me by Ellen Taliaferro, M.D., coauthor of *The Physician's Guide to Domestic Violence,* Volcano Press, 1995.

ing in domestic violence.

Although this example may seem dramatic, it highlights the trouble that is created when well-intentioned providers assume they should never relinquish their position of dominance, even if it is met with resistance.

Do Not Seek to Dominate a Major Life Choice

Whenever a therapist seeks to dominate clients' major life choices, such as telling a couple they should get divorced or telling people they should quit their job, the outcome may be disastrous. If the client is not fully prepared to do what the therapist is insisting upon, and does not know how to resist the coercion, then the result is likely to be a muddled and unhappy outcome.

For example, a friend of mine communicated great sadness over the loss of her marriage as she explained, "Looking back, I think we could have made it work. But we were in couples counseling, and our therapist told us we should divorce, so that is what we did." She was telling me this nearly 20 years after the fact, and in all that time, she had not remarried and was horribly lonely. In this case, the therapist crossed a boundary that should not have been crossed.

It is not appropriate for a care provider (who only sees a person one hour a week) to tell a client what to do with the rest of his or her life. Though it might be useful to tell the client to consider one issue or another, or perhaps to even experiment with some new behavior for a week, these are short-lived events that do not have such massive consequences associated with them.

Unfortunately, the larger the life event, the less likely it is that a conflicted individual will want to accept responsibility for the decision that must be made.[452] When clients make a direct request for advice about big decisions, such as whom to marry, whether to divorce, or what religion to choose, my tendency is to confess that I have no way of knowing what will be best for them. No matter how skilled therapists may be, it remains impossible for them to know all of the circumstances surrounding the client's situation or to predict how other people (whom the therapist has never met) will respond to the client's decision. While therapists should be prepared to help clients evaluate options and reflect upon relevant life experiences, the final decision is left with the clients. In this way, therapists do not have to accept responsibility for outcomes they can neither control nor fully predict.

---

[452] Making a choice can be threatening to the self because a poor outcome can undermine one's sense of competence as a decision maker (Larrick, 1993).

Coercive Dominance Is Most Likely When the Therapist Is Struggling With Feelings of Powerlessness

Assuming that it is never the intent of a therapist to make the client feel bad about him- or herself, then one might wander why overt and even hostile forms of coercive dominance are sometimes used by therapists. Part of the explanation might be that during those moments, the therapist is struggling to offset personal feelings of powerlessness.[453] In the same way that a wounded tiger is more dangerous than one that is comfortable and well-fed, individuals who feel overly powerless are more threat-sensitive and tend to lash out aggressively when challenged.[454]

What might cause a threat-sensitive care provider to feel challenged will vary from individual to individual. I had one client complain that his previous therapist (whom he referred to as the "old hag,") became agitated when he called his medication "dollies." According to this client, after listening to all of her reasons why he was not supposed to call his pills "dollies," he became exasperated and pitched his list of medications to the floor. Allegedly pointing her finger to the ground, the therapist demanded he pick the paper up off *her* floor. As unhappy as he was with her command, in the end he submitted to her dominance and retrieved the paper. Of course, that relationship did not last beyond the first visit.

With minimal training, it becomes obvious to most that showing appreciation for what the client has to say is important. Even so, there are still many instances in which clients are interrupted, dismissed, or made to feel that their insights are not as important as the point being made by the therapist.[455] My own struggles to resist subtle acts of coercive dominance are most likely to occur when clients do not seem to be cooperating with fundamental therapy processes.

For instance, I have had some clients talk for 45 minutes without pausing for air. As I sit and watch the therapy hour slip away, there is a strong temptation to interrupt. Other clients will stutter as they make their point, drawing each sentence out into a five-minute ordeal. In these instances, the temptation is to help them along by finishing their sentences

---

[453] Research has shown that perceived powerlessness within relationships tends to result in coercive relationships (Bugental, Blue, & Cruzcosa, 1989; Grusec & Mammone, 1995).

[454] The same behavior can be seen within the family hierarchy. Parents characterized by a more harsh and coercive parenting style tend to view themselves as having less power than their children (Bradley & Peters, 1991; Bugental, Blue, & Cruzcosa, 1989; Kipnis, 1976).

[455] It seems that therapists, as a whole, interrupt female clients more than male clients, thus reflecting the role-related nature of the problem (Werner-Wilson et. al., 1997).

for them. However, interrupting the client sends a subtle message: "What you have to say is less important than what I wish to say."

Whether clients are hoarding the talk time by activating a slow stutter or by being incredibly circumstantial, it is important to remember that clients are more likely to benefit from an atmosphere of acceptance that allows them to open up than an atmosphere of control that causes them to feel shut down. When clients are striving to let the therapist know something important about themselves, then they should be afforded plenty of time to make their delivery; otherwise, there is no way to know what might have been said.

Another common difficulty occurs when the therapist is trying to conform to the procedural requirements of a third party (e.g., an employer or insurance company), and the client refuses to cooperate. These systemic tensions tend to reduce the amount of flexibility afforded to the client.

Therapist: "I need your social security number."

Client: "I do not give my social security number to anyone."

Therapist: "Because your insurer has outsourced the mental health benefits, your regular I.D. number will not work. Therefore, you are going to have to give me your social security number."

Client: "I've been told not to trust anyone who demands my social security number, because of the risk of identity theft."

At this point the therapist is thinking, "Why are you making this situation so impossible?"

That sort of interpretative bias is the curse underlying the use of coercive dominance. Ironically, it is the dominant individual who ends up feeling victimized by the situation.[456] Perhaps the most insidious part of the problem is the fact that the care provider's intentions remain positive, even as he or she engages in unproductive behavior. Therefore, in any instance in which the therapist plans to assume a dominant position within the encounter, there should be a strong appreciation for what needs to be achieved relative to the client's subjective experiences. In the above example, the therapist might respond, "It is important to protect your identity, and I certainly do not wish to compromise your privacy. So I am going to call your insurer and see if we can get a representative to help us figure this out."

Meet Resistance With Flexibility

This brings us to the concept of resistance. Those who are in the dominant role, but experience low personal power, are most at risk for creating

---

[456] Research in parent-child relations indicates that adults who engage in coercive parenting styles see the children as causing the negative relationship and themselves as the victims (Bugental, Blue, & Lewis, 1990; Bugental et al., 1993; Bugental, Brown, & Reiss, 1996).

power struggles. An escalation in aggression is likely to occur any time there is the perception that a subordinate is intentionally resisting his or her influence, thereby increasing feelings of powerlessness.[457] That is why in therapy, rather than seeking to overcome resistance with persistence and intensity, it is better for therapists to respond to clients' uncooperative behavior with flexibility. In other words, the therapist needs to focus his or her greatest efforts on accepting the client's behavior rather than seeking to dominate or control it. Being flexible helps prevent a waste of time and energy on unproductive power struggles. Furthermore, for therapists to maintain a position of influence, they should avoid arguments they cannot win.[458] This type of skillful maneuvering requires an ability to anticipate when resistance is likely to occur.

While skepticism or resistance to treatment efforts can vary according to individual personality factors, there are several situational factors that increase the probability of resistance. Research in social psychology has shown that people tend to resist persuasion when they are warned in advance of someone's persuasive intent,[459] when they feel that a persuasive message threatens their personal freedom,[460] and when their original attitudes are strongly held.[461] Therefore, if before coming to therapy, a prospective client is chided by a controlling partner, with comments such as, "Why are you paying money to have some therapist tell you what to do?"; during therapy, the care provider utters the words like, "This is something you cannot disagree with"; and the client truly believes in his or her own position, then all three conditions have been met, and any efforts at persuasion are highly likely to be resisted.

Resistance, when it occurs, will take one of two general forms: covert or overt. In the first type, the client may sit and listen politely, while privately dismissing each remark that is made.[462] If the client is not going to

---

[457] Research on parental caregivers with low perceived power indicates that a belief in the child's deliberate unresponsiveness is related to aggressive and harsh forms of discipline (Martorell & Bugental, 2006).

[458] When people successfully resist a persuasive message, the certainty with which they hold their original attitude can increase (Lewan & Stotland, 1961; Lydon, Zanna, & Ross, 1988; Tormala & Petty, 2002).

[459] This resistance is created by providing information about the topic and position of the upcoming communication, or information about the communicator's persuasive intent (Hass & Grady, 1975; Papageorgis, 1968).

[460] For example, freedom of thought is threatened when communicators tell their audience what conclusion must be drawn. Telling listeners what to think will create significant resistance to attitude change (Brehm, 1966).

[461] By contrast, some attitudes are highly persistent only if they are not challenged (Petty & Krosnick, 1995).

[462] For this reason, it is important to probe for the client's opinion following a persuasive message, rather than assuming there is automatic concurrence.

refute openly the therapist's persuasive message, instead privately discrediting the source of the persuasive message, then the client's resistance is easily maintained.[463] On more than one occasion, I have listened to clients scoff at remarks made by previous therapists. When asked if they shared their misgivings so that the therapist would have a chance to address them, the response is often, "No." After which, I sympathetically comment, "Please help clue me into what is happening if I make any silly remarks and do not seem to recognize it." The reason this request for feedback is so important is because a losing argument requires a shift in energy, and it is only after the resistance is exposed that it becomes more clear which direction to proceed.

In other instances, with those who feel less compelled to submit to authority figures, the resistance is exposed through overt disagreement. When clients make it clear that they are firmly entrenched in their efforts to defend a particular attitude, the most productive approach is to accept the associated beliefs as absolute truth and then change the topic, while remaining oriented to the overall goal of promoting the client's wellbeing.[464] The analogy that helps me conceptualize this type of maneuverability is that of a traveler who is trying to arrive at a certain destination. One method is to point oneself straight at the desired target and never veer off course. However, this method does not leave any room for obstacles. Another, more skillful orienteering strategy is to find a sort of beacon that is located at the desired end point and keep it in sight, so that it is possible to zigzag around any obstacle and never become lost. In other words, if you know what you are seeking to accomplish in the end, it is not difficult to circumnavigate points of resistance as you search for a different means to the same end.

As an example, during my first weeks as a school psychologist intern, I had the task of introducing myself to students who were on my caseload and letting them know that I would be available for support and consultation throughout the school year. My general intent was to encourage the students to feel capable as they made good use of their resources, in whatever form those resources may be. When I approached a high school senior who was slated for services, my invitation for a brief meeting was rebuffed.

---

[463] A third method for resisting persuasive messages is to strengthen the original belief before it is attacked. This method of immunizing beliefs from attack has proven more effective than seeking to restore discredited concepts (Tannenbaum, Macauley, & Norris, 1966). This method can be used in therapy to help protect clients from toxic messages coming from outside the office.

[464] In addition to reduced persuasion and increased counter argumentation, further debate can reduce favorable thoughts about the idea being communicated (Brock, 1967; Petty & Cacioppo, 1979).

He informed me that he would not come unless he could bring along his friend. The student he wished to accompany him was also on my caseload, so I decided to be the first to cooperate. I agreed to his terms.

Of course, once inside the office, the two boys had more to say to each other than to me. After awhile, I turned to the first student and asked if last year's intern had been able to get much out of him. He boasted that the intern was never really able to get him to talk about himself. I responded with intense curiosity and amazement. "How did you pull that off? Last year's intern was supposedly pretty good." The student then proceeded to describe his psychological defense mechanisms, until interrupted by a backhanded slap on the shoulder from his companion. "Hey dummy!" the second boy said. "You are telling him all of your secrets!" The comment caused the first boy to shut down.

So I turned to the second student and said how much I admired his willingness to defend his buddy's interests. I asked if there was anything that was too uncomfortable to be shared between friends. They assured me there was not anything that could not be discussed between the two of them. After further discussion about the value of their friendship, I secured their commitment for them to use one another as a resource throughout the school year and then asked if they would be willing to come to me with any trouble they did not feel able to resolve between the two of them. Both agreed, and both later returned for individual counseling.

There was no need to make the first student perform according to my expectations. The resistance I encountered from the moment I first approached the first student was not a problem. In fact, it only increased the probability that he would be more deeply persuaded by any ideas that he came to accept.[465] I was able to maneuver around the initial obstacles because I was willing to be flexible and I had my eye on a more distant objective, which was to encourage the student to make good use of whatever resources he had available to him.

As with any other rule, there is an exception to the prohibition of coercive forms of dominance. Coercive dominance can be useful if the therapist is seeking to achieve failure for the sake of progress. This is best illustrated in a case with a 14-year-old boy who was brought in for help with impacted bowels. No matter what the parents or pediatrician tried, they could not get the boy to eliminate with regularity. He refused to use public toilets and only defecated at home once every two weeks. This behavior had enraged the stepfather, who punished the boy harshly and routinely. A doctor

---

[465] Rucker and Petty (2004) found that when people try, but fail, to resist persuasion, they can reflect on this outcome and become more certain of their newly changed attitudes than they would be if they had not tried to resist in the first place.

had attempted to solve the problem by prescribing an adult laxative at four times the typical dose, resulting in a humiliating accident at school.

After all this, the boy still resisted defecation to the point of developing blood toxicity, such that his skin would turn yellow,[466] and on at least one occasion he experienced a transient loss of consciousness. Whenever elimination did occur, it was painful and bloody because of the compacted feculent material. The pediatrician suggested that it might be necessary to alter surgically the boy's rectum. Before doing this, the mother decided to try counseling.

During the counseling intake, I discovered that the stepfather was constantly criticizing the young adolescent. Although he was not physically violent, the stepfather had a tendency to yell and scream when denied his way. Both the mother and the son were scared of his anger. When asked if she would consider leaving the unhappy marriage for her son's sake, she sheepishly replied, "I just need [her son] to stop being so stubborn about going to the bathroom because it is enraging his stepfather." The mother explained that other than this single act of defiance, there were no other problems with the boy's behavior. His demeanor was gentle and kind. However, if he did not find another way to exert his will and maintain his sense of personal power, then his rectum would soon be carved wider by the surgeon's knife.

Given these circumstances, it did not seem likely that I or anyone else would be able to talk the boy into altering his behavior. Just to make certain of this, during his first and second visits, I gave him several direct suggestions for how to make the task of elimination less difficult. By the third appointment, he confessed that he had not followed through with any of my suggestions. My assumption was that in addition to the need to exercise control over his body, he also needed the experience of acceptance from a respected authority figure, even when he was not in compliance with that person's wishes. In other words, proper therapy for him would need to provide an opportunity for him to defy my direct commands.

So I ordered my young client to *keep his eyes open and on my face,* and to listen to what I had to say. Accordingly, he shut his eyes and stopped listening to me. Although I had winked at the mother while giving him these strange commands, the mother took my statements very seriously. Seeing that her son's eyes had closed, she began to shake his arm, saying, "Look at the doctor, you are being rude!" I told her that it was all right and that he had gone into a trance. She looked at me with disbelief. "But he does this all the time, going to sleep when he should be listening." After I

---

[466] These symptoms suggest that the blockage in his intestines led to an excess accumulation of bilirubin in the blood.

pointed out that he was not going to awaken, she released his arm and slid back to her side of the couch.

I explained to the mom, "The earlier interventions have not worked because we have put too much pressure on him." Turning to the boy, I spoke slowly and clearly. "This time we are going to put the pressure on me and your mom. So for this solution to work all you have to do is *nothing*. Just be you. That's all you have to do."

After making certain that he understood me, I continued, "Rather than encouraging you to make progress, I am actually going to tell you not to *think about progress*. So your order from me is not to change this week. I am ordering you not to change this week!"[467]

A little later, I explained to his mother her part in this new approach. "Each day, you are to tell him, 'This is not the day I have chosen for you to make your breakthrough!'"

At the end of the session, when we were engaged in casual conversation, the boy noted that this was his last week of school. I replied, "This is interesting! School is out in three days. So if I order you not to change this week, that takes away your right and ability to solve this problem as an eighth grader." The boy already knew that I thought he had a great deal of ability, because during the first ten minutes of the session I had interpreted his resistance to my earlier intervention saying, "One thing that is happening is that your unconscious mind is showing that it is not going to be bossed around. I think there is a strong spirit inside of you!"

Two days after the appointment, I received a phone call at my home number. It was the boy's mother. In a sheepish voice she apologized for calling me after hours, but said that her son was unrelenting in his insistence that she call. "He wanted me to tell you that it was not one full week; it was only two days, if that makes any sense to you." I told her that it did and asked her to tell him that I was very impressed by *his* accomplishment and by what he had proved himself capable of doing.

One month later, during his fifth and final visit, there was no longer a need to discuss his bowels. They were no longer impacted. Instead, we spent the entire session discussing how he could assert himself with others in such a way that it would be difficult for them to become angry with him.

Although I used coercive dominance during a small portion of the

---

[467] At first glance, this could look like a risky suggestion. What if the boy did not have a paradoxical response? However, if you examine the details of the statement closely, you will see that I was not suggesting anything that was not already occurring. So the worst the suggestion could do was to affirm and provide an outside excuse for his current behavior. Even if my approach failed, it would still would help take some of the pressure off the child, allowing him to think, "It's the therapist who made me do this!"

third meeting, I did not make it my goal to control the client's behavior. On the contrary, my primary objective was to help him arrive at the realization that he could make the necessary adjustments for his health without me or anyone else forcing him to do so. From this child's perspective, my behavior would not have felt uncomfortable, given the type of abusive dominance to which he was accustomed. In fact, there are instances in which therapists might feel that they are acting in a very dominant manner when, in fact, the behavior is hardly perceptible to the client.[468]

It Is the Therapist's Responsibility to Protect the Therapeutic Alliance and Maintain a Safe Relationship

Whatever houses I may visit, I will come for the benefit of the sick, remaining free of all intentional injustice, of all mischief and in particular of sexual relations with both female and male persons, be they free or slaves.
—Hippocratic Oath, 400 B.C.

At some point, a study of healthy relating will naturally overlap with a discussion on ethics. And more than anywhere else, it is between the subjects of power and individual responsibility that the overlap occurs. It could, in fact, be argued that commonly agreed upon ethical principles—such as beneficence, justice, fidelity, and respect for autonomy—are core components of any transformational relationship. While the primary ethical principle in all helping professions is to do no harm, the explicit application of this principle for therapy is to protect the therapeutic alliance and maintain a safe relationship. Because most clients lack the skills needed for building therapeutic relationships, this responsibility belongs to the professional.

When the client does not respond favorably to the therapist's efforts to engage, the problem is, unfortunately, often attributed to the client: "This client is too resistant." There is also an equally disempowering tendency to attribute the problem to fate: "I am going to have to refer this client to a different therapist because we simply do not have the right chemistry."[469] These biases can lead to a premature abdication of the professional's responsibility to build a positive working alliance. As demonstrated

---

[468] Women in particular are most likely to overestimate their overt displays of dominance (Moskowitz, 1993).

[469] The latter is a person × partner causal attribution—the notion that a fit between one's own traits and their partners' traits acts as the sole determinant of relationship quality. However, this view does not take into account the impact of the physical and social environment on relationship formation or the effect of interpersonal dynamics under volitional control (Berscheid, 1999).

throughout the pages of this book, it is not necessary to blame the client or automatically refer out when the therapy relationship is not flourishing. The other option is for the therapist to change his or her approach.[470]

Just as ignorance is no excuse under the law, one of the first steps in meeting one's professional obligations is to increase awareness. As such, it is extremely important for care providers to monitor closely the client's responses to the therapy relationship. Because many clients automatically assume a compliant posture, the therapist is not likely to be warned in a proactive manner when the relationship is in trouble. As a result, many therapists do not realize that the client is seriously dissatisfied with therapy until after it is already too late.[471] Therefore, it is the therapist's responsibility to develop a reliable and routine means of assessing client satisfaction.[472] The early detection of problems increases the therapist's opportunities to repair alliance ruptures and to make adjustments to treatment strategies before dropout occurs.[473] My experience has been that a brief rating of client satisfaction at the end of each visit serves this purpose well.[474]

One of the first lessons I learned as a young therapist is to take the initiative in exploring any uncomfortable feelings the client may have about therapy.[475] Although it is natural to avoid conversations that may lead to clients saying outright that they do not like you or your therapy style, it is better to deal directly with problems inherent in developing intimate relationships.[476] I got a lot of practice with this early on in my career because most of my clients were court-mandated and, in that regard, were a captive audience. However, after listening to the client hint that I may not know what I am talking about, I found the client's response to direct investiga-

---

[470] Unfortunately, when therapists were asked how they handle failing cases, 30% said they refer to someone else, 41% continue with the same treatment, and only 26% said they change their treatment (Kendall, Kipnis & Otto-Salaj, 1992).

[471] In most instance clients will not reveal their dissatisfaction until after having made the decision to quit therapy (Hill et al., 1996; Rhodes et al., 1994).

[472] Obtaining the client's perspective using a reliable measure is particularly important since therapist's ratings of the strength of the alliance do not correlate with outcome as well as client's ratings do (Bachelor & Horvath, 1999; Horvath & Symonds, 1991).

[473] This type of monitoring and feedback has been shown to be helpful in improving treatment outcomes (Ackerman, et al., 2001; Miller, Duncan & Hubble, 2004).

[474] Client-satisfaction surveys have long been used to successfully predict early treatment dropout (Larsen et al., 1979).

[475] The capacity of the alliance to rebound from damage is associated with client improvement (Stiles et al., 2004).

[476] Evidence from research with couples suggests that the most effective problem-solving style is one that combines active engagement of the issues with a positive, supportive approach. This style produces greater satisfaction and agreement between partners (Miller et al., 1986).

tion was often favorable.[477]

For example, my question, "Do you currently feel like it is a waste of time talking with me?" was often met with reduced defensiveness: "I know it is not your fault that I have to be here talking to you. You seem like a fairly decent fellow, and there might be something that you say that I actually need to hear." There are often negative feelings about the therapy or the therapeutic relationship that clients, especially neurotic individuals, are reluctant to describe for fear of the consequences.[478] So anytime the therapist suspects that a rupture to the relationship has occurred, it is important to take the initiative in addressing the issue.[479] These types of discussions serve as opportunities for modeling the fundamental skill of finding resolution for discord in close relationships.[480] Rather than being interpreted negatively, paying attention to relationship ruptures allows the therapist to demonstrate to the client the importance of the relationship.[481]

Standards of Care Are the Responsibility of the Therapist

In order to make certain that the therapeutic relationship remains safe, the care provider has a duty to make certain that his or her primary relationship needs are met else where. The therapist must not position the client as a romantic figure or as a mother or father figure. And to a more subtle extent, the therapist must not seek to impress the client or defensively bolster his or her own ego.[482] Instead, a different type of attention is projected outward. The therapist's personal agenda is set aside as awareness is centered squarely on the immediate and long-term needs of the client. If there is any type of agenda on the mind of the therapist, it is simply to ensure that the

---

[477] Also, qualitative analyses of working alliance "breach" events suggest that beneficial outcomes ensue if therapists respond by focusing on a here-and-now exploration of the relationship and the client's feelings toward the therapist (Safran, Muran, & Wallner-Samstag, 1994).

[478] Hill, Thompson, Cogar, and Denman (1993) found that therapists are often unaware of patients' unexpressed reactions to therapy. Furthermore, 65% of the patients in the study left something unsaid (most often negative), and only 27% of the therapists were accurate in their guesses about what their patients were withholding.

[479] While addressing ruptures to the alliance, it is important to respond in an open and nondefensive fashion and to accept responsibility for one's contribution to the interaction (Safran et al., 2001).

[480] Safran (1993) has contended that it is precisely by working through therapeutic-alliance ruptures that patients come to redefine and redevelop their sense of their ability to maintain relatedness in the face of hurt and anger.

[481] It has been found that moments of direct action to repair weakened alliances were followed by the highest levels of patient-alliance ratings (Lansford, 1986).

[482] This behavior has long been studied as countertransference and is usually seen as harmful, since it distracts one from attending to the client's needs (Gelso & Hayes, 2001).

client is better off for having entered into the therapeutic relationship.

More than inhibiting one's own impulses, this ethical responsibility requires a proactive approach that does not allow anyone to initiate a romanticized relationship. Considering the degree of relational deprivation that often characterizes those who seek counseling, and the presence of a warm and caring provider, it is to be expected that clients will sometimes develop strong feelings for their therapist. When this occurs, the therapist must not be operating from a submissive posture or responding in a consensual manner; otherwise, great harm is likely to occur.[483] The therapist cannot take on the role of lover or best friend. There is good reason why, after a century of psychotherapy's existence, romantic relationships between therapist and client remain strictly forbidden.[484]

When considering other areas in which the therapist is primarily responsible and, therefore, must remain dominant, one could add anything that falls under standards of practice. In other words, because current standards of practice require documentation in the form of clinical notes, the client does not get to decide whether or not the therapist will take notes.[485] Similarly, the client does not decide if test materials will be taken home when the psychologist has used a published instrument that must be kept secure. And when working with individuals who have been referred by a friend that is also in treatment, issues of confidentiality and privacy are the responsibility of the therapist, not the client.

It is also the therapist's responsibility to know when to refer out. Although the aim of this book has been to increase the range of personalities with which the therapist can successfully engage, there are limits to every therapist's skill and expertise. When confronted with a serious problem (e.g., suicidal ideation) that exceeds the care provider's level of expertise, referral to a specific care provider who is equipped to deal with the problem is indicated.[486] It may also be necessary to end therapy, regardless of the client's wishes, if there is evidence that the client's condition is continuing

---

[483] Therapeutic relationships should never be sexualized. Problems of sexualization range from viewing attractive clients as seductive to actually engaging in sexual relationships with them (Pope, 2001).

[484] Sexual contact between a psychologist and client is a clear violation of the ethical code of conduct of the American Psychological Association (APA; 2002a) and is illegal in many states.

[485] The treating professional has a professional and ethical responsibility to develop and maintain records (APA, 2007).

[486] As indicated in the ethical standards (APA, 2002, 2.01) for psychologists, therapists should provide services only within the boundaries of their competence, based on their education, training, supervised experience, consultation, study, or professional experience.

to deteriorate.[487] If there are unexplained physical symptoms, such as head-aches, dizziness, or fainting, then an in-depth medical evaluation may be required.[488] If the deterioration seems to be related to gaps in service, then outpatient treatment may not be a suitable option.

Finally, one should recognize that there may be instances when the client's motives for therapy are less than honorable, and therefore, the continuation of therapy is not appropriate. For instance, I was approached once by a rough-looking male who wanted me to train him in how to be more dominant. Since he already had a fairly tough-looking exterior, I asked why he wanted this. His reply was, "In my business, I deal with people who sometimes try to intimidate you with guns, and I am not really in a position where I can call the police, if you know what I mean." My response was initially incredulous: "You want me to help you become a better drug dealer?" And when he responded in the affirmative, I refused further contact.[489]

A Submissive Posture Is Complementary to Those Seeking to Protect Their Resources or Expand Their Power

A wolf has enlightened me: not so that your enemy may strike you again do you turn the other check toward him, but to make him unable to do it.
—Konrad Lorenz, 1952

When facing a creature that cannot be outdominated, one might reasonably wonder what will happen when a complementary response is produced.

I was able to observe the answer to this question while visiting a wild animal park that has achieved national acclaim for its display of natural animal behavior combined with human interaction. In one such instance, the owner of the park, Dean Harrison, stood inside an enclosed arena with a large carcass of meat 25 feet behind him. Further back, a Bengal tiger came bounding into the arena and jumped onto the rock formation where a slab of

---

[487] Although it is not frequent, 5 to 10% of patients do deteriorate while in psychotherapy (Lambert & Ogles, 2004).

[488] Any time there is a pattern to physical complaints—such that they always occur in a certain location or during specific events; if they are linked to dates on a calendar; if the physical distress is perfectly symmetrical, covering equal portions of the body; or if the distress is linked to secondary gain, such as receiving pain medication—then is it likely that the physiological symptoms are linked to psychological factors (Hersen, Kazdin, & Bellack, 1991).

[489] The Ethical Standards for Terminating Therapy (APA, 2002, 10.10, a) state, "Psychologists terminate therapy when it becomes reasonably clear that the client/patient no longer needs the service, is not likely to benefit, or is being harmed by continued service." My belief is that therapy should also be terminated when it becomes apparent that the services are being used by the client to harm to others.

meat lay. With my attention riveted to the massive predator, I half listened as the man spoke of the importance of dominance and submission in communicating with animals. Stating the obvious, he explained how dangerous it could be to approach a hungry tiger while it is eating its meal. He then told the crowd to say stop when it seemed he had gone as close as he should to the hungry carnivore. With that, he turned around and walked toward the tiger, staring directly into its eyes. He had not moved more than a few feet before the tiger jumped up with a violent roar. Urgently, the audience called out, "Stop!" The man froze and then slowly and carefully backed away, diverting his gaze to the ground, never turning his back to the tiger. After the threat was removed, the tiger settled back down to its lunch.

Coming to stand outside the enclosure, the owner of the park urged the crowd not to make any noise or sudden movements as he sent his wife, Prayeri, into the arena. She was going to demonstrate the proper way to communicate with an untamed tiger.

She began her slow journey toward the 750-pound animal with her head bent forward in a submissive posture, her shoulders rounded downward, and her hands extended down in front of her with fingers overlapped. As she walked, her eyes never left the ground. With a soft voice, she repeated, "I do not want your food. I have not come for your food." When she was approximately six feet from the tiger, she slowly turned to face the audience, with her back to the animal. Although it kept its eyes on her, the tiger did not seem to be bothered by her presence as it continued to tear at its meal and crack bones with its teeth. The owner explained that her submissive posture signaled that she was not a threat to the resources the tiger was seeking to protect.

Just as dramatically, Konrad Lorenz (1952) describes a fight between two wolves that was likely to result in the death of the younger. However, the fight was suddenly halted by the "underdog" as he turned to expose this throat. "Less than an inch from the tensed neck-muscles, where the jugular vein lies immediately beneath the skin, gleam the fangs of his antagonist from beneath the wickedly retracted lips," Lorenz said (p. 175). As long as one wolf remained in the submissive posture, the other wolf remained unable to attack. Lorenz believed this dynamic to be true of most animal species and most humans. Referring to the teaching of Jesus Christ (Luke 6:29), "If someone strikes you on the cheek, offer the other cheek as well," Lorenz notes that since the beginning of recorded history, when people fully surrender to an aggressor and remove all obstacles to their own destruction, the dominant individuals experience some change in the central nervous system that prohibits them from continuing the aggression.

My experience has been that total surrender is not always necessary to achieve influential results. However, some degree of submission may be needed when working with individuals who will not, under any circumstances, surrender the dominant position.

In one such instance, a 40-year-old female and her 33-year-old husband had been given my name by another therapist. The woman had been seeing this counselor for individual therapy, but now she wanted to try couples counseling, and her counselor was not willing to work with this couple. Without having any other details, I scheduled a couples session and said that I would do my best to help them.

After hearing the opening remarks made by the husband, my optimism vanished. He was consumed with an unrelenting need to blame her for all the misery in his life. They had only been together for five years, marrying after a very brief courtship. My concerns increased when he accused her of being dangerous. Although his verbal message implied he was in a disadvantaged position, his demeanor indicated an underlying narcissistic self-grandeur. However, the thing that worried me most was the sideways stare he used to capture her in his field of vision.[490] Although I had on many other occasions confronted clients for indulging in counterproductive diatribes, I did not want to challenge this man. Whenever he spoke, I let him continue uninterrupted. Whenever I used confrontation, it was aimed at both of them so that my remarks would not be interpreted as a direct challenge, one man to another.

For example, I said, "I have to tell you both something that I am certain neither of you wants to hear. But listening to you both, I get the strong feeling that not only is couples counseling not going to work, I am afraid that someone is going to get hurt. Based on comments that both of you have made, it sounds like you have a dangerous relationship and fighting that is leading to greater and greater tension. And you have guns in the house. I am afraid that someone is going to get killed."

Knowing that this man would not respond well if he got the idea that I was telling his wife to leave him, I was careful to repeat more than once, "It is not a counselor's place to tell a couple to end a marriage, and I would never tell either of you that you must leave this relationship. But I must tell you that I am very concerned that if you two choose to stay together, some-

---

[490] Police academies warn cadets about the increased probability of violence from those employing "the evil eye" (i.e., individuals shifting their head to the right, casting a stare from the left eye). The neurological explanation for the connection seems to be that the right hemisphere processes strong primary emotions, such as anger, and, due to contralateral pathways, the left side of the field of vision provides the most concentrated form of sensory input to the right side of the brain (Ross, Homan, & Buck, 1994).

thing really bad is going to happen."

The session ended and no further appointments were made.

Two days after the initial visit, I got a call from the woman. She said she wanted to thank me for my candor during the meeting. She was grateful that I had not sided with her husband against her. She said that she could not allow herself to seriously consider leaving the relationship until after giving counseling a try and now that someone had said that the relationship was dangerous she felt empowered to leave. And then she added, "Did you know that after we left your office I found out he was carrying a handgun in a holster under his shirt? He told me that no one is going to tell him what to do, but I did not realize he was going to bring a gun to the appointment." Later, when I was describing the seriousness of the threat he represented toward her, she added, "He is always bragging about his uncle who is in prison for manslaughter. He absolutely idolizes that man."

Having heard the uncensored version of the story, which included disturbing acts of psychological violence, I made certain she understood that couples counseling with me or anyone else was not safe, for many different reasons. Because she had made it clear that she was going to leave, I warned her not to attempt a face-to-face breakup, but instead to leave secretly with her daughter to an undisclosed location when he was not at home. She did exactly that. After finding that she had secretly left with her daughter and her pets, he left a message on the back door to her townhome. The door was taken off its hinges and placed in the garage, with over 100 bullet holes in it. Fortunately, she was able to obtain a divorce and safely relocate in a different state. Although there is no way to know for certain, my belief is that this man would have responded viciously if I had attempted to outdominate him rather than engaging in the strategic use of temporary submission and deference.

Although it may be exceedingly rare that a client comes to therapy equipped with a gun, it can be just as frightening to use too much dominance while seeking to influence someone who has dissociative tendencies. Any client who has been exposed to painful or frightening experiences while interacting with a brutal and dominant individual has the potential to be retraumatized when the other member of the dyad is overly dominate.

Unfortunately, this very scenario occurred while I was demonstrating the power of nonverbal techniques to a group of trainees. Halfway through my demonstration, the woman who volunteered to serve as a subject gave subtle indications that she was ready to quit the exercise and return to her chair. Having just achieved miraculous results with the previous demonstration subject, I became overly confident in my abilities and insisted that she continue. The task she had been given was to take four steps toward a male volunteer. The assignment was not so terrible, but my refusal to allow her to escape from the task proved to be disastrous. After taking only two steps, the woman began to shake and tremble. Then, suddenly struck with a blank stare, she went into what appeared to be a brief catatonic stupor. After approximately 10 minutes, she recovered her ability to talk and move about the room, but she seemed fearful and remained withdrawn. Needless to say, she avoided further contact with me, as did most everyone else in the room. My failure on her behalf was difficult for me to accept and was an exceedingly painful way to learn my lesson. While trying to make her step forward with confidence, I failed to recognize the tremendous importance of knowing when I should take a step back in humility.

An interesting point that should not be missed, from this and other examples of submission, is the power that can be exercised from the one-down position. As Jay Haley (1986) notes, "Power tactics are those maneuvers a person uses to give himself influence and control over his social world and so make that world more predictable," (p. 37). As it turns out, this social structure can be created from either a dominant or submissive position.

A fascinating example of the influential power of submission comes from historical accounts of the meeting between Octavian and Herod in 31 B.C. Octavian had just crushed the combined armies of Antony and Cleopatra, becoming Caesar Augustus, first emperor of Rome. Because Herod had been a close friend and ally to Mark Antony, his reign over Judea and his life were both likely to end. However, Herod rushed to the island of Rhodes, where he met the new emperor and presented himself *without* his crown, but with all his kingly dignity, which included his royal attire, numerous servants, and other symbols of wealth and power. In a submissive, but powerful, declaration he promised to serve his new master, Octavian, with the same loyalty he had shown Mark Antony.[491]

In the same way that aggression is sometimes confused with dominance, it is also common for submission to be mistaken for weakness. From the examples above, one should recognize that submission is not synonymous with weakness. Similarly, a display of weakness and desperation are not synonymous with effective submission. Like dominance, submission can be coercive and deceitful or prosocial and positive. When coercive submission is used, it traps others, exploiting altruistic instincts by means of victimization or deceit. While the power of victimization is legendary among

---

[491] Historical records indicate that Octavian was impressed by Herod's poise and confirmed him king of Judaea. Octavian later added other territories to Herod's realm (Mueller, 2008).

certain groups of clients, it is not often that such an individual will admit to the coercive intent of the submissive behavior. As a unique exception, I had one client explain to me, "I just love going to the cafeteria at the mall and filling my tray with all sorts of plates and cups. After paying for the meal, I then stumble and fall to the floor, sending all of the food and plates flying in all directions. I then ashamedly pick myself up off the ground, repeatedly saying, 'Oh my, oh dear, I am so sorry. I have created a terrible mess.'" He went on to explain, "It is so delightful how everyone rushes to help me up. They insist on helping clean up the mess and tell me that I should not worry about it." In these carefully orchestrated mini dramas, his posture was very submissive. However, the power he exercised over others was both intentional and highly effective. Given his ability to use this type of skillful maneuvering, combined with his history of suicidal behavior, this was clearly not a client who could be bullied by a therapist or handled with too much dominance.

As one might imagine, coercive submission should not be used by a therapist, just as coercive dominance should not be used. The more prosocial version of submission still communicates the deferral of one to another, but without degrading either participant. *Humility* is the term I use to describe this more prosocial type of submission. For example, while working with the individual who would intentionally fall and spill things, I would humbly confess, "I might not have the skill that is needed to help you with all that you want; however, I am willing to give it my very best try. I just ask that you tell me if I have missed something important or if I say something that some how upsets you." Rather than provoking the client, these types of humble statements enabled me to use submission to define how the relationship would operate, while positioning him to use a more direct and honest approach to interpersonal relations.[492]

To maintain healthy structure within the therapeutic relationship, there is a variety of interpersonal demands that are best met with a posture of submission. The type of submissive behavior described in this section is likely to be subtle and delivered with confidence rather than self-deprecation. In many instances, the behavior used to signal submission will escape the client's conscious awareness, yet it still can produce a significant effect. For instance, allowing the client to have the last word or formally agreeing with an opinion that the client has framed as contrary to your own are forms of submissive yielding. Submissive posturing might include sitting in a smaller chair, collapsing one's posture, or softening one's voice.

---

[492] My work with this client continued happily for nearly two years. He had come to therapy with a long list of prior therapists, each of whom he had managed to scare off after only a few visits. One had allegedly met with him for less than an hour before declaring that she could not work with him.

What should be recognized is that none of these actions require the abandonment of self-determination, nor do they mean that the client has now taken charge of the total situation. However, this type of flexibility does require some humility. Also, therapists must have enough self-confidence to be able to surrender the one-up position, to not always have to be right, and to admit they do not have all the answers. In fact, it is more likely that clients will respect the therapist's intelligence if they are able to persuade the therapist to think differently on some issues.[493] And perhaps most importantly, the skillful care provider does not feel a need to take credit for all of the client's therapeutic accomplishments.

Dominant Clients who View Authority as a Threat Respond Well to Those who Can Assume a Submissive Posture

Now that flexible relating has been established as more productive than a rigid insistence on maintaining the dominate position, it is now necessary to determine under which circumstances a submissive posture is more helpful than a dominant one. Perhaps the most obvious need for this type of shift occurs when seeking to establish a complimentary interaction with clients who have a strong need for dominance and are, therefore, unwilling to subjugate themselves by seeking guidance or help.[494]

It is important to remember that people come to therapy seeking to establish a relational connection using the means they know. If the client is able to experience comfort or safety only while assuming a dominant posture, then that need should be recognized and respected. And, as mentioned earlier, if individuals experience a great deal of personal powerlessness early in life, then the type of dominance they use is likely to be coercive and aggressive.

For example, I had a client who, after entering my office for the first time, refused to sit on the couch commonly used by my clients and instead wanted to sit in the chair set aside for the therapist. I readily agreed to surrender my chair, and as I moved toward the couch, the client informed me that he wished to remove his shoes. I told him that he had a right to get as comfortable as he would like, so he took off his shoes. With a look of intense agitation, the client then launched into a twenty-minute diatribe. I

---

[493] Cialdini, Braver, and Lewis (1974) demonstrated that influencing agents regard a target person as more intelligent and likable if their attempts at persuasion were successful than if the attempts were unsuccessful.

[494] Some individuals, seeking to avoid feelings of devaluation or infantilization, resist defining themselves as "patients" in need of help from a stronger or wiser person (Farber, 1995).

listened quietly as he told me how he wished he could tell the doctor who had referred him to me to "fuck off," how he wished he could tell his old boss to fuck off, how he wished he could tell the IRS to fuck off! And, he let me know that if I did not agree with him, then I could fuck off as well. By this time, he was no longer sitting, but had stood up and started pacing back and forth in the small office.

With a relaxed posture and easy tone, I asked if he would mind sharing a little bit with me about his childhood experiences. He then told a tale of horrific violence, of a father who often became drunk and abused his mother during the late hours of the night. The screaming and crashing noises terrified him. Then one night, his mother ran into his room with a handful of shotgun shells and pleaded, "Your father is going to kill me. Please hide these in a place where he will not find them!" My client described the hiding place he had picked for the ammunition and exactly why he had chosen that spot. Of course, this experience explained a great deal about why this person felt so powerless while in the presence of authority figures.

Although I was initially submissive (allowing the client to sit in my chair, speak uninterrupted, and criticize whomever he pleased), I knew this client would not be content with a nondirective approach throughout the entirety of the first visit. I did not feel that he would return for a second visit unless I somehow proved my abilities to him. So when he put the question to me, "Why should I waste my timing coming in here and telling you about something that happened years ago?" I shifted to a position of dominance, replying, "Because I might know more about you than you know about yourself."

With a look of smugness and absolute amusement, the client responded, "Oh yeah? Is that so?"

Looking him deeply in the eyes, I said, "I bet I know what you spent your entire life wishing to say to your father, but never did."

Showing a little uncertainty, he asked, "Yeah, what is that?"

And with a voice of absolute confidence, I told him, "You wanted to tell your father to fuck off!"

Hearing that, he sank back into the chair, almost limp, "You are right."[495]

From that point forward, the client was highly responsive to any suggestion I offered. Over the next several years, he returned to my office anytime he needed help or advice. He eventually brought in his wife, his adult

---

[495] My guess was a safe bet because he showed signs of a strong transference pattern. As research has shown, individuals will actually lose track of the identity of the immediate interaction partner when it is the structure of the relationship that has become most salient (Fiske, Haslam, & Fiske, 1991).

son, and his daughter-in-law, telling each of them to just be honest with me and that I would help them with their problems.

One of the major social benefits of surrender is that it stops aggression. Anyone who has witnessed dogs fighting knows that when the disadvantaged animal drops to the ground with its belly up, the attacker will instinctually end its assault. Submission is how societies of animals and people are able keep from destroying one another. Similarly, I have found that it is often helpful to be able to say to someone who is becoming more and more verbally aggressive, "I cannot argue with a single word you have said." The startled response is often, "You agree," which, if affirmed, is then followed by greater calmness.[496]

However, it is important to recognize that acts of submission invite greater dominance from others. Therefore, if the interaction is being led down an increasingly destructive path, it may not be wise for the therapist to remain in the submissive role. Under such circumstances, submission is simply used as a disarming strategy. In other words, a brief moment of submission is used to halt an attack, but then it is quickly followed by acts of prosocial dominance.

An example of using submission as a disarming strategy comes from when I was giving a lecture to a room filled with women who had experienced domestic violence. I had been asked to talk about my work with men who had come to counseling as perpetrators of domestic violence. Feeling enthusiastic about my work, I was sharing the results of outcome data collected from the men's partners when my talk was interrupted by a woman who stood up in the audience and began to shout. She accused me of falsifying my data and of putting dangerous ideas into everyone's minds about how easy it is to get a violent and controlling male to suddenly become a new person. Judging from the redness in her face and the velocity of her voice, I could tell this was a fight I was not going to win. So I waited for her to finish and then conceded, "You are right! I have made a terrible mistake here, and I want to thank you for pointing it out." This reply stopped her verbal attack. Then I quickly slipped back into the dominant position and continued my lecture, "In fact, my statistics do not represent what happens with all men. Many men never bother to seek out help, and of those that do, many more never come for more than one session. So the positive outcomes I am describing only occur for the small percentage of men who have the dedication and courage to continue working on themselves for a long pe-

---

[496] My tactic is to initially switch over to their position, declaring them the winner, and then I begin to debate their position for them in such a way as to move toward the point I originally wished to make, while at the same time describing their comments as valuable. When done correctly, this maneuver is extremely effective.

riod of time." As I continued on with my talk, the woman settled into her chair and made no further comments. If she had been a client in my office, then I might have remained in a submissive posture for a greater period of time, in order to draw her out and make the relationship feel safe.[497]

When the Client Believes He or She Has Been Wronged, Therapists Should Show Remorse and Adjust Their Behavior

An interesting thing to consider from the previous example is why a person who was sitting silently in an audience would (without any formal invitation or permission from the group) suddenly refuse her subordinate role, instead seeking to commandeer the audience's attention. My experience has been that it is common for individuals to experience a tremendous boost in personal power if they reach a point of self-righteous indignation. In other words, a person who is otherwise compliant or passive will suddenly shift to a strong and dominant posture if he or she believes that an injustice has occurred and that the injustice is intolerable: "Nobody has a right to do that!" This human tendency seems to account in large part for the revolutionary birth of the United States ("Give me liberty or give me death!"). Within the therapeutic context, this sudden switch to a dominant posture is likely to occur when clients get the idea that they have somehow been wronged. When this occurs, it is vitally important to respond in a complementary manner; otherwise, the relationship is not likely to last.

As in the example above, the first action to take is one of verification. Although verification is not synonymous with submission, when the act of verification involves admitting to a mistake, then a form of surrender has occurred. Because it is impossible for the therapist to have a perfect understanding of all the client's needs, sensitivities, or areas of intense vulnerability, it is likely that on occasion something will be said or done that leaves the client feeling threatened or in some way violated. The more weak and vulnerable the client feels, the more likely this is to happen. Even if the therapist does not believe he or she has made a mistake, it is still important to validate the client's understanding of the situation and offer an apology.[498] This type of submission significantly reduces the client's sense of self-righteous indignation while increasing his or her feelings of safety.[499] Furthermore, if the

---

[497] Clients presenting with high resistance have been found to respond better to self-control methods and minimal therapist directiveness (Ackerman et al., 2001).

[498] Apologies have been shown to reduce the negative thoughts, feelings, and behaviors associated with not forgiving and to help restore damaged relationships (Darby & Schlenker, 1982; Exline & Baumeister, 2000; Weiner, Graham, Peter, & Zmuidinas, 1991).

[499] Research has shown that social verification that one is correct about one's interpretation of an event may reduce the threat associated with the transgression and help individuals become more forgiving and less vengeful (Eaton et al., 2006a).

client has experienced some form of discomfort, and the therapist is able to communicate genuine regret,[500] then the client is afforded a better opportunity to recognize his or her own value within the context of the relationship. (We do not apologize to others unless they have significance.) When handled appropriately, almost any mistake can be used to further the therapeutic relationship.[501]

While this type of interpersonal flexibility may seem straightforward enough, it is not always easy to implement. Those who have been classically trained might find it difficult to shift from the posture of dominant caregiver to that of submissive caregiver. What is more common is for the therapist to increase the use of dominance once he or she learns that the client is having a negative reaction to the therapy.[502] For example, starting in 1905, Freud emphasized the importance of using transference interpretations to address negative reactions to the care provider. As well intentioned as it may be, this type of response further emphasizes the therapist's dominant status while weakening the position of the client, who is already struggling with feelings of vulnerability and inferiority.[503] For those who are not trained in psychodynamic theory, there are many other variations, all of which serve as a means of maintaining dominance over the care receiver. For example, in cognitive therapy, when a client expresses dissatisfaction or disappointment with the therapy relationship, a therapist seeking to maintain a position of dominance might become more engaged in the act of challenging the client's distorted cognitions.[504] I use these two examples not as an argument against well-established models of care, but rather to illustrate the transtheoretical nature of the problem. Unhelpful dominance is not limited to transference interpretations or analysis of cognitions, but rather includes any form of one-upmanship that causes clients to regret their disclosures.[505] By contrast, if therapists will respond nondefen-

---

[500] When a transgressor expresses remorse, it increases the probability that the victim will seek to restore the relationship (McCullough et al., 1997).

[501] Apologies not only improve the victim's impression of the transgressor (Goffman, 1971), but also increase empathy toward the transgressor (McCullough, Worthington, & Rachal, 1997; McCullough et al., 1998).

[502] In fact, numerous studies have shown that therapists' awareness of patients' negative reactions often prove to be detrimental to therapy outcomes (e.g., Fuller & Hill, 1985; Martin, Martin, Meyer, & Slemon, 1986; Martin, Martin, & Slemon, 1987).

[503] In fact, research has shown that the more transference interpretations are used, the poorer the alliance between client and therapist is (Piper et al., 1991).

[504] Increased adherence to the cognitive model during alliance ruptures is associated with poor-outcome cases (Castonguay et al., 1996).

[505] In this type of scenario, the session will often end with the subjugated client agreeing to continue treatment as recommended by the therapist, but he or she does not return (Piper et al., 1999).

sively and allow the client to tell them what he or she needs from therapy, then rifts in the relationship are more readily repaired.[506] If therapists are able to surrender control and adjust their behavior in ways that can be verified by the client, then the client is much less likely to feel threatened by the relationship.[507]

Having argued for the reasons why one should be able to shift into a submissive posture to disarm escalating tensions, I would like to point out once again the benefits of maintaining a dominant posture under certain circumstances. In other words, it is not always helpful to apologize or reorganize one's behavior in response to the client's display of distress. In fact, under certain circumstances, it is more likely to create problems for the relationship if the therapist does not maintain the dominant role in the relationship, such as when the client has learned to use displays of distress to manipulate and exploit others. Individuals who resort to this style of interaction are most commonly diagnosed with personality disorders such as borderline or narcissistic personality disorder. Not only are these individuals not likely to *forgive* when apologies are offered,[508] but they also tend to become more self-righteously angry as they berate the professional for having failed them.[509]

Do Not Compete With Clients in a Domain That Is Important to Their Sense of Self (Unless You Plan to Lose)

Another set of circumstances in which the therapist should consider switching to a submissive posture is when a competition develops between the client and therapist in a domain that is of great importance to the client's self-esteem. For instance, if the client considers himself a great fisherman, the therapist should not relate stories of his own amazing catches while fly-fishing. Or if the client is especially proud of her quick wit and good humor, it might be counterproductive to make a sly remark that catches the client off guard.

The reason for this caution is because it is upsetting to be outperformed by another person when the performance involves some ability that

---

[506] It has been found that when therapists directly addressed the patient's negative feelings towards the therapist, the alliance improved (Foreman & Marmar, 1985).

[507] When there is evidence that an offender is not likely to commit similar transgressions in the future, then the victim is more likely to forgive (Gold & Weiner, 2000).

[508] Researchers found strong evidence that narcissists were less likely than nonnarcissists to forgive others for interpersonal offences (Exline et al., 2004).

[509] Researchers found that individuals with narcissistic tendencies were less forgiving toward a transgressor and that apologies can actually make this group less forgiving and more likely to retaliate (Eton, et al., 2007).

is important to the self-concept; the emotional distress is further magnified if the other person is a close acquaintance.[510] That is why it can be especially tricky providing expert care to other therapists who meet their self-esteem needs through their self-perceived problem-solving abilities. Providing a skillful response to a difficult problem faced by such an individual could prove to be disastrous for the relationship and further progress in therapy.[511] But when the informational or emotional support can be provided indirectly, there is less risk of rupturing the relationship.

For example, during group therapy, one woman, who was not a therapist, but who took great pride in her ability to develop her own solutions, shared details about a crisis situation that had left her overwhelmed and horribly depressed. I expressed a shared concern about the seriousness of her situation and my sympathy for her distress, then I moved the conversation along to other members of the group. This redirection served two purposes: one was to buy me some time to think about the details of her dilemma, and the other was to make my intervention less obvious. After five or ten minutes, I realized what she needed to do and then announced to the group how to handle a complex situation that involved the same set of circumstances she had just described. Later, when the group session was about to end, this woman suddenly announced to everyone in the room that she had just realized what she needed to do. The woman went on to relate the same solution I had suggested earlier. She left the session looking much less distressed. During a private supervision meeting with my intern (who had been present for this group session), the intern noted, "She repeated back, word for word, everything you had said without realizing it was your idea. That was really weird."

Another, simpler strategy to use with those who pride themselves on their problem-solving ability is indirect suggestion and role-play. For example, I had one client who came to therapy having just graduated with a doctoral degree in clinical psychology. He had recently married, and his parents, who were an exceedingly important part of his life, had come to town in order to help celebrate his marriage and graduation. The two weeks with his parents had been wonderful for him, but unfortunately, as they were driving out of town, a truck hit their car, killing them both. After

---

[510] In contrast, if the performance involves a domain that is not important to one's self-definition, then a friend's success can produce vicarious enjoyment (Cialdini et al., 1976; Tesser, 1991).

[511] Research on close social relations has shown that individuals will distance themselves from a friend who has out performed them in a domain used to define the self, or they might defensively devalue the importance of the domain, or sabotage the friend/competitor's performance (Tesser & Smith, 1980).

three weeks of intense mourning and depression, my client was finally able to make the call and get himself to my office.

After having him tell me about some of his happiest memories with his mother and father and what type of role they had played in his growth and development, I asked the young therapist to consider what he might say or do if someday he were to have a client come to him with the exact same set of circumstances. He was absolutely intrigued by the idea. So I surrendered my chair and had him role-play the most important parts of the session with this imaginary client. When he finished, I saw that a faint smile had returned to his face. I then verified the quality of his work and pointed out that I probably would not have been able to address his needs as adequately and skillfully as he just had. Although I had other interactions with him in professional settings, that was the only therapy session that he required.

The general point to be recognized is that any attempt to compete with a client and win is likely to be experienced by the client as dominant behavior. However, if a therapist conducts a competition with the client in order to acknowledge the client's superior performance, then a submissive posture has been utilized.

Some Clients Need the Experience of Successfully Standing Down an Authority Figure

One of Carl Roger's major contributions to the field of psychology was his elaboration on reasons why it is not always helpful to dominate the client. Though his utopic ideas about an entirely egalitarian society did not hold up in the end, he did demonstrate some of the benefits of allowing the client to take the lead during therapy. As Rogers (1951) says, "The primary point of importance here is the attitude held by the counselor toward the worth and the significance of this individual . . . [D]o we respect his capacity and his right to self-direction, or do we basically believe that his life would be best guided by us?" (p. 20). Indeed, it was Rogers who popularized the word *client* (versus *patient*), thereby granting a higher status to those seeking to have their needs met. After all, in a free marketplace, the customer is not automatically expected to submit to the wishes of the service provider.

My experience has been that some clients come to therapy having never had the experience of standing their ground with an authority figure. These individuals often have very aggressive and domineering parents who have done very little to empower their children. As a result of this conditioning, these individuals lack the capacity to identify their own needs, actively seek support, or to set clear boundaries. Thus, their interpersonal relations with other adults are debilitated by excessive feelings of anxiety, resentment, and self-doubt. In this weakened condition, the client is easily exploited or otherwise abused by others. For such individuals, I have found it helpful to provide the experience of successfully standing down an authority figure. Within the context of individual therapy, the therapist is the most readily available authority figure.

The boost in strength that comes from prevailing in a match against an authority figure,[512] such as a therapist, is beneficial not only for those who have been overly subjugated, but also for anyone who is taking on a great challenge and thus needs a feeling of empowerment. By means of strategically timed acts of submission, a therapist can help legitimize the will of the client in a way that cannot be achieved from a dominant position.

For example, while working as a college advisor to students with special needs, I encountered a student who had all the odds stacked against him. His father was already deceased, and he had no social network of friends. When I took his folder to my supervisor and showed her the IQ scores, she responded, "He never should have been admitted into a four-year college. Even with all of the accommodations that we can arrange for him, his IQ is too low for him to be able to succeed here. You are going to need to talk him into transferring to some type of vocational school." The reason I had gone to my supervisor for advice was that some of his professors were already coming to me, expressing concern. The band director had told me that this student created delays for the education of other students; therefore, as his academic advisor, I would have to tell him that he could no longer participate in the band program. I really liked this student and knew that he was willing to work harder than any of the other students.[513] His motivation to succeed came in great part from his love for his mother and his promise to her that she would someday watch him perform in the college marching band. As best as I could tell, this dream of someday joining the university marching band served as the inspiration he needed to get through very difficult circumstances during his high school education.

Although I did not like what I had been told to do, I complied with my instructions and called the student to my office to show him various options for vocational schooling. Of course, he would hear nothing of it. Al-

---

[512] Research has shown that the experience of successful dominance (winning) serves to increase levels of testosterone release in human and nonhuman primates (Miczek & Tornatzky, 1996; Sapolsky, 1991).

[513] The staff running the testing center had commented that, while he was taking an untimed test, he spent six hours working on what should have been a two-hour exam, forcing them to keep the center open long past its normal hours of operation.

though I had previously had good rapport with him, hearing these recommendations he became angry, shouting, "No! You are wrong! You are wrong!"

After listening quietly, to all the reasons he felt I was wrong, I hung my head and admitted that I could be wrong. I further added that he seemed too courageous to allow me or anyone else to make him do something he did not want to do.[514]

Following that meeting, the student went on to prove the professors wrong. His determination to succeed was absolutely unyielding. Although none of his grades were impressive, they were passing grades. When the band instructor returned to ask me why the student was still coming to his class, I explained that I was unable to convince him to quit. When the time came, the student did march with the band. This individual's fierce determination was certainly present before my intervention. However, if I, someone he trusted, had used all of my intellectual capacity to debate him (acting as if I believed that his life would be best guided by me), then he would have left my office in a weaker condition. He would not have been as prepared to stand down the other authority figures he would have to confront.

Strategic Submission Does Not Decrease One's Ability to Influence Outcomes

In the descriptions of different circumstances in which partial or temporary submissiveness by the therapist may prove beneficial for the therapy relationship, it should be recognized that submission is not the same as helplessness. Most are familiar with the adage, "Sometimes you have to lose a battle in order to win the war." If the therapist accepts that he or she remains capable of influencing outcomes, even as the client begins to exercise some dominant behavior, then professional responsibility for outcomes is not abandoned or abdicated to the client. At some level, the therapist continues to remain in charge of what is happening during therapy, regardless of the interpersonal posture that is adopted.

The power that is retained by the therapist, even while the therapist is temporarily surrendering to a client's assertions, is illustrated in the following example. The woman I was working with was 53 years of age and severely traumatized as a child by acts of violence from her mother and sexual abuse by multiple perpetrators. We had established a good working relationship, and now she was returning for her 21st visit. Having arrived late,

---

[514] Research suggests that those who believed they have acted courageously experience a positive change in their sense of self (Staub, 1974).

she discussed various items and then timidly explained why she was unhappy with her last session.

"I appreciate all of your help and you have done a lot for me, yada, yada, yada, but every once in a while, something has crept into your feedback that sounds like it's from the worst part of the mainstream, such as when you told me that I was muttering."

Immediately I took her side on the issue. "*Muttering*—that sounds like a criticism. It sounds like a very critical remark." I then asked if she remembered any more details from the discussion or the context in which the remark had been made.

Her reply was dominant, but kind. "You were making several remarks that were actually very helpful, and also you were crunched for time." (She had arrived 35 minutes late for that appointment.) "It just came across as really derogatory, and I thought you ought to know because that is not you." As she continued to control the conversation, explaining the reasons for her drop in vocal volume during the last session, I sat in a submissive posture and listened silently. She spent several minutes detailing the ways in which she had struggled for a lifetime to "find her voice." Then she paused and looked at me, waiting for a response.

Because she had laughed and seemed comfortable returning to her position as care receiver, I returned to a dominant position. "I am glad you brought this up. I am really glad you brought this up. Obviously, I would have preferred not to make the mistake that I did, but given that I did make the mistake, the fact that you were able to turn it around a week later and *find your voice* and tell me about it, is nice, this is really a nice development!"[515]

Smiling, and with her eyes becoming watery, the client thanked me for being an easy person to "give feedback to." After that event, she showed much greater comfort with my provision of care. Had I responded defensively, as would be expected in general society, then her expectation that no one would ever listen to her would have been reinforced.[516] Yielding at a strategic moment, I helped her realize new possibilities for relating with others.

Similarly, there are certain instances when it is easier to take charge of the total situation after having surrendered to the client. It is possible for clients to be highly ambivalent about their role as someone who is submitting to psychological care, and yet also believe that they have no reservations. In other words, they are only aware of the positive half of their am-

---

[515] Evaluating others' actions, whether critically or approvingly, is a dominant role.

[516] An individual experiencing transference may elicit from the new partner behaviors that confirm the transference-based expectation. In this case, representations of past relationship partners provide the expectancy seed for behavior confirmation in present relationships (Snyder & Stukas, 1999).

bivalence and do not recognize the existence of negative attitudes that can impede their willingness to comply.[517] Under these circumstances, a confusing set of interpersonal dynamics can occur. Such clients may announce that they are ready to comply with the treatment they desperately need, but then respond with resistance to any procedure requiring compliance. Thus, it is possible for client to believe that they should submit to care while not noticing that they do not feel like being dominated by the therapist.[518]

Statements that reflect this sort of ambivalence contain both the stated intention to submit and an expression of dominance. For example, the client's statement "You just need to tell me what to do" seems to indicate a readiness to submit, but it is, at the same time, a command. Equally dominant is the statement "I want you to hypnotize me right now and make me stop thinking these thoughts." My experience has been that if the therapist acts on the explicit message, clients automatically shift their energy to the implicit imperative, which is to resist the process[519] (e.g., "I'm sorry to interrupt you again, but I suddenly realized I need to go to the bathroom").

However, if the therapist first assumes a dominant posture by applying a technique (e.g., offering advice, using hypnosis, replacing dysfunctional thought patterns) and, when progress is not forthcoming, switches to a submissive posture by admitting failure, a surprising thing occurs: the resistance disappears. In other words, if the therapist meets the client's needs at multiple levels, by offering behavior that is both dominant and submissive, the ambivalence is nullified.

Accordingly, on more than one occasion, I have listened to a keynote speaker or other equally prominent therapist describe a seemingly inexplicable turn of events that occurred with a highly resistant client (who seemed to want help, but whose symptoms got worse) when the therapist finally admitted to being powerless. In each instance, this act of surrender was followed by evidence of remarkable progress.[520] When I encounter a

---

[517] When highly inconsistent cognitions are rendered simultaneously accessible, negative affect is experienced (Newby-Clark, McGregor, & Zanna, 2002). Because this affect is aversive, there is an intrinsic drive to avoid awareness of the cognitive inconsistency.

[518] In cognitive validation, the attitude is tagged as either true or false (e.g., "It is right to comply with treatment requests--true"). In affective validation, the attitude is associated with positive or negative affect (e.g., "This situation feels good," or "This situation feels bad"). Because these processes are presumed to reside in independent mental systems, the two attitudes can be affected and act independently (Petty & Brinol, 2006).

[519] Interpersonal antecedents have been shown to influence subjective feelings of ambivalence; furthermore, this influence is greatest for high-importance topics, and the valence of the relationship moderates whether the influence is positive or negative (Priester & Petty, 2001).

[520] As an example, one can listen to the keynote address by David Burns at the 2008 Brief Therapy Conference in San Diego, sponsored by The Milton H. Erickson Foundation, www.erickson-foundation.org.

client who insists on receiving direction and responds with resistance, my tendency is to isolate my initial display of dominance to a small component of therapy (i.e., any formal technique or procedure). Afterward, I am able to affirm the client without having to discount myself or the goodness of the total therapy relationship. For example, I might say, "After having given it a good try, I find that I am unable to hypnotize you. It seems that you are just not that susceptible to suggestion from others. Are you willing to give regular counseling a try?" When I've secured the client's confidence in this way, the resistance typically vanishes. Once again, the submissive posture of therapist is temporary and timed to occur at a strategic moment.

In Healthy Relationships, the Power Structures Are Flexible and the Interdependent Participants Are Willing to Negotiate Positive Outcomes

Beginning with Freud and continuing on through Rogers, there have been ongoing attempts to determine the best therapeutic posture for interacting with clients. For those instances when therapist and client cannot relate as perfect equals, the question arises, "Who should be the dominant member of the dyad?" This question cannot be given a definitive answer because it is too simplistic. Not only does it imply that there are no individual differences among clients, but such a question also ignores the issue of timing and the fluidity of healthy interpersonal relationships.

Therefore, discerning therapists develop an understanding of when to move between a dominant or submissive posture, based on the evolving needs of the client. In this way, therapists are neither dominant nor submissive, or at least not entirely so. As indicated in the ancient text[521] of the *Tao Te Ching*, "If the sage would guide the people, he must serve with humility. If he would lead them, he must follow behind" (p. 66). This juxtaposition of guiding and serving or leading and following represents the vast range of potential action that is available when looking beyond the confines of orthodox roles. It is this perspective that fosters the flexibility needed to implement varying degrees of dominance or submission strategically, based on the needs of the immediate situation.

Supportive Relationships Are Characterized by Collaboration Rather Than Power and Control

Once this level of flexibility is achieved, there must be some means of determining how dominant or how submissive to be at any given moment. Obviously, if therapists are not dominant enough, they will suddenly find

---

[521] *The Tao Te Ching* was probably written around the 6th century B.C., in a province of China.

themselves following rather than leading. However, if the intensity of the dominance is too high, the client's satisfaction with the relationship is likely to suffer.[522]

While it might seem that the level of dominance could be adjusted in accordance with the client's compliance with treatment, it is important to recognize that this approach sets into motion subtle, undesirable dynamics of power and control. In other words, if the therapist is operating under the rule that "I will increase my dominance until you comply," then the expression of individuality on the part of the client could quickly lead to disproportionate levels of dominance, which would eventually undermine the strength of the alliance. Relationships based on power and control operate in such a way that the will of the more powerful person becomes the will of both. This type of unilateral action against the client is the opposite of what needs to occur in therapy. Complementarity alone is not sufficient for the formation of transformational relationships,[523] but instead there must be evidence of a joint effort to achieve the client's goals.[524]

What is needed is a collaborative relationship in which the response capacities of the client are recognized and accommodated by the therapist. If the client is able to exercise dominance only in small degrees, then if and when the therapist sees the need to take charge, he or she should respond with a mild form of dominance. For example, the therapist might say, "You made some really good points. I am very impressed. Do you mind if I offer one or two additional points to consider?" If clients enter the office like bulls, ready to knock down anything that stands in their way, then the therapist, in order to be taken seriously, will need to use a more intense form of dominance. For example, the therapist might say (in a strong voice), "I sat here and listened to everything you had to say. I did not interrupt you once, not even when I did not like what you had to say. Now I am going to ask you to show me the same courtesy and respect. Are you willing to do that?" In both examples, there is a clear statement of intention to take charge of the conversation. And in both instances, there is an attempt to obtain the client's com-

---

[522] Under controlled conditions in which complementarity was observed and measured by a third party, satisfied participants judged their partners to be similar to themselves in dominance, and dissatisfied participants judged their partners to be dissimilar. These results suggests that for satisfied individuals, the differences were so slight that most participants did not detect them (Dryer & Horowitz, 1997).

[523] The dominating behavior of one person together with the submissive behavior of the other is no guarantee of partner satisfaction; a person's goals must be considered as well (Dryer & Horowitz, 1997).

[524] The alliance speaks to both therapist and client contributions and emphasizes the partnership between the client and therapist to achieve the client's goals (Bordin, 1979).

mitment to allow this action to take place.[525] Because of the latter, the interpersonal exchange is defined as more voluntary than coercive.

Because healthy relationships create space for the expression of individual personality and independent will, therapists should always be ready for the client to say no to a request for compliance. If this occurs, therapists do not forfeit their opportunity to intervene, but rather seek to negotiate a collaborative exchange along some other pathway.[526] In this way, the interaction between client and therapist is characterized by creativity and appreciation for the idiosyncrasies of the client. There needs to be enough respect for the will of the client that he or she can refuse certain tasks and enough altruism on the part of the therapist that the motivation to help is not deterred.[527] In contrast to relationships based on dynamics of power and control, the collaborative model recognizes that clients and therapists need each other to achieve their goals. Because therapists cannot succeed on their own, there is some degree of interdependence in the therapy dyad. And it is this sense of interdependence that compels the therapist to learn as much as possible about the client as an individual.[528]

As a concrete example of the process of negotiating an interdependent relationship between client and therapist, I can describe some work with an individual who was both overly dependent on others for care and deeply resentful of anyone who sought to manage him. Much of his emotional turmoil was somatized and experienced as intense gastrointestinal distress. He had stopped eating solid foods, and his face and arms had an emaciated appearance. His anxiety was such that he refused to cooperate with the caring individuals whom he engaged with provocative displays of helplessness. As an example, the client had called his brother on the phone, saying that he was suicidal and thereby alarming the brother, who phoned the police for assistance. However, when the police arrived, the client became violent and was eventually led away from his house in handcuffs. The end result was intense rage and a decision to never again speak to his brother. Similarly, he initially bragged about the wonderful skill of his psychiatrist and then fumed over a single remark by the doctor that he interpreted as being overly dominant. In the client's words, "He has no right to tell me

---

[525] Forming an alliance involves not only a sympathetic, accepting disposition toward clients, but also the ability to develop a sense of shared commitment to the goals of treatment (Hatcher, 1999).

[526] The pathways to collaboration include efforts to explore, understand, and join (Siegel & Hartzell, 2003, p. 89).

[527] Even among strangers, familiarity leads to increased helping, as does a sense of interpersonal dependency (Pearce, 1980; Schoenrade et al., 1986).

[528] The formal recognition of interdependence has been found to increase the variability of impressions across people, resulting in more idiosyncratic perceptions (Fiske, 1993).

how to feel about something!"

Continuing with this pattern of excessive dependency and resentment, he requested that I hypnotize him and make him start eating again. Obviously, this was not going to work unless I was able to some how define the relationship as a safe collaborative endeavor.

With this in mind, I sought to verify his overall position by talking about a time when I had been a reluctant patient for doctors who were seeking to save me from an ulcer that cut into a major artery.[529] My hope was that he would find humor in my confession while indirectly recognizing that it would be silly to resist my attempts to help.

Unfortunately, the client perceived my action as a terrible threat. Shaking his head, he nervously said, "That particular example did not help. It really did not help because now my stomach is burning, and I am worried about an internal bleed!" I had been attempting to take charge of the conversation, but as a result, his anxiety had skyrocketed.

So I searched for a different pathway. "Okay, so if you are that susceptible to suggestion—"

Still refusing to submit, he interrupted, "I really am!"

Accommodating my approach to his responses, I continued, "Then I can suggest that there is nothing wrong with your stomach, that it is no worse off now than it was ten minutes ago, so you can feel just as good now as you did when you came in."

Because I had accepted every remark he had made without becoming frustrated or more intensely dominant, the client cooperated. "That is making it feel better. Thank you."

Because he had allowed me to take a leadership position and intervene successfully, I reinforced his compliance by spending some time discussing all the ways he had done a really good job as a husband and a father. These responsibilities were exceedingly important to him. Although I was careful to point out that he did not have to be affected by any misstatements on my part, the client continued to exercise his ability to object to my requests, and in each instance, I treated his statements as valuable information and corrected my behavior. For example, after I suggested that he could focus his attention on his stomach and experience it getting better, he responded, "I cannot do that." So I asked where he felt that we needed to start, and he indicated that it should be out on the periphery of his stomach. Each time I

---

[529] My condition was such that I required several liters of blood, but I was uneasy with the idea of having someone else's blood pumped into my veins. When I asked about my options, the doctor bluntly said that I could sign the consent form immediately, or I could refuse, and he would wait until I passed out and then give me the blood transfusion anyway.

took his comments into account, he responded positively. By the end of the session, he was insisting that he felt no further discomfort.[530]

What should be apparent from this example is that interdependency demands power sharing. This power sharing should be regulated along lines of ability and responsibility. It is undesirable for the therapist to remain entrenched in the role of rescuing the client. There must be some space within the relationship for the client to exercise power. Because the client is the only one who can directly control therapy outcomes, the skillful therapist is careful to defer to the will of the client. It is this recognition of ability and responsibility that regulates power sharing within the therapeutic relationship.

---

[530] Two days later, the client called to cancel his next appointment. He told me that he felt remarkably better and described the therapy as amazing. He indicated that he was eating normally and had no further need for treatment. One year later, I received a card informing me that he continued to do well and was grateful for the therapy.

PART II

STANDARDS OF THERAPEUTIC RELATING

Therapeutic Relationships Are Defined by Supportive Experiences Not Readily Available (or Recognizable) in Childhood or General Society

What torments my soul is its loneliness. The more it expands among friends and the daily habits or pleasures, the more, it seems to me, it flees me and retires into its fortress.
—Eugène Delacroix[531]

During my childhood years, I witnessed more than one person destroy themselves. The most sad of these was a good friend from fifth grade, whom I had initially envied because of his above average social skills. However, by the time he turned 16, his experience of himself had somehow darkened. His self-esteem was low, he seemed to be very lonely, and his expectations for the future were primarily negative. During a moment of palpable desperation, he confided to me his worst fears, "Dan, I am afraid what will happen when I die. I am afraid that I am going to hell!" By this time, he had started to engage in a shadowy, high-risk lifestyle, and our paths diverged. Two years later, I found myself standing in front of his coffin, looking down at the pale, lifeless features of his face. He had overdosed while snorting a drug that was more lethal than he realized. That desperate statement from him was the last real conversation we had shared. I had wanted to help my friend, but did not know how.

There is a universal need to be known by at least one other caring human presence.[532] This is an absolute necessity. Sadly enough, being liked or loved by others is not always sufficient. The boy mentioned above became increasingly isolated and was certain of his impending demise, yet he had

---

[531] For much of his life, Eugène Delacroix (1798–1863) was one of the most prominent and controversial painters in France.

[532] Virtually every study of human happiness indicates that there is nothing people consider more meaningful and essential to their mental and physical well-being than satisfying close relationships (Berscheid & Reis, 1998).

numerous friendships, romantic relationships, and loving parents who wished to be a part of his life.[333] However, these relationships were not sufficient because none provided the type of support he required. Accordingly, in addition to understanding the core principles of complementarity, a well -trained therapist should also know the defining elements of transformational relationships. While the dynamics of verification, affect attunement, reciprocity, attachment, and structure occur in any successful relationship, the therapeutic relationship offers something more. It is an individually tailored relationship that strategically cultivates vital supportive experiences not readily available in childhood or in general society.[334]

As stated by Norcross (2002), "It trivializes psychotherapy to characterize it as simply a good relationship with a caring person" (p. 13). On the contrary, a great deal of skill and discernment are required to achieve complex therapeutic goals.[335] When a relationship is developed with discrete outcome objectives in mind, then it is a strategic relationship. In other words, in strategic relationships, the outcomes are intentional rather than random or spontaneous. Because it is within a professional context, the interpersonal connection that develops between a client and therapist is goal directed and time limited. Unfortunately, it is not possible to list the precise objectives that should govern the behavior of the therapist during all therapy encounters. Even when multiple clients share the same diagnosis, one client might need nurturing, another need clear guidance, another need encouragement to try something new, while others may need a sounding board or even a worthy opponent. During the ongoing process of discovery, skillful therapists remain as fluid as possible in their application of technique, as needs differ from person to person and moment to moment. For these reasons, philosophical discussions about how and why change occurs, or academic debates about which school of psychotherapy offers the most evidence-based techniques, do not yield as much practical benefit as one might hope.

When a relationship is developed in accordance with some predeter-

---

[333] Social isolation and loneliness are not highly correlated. For example, a person who has a large social network can experience intense loneliness, while a person with only a few close social ties may not feel lonely at all. Because lonely and nonlonely people do not differ markedly in the amount of time they spend with other people, it is the quality (vs. quantity) of social interactions that is associated with health (Cutrona, 1982; Jones, 1981; Peplau & Perlman, 1982; Reis et al., 1985).

[334] Meaningful social support is considered to be one of the major benefits of close relationships (e.g., Cunningham & Barbee, 2000).

[335] Expert psychotherapists have been found to be highly disciplined improvisationalists who have stronger self-regulating skills and more flexible repertoires than novices (Schacht, 1991).

mined protocol that prescribes a specific doctrine of change, then the relationship can be classified as orthodox. From this perspective, it is the actions of the therapist that become the focus of attention rather than the outcome that is achieved. For example, if the therapist is working from a treatment manual that prescribes certain behaviors at the beginning, middle, or end of the relationship, then it is the orthodox application of these prescribed behaviors that serves as the standard by which the relationship is defined. If the therapist does everything the way he or she is supposed to, then he or she can feel successful, regardless of how the client responds. Even Carl Roger's general principles of therapeutic relating encourage orthodoxy, such that if therapists meet the three prescribed conditions,[536] then they have done their job well. If the client responds poorly, then the client is considered resistant to treatment.

Strategic relationships turn this logic on its head by maintaining that the actions of the therapist do not matter as much as the client's response. Therefore, it is not the actions of the therapist, but instead the client's response that serves as the standard by which the relationship is defined. For example, rather than prescribing what therapists must do to be empathetic, the focus is shifted to the clients and whether or not they feel cared for and understood. In orthodox relationships, it is the means that is studied and rehearsed, whereas in strategic relationships, it is the end that serves as a foundation for independent decision-making.[537]

In the focus on client outcomes, it is possible to highlight certain relational objectives that are closely correlated with successful outcomes.[538] From the broadest perspective, counseling or therapy[539] is essentially a relationship between individuals, in which one lends support to another who is in need.[540] Therefore, it is the client's experience of feeling supported that matters more so than the experiential reality of the therapist. In other words, therapists do not respond to the client's actions or words in a self-

---

[536] He persuasively argued that empathy, positive regard, and genuineness toward the patient are the essential therapeutic conditions for change (Rogers, 1951).

[537] This is a matter of perspective rather than an ethical code and, therefore, should not be confused with the argument that the end always justifies the means. Also, one should recognize that absolute statements of any kind are inherently flawed.

[538] A recognition of such objectives provides clinical heuristics that can help guide decision making during the course of therapy (Goldfried, 1980).

[539] Therapy is commonly defined as the attempted remediation of a health problem, usually following a diagnosis, and is, therefore, closely associated with the medical model of treatment; counseling is defined as an attempt to increase the client's ability to solve problems and make decisions and is, therefore, closely associated with learning and education.

[540] It has long been argued that every form of psychotherapy incorporates interpersonal-relationship factors to some degree, regardless of the theoretical underpinnings (Frank, 1971; Strupp & Hadley, 1979).

oriented manner. Therapists do not compliment the client because they have a personal desire to be liked. They do not confront the client because they feel that they should be shown more respect. Similarly, they do not express affection for the client because they feel attraction. Each of these actions are natural social behaviors that characterize many types of relationships. However, this type of spontaneity could potentially be at odds with the immediate needs of a given client. As will be seen, the objectives that define the therapy relationship are not aimed at the personal needs of the therapist. Rather, the main concern of any therapy relationship is the client's psychological well-being.[541] Similar to the concept of delayed gratification, therapists temporarily put aside their immediate personality needs because, by definition, it is the care receiver's needs that are more urgent.[542] During therapy, all of the therapists' interpersonal functioning is measured against this singular purpose.

The tactics that a therapist uses to pursue this overarching objective are, in some ways, similar to those used by any other professional who is highly skilled in interpersonal relations, such as a politician or salesperson. However, the main difference is the intent to provide support. In therapy, the type of support offered is typically informational support[543] or emotional support.[544] Yet the type of helping relationship described in this book is different from other relationships that also offer information (such as a teacher-student relationship) or positive emotional experiences (such as a romantic relationship). So a more nuanced understanding of relationships is required.

In an effort to identify the core components of psychotherapy, Wampold (2001) described four essential elements: (1) an emotionally charged confiding relationship, (2) a belief that there is a care provider who will work in the client's best interest, (3) a rationale for treatment that is con-

---

[541] From a legal perspective, the therapist serves as a fiduciary, which means that his or her aid or advice has been sought by a person in a position of vulnerability who is acting on trust and good faith. In such a relation, it is necessary to act at all times for the sole benefit and interests of the principal (i.e., the client).

[542] Strategic relationships do not require an emptying of the therapist such that no traces of human need are left; rather, this interpersonal process is an act of self-transcendence that ultimately provides the rewards of professional achievement. Being able to help someone by providing a transformational relationship allows therapists the long-term satisfaction of knowing they made a difference in someone's life.

[543] Informational support refers to the provision of relevant information intended to help the individual cope with current difficulties. That information typically takes the form of advice or guidance in dealing with one's problems (Cohen, 2004).

[544] A third category, instrumental support, is not addressed in this book, as it is more commonly associated with social work, which provides tangible goods or direct assistance with tasks (Collins et al., 1993).

sistent with the client's worldview, and (4) a procedure or ritual that is consistent with the rationale of the treatment and requires the active participation of both client and therapist.[545] This is an eloquent contextual model that highlights the interdependent functions of relationship, therapeutic technique, and client expectancy. However, it still does not shed much light on the strategic relational objectives, other than the fact that the relationship should be intimate and emotionally charged. Because a romantic relationship is also one that is intimate and emotionally charged, a greater level of discernment is still required to set the therapeutic relationship apart.

The key to understanding the uniqueness of therapy relationships is to recognize the interpersonal dynamics that generate ongoing transformation. In other words, it is possible to create a relationship that will bolster the resources of the client by producing increased emotional resiliency, expand the client's capacity for growth and problem solving, utilize the client's lifetime of learning, and uncover previously unrecognized emotional or intellectual potentials.[546] As will be thoroughly outlined in the following section, there are numerous studies documenting that these types of results can be achieved when certain conditions are met. In an effort to organize and consolidate this information, I have listed three relational objectives associated with a transformational event: (1) an increase in self-awareness and self-trust, (2) the development of a positive self-concept, and (3) a general movement toward increased autonomy rather than dependence.[547] This is not meant to be an exhaustive list, but rather a starting point that offers a general understanding of what differentiates therapeutic relationships from other types of intimate or influential social relationships. The following chapters offer a more detailed examination of these basic contextual elements and the science behind them.

---

[545] A very similar model was first proposed by Frank and Frank (1991).

[546] Strupp and Hadley (1979) suggested that the core components of therapy include a confiding relationship, a compassionate explanation of the client's distress, psychoeducational information regarding alternative ways of dealing with problematic situations, enhancement of perceived mastery and interpersonal competence, the arousal of hope, or facilitation of emotional arousal and motivation for change.

[547] Notice that the focus is on subjective realities occurring within the client rather than what is done to the client. Thus, this is a strategic versus orthodox perspective.

Chapter 6

Transformational Relationships Promote Awareness of Internal Experiences and Needs

Every great and deep difficulty bears in itself its own solution.
It forces us to change our thinking in order to find it.
—Niels Bohr[548]

Since its conception, psychotherapy has distinguished itself as a unique supportive endeavor that draws its effects primarily from the internal resources of the helpee.[549] A general knowledge of human behavior, such as found in this book, is necessary for therapeutic proficiency, but it is not sufficient for achieving transformational experiences. Therapeutic engagement requires getting to know clients well enough to recognize what they are uniquely capable of achieving, yet, without support, will not attempt. Even more importantly, transformational relationships promote the client's awareness of internal experiences and needs so that mechanisms of self-governance and problem solving are more fully employed. When a relationship promotes self-awareness and self-trust, then instinctual knowledge and the client's lifetime of environmental learning become available for use. This product of the therapeutic relationship is uniquely transformational because the scope and availability of these internal resources far exceed anything that could be provided by an external agent of change.[550]

Unfortunately, the clinical objectives used to guide the therapy process too often depend on external sources of information, such as the ideas of brilliant theorists, the evidence-based conclusions of academic researchers,

---

[548] Niels Henrick Bohr (1885-1962) was a 1922 Nobel Prize winner for his work with quantum physics.

[549] In this regard, Freud virtually invented new social roles: that of the patient as a vital source of knowledge and the physician as a special kind of listener (Homans, 1995).

[550] Similarly, research has shown that being invited to develop one's own ideas about the causes of events promotes greater learning than receiving external feedback alone (Siegler, 2005). Thus, during therapy, the client should be actively engaged in the process of analyzing experiences and developing causal explanations.

or the clinician's firsthand experience with prior clients. Like alcohol, these sources of information are not bad when used in moderation. However, externally derived information cannot form the basis of the client's connection to his or her internal resources. That is why the process of therapy is squarely rooted in an intimate examination of the client's subjective realities.[551] When an empathetic understanding of the client's memories, beliefs, and emotional experiences is achieved, then increases in self-awareness are certain to follow. This means the therapist will really need to get to know his or her clients, developing a thorough understanding of their views of the problem, their hopes, their fears, their ways of dealing with people, their sources of energy, and most importantly, the things driving them to seek help. In order to hand-tailor the therapy objectives to match the needs of each unique individual, the therapist must turn to the client as the primary source of information.

A stronger sense of self is experienced by clients when they are given permission to access their own inner resources, rather than having a technique or doctrine of change put upon them. As one client explained to me, "I like what you just said—that I have problems and I have a right to solve them *my own* way. That's powerful. I never thought about it that way because no one ever told me that. These doctors I have been seeing have made me feel that it is their way or the highway! And that doesn't work for me." Thus, the starting point for any transformational relationship is a careful exploration of the client's self-perceived needs and subjective distress so that matching support can be offered.[552]

Just a casual remark, such as, "You are not going to be able to find something unless you know what it is you are looking for," can have a dramatic impact if it promotes increased self-awareness in crucial areas. This particular comment left one client momentarily speechless. When she replied, her voice was full of energy. "Dr. Short you have done it again! I am really going to spend some time thinking about this!"

For most others, this comment would not have seemed so special. However, for this person, the words tapped into a lifetime of confusion, desperation, and loneliness. This particular client had been forced to move almost every year of her childhood, resulting in numerous painful separations and constant disorientation. As a 50-year-old adult, she suffered from

---

[551] It has been noted that prerequisite skills for caregiving include (a) the ability to empathize with and take the perspective of distressed individuals and (b) social skills that assist caregivers in orienting them toward others and recognizing others' needs (Feeney & Collins, 2001).

[552] The matching hypothesis states that the effectiveness of social support is determined by whether or not the support provided matches the support needed and desired by the distressed individual (Cohen & Willis, 1985).

chronic depression and still had not been able to establish a sense of home. The more we talked, the more it became apparent that she did not know where to live or what to do with herself. So I asked her to list ten things that she felt made a place home. After we spend approximately twenty minutes of exploring her thoughts on what home might look like, I made that brief statement that illuminated the importance of her increased self-awareness. Looking deep within, she suddenly became aware of both the problem and the solution.

When I'm conducting workshops, a common question from the audience is "How did you know what to say to that particular client?" My answer is that I do my best to start with the assumption that I do not know what this person needs. This attitude is important in order to avoid the blind spot created by the assumption that one knows what *this type of client* needs.[553] The risk of biased processing becomes even greater if the client's situation reminds therapists of a problem or disorder that they have experienced themselves. This familiarity can trigger the type of self-referencing that causes the care provider to overlook subtle clues pointing toward the individuality of the client.[554] By contrast, when working from the assumption that one does not know what the client needs, it is easier to really listen and make adjustments to one's approach.[555]

For example, when I'm working with two separate individuals who are both male and both depressed, there are numerous strategies that might be employed. With one, I might spend a majority of the session sharing advice, and with the other, I might simply listen and not say a word. The treatment is highly individualized as a result of my having listened to what each client had to say about his needs. The client receiving advice will have made some brief, passing comment, such as, "I hate not knowing what to do. I wish I had more answers." If, as I am sharing information, the client leans in and looks intensely interested, then my interpretation of his immediate need was probably correct. In contrast, the second client might have commented, "I have a friend that keeps trying to give me advice. I wish somebody would just listen to me." For this individual, it is probably a mistake to give advice about functional versus dysfunctional thinking patterns or any other method of fighting depression, even if the method is research based. Instead, this client would need a therapist who is willing to stop

---

[553] A well-supported finding is that stereotypes dominate unless the perceiver spends more time learning about the person's unique attributes (Fiske, 1998).

[554] This is known as the false consensus effect, which is the tendency for people to perceive similarity, to assume that others feel, think, or behave as they do (Sherman, et al., 1983).

[555] Discrepancies between what the client needs and what the therapist is seeking to accomplish may hurt the therapeutic relationship (Goldstein, 1962).

talking and just sit and listen.

When there are not any revealing statements such as these, and therapists do not assume they already know what is needed, then their natural response is to ask the client, "What is it that you need from therapy today?" My experience has been that most clients are intrigued by the question because of the inner awareness and self-determination it promotes. Thus, the skillful therapist responds to the problem of not knowing what the client needs by asking questions and seeking to learn more about the uniqueness of this particular individual.

The Client Is Treated as the Final Authority on His or Her Needs

It is important to recognize that the client is responsible for all matters related to self-determination. Accordingly, the client must be treated as the final expert on his or her needs. From this perspective, the therapy relationship is viewed as a catalyst that sparks the process of change, but it is the client who ultimately decides what issues need to be addressed.[556] Similarly, Rosenzweig (1936) argued that therapist formulations of the problem, rather than being viewed as totally "adequate," need only have enough relevance to motivate the client to begin the process of change. The act of deciding how one should live his life or who she should become is a tremendous responsibility that really does not belong to a therapist. Therefore, great care is taken when seeking to help clients decide what parts of their lives will be targeted for change.

Unfortunately, there is a subtle temptation for care providers to exert their will over the lives of those who profess to having some problem. The effort to "cure" or "treat" a client can lead to coercive scenarios. Part of the problem is that in order to accomplish a cure, there must be some standard of how the person "should be," and often the standard is derived from sources that are external to the client, such as theories from a textbook or statistical norms. Any attempt to "make the client be more healthy" could convey to the client the idea that he or she is not a distinct and consequential entity. While it may be the job of the justice system to impose external standards on individuals, therapy is ultimately driven by internally derived standards. This is a fundamental principle that distinguishes therapy from brainwashing or mind control. In fact, it could be argued that any therapist who does not appreciate the importance of respecting the client's right to

---

[556] Not only is the strength of the therapeutic alliance associated with greater self-disclosure, but the clients' ratings of the relevance of their disclosures also predicts positive outcomes (Farber, 2003).

freedom of thought and choice should not be allowed to practice.[557] Rather than imposing one's self on others, a skillful care provider will focus intently on what can be discovered in relation to this other individual. There is a manifest acceptance of the individual's right to self-expression, including a recognition of the individual's need and right to participate in decisions about his or her welfare.[558]

Another direct implication for therapy is that all treatment planning should be based on a utilization of the client's will. Rather than relying on a sophisticated treatment model or deep philosophical knowledge, a provider of psychological care is most interested in finding ways to promote the utilization of the client's inner resources and potentials.[559] As Milton Erickson (1964) argued, the therapist needs to find a means "of deliberately shifting from the therapist to the patient the entire burden of both defining the psychotherapy desired and the responsibility for accepting it" (p. 271). In this way, clients are empowered as they begin to recognize their role as a vital contributor to the therapy process.[560] Furthermore, the establishment of a strong sense of self-determination helps promote effortful striving on the part of the client in therapy.[561]

Work Within the Parameters of the Client's Subjective Realities

Not only is it important that therapists make efforts to understand their clients, but this understanding should also seem both obvious and clearly aligned with the self-perceived needs of the client. This means therapists do not insist on promoting ideas that contradict the beliefs of the client. Similarly, therapists do not seek to make the client accept a disliked object or event. Nor do therapists hide their motives while working toward a specific outcome. When someone with an ideological agenda seeks to make others adopt a new belief, that is called *indoctrination*. When someone has an agenda that includes having the target person experience a desire for a specific object, that is called *seduction*. When someone elicits a target behavior

---

[557] One of the core ethical principles guiding professional helping relationships is that the caregiver should strive to protect the autonomy of the client (Kitchener, 1985).

[558] Increased choice for the client is considered a core component of the relational model for therapy (Duncan, 2002).

[559] Tallman and Bohart's (1999) review of outcome research indicates that the client is the single most potent contributor to progress in psychotherapy.

[560] Reach indicates that the active participation of clients in therapy is associated with increased empowerment (Moradi, Fischer, Hill, Jome, & Blum, 2000).

[561] Self-determination theory maintains that an understanding of human motivation requires a consideration of innate psychological needs for competence, autonomy, and relatedness (Deci & Ryan, 2000; LaGuardia et al., 2000).

while hiding his or her true motives, that is called *manipulation*. These tactics can produce behavioral change; however, therapists wishing to establish a supportive relationship do not seek to indoctrinate, seduce, or manipulate the client. Instead, there is a profound respect for the subjective realities operating within the client's mental world.

Although the task of supporting and validating the client's psychological realities might seem simple, the process quickly becomes complicated when the client starts to assign negative feelings or negative intentions to the therapist.[562] For example, the client may insist, "I know you do not want to hear my problems. Nobody could want to sit and listen to all of this." Though it might seem counterintuitive, one effective response is to affirm the client's statement. As I said to one client, "You are right. Please do not talk any more about this man who is clearly mistreating you. I think a much more helpful topic would be a discussion about your value and worth. I think there are some things we can do in here to help you feel better about yourself." The outcome of my reply was that, on the end-of-session feedback form, this client wrote, "The most helpful part of this session was Dan stopping the conversation and not wanting to hear about [John Doe]."

Offering this type of acceptance is even more difficult if the client is insisting on an emotional reality within the therapist that confirms the client's lack of value. In other words, it is possible for the therapist to feel very strongly about the intrinsic worth of the client and the goodness of the relationship, while the client might, in turn, feel that he or she means very little to the therapist.[563] Therefore, the perception of acceptance must start with a validation of the client's reality and then spread to the perception of new possibilities for future experiencing. As an example, the therapist might respond to such a comment by empathetically saying, "You are right. I have not gotten to know you well enough to fully appreciate your intrinsic worth as another human being, but I honestly want to try. I am not ready to give up. I think that the more I get to know you, the more I will like and appreciate you." Rather than arguing with a practiced and well-established belief, it is better for the therapist to offer new possibilities that the client has not yet considered.

---

[562] Due to a biased interpretation of social interactions, some people will perceive others as unsupportive even when others are, in fact, being supportive (Lakey & Cassady,1990).

[563] Low self-esteem individuals are often unhappy in relationships with caring others because they underestimate how much their partners value and care for them (Murray et al., 2002).

The Client's Reactions Are Explored Rather Than Controlled

Promoting increased self-awareness in response to those who think that you may not like them requires some skill, but doing the same for individuals who are momentarily certain they do not like you requires both skill and resolve. While it is generally true that there is less resistance when clients feel that their needs and desires are understood, negative experiences from past relationships can still enter into the therapy relationship, resulting in the arousal of strong emotions. However, rather than being concerned about the possibility of the client becoming angry or fearful during therapy interactions, the skillful therapist views this situation as an important opportunity.[564] When strong feelings are aroused within the client and then explored by the therapist without judgment or negative reaction, a new experience of intimacy is created.[565] This more positive experience can lead the client to have more productive expectations for interactions in general society. When relationships outside the office start to improve, then the pervasiveness of the client's relational support is greatly expanded.[566] As a female client recently told me, "I now find myself more comfortable while talking to men, and I am really enjoying myself."[567]

Even more importantly, this experience of acceptance and reflection on emotion leads to a reorganization of emotional experiencing.[568] The care provider's behavior toward the client will serve as a model for new interaction patterns that the client can internalize for use in self-referential processing (i.e., the client's relationship with him- or herself). In other words, the therapeutic relationship helps clients explore and make sense of the

---

[564] Research has shown that the arousal of emotions followed by cognitive processing of the emotional material is associated with a greater reduction in clinical symptoms than one process alone. In other words, therapy is enhanced when client emotion is vividly produced and reprocessed in a controlled and differentiated manner (Missirlian, et al., 2005).

[565] As Hobbs (1962) explains, "It is the fact that the client has a sustained experience of intimacy with another human being without getting hurt and that he or she is encouraged, on the basis of this concrete learning experience, to risk more open relationships outside of therapy" (p. 743).

[566] One study found that clients who manage to increase the availability of support from their social network tend to report fewer psychological symptoms at the termination of therapy, regardless of change that has occurred in the working alliance, whereas clients who improve the working alliance, but not the level of social support, tend to report little corresponding reduction in symptoms of distress (Mallinckrodt, 1996).

[567] Similarly, research has shown that people with high levels of intimacy motivation tend to enjoy higher levels of happiness and subjective well-being (McAdams & Bryant, 1987).

[568] Active attention to and reflection on emotional experiences, within an interpersonal context, seems to be necessary for emotion schemes to be changed and restructured (Greenberg, 2002; Greenberg & Pascual-Leone, 1995, 1997).

complex array of feelings they may have *about themselves*, including anger, fear, and the need for love.[569]

This process of exploration, which begins with a nondefensive acceptance of one emotion, such as anger, often leads to the discovery of other powerful emotions, such as disappointment and hurt over having been failed by the therapist or the intense shame surrounding events that have been disclosed during therapy.

On one such occasion, a polite, but proud Castilian woman was suddenly over come with rage. Sitting just across the desk from me, she raised her hand up in the air as if threatening to strike. "I am feeling so angry at you and my psychiatrist! I do not know why, but I just feel like slapping you across the face!"

My response was to acknowledge that the personal history she had been sharing was a difficult story to tell and that its disclosure required a great deal of courage.

With her face blushing and her eyes shifted toward the ground, she replied, "I just feel so much shame having told you that I was born an unwanted bastard and that my mother came from a brothel." As the interaction continued, her awareness moved through her feelings of anger at me to more vulnerable areas (i.e., a child's desperate wish to be loved and respected). The safety she experienced in therapy helped her be less avoidant of her own internal processes.[570] Following this session, she became more confident of her abilities and more certain of her plans for the future.[571]

For those who use suppression as their primary emotional coping strategy, the emotional reaction created by the therapy relationship may not be as obvious as a slap across the face. On the contrary, clients may remain highly agreeable and compliant while experiencing distress that they attribute to the therapist's actions. This type of alliance rupture is likely to result in clients silently withdrawing from therapy. Therefore, when therapists are working with someone who shows signs of having an avoidant attachment style, it is particularly important that they watch for any signs of withdrawal.

To illustrate, a 23-year-old client, *who routinely scheduled his visits at*

---

[569] When clients disclose their thoughts, emotions, desires, and actions and are met by the therapist's empathy, understanding, and acceptance, they learn to be more accepting of themselves (Goldfried, 2004).

[570] Typical avoidant operations that emerge in therapy often come from the fear of being too aggressive or too vulnerable—fears associated with the expectation of retaliation or rejection by the therapist (Safran et al., 2001).

[571] Processing emotions completely, within conscious awareness, makes available for clients vital information about their needs, action tendencies, and previously untapped sources of motivation for change (Greenberg, Rice, & Elliott, 1993).

the end of each session, gave no indication of unhappiness with me other than to end a difficult session saying, "I'll call to schedule the next visit." Unfortunately, he did not call back, and I failed to initiate a call to him. Two months later, he wrote a suicide note indicating that no one in the world cared if he lived or died, that he had already been abandoned by a biological mother, who gave him up for adoption, and by his adopted mother, who died of cancer after he had been sent away for boarding school. His adopted father, whom he routinely begged to love him, was no longer returning his calls, and thus, he felt unbearably empty and alone. He had bought a gun and was preparing to end his life when he received a call from the mother of a friend. As a matter of coincidence, she had just discovered her son was suicidal and wanted someone to go stay with him until she could catch the next flight out from California. My client agreed to help out, and while trying to convince his friend not to take his own life, he experienced a shift in his own thinking.

The next day he called my office and left a message that was garbled and impossible to understand. Hearing both urgency and confusion in his voice, I called back and left a message instructing him to come as soon as possible. When he entered my office, he threw his arms around me, and pulling me to his chest, he muttered that he missed me. When I asked him why he did not come back earlier, he shared that on the last visit he felt I was disappointed in him and no longer wanted to meet with him. He had perceived that I did not speak in as "friendly" a tone as usual and that I did not sit in the same chair as usual. These perceived differences in my behavior had left him feeling frightened and distraught. However, these feelings were not available for discussion at the time they occurred and may not have fully entered into his conscious awareness until days or weeks later. Once he was able to articulate his concerns, I was able to respond with an unambiguous display of care and concern.[572] Even more important for his emotional adjustment, we began to address his deep-rooted fear of abandonment.

The reason I mention this case is because it illustrates the delicate balance that must be achieved between respecting the individual's right to privacy and the ongoing need for client assessment.[573]

In order to develop the type of therapeutic environment that is needed

---

[572] Withdrawal ruptures are addressed by seeking clearer articulations of discontent (what the client does not like) to self-assertion (what the client needs from the therapist), during which the need for personal agency is recognized and validated by the therapist (Safran et al., 2001).

[573] It has been suggested that therapists should actively pursue material that is difficult for the client to disclose because of the relief that disclosing it produces and because keeping secrets inhibits the work of therapy (Farber, Berano, & Capobianco, 2004). However, reluctant individuals are likely to experience disclosure as an additional stressor when they are made to engage in it (Taylor et al., 2007).

for adequate disclosure of emotion, it is helpful to give the client overt permission to explore any feelings. Even so, some individuals will still express doubt: "I am afraid of what I will do once I really start to feel what's inside of me." For clients who are afraid of their response to an increased awareness of their feelings, I like to point out the difference between feeling and doing. Because of the painful consequences that have been associated with strong emotion, such as lashing out in anger or breaking down into uncontrollable sobbing, these individuals seek to block both the emotion and the behavior. Rarely has such a client had the experience of focusing on a strong feeling for a sustained period of time, but without acting on it. As I sometimes explain in therapy, "There is a big difference between feeling and doing. I can feel like soaring across the sky, but that does not mean that I am going to be jumping over the edge during my next visit to the Grand Canyon." Therapists can show the client how to practice this skill by having the client allow some feeling to come into awareness, perhaps even locating the associated sensations within the body, holding the emotional experience in awareness as long as possible, and then witness it subside without much physical movement or discussion. My experience has been that as the client becomes more adept at emotional experiencing, the breadth and range of his or her problem solving also increases.[574]

In addition to exploring the internal world of emotion, supportive relationships also expand conscious awareness of and trust in one's own thoughts. Because choice is closely linked conscious thought, the elaboration of thought can increase one's capacity for self-governance and meaningful action.[575] As mentioned earlier, my tendency is to help clients discuss the nature of the problem in great detail. During this exercise, the client engages in the type of slow and effortful cognitive processing that produces changes in perspective or new insight. In one such instance, a client spent 45 minutes reviewing the timeline of events leading to his realization that his wife was lying to him. During this discussion, he surmised that she was probably involved sexually with some other man. Afterward, he indicated that this review of events was the most helpful part of the session. This feedback is interesting because the discussion consisted of nothing more than him examining what he already knew.

The dynamic is illustrated even more clearly with a different client whom I gave permission to sit quietly and explore her thoughts in silence. Relaxing back into the couch and closing her eyes, she spent approximately

---

[574] It has been argued that emotion schemes inform one's perception, experience, and anticipation of future events; thus, they increase the individual's readiness for dealing with the world (Greenberg & Safran, 1987).

[575] Awareness creates the possibility of choice (Siegel & Hartzell, 2003, p. 70).

15 minutes exploring her thoughts. During this time, I did not make a single remark. When she finally opened her eyes, her body appeared to be more relaxed. Her rate of breathing changed with a deep slow release of air as she opened her eyes. Even more significantly, she began smiling for the first time since entering the office. The reason I thought this experience might be needed was that the client had indirectly told me as much. Prior to the exercise, while speaking rapidly, with agitation in her voice and tears in her eyes, she said, "I wish [my husband] was not always saying things to confuse me! I wish I did not doubt myself so much. I need people to stop talking at me!" Taking that statement as my cue, I decided not to talk for a little while. After the session was over, on a feedback form, this client wrote, "The most helpful part of this session was [the] quiet time with [my] thoughts." On the same form, she also noted, "After this session, I am more likely to be aware of how I [unnecessarily] doubt myself." What this client needed more than advice, or words of encouragement, was a safe relationship that fostered increased self-awareness.

Finally, after we recognize the importance of exploring the client's thoughts and emotions, it naturally follows that, when possible, the client's behavior should be explored rather than controlled or manipulated. Because the therapy relationship is temporary, any success achieved through the external manipulation of behavior is short lived, unless internal methods of behavioral regulation are established. The effectiveness of behavior modification has been scientifically established, but its popularity is greatest in institutional settings, where environmental factors can be regulated and maintained. Psychotherapy, by contrast, seeks to establish an internal transformation that will generalize across time and place. Therefore, whatever problem situations the client brings into the discussion are ideally used as a context for the client's discovery of internal problem-solving skills, rather than as a problem to be resolved by the therapist. The importance of this approach is expressed in the popular adage "Give a man a fish, and he will eat for a day. Teach a man to fish, and he will eat for a lifetime."[576] Of course, no solution will work until the client develops enough trust in him- or herself to attempt some type of problem solving.

As an example, a 25-year-old college student came to my office for help with chronic depression, confusion, a lack of concentration, and rapid emotional shifts. Her experience with therapists and psychiatrists dated back to seventh grade, when she first started feeling depressed. After her second visit to my office, she realized that her sudden weight gain and emotional

---

[576] Some have argued that this expression might have been inspired by the Chinese proverb 救急不救穷, "To relieve emergency does not relieve poverty."

volatility might be caused by pregnancy. The pregnancy was confirmed by a doctor the morning before her third session with me, during which she was experiencing both shock and horror.

"I can't possibly think of going through with it [having a baby]," she said. "Every part of me tells me that I can't handle this!"

When I asked her how much time she had to consider her options, she said that the doctor told her the abortion would need to be performed within one week. This physician had assured her that the abortion would not be as scary or complicated as my client was thinking.

When I asked if the physician had encouraged her to speak with anyone about this big decision or discussed any other options such as adoption, she replied, "No. What she gave me was the name of a website that supposedly has good information about abortions." When I asked if she was planning to tell her family, she said she did not want to because her older, married sister was currently trying to get pregnant. And, because of her parents' religious beliefs, she was certain she would be treated with scorn. "The last thing I feel like dealing with is the judgment from my family."

I did not insist that she tell her family members about her predicament, but I suggested it would be wise. "You know, sometimes people can really surprise you with their reactions."

A week later, during her forth visit, she began the session by saying, "I told my family. Their reaction really surprised me. They were excited about the baby. My father kept talking about becoming a grandfather. And my mother's reaction was most surprising—she remained neutral! She talked with me about the possibility of abortion and did not become critical."

Once the initial shock of learning about her pregnancy had worn off, this young person was feeling very confused. "I let myself think of the other side. I can see myself having a baby."

Her history included the onset of childhood depression when her father suddenly became withdrawn and emotionally unavailable, compounded by further alienation in adolescence following an episode of forced sex with an older man who was attending a high school party, resulting in public scorn by the females at her school and the onset of suicidal ideation. Her list of medications included Effexor, Wellbutrin, Adderall, and Lithium. Given these circumstances it seemed to me that the thing she most deeply desired was to reconnect somehow with her family, once again experiencing their love and approval as a normal member of the group. But first she had to figure out how to make a decision that she could live with and for which to love herself.

What I did was to help her thoroughly explore her ambivalence. "You can go to different spaces in your mind by going to different spaces in a room," I told her. "So I am going to set one chair over here, and that is going to be the part of you that wants to be a mother. And this other chair over here is going to be the abortion chair." When asked to choose which side to begin with, she responded, "I guess the abortion side."

What followed was an emotional exploration of her thoughts and feelings surrounding the idea of abortion and motherhood. She pleaded with herself as she explained why she could not let this "thing" ruin her chance at finishing college and how unlikely it was that the biological father would have anything to do with her or the baby. After switching chairs, she began to cry as she softly confessed how desperate she was to give and receive love. She also indicated that she knew in her heart she could be a good mother, even if no one else believed in her.

After fully exploring each side of her ambivalence, I affirmed her efforts. "I want to comment on how lucky you are that you have both sides of you, because you put it all together with a lot of really smart thinking." Following that suggestion, I offered her the opportunity to listen to the audio recording of the dialogue. So for the next thirty minutes, she listened as an outside observer as the two parts of her debated the fate of an unborn child. During this part of the session, she did not show much emotion, but was obviously absorbed in the experience, as her eyes shot back and forth between the chairs and her jaw clenched and unclenched. By the end of the session she still was not ready to make a decision, but she indicated that the session had been very helpful to her.

It was a week later that she announced her decision to keep her baby, and it was only after the baby was born that she shared her full satisfaction with herself. "For the first time in years I feel like I trusted myself and made a really good decision!" Up until that moment, she had experienced her life as a series of tragic missteps. The exploratory work in therapy allowed her to recognize her emotional needs and her capacity for self-governance. This one decision then transformed her view of herself and her future possibilities.

The Therapist Does Not Always Have to Know What the Client Needs to Discover

While therapists are seeking to guide the client to greater levels of self -awareness, it might seem that they should know where they are going. However, unlike leading a hiker to base camp, exploration in psychotherapy has an unlimited number of important destinations and very little chance of becoming lost. If therapists are skillful observers and have developed a high degree of emotional attunement, then they will find their way to psychological territory that needs to be explored, even without knowing what is about to be discovered.

I learned this lesson early in my career. While studying for my master's degree, I enrolled in a seminar on hypnosis. The three-day workshop included numerous experiential exercises, during which the participants practiced the new skills on one another. During one such exercise, we were told to help the subject enter into a relaxed state. So I asked my practice partner to tell me about an experience that has been very important to her and highly enjoyable. Without hesitation, she replied that floating down the river in a boat with her husband was undoubtedly the most enjoyable experience she knew. So I told her that I would suggest some relaxing imagery using that theme, but before I could begin, she asked if it would bother me if she laid on the floor. I indicated that it would be fine, so she positioned herself on the ground, with her head facing straight up and her arms folded across her chest. The room was already dark so the corpselike pose that she assumed was slightly eerie. However, I forged onward, spending approximately fifteen minutes describing the bliss of floating down the river with someone you love.

When it came time to end the exercise, I decided to make a statement that fit the immediate set of circumstances: "From the smile on your face, I can see that you have enjoyed this experience. But *all good things must come to an end.*" Hearing this statement, the woman responded with a dramatic change in affect. She covered her face with her forearms and wept uncontrollably for several minutes. The other students, who had previously seemed impressed by my technique, glared accusingly at me, as if to say, "What have you done to this nice person?" Since I was not yet certain of how to respond to this type of scenario, I decided I would just sit quietly and wait to see what would happen next.

Eventually, my partner regained her composure, and before speaking to anyone else, she looked me in the eye and said, "Thank you! My husband is in the hospital as we speak. They are going to attempt a quadruple bypass surgery, but the doctors do not expect him to make it. He was in the hospital three years ago for heart surgery. I have been telling myself that this time will be just like last time and that he will come home with me. I have not allowed myself to consider the possibility that he could die. You have helped me break through this denial. I really need to get things in order and prepare for the possibility of his death." Evidently, others had already tried to encourage her to prepare for the loss of her husband. However, she needed a means of psychologically preserving the goodness of what she had before dealing with the sadness of its loss.

When I began the interaction, I could not have predicted where we would end up.[577] Once she arrived at this particular insight, all of her previous behavior made perfect sense.

For individuals who are highly sensitive to judgment, it may be necessary to delay any type of emotional probing or problem-solving conversations. When the client's privacy is protected by the therapist in this manner, it does not mean that self-discovery will not occur, but rather, that a safe space is created—one that later acts as a container for any new insights that may emerge.

When just beginning therapy, some individuals have indicated to me that, after just 15 minutes of casual conversation, they are starting to feel overwhelmed and are, therefore, ready to end the session. One such client was new to therapy and assumed that she might feel more comfortable with a female therapist. She had come for only two visits with me and had spoken no more than 15 minutes in each session, making only vague reference to her problem situation. However, I congratulated her on her ability to speak up and voice her needs, and I agreed that, for whatever reasons, it might easier for her to meet with a female therapist.

After leaving to try a different therapist, she called me on the phone and made a desperate plea to return to therapy with me. "Oh my god! Dr. Short it was awful! This woman made me sit in different chairs and pretend to be different parts of myself. There was just no way I could do this, but I felt like I had to because she was so insistent. I could hardly wait to get away from her."

As mentioned in the chapter on attachment, just being in the presence of someone who is considered a safe haven will produce psychological benefit. With adults, a symbolic connection such as a handshake or a photograph with two people standing together is emotionally beneficial. A direct discussion about one's problems is not always necessary. Indeed, for individuals coming from cultures or family environments that value privacy over self-disclosure, implicit social support produces the benefits of social support[578] without forcing the individual to "lose face" or "burden others"

---

[577] When I've shared this case with others, some individuals have expressed doubts about the use of hypnosis, arguing that it is a potentially disturbing technique. I think this is an incorrect interpretation of events, since it was not the hypnosis that caused this woman's distress, but rather, it was the impeding death of her husband that underlay her emotional outburst.

[578] Implicit social support is defined as the emotional comfort one can obtain from social networks without disclosing or discussing one's problems or specific stressful events.

with personal problems.[579] When focusing on the importance of forming a relationship, rather than the importance of using a particular technique, the therapy endeavor becomes more expansive and more likely to be guided by the tremendous range of individual needs brought by a diverse clientele.

---

[579] There is evidence to suggest that certain groups, such as Asian Americans, are more likely to use and benefit from forms of support that do not involve explicit disclosure of personal distress (Kim, Sherman, & Taylor, 2008; Taylor et al., 2007).

Chapter 7

Transformational Relationships Encourage a Stable and Generally Positive Self-Concept

The fundamental datum for our science is a fact that . . .
all organisms like to 'feel good' about themselves. . . .
Thus in the most brief and direct manner,
we have a law of human development, . . .
the Principle of Self-Esteem Maintenance.
—Ernest Becker, 1968[580]

Starting with Alfred Adler and his conceptualization of the inferiority complex,[581] psychotherapy in general has been characterized by a recognition of the importance of ego support.[582] Later, Kohut (1971) argued that a strong sense of identity, value, meaning, and permanence was important for preventing people from becoming focused on their deficiencies, extremely vulnerable to criticism and failure, and overwhelmed by negative emotions, pessimistic thoughts, and feelings of alienation and loneliness.[583] To date, there is a tremendous amount that has been said[584] about the importance of

---

[580] Ernest Becker was an anthropologist who won the Pulitzer Prize for his 1973 book, *The Denial of Death*.

[581] The inferiority complex refers to an intense and chronic feeling that one is inferior to others. While sometimes subconscious, the inferiority complex was thought to cause individuals to overcompensate, resulting in spectacular achievement, extreme antisocial behavior, or both (Adler, 1927).

[582] In more recent studies, it has been shown that people with low self-esteem have been shown to have less emotional stability and greater amounts of anxiety, depression, and loneliness (Hokanson, Rubert, Welker, Hollander, & Hedeen, 1989; Jones, Freemon, & Goswick, 1981; Judge, Erez, Bono, & Thoresen, 2002; Leary & Baumeister, 2000; Pyszczynski & Greenberg, 1987; Robins, Hendin, & Trzesniewski, 2001; Tennen & Herzberger, 1987; Tarlow & Haaga, 1996; Watson, Suls, & Haig, 2002).

[583] In independent investigations, it has been found that individuals with high self-esteem deal better with negative events, having less stress and negative affect afterwards (Brown & Dutton, 1995; DiPaula & Campbell, 2002; Greenberg et al., 1992; Moreland & Sweeney, 1984; Steele, 1988).

[584] There are more than 25,000 articles, chapters, and books in the modern psychological literature on the topic of self-esteem (Rodewalt & Tragakis, 2003).

the amount of value placed in one's self.[585] Although there is still some debate over the absolute benefits of self-esteem, most researchers agree that developing high self-esteem, or avoiding low self-esteem, is an important contributor to health and well-being.[586]

When therapists provide psychological care for those who have been completely demoralized, it is imperative that they strengthen the client's core sense of self.[587] While efforts to improve the self-concept are most likely to be appreciated by those who are troubled by self-perceived flaws,[588] it is necessary to shelter the overall self-concept of all clients while addressing problematic areas, so that self-esteem does not fall below moderate levels.[589] Where there is a significant relationship, there will be some degree of influence on self-perception.[590] Regardless of theoretical orientation, every therapist is responsible for using this influence wisely.[591]

William James (1890) observed that one's core self-evaluation does not always alter with changing circumstances. In his words, "[T]here is a certain average tone of self-feeling which each one of us carries about with him, and which is independent of the objective reasons we may have for satisfaction or discontent" (p. 306). In contemporary literature, when an idea about one's self becomes so strong that it is capable of defining one's experiences, then it is referred to as an attitude.[592] When thinking of the self-concept as an attitude,[593] it becomes apparent that there is an entire

---

[585] Rosenberg (1965) provided a widely accepted definition of self-esteem as the value that one places on the self.

[586] For example, people with high self-esteem have more positive and fluid views of themselves and a greater sense of subjective well-being and happiness than people with low self-esteem (Baumeister, Campbell, Krueger, & Vohs, 2003; Campbell, 1990; Cheng & Furnham, 2004; DeNeve & Cooper, 1998; Diener & Diener, 1995; DuBois & Flay, 2004; Taylor & Brown, 1988).

[587] There is evidence to suggest that self-esteem, locus of control and generalized self-efficacy combine to create the core self (Judge, Erez, & Bono, 1998).

[588] Contemporary research suggests that therapeutic attempts to produce a strong self-concept might be most relevant for those who struggle with neuroticism, dispositional depression, daily sadness, and loneliness (Sedikides, et al., 2004; Watson & Clark, 1984).

[589] Most participants in functional society have moderate to high levels of self-esteem (Banaji & Prentice, 1994; Baumeister, 1998; Greenwald, 1980; Taylor & Brown, 1988).

[590] The influence of a relationship on self-perception can be both immediate and long lasting (Baldwin, Carrell & Lopez, 1990).

[591] The influence of immediate relationships remains important because the self-concept remains malleable throughout the life cycle (Bem, 1967; H Markus & Kunda, 1986; HR Markus & Wurf, 1987; McGuire & McGuire, 1988).

[592] More specifically, an attitude that is central enough to guide behavior and information processing, and it remains stable over time and resistant to change (Krosnick & Petty, 1995).

[593] An attitude is defined as a summary evaluation, ranging from positive to negative, of some object, such as an idea, a person, or a thing. Attitudes can be based on thoughts, feelings, or behaviors connected to the attitude object (DeMarree, Petty, & Brinol, 2007).

range of thinking, feeling, and doing that cumulatively produces a pervasive and stable sense of self. So when a person thinks "I am a good person" (cognition); looks in the mirror and smiles (affect); or accepts a promotion at work, taking on greater responsibility and increased opportunity (behavior), any and all of these would contribute to a positive self-concept. From a social-learning perspective, it could be argued that feelings of self-esteem, self-efficacy, and locus of control are sustained by attitudes that have been acquired through interaction with others. Because attitudes do not change quickly and easily,[594] it will be necessary for the therapist to work with the client's global values, which have been produced by a lifetime of learning and experience, so that it is the core self that is affirmed. For the therapist to be effective in this realm, he or she should have some understanding of attitudinal change.

One of the most common approaches to changing attitudes is to modify existing thoughts or introduce new ideas.[595] So it is logical to assume that dialogue about the client's thoughts and ideas about self will play a central role in the process of transformation.[596] In order for their attitude to change, clients who have low self-esteem need information designed to help affirm their value as a person. Clients who have low self-efficacy need information designed to highlight their capacity for achievement. And clients who have a generally external locus of control need information designed to connect outcomes with personal effort and initiative.

In summary, a healthy self-concept comes in large part from encouraging experiences with other people whose opinions are considered important. The effects are even more pronounced if the information is communicated in a way that is memorable and highly persuasive.[597]

Self-esteem Is a Ratio of Positive to Negative Ideas

If we accept the basic premise that healthy individuals still have occasional critical or negative ideas about themselves, it is easier to recognize

---

[594] In contrast to momentary feeling states, self-esteem is an enduring evaluation, or attitude, towards the self (Campbell et al., 1996; Eagly & Chaiken, 1993; Tesser, 2000, 2001; Wright, 2001.

[595] In persuasion research, attitude change is often mediated by the thoughts a person has about the attitude object, so intervening statements are directed at the person's thoughts about the attitude object (Petty & Cacioppo, 1981/1996).

[596] Accordingly, social-psychology research has shown that attitude change is often mediated by the thoughts a person has about the attitude object (Petty & Cacioppo, 1981, 1986; Petty, Ostrom, & Brock, 1981).

[597] Research has shown that the more persuasive information a message contains, the more persuaded people tend to be (Calder, 1978; Calder, Insko, & Yandell, 1974; Chaiken, 1980; Maddux & Rogers, 1980; Norman, 1976).

why self-esteem enhancement is not an all-or-nothing proposition. By contrast, it should be viewed as a matter of readjusting the balance of positive-to-negative self-evaluations. Those who have high self-esteem do not achieve a complete absence of self-critical ideas, but rather their negative self-evaluations are overshadowed by a generally positive self-attitude.[598] Thus, the implication for therapy is obvious: rather than seeking to strip away self-critical thoughts, the therapist can focus on counterbalancing negative evaluations with a greater supply of self-affirmational resources.

While a therapist verbally validates the client's negative remarks, it is helpful to strive for a three-to-one ratio, making three positive remarks for each negative idea the client has about him- or herself. As clients continue down the path of acceptance, they are subtly conditioned to find three positive factors about themselves for each negative. Progress is further promoted by giving clients the explicit task of self-monitoring,[599] so that when they are verbally critical of themselves, they follow up with a conscious effort to search for three other items they can feel good about.

I gave this task to a woman whose self-concept had been battered by childhood sexual abuse, neglect, abandonment, verbal abuse, her own extreme obesity, and a divorce. Three weeks later, when she returned for her second visit, she reported that she "sort of" failed to use the intervention. "There was just this silence in my head. For the first time in years, [the self-criticism] stopped. It was amazing. After all the years of therapy, this was the first time I have experienced this type of peace."

I joked with her that her response was not unusual and that sometimes just the thought of having to compliment ourselves is enough to scare us out of being so self-critical.[600] My general experience has been that when this corrective action is linked to habitual patterns of self-criticalness, there is both a retraining of the attentional processes and a probable decrease in the number of instances when the self-critical focus occurs.

While therapists seek to create a surplus of positive self-referential ideas, it is helpful to note that the positive ideas can come from any part of

---

[598] This attitudinal bias is the result of an abundance of positive self-conceptions (Steele, Spencer, & Lynch, 1993).

[599] Behavior therapists, in an attempt to use self-monitoring procedures for assessment purposes, discovered that their clients changed merely as a result of observing their own behavior. It has since been established that when individuals begins paying unusually close attention to one aspect of their behavior, that behavior is likely to change in a positive direction (Mc-Fall, 1970, p. 140).

[600] It is important to validate the clients' accomplishments even if they fail to perform a task in the manner it was intended.

the client's total identity.[601] In other words, if a client decides, after having an abortion, that she is a terrible mother, her self-esteem can be repaired by providing evidence of her success as a loyal and dedicated daughter (especially if parental influence was involved in her decision to abort). She does not have to be convinced that she is a good mother, which would obviously be impossible if she has not given birth to any children. When individuals have difficultly liking themselves because of behavior that is contrary to personal values, it is necessary to neutralize the effect of past behavior by calling attention to a favorable behavior in a different domain. In other words, it is possible to counterbalance negative self-evaluations.[602]

Although there are instances when the client will need some help finding a counterbalance, it is not uncommon for a client to list his or her positive attributes defensively.[603] When clients make this type of image-restoring attempt, all that the therapist needs to do is endorse their conclusions.

For example, I encountered a 74-year-old woman who was so ashamed of her addiction to cigarettes that she hardly felt able to sit in my office (for fear that she would leave an unpleasant smoke odor). Before I was able to decide what to say so that she would return to therapy, she commented, "For people who insist that I am a criminal because I smoke, I ask, 'Which would you choose: to be locked in a garage with a car that is running or locked in a garage with someone who is smoking?' It is not secondhand smoke that creates so much trouble for people's breathing. It is all the cars on the road!" Because she walked nearly everywhere she went, including to my office, her assertion was a perfect means of protecting her self-concept. All that was required from me was a willingness to affirm the goodness of her preference for walking. Had I offered different affirmations, in too large of a dosage, there is the possibility that she would have become increasingly anxious.[604] Once again, it should be recognized that people welcome positive ideas if they can find a way to make them fit within the established system of beliefs.

---

[601] It has been shown that negative ideas do not need to be counterbalanced with positive ideas from the same domain (Steele, 1988; Tesser, 2000).

[602] As researchers have demonstrated, the self-evaluative system is flexible, and there is interchangeability among the positive and negative points of self-conceptualization (Tesser & Cornell, 1991).

[603] As noted by several researchers, there is evidence that healthy people automatically respond to threats to a specific self-concept domain by inflating their self-presentations in an unrelated domain (Baumeister & Jones, 1978; Brown & Smart, 1991; Greenberg & Pyszczynski, 1985).

[604] As demonstrated experimentally, large amounts of positive feedback cause people with low self-esteem to become anxious, but small doses help reduce anxiety (Swann, Wenzlaff, & Tafarodi, 1992).

As paradoxical as it may sound, sometimes it is possible to use a client's experience of shame as a counterbalance for egregious behavior. For example, a client I worked with early in my career had beaten his wife so severely that she fled with the children to an undisclosed location in a different state. Long after her departure, he remained remorseful and commented that he could not bear to live with himself after doing so much harm to her and two daughters. My memory is that he spoke with great sadness about the fact that he could never again visit his daughters and that they would grow up thinking of their father as the monster who nearly killed their mother.

As he stared at the ground in a semidespondent state, I affirmed his basic position and added that I was glad to see that he felt so terrible about his behavior. My response was not what he had expected, so he sought clarification. I explained that had he done these things and *not* felt any remorse, it would mean that he had no conscience. My statement was something to the effect of, "The amount of pain that I see in you tells me that you are a person with character and that once we are able to strengthen that character, you will be able to devote yourself to the well-being of others with much more tenacity than the average man." Rather than seeking to make him feel good about himself as a father, I built up an appreciation for his potential as a friend to others. The indictment in the first statement made the therapeutic suggestion in the second all the more compelling. Because he felt bad about himself, this individual was more highly motivated to improve future relationships.[605]

Of course, in therapy it is sometimes necessary to have a frank discussion about poor decisions and problematic behavior. While doing so, the therapist can model the sort of corrective dialogue that needs to be internalized. Clients with low self-awareness and limited self-control[606] do not benefit from dialogue with a therapist who offers only praise and acceptance. As a prime example, pathological narcissists often use blame,[607] projection,[608] and

---

[605] Steele (1975) found that after being called "bad drivers," subjects were more willing to help with a community food co-op, even though this service could not remove the specific stigma of being labeled a bad driver. These findings seem to suggest that people are motivated to do other things to enhance their self-image, after it has been threatened, even if the action cannot rectify the specific threat.

[606] Known collectively as executive functioning, these cognitive systems are invoked when it is necessary to override responses that may otherwise be automatically elicited by stimuli in the external environment (Norman & Shallice, 2000).

[607] Narcissism is closely associated with self-deceptive enhancement, arrogance, and hostility, particularly after failure (Johnson, Vincent, & Ross, 1997; Paulhus, 1998; Rhodewalt & Morf, 1998).

[608] Projection is the act of attributing characteristics of the self to others (Freud, 1924/1956).

denial[609] to keep attention away from personal defects. As a result, they loose their ability to self-correct and are prone toward serious miscalculations when seeking to determine what they can accomplish. In addition to many offensive behaviors,[610] they lack the amount of empathy, gratitude, and transparency needed for successful intimate relationships. Therefore, it is often necessary to teach such people how to feel comfortable with rudimentary self-corrective mechanisms, such as learning from mistakes and feeling remorse after hurting someone.

Thus, the overall objective of building a positive self-concept does not require the therapist to remain mute on the issue of faults. Instead, there is judicious acknowledgement of what is wrong, followed by equally honest feedback about all that is right and good about the individual. While improvement is sometimes contingent on critical feedback,[611] positive ideas should outweigh the negativity by a three-to-one ratio. This way, negative feelings are felt for a limited amount of time and are related to feedback about a specific situation.[612] Skillful therapists spend more time discovering what is right about the client than finding flaws. By the end of the session, the client should have a strong feeling about his or her goodness as someone willing to work on difficult issues in therapy.

People With Low Self-esteem Respond Poorly to Overly Positive Feedback

Before leaving the subject of self-esteem enhancement, it should be pointed out that some clients might respond poorly to encouragement to feel better about themselves. This reluctance is often rooted in the need for a stable sense of identity. In some cases, the resistance may also be reinforced by moral teachings, such as a belief that self-esteem is synonymous with conceit, selfishness, and lack of humility.[613] Others are uncomfortable with the idea of self-liking because of excessive parental criticism during

---

[609] Denial is essentially an act of repression in which information that is not accepted as part of a positive self is dissociated from other self-aspects.

[610] These individuals are often characterized by competitiveness, exploitive behavior, hostility, and mistrust of others (Morf & Rhodewalt, 2001; Rhodewalt, 2001; Sedikides et al., 2002).

[611] It has been suggested that low levels of negativity may be necessary for people to flourish and obtain optimal functioning (Baumeister et al., 2003).

[612] As opposed to global character assignations (Fredrickson & Losada, 2005).

[613] There are numerous religious articles posted on the Internet warning that the self-esteem movement is an attempt by Satan to turn people away from God. Therefore, while working with some religious individuals (of various faith backgrounds), therapists must be careful about the use of psychological jargon that religious leaders may have paired with negative or frightening ideas.

childhood, which has resulted in a belief that they have no right to think highly of themselves. Other negative reactions to self-esteem enhancement might include an achievement-oriented value set that demands the attainment of exceedingly high aspirations or unrealized potential before having any positive feelings about self. Finally, there are those who simply believe that a damaged sense of self can never be repaired.

Regardless of the cause of a client's low self-esteem, it is important for the therapist to recognize when the use of positive, affirming comments is having a negative impact on the client.

While conducting therapy, I have had some clients respond with a motionless stare, seemingly in a state of shock, after I mentioned the possibility of helping them feel better about themselves. These clients will then change the subject or openly disagree with my suggestion.[614] The fact that a suggestion is positive and affirming does not justify its use. When an idea is met with this type of resistance, it is necessary to rethink one's approach; otherwise, there is a real risk of damaging the relationship.[615] After all, even those with low self-esteem are not going to like having threatening ideas forced upon them.

Acceptance Is the First response to Excessive Self-criticism

Unfortunately, there are some clients who do not like *anything* at all about themselves. While I was once speaking to a group of women, there was one such individual who fell into a heap of sobbing tears after I asked her to consider one small thing she might like about herself. The woman's response was, "I hate everything about me. I hate every single cell in my body. I hate the fact that I was ever born!"[616] What this type of person needs most at the start of therapy is the experience of acceptance. Paradoxically, the best place to begin accepting such a client is with her right to self-criticism or even self-hatred.

To understand the importance of verifying the client's right to self-criticism, it is helpful to consider the problems created by rejecting nega-

---

[614] Along these same lines, research has shown that when people with low self-esteem receive direct positive feedback, they will likely dismiss it (Shrauger & Lund, 1975; Swann et al., 1987) or reinterpret the statements to make them more in agreement with existing negative ideas about self (Andrews, 1993; Swann & Read, 1981).

[615] If those with low self-esteem are not able to dismiss the positive statements or reinterpret them (because the source is too credible), they are likely to become exceedingly anxious (Swann, Wenzlaff, & Tafarodi, 1992).

[616] This woman had been physically and sexually abused since childhood. She was currently working as a stripper who, up until this day, had watched helplessly as her boys were verbally and physically abused by her former boyfriend.

tive self-evaluations. For instance, telling a client "You should not be so self-deprecating" ironically begs the response "I'm sorry. I know how terrible it is to listen to this. I hate the way I talk." In this example, the therapist's admonition sets the client up to experience failure during the interpersonal exchange. Similarly, telling a client "You should not be so critical of yourself" creates a negative double bind. The client must now feel critical of him- or herself for being so self-critical. As a general rule, the use of confrontation (e.g., "You should not be so self-defeating,") and demands for conformity (e.g., "You must now think and talk about yourself using my set of evidence-based encouragement-oriented techniques") is contraindicated when seeking to help a client move in the direction of greater self-acceptance. Imagine the confusion that is created when a client is given the explicit message "You should accept yourself exactly as you are," followed by the implicit message "So now change how you think about yourself." Therefore, when the client says to the therapist, "I hate everything about me. I want a complete overhaul," an affirming response would be to ask, "What part of yourself do you dislike most?" This type of question not only communicates acceptance, but it also points the client in a positive direction by very subtly implying that there might be other parts of self that are not disliked so intensely.[617]

As thinking creatures with the capacity for self-reflection, each human not only has the right to think self-critically, but also a need to reject foreign ideas that are too destabilizing. In therapy, it is important to recognize the universal need to feel good about one's self, but it is just as important to respect the client's beliefs, whether they are negative or positive.[618] Therefore, when the client says, "I just hate the size of my nose," an attitude of acceptance is warranted. For example, a therapist might respond, "You have a right to dislike certain parts of your body. You might continue to dislike that part of your body, even as you progress and become more self-accepting." In addition to communicating acceptance, this type of statement also communicates the possibility of change. The client may or may not dislike this part of the body for life. When given this type of nonthreatening opportunity, the client will almost always seek to adopt and confirm

---

[617] Although individuals with low self-esteem are generally more accepting of negative information about themselves than those with high-esteem, they do accept positive ideas when they believe those ideas can defend the more favorable self-image (Brown, Collins, & Schmidt, 1988; Dykman et al., 1989; Schlenker, 1985).

[618] Research indicates that low self-esteem individuals do not lack the desire to feel better about themselves, but rather, they experience a conflict between the wish to enhance feelings of personal worth and the need to maintain a consistent (negative) self-view (Swann, 1987).

more positive self-attitudes.[619]

Another important point to be recognized is that a thorough examination of all the client's ideas (good and bad) provides a more solid basis for eventual adjustments to the self-concept. If the therapist seems unwilling to hear or accept the client's negative self-evaluations, then the client is left with the idea that "If he truly knew me, he would not think so positively about me." By contrast, when client know that they and the therapist together have carefully considered all sides of the issue, clients are in a better position to embrace the positive conclusions that eventually develop.[620]

Encourage the Client to Do Things That Are Important to the Core Self

Most of what I know about good self-esteem can be communicated in a single persuasive message: "You are more good than bad." As will soon be discussed, in order for this idea to take root in the mind of the client, it will need to be substantiated through action and validated by at least one external witness.[621] What this means for therapy is that self-concept change can be achieved by facilitating the activation of new behavior and its subsequent recognition.[622] As shown experimentally, people appear to internalize the implications of their behavior, so that acting in a certain way leads to thinking of oneself in that way.[623]

The pioneering psychotherapist Milton Erickson commented, "The secret to psychotherapy is to get the client doing something he wishes to do but otherwise would not."[624] This statement brings to light the importance of encouraging behavior that is congruent with the client's core values. That way, once the behavior is performed, the client can rely on deeply ingrained beliefs to help reorganize fundamental ideas about self. Consider-

---

[619] In fact, research indicates that low self-esteem individuals will resist negative self-relevant information even more strenuously than those with high-esteem, when they believe they can get away with it (Steele, Spencer, & Lynch, 1993).

[620] Accordingly, research on attitude change has shown that the perception that one has carefully considered both sides of an issue before arriving at a judgment can increase the certainty of newly formed beliefs (Rucker & Petty, 2004).

[621] Research indicates that thinking and feeling tend to align with action, both for the sake of internal consistency and interpersonal impression management (Baumeister & Tice, 1984; Paulhus, 1982).

[622] This process has been referred to as internalization.

[623] Internalization is most apparent when individuals express a willingness to perform the given behavior, as opposed to reluctant compliance (Jones et al., 1981).

[624] This remark was made during a recorded conversation with Ernest Rossi and later quoted in a book about Erickson's therapeutic strategies (Short, Erickson, Erickson-Klein, 2005, p. 41).

ing the maxim "You discover who you are through the things which you do," a strong argument can be made for the importance of one's daily activities to be congruent with the values and priorities acquired through a lifetime of learning. To move the client in this direction, the first step is to probe for such values (e.g., "What is it that is most important to you?"), and then follow with relevant behavioral adjustments.[625]

This approach was surprisingly effective when I counseled a 21-year-old man suffering from intrusive thoughts. He described himself as feeling hopeless, despondent, and as if he were about to go insane. He had already seen another therapist, but wanted a second opinion. He had been molested as a young child and many years later, as an adult, developed intense distress after being surrounded by children in someone else's home. Intrusive ideas and sexual images began to flood his thoughts. Like someone struggling against quicksand, the more he tried to resist the images, the more ensnared he became in the neurotic complex.

The therapist before me had taught him a thought-replacement technique, which had produced positive results. However, his core identity remained damaged. Behavioral modification alone was not enough. So during his visit with me I sought to create a sense of hope. By the end of the session, he said, "I am just now starting to realize that this problem can be overcome."

Interestingly, he did not return for the next scheduled appointment, so I assumed the therapy had failed to meet his needs. However, five months later, he returned for a second visit. He explained that he was now doing much better and that he had used what he learned in therapy to manage the intrusive thoughts in a satisfactory way. However, as he explained, "It is the fact that I would ever have such a thought that is really bothering me."

Seeking to work more directly on his self-concept, I explained that his personal values seemed to be very strongly oriented around the well-being of children. He readily agreed. Then I offered specific instructions: "Each time this thought pops into your head, you can put one dollar toward feeding children in third-world countries." After he joked, using self-derogatory humor, "I might go broke," I explained, "Instead of just trying to keep something bad from happening, let's turn it into an asset of yours. Let's make it an important part of who you are [and] how you become who you want to be." He had come to therapy fearful that he *could* harm children (in the same way he had been harmed), so I got him to do something that *would* help children. These children were on the other side of the globe, so he did

---

[625] Because people have different values, often derived from a different culture or subculture, their self-esteem will sometimes benefit from doing things that the larger society disagrees with (Andreas, 2002).

not have to worry about his potentially damaged boundary system. Once he followed through with behaviors connected to core values, he had new reason to believe in his overall humanity.[626]

An important point about this case is that this man could not have remained isolated in his struggles and still made progress. He had been struggling alone with terrible shame since he was a child. Sending money to organizations that serve children would not have repaired his damaged self-concept if it had been performed in isolation. It was vitally important that he have someone to confess his problem to and someone to witness the reality of his charitable behavior.[627] So while verbal persuasion may be used to seed an experiential process, it is the relationship that acts as a fertile bed in which the self-concept takes root.

In some cases, the high value behavior is already in place and merely needs to be pointed out. For example, while I was working with a 67-year-old retired school teacher (and former nun), a single comment appeared to have had a substantial impact on her self-concept. She was an intelligent and capable individual who felt exceedingly anxious about her relationships with others. The subsequent emotional stress manifested itself somatically in the form of irritable bowel syndrome (IBS). One day, after hearing about her post-retirement work as a substitute teacher, I commented on her handling of a special-needs student who had been challenging her authority. The boy had been seeking attention using loud and hyperactive behavior. She responded to him in a way that was effective. So I provided an enthusiastic endorsement of what I considered to be skillful classroom-behavior management.

With her attention riveted to my comments, she asked me to explain more about what I meant. I explained how rare it is to find a person who can set firm limits without becoming angry and while simultaneously initiating acts of kindness and encouragement. I then added that this skill of hers was a special type of strength that was undoubtedly a great asset to her daughter and young niece, both of whom she cared for deeply. This woman had dedicated her life to teaching. The only thing she valued more than teaching was her role as a mother.

In the weeks following this conversation, there was a noticeable de-

---

[626] One month later, he returned for a third visit, saying that he was satisfied with the results and did not wish to continue with ongoing psychotherapy. To date, I have heard no more from him.

[627] Accordingly, research has shown that internalization occurs only with public displays of behavior. In other words, there must be an ongoing interpersonal process or relationship for high-value behaviors to enhance the self-concept (Schlenker, Dlugolecki, & Doherty, 1994; Tice, 1992).

cline in the amount of anxiety that she experienced in relation to her own well-being and the well-being of her extended family. Although I had already used direct hypnotic suggestion to help decrease the frequency of the gastrointestinal symptoms, it was only after this session that she reported no further difficulty with IBS. Also after this visit, she began describing herself as a strong person, something she had not done in prior conversations. Although I had done a lot of earlier work had with this woman, I believe one of the most important influences was my use of persuasive dialogue to connect long-established global values to the core self.[628]

Help Clients Value Domains at Which They Excel

While the initiation of new behavior can contribute to a positive self-concept, another useful strategy is to help clients develop new values that are tailored to existing behavior. James (1985) persuasively argued that the secret to feeling good about oneself is selectively valuing those dimensions at which one excels. In other words, low self-esteem often results from a discrepancy between the importance of an area of self-definition and one's perception of competence in that area. For example, if a little boy decides that he will be defined by what type of runner he is, then his speed relative to other children will result in either low or high self-esteem. Or if a young woman decides that she will be defined by her beauty, then the shape and style of her body will greatly affect her self-esteem.

Whereas self-determination is a matter of getting oneself to the right place at the right time,[629] productive self-confidence starts with a decision to value domains of performance that fit within one's range of ability.[630] Of course, it is within the context of close relationships that a person decides which activities are most meaningful and praiseworthy.

As an example, a mother found herself struggling with an angry and unmotivated 14-year-old son who had a history of failing grades at school. In an effort to get him to take her seriously, she contacted the school administration and insisted they have him repeat eighth grade. During the fall

---

[628] As stated in Steele's (1988) self-affirmation theory, the main consideration in selecting an affirmational resource should be its positivity and centrality to the self.

[629] Because we do not have absolute control over the events that occur around us, self-determination often depends in great part on finding our way to environments that are responsive to our needs. In other words, a person who has been caught in the middle of a tornado will not have nearly as much opportunity for self-determination as the person who was able to avoid being in the wrong place at the wrong time.

[630] Accordingly, Pelham and Swann (1989) found that healthy individuals who consider themselves intelligent or attractive tend to value intelligence or attractiveness more so than people who consider themselves unintelligent or unattractive.

semester, I met with her son in private and watched him cry as he described the humiliation of being held back. Yet his mother remained absolutely unconvinced that he had any real concern for his grades. "He still refuses to study at home," she told me. "He lies about his grades, and he complains constantly about how unfair we are, insisting that we love his sister more than him. What I have tried to explain to him is that his sister is not being held back because she has straight *A*'s. His sister is not being grounded from playing with friends because she finishes her homework each evening, without having to be told to do it."

The father was also angry at his son because during their discussions the boy refused to place any value on academic achievement.[631] In response, the father told the boy that his problem was that he was lazy.

The mother recognized the counterproductive effect caused by the parental shaming, but did not feel that they had any other options. "When the kid will not do anything, it is hard to think of him as anything other than lazy!"

Although the mother was firmly entrenched in this negative conceptualization of her child, she did like to think of herself as a fair person. So I confronted her in a way that would allow her to demonstrate to me how much she valued fairness. With a stern gaze, I asked her, "Are you absolutely certain that you have treated your son fairly?"

She accepted my challenge. "If I have not been fair, then I would like to know what I should do differently."

So I started to build my argument. "Your son practices basketball three to four hours daily. He has been recognized as the team's most valuable player. Are you absolutely certain that it is fair to say that he does absolutely nothing?" I was using facts she had provided so there was little to argue against.

"Alright, I have to admit, he is a really great basketball player. But there is more to life than basketball!" she said.

Then I continued, "Your daughter is a happy child with really good self-esteem. Because she has such high self-esteem, she is self-motivated and does not engage in any self-sabotaging behavior." The mother agreed, so I finally made my point, "What would happen to your daughter's self-esteem if her parents treated basketball as the ultimate definition of success and personal value. What if you demanded that she step up to the free-throw line and make the same number of baskets as her brother and if she didn't she would be given the same harsh treatment as he has received?"

---

[631] This was most likely a defensive maneuver. Research has found that when targeted with negative stereotypes, individuals tend to devalue the dimensions on which they are faulted, presumably to render those stereotypes innocuous (Major et al., 1998).

At this point, the mother laughed at the image forming in her mind. "His sister could not make a successful shot [with the basketball] to save her life!"

To make certain I had made my point, I continued, "So do you understand? She is naturally good at academics. He is naturally good at athletics. If their genetics had been switched, it would be your daughter who would be struggling to believe in herself, and your son would have it made."

The mother let me know that she did understand. So I applauded her for her fairness and intellectual openness. I then got her to agree that as long as he brought home passing grades, she would stop making such a big deal about academics and instead emphasize the goodness of his athletic ability. Following this conversation, her son became much less depressed and less rebellious. The family learned that, for the sake of their son's self-esteem, basketball needed to be held in just as high a regard as his sister's academic accomplishments.[632] After this conversation, no further therapy was needed.

The application of this information to therapy challenges some aspects of conventional thought. Some clients may not benefit from an expanded view of self nearly as much as a more selective view focused on underutilized talents and abilities. In short, the therapist helps the client construct a value system that overlays existing talents and abilities. Under these conditions, the emphasis of therapy shifts from behavior modification to value elaboration. This shift begins with an inventory of existing strengths and behavioral assets: "Let's see if we can make some time for you to concentrate on the things you do well." I have had several clients respond to this statement in an almost stunned state: "Wow, I don't think I have ever stopped to think about what I might be good at! I spend all my time thinking about what I need to fix."

After existing strengths and behavioral assets have been assessed, the next step is to expand upon the value of a given behavior. One of the most brilliant examples of this strategy comes from Viktor Frankl (1996), who successfully convinced a grief-stricken widower that his capacity to survive his beloved wife was an extraordinarily high value behavior because it spared her from the misery he was now experiencing. The type of heroism offered by Frankl fit so perfectly with the man's existing value scheme that the man's self-concept was automatically enhanced and no further therapy was needed. My experience has been that when this strategy is used, not

---

[632] When confronted with a task, most individuals tend to focus selectively on a single dimension in which they posses some degree of skill, thereby creating the feeling of being above average (Constantino & Castonguay, 2003).

much follow-up is required due to the cycle of achievement that is created.[633] In other words, once the self-esteem begins to increase, a self-reinforcing cycle is set into play. (The better you feel about yourself after performing a high value behavior, the more likely you are to repeat that behavior, resulting in better feelings about the self.)

The Realization of Existing Capabilities Promotes Tangible Action Through Which Ideas About the Core Self Are Sustained

Most people can remember at least one instance when something that was said significantly altered their confidence and perhaps the course of their life. I can recall the day I came home from first grade to show my mother my "dinosaur book," which I had authored. Made from construction paper and crayon, it was my greatest achievement to date. My mother responded with encouragement that made me feel I was a capable writer. She then helped me create a second book on space travel, which we both illustrated.

Unfortunately, as I got older, my problems with dyslexia became more apparent and my writing assignments were returned with comments such as, "A for creativity, F for grammar and spelling." At first, I tried to defend myself, arguing that in most instances I had the right letters, just in the wrong order. However, after accumulating a number of low grades from a variety of teachers, I lost all confidence in my ability to pursue my dream as a writer. Then, during my last year of high school, an astute English teacher pulled me aside and asked why I was not trying in her class. I explained that it was difficult to put much effort into writing when I knew that I would never be any good at it. With a look of certainty she told me, "You can become highly skilled at whatever you want to do. And if you really want to become a writer, then that is what you will do!" Her confidence in me was so absolute that I experienced temporary shock. Like gum on a shoe, her words stuck in my head. Eventually, I decided to prove that she was right. My experience has been that it is much easier to fight against life's many discouragements when at least one other person is willing to state his or her belief in your ability. The result is an increase in self-efficacy.[634]

---

[633] Sustained achievement motivation is produced by action that is central to the personal identity, such that good self-feelings result from success in this domain, along with the perception that progress is possible (Steele, 1997).

[634] According to Bandura (1986) self-efficacy refers to "people's judgments of their capabilities to organize and execute courses of action required to attain designated types of performances" (p. 391). It has also been described as a person's estimate of his ability to succeed in the face of adversity.

Albert Bandura (1977)[635] argued that regardless of theoretical orienta-tion, all effective psychotherapies promote the client's sense of mastery while reducing maladaptive defensive functioning. Accordingly, he believed that the overarching objective in therapy should be to increase feelings of self-efficacy, which determines whether coping responses will be engaged, to what degree, and for how long.[636] Bandura (1986) used an impressive body of research to demonstrate that the will to commit to a highly de-manding undertaking is dependent in large part on a belief in one's capacity to mobilize the physical, intellectual, and emotional resources needed to succeed. By adding an appreciation for the importance of self-efficacy to the process of encouragement, a more nuanced view is created, allowing indi-viduals to recognize the difference between helping someone feel better about themselves versus positioning them for success.[637]

If the idea that clients just need to be told encouraging statements, such as "You can do it," seems too simplistic, that's because successful ef-forts to increase self-efficacy are more complex. For example, one level of needed encouragement might be to help a man value his role as a husband, while at another level he needs to be equipped with the skills needed to be a better husband.[638]

That having been said, I have spoken with numerous individuals who attribute major developments in their life to an encouraging remark made by the right person and the right time.[639] As one client, who had spent most of her life in abusive relationships, phrased it, "I really took care of myself [during the last couple of weeks] because of what you said. You told me that I have both the right and the ability to take care of myself."[640] When a

---

[635] The chief architect of social learning theory and the fifth most-frequently cited psycholo-gist of all time (Haggbloom, 2002).

[636] It has been argued that helping demoralized people regain a sense of self-efficacy is the noblest and most effective form of help because it prepares people to help themselves (Eden & Aviram, 1993).

[637] While self-esteem enhancement seems to affect broad indicators of wellness, such as de-pression, it is often unrelated to performance (Torrey et al., 2000).

[638] For example, avoidant adults may be unresponsive and controlling caregivers at least partly because they lack knowledge about how to support others, they lack empathy and communal orientation, and they fail to develop the deep sense of relationship closeness, commitment, and trust that appear to be critical for the motivation of deep sense of rela-tionship closeness, commitment, and trust that appear to be critical for the motivation of caregiving behavior (Feeney & Collins, 2001).

[639] Similarly, research studies have shown that the potential to succeed can be significantly increased using brief personal interviews in which subjects are credibly informed that they have high potential to succeed at the task before them (Eden & Ravid, 1982).

[640] Accordingly, it has been found that generalized self-efficacy mediates the relationship between social support and mental health (Cheung & Sun, 2000).

client is offered permission, from a respected authority, to believe in some ability residing inside the self, it is highly likely to be experienced as a memorable encounter.[641] These types of supportive statements often do not need to be repeated. As was the case with this client, changes in self-efficacy tend to be self-sustaining.[642]

The point to be appreciated here is that a sense of self-efficacy is dependent in large part on the perception that existing parts of the self are a vital and are sufficient resources for confronting life's immediate challenges.[643] It is the communication and acceptance of this idea that qualifies a relationship as being truly transformational.[644]

Provide Positive Labels for the Acknowledged Activities of Self

Using principles described in the first section of this book, we can now consider some of the more nuanced ways in which individuals' belief in their capabilities is subtlety influenced. To begin with, encouragement is more effectively communicated when emphasis is placed on the verification of existing ideas of personal ability, rather than emphasizing the need to change one's self-concept. It is particularly important to verify existing positive self-views when clients feel uncertain about those self-views.[645] This verification helps strengthen the idea so that it will last longer, hold up better when under attack, and have a greater impact on the client's judgments and future behavior.[646] So when the client hesitatingly says, "Sometimes I am able to be bold and say what I need to say," all that is required is verification: "Yes. You do have this ability. I noticed evidence of it from the first day I met you."

Even more strength is added if the behavior that is being referenced is labeled by the therapist as a pervasive character trait: "You really are a courageous person." If, after taking a bold action, people are told they are courageous, they will act more courageously in the future than someone who

---

[641] There is evidence that positive self-views tend to be the most subjectively important self-views (Pinel & Constantino, 2003).

[642] Similarly, research has shown that enhancements to self-efficacy increase the likelihood that positive changes will be maintained over time (O'Leary, 1985).

[643] As Bandura (1986) explains, self-efficacy "is concerned not with the skills one has but with judgments of what one can do with whatever skills one possesses" (p. 391).

[644] As demonstrated by social scientists, people tend to behave in a way consistent with their relationally defined self-perceptions (Berk & Anderson, 2000; Fazio, Effrein, & Falender, 1981).

[645] In this way, subjective certainty is increased (Pinel & Constantino, 2003).

[646] Research on attitude certainty has shown that attitudes about which we are certain have these characteristics because they are stronger than attitudes about which we are doubtful (Petty & Krosnick, 1995).

did not receive such a label.[647] The use of affirming labels both solidifies the positive identity and leads to greater generalization of desired behaviors.

Ironically, clinicians have an unfortunate reputation for assigning negative labels—such as *anal retentive, dysfunctional,* or *incongruent*—to individuals. The general public has come to expect and dread this behavior. This was made clear to me during an internship as a school psychologist. The district in which I worked had master's level diagnosticians who conducted the intelligence and achievement testing and doctoral level psychologists (and interns) who tested for emotional disorders while also providing educational counseling to those in need. During lunch breaks, I sought to sit among the teachers in order to build relationships. However, each time I would sit at a table, they would either eat quietly without comment or suddenly notice someone else they wished to greet and move to another table.

One day, after sitting at a table with several teachers, who shortly vacated it, I jokingly called out across the room to the diagnostician who was surrounded by company and insisted on knowing why no one would sit next to me. (She was a well-respected member of the staff whom I trusted would provide an interesting answer to the question.) Laughing, she explained, "No one wants to talk with you because you are a psychologist." Still not satisfied, I countered, "But you do psychological testing, and they still sit next to you." The diagnostician, who understood the self-consciousness of the younger teachers, explained, "The type of testing I do is not as threatening as what you do. They do not have to worry about me secretly analyzing them." As I learned, it takes time and effort to show others that, as a psychologist, you are not there to judge them or to assign negative labels.

Fortunately, some prominent members of the professional community have begun to argue the importance of assigning positive labels. For example, in trauma work, it is now more common to hear the client labeled as a *survivor* rather than *victim*.[648] The new terminology is important because it suggests the presence of strength rather than helplessness. The use of labels that carry more positive implications is not a technique that belongs to one type of therapy, but rather a principle that should be applied to all helping relationships.[649]

---

[647] This is because people tend to act in accord with the labels that have been placed on them (Dienstbier, Hillman, Lehnhoff, Hillman, & Valkenaare, 1975; Jeson & Moore, 1977; Toner, Moore, & Emmons, 1980).

[648] This particular recommendation was made by Herman (1992).

[649] In the study of relationships in general, it has been found that constructive relationships are characterized by a willingness to acknowledge others' positive qualities using statements that attribute positive behaviors to stable personality characteristics or to intentional causes (Crowell et al., 2002).

By contrast, unproductive distress is created by attributions that attach negative behaviors to the individual self. Examples of unhelpful labeling that occurs in therapy include "You failed to assert yourself with your boss because you are an anxious individual" or "You are responding with 'yes-but' statements to all of my advice because you are resistant." The problem with these statements is that they imply deep-rooted inadequacy. By contrast, a relationally oriented therapist actively seeks to make encouraging remarks, even if the client does not seem to be cooperating: "That was a very challenging statement you just made. You are insightful."

An interesting finding in the classic studies on learned helplessness is that failure is more damaging when it is attributed to a lack of self-agency.[650] But even more interesting is the fact that damage produced by learned helplessness can be reversed by merely affirming or verifying existing ideas of personal ability.[651] In other words, a willingness to acknowledge others' positive qualities can shield them from symptoms of depression associated with helplessness. The implications for therapy are very straightforward. Negative attributions tend to be harmful. Therefore, it is generally better to offer self-enhancing attributions while attributing negative behaviors to circumstantial or unintentional factors. For example, the same client behaviors that received negative labels could have contained positive attributions, such as, "You were just caught off guard yesterday. Next time you will know what to say to your boss. You tend to be a good learner" or "I like the way you are able to critically analyze the information I am sharing with you. You are an astute listener."

Foster Pride in Unique Attributes and Capacities

In order to initiate a course of action that has special significance, the person performing the task must have at least a partial belief that there is something special about him- or herself.[652] Thus, the development of a strong pride in unique personal attributes can produce long-lasting results.

As a humorous example, I can recall my experiences as a very young child when I had to receive an injection. The nurse informed me that I would need to receive the injection in the backside, which I protested due

---

[650] Abramson, Seligman, and Teasdale (1978) observed that more severe symptoms occurred when the experimental condition of uncontrollability was attributed to the self as opposed to outside circumstances.

[651] Researchers reversed the negative effects of experimentally induced helplessness by affirming a valued self-image, thus decreasing feelings of personal inadequacy (Liu & Steele, 1986).

[652] Those who perceive themselves as having unique talent enjoy not only higher self-esteem, but also an increased readiness to act (Campbell, 1986; Suls & Wan, 1987).

to the increased feeling of vulnerability that comes from having to drop your pants. As I recall, the nurse responded with a verifying comment, such as, "Well, to tell you the truth, I would rather not have to give you the shot in your bottom because looking at the size of your muscles I am a little concerned that you will bend my needle. However, the doctor says I have to give the medicine at that spot." After having the unique goodness of my buttocks affirmed, I was ready to receive my injection. Not only that, but I also recalled the seemingly casual comment during future childhood ordeals and decided if my body was uniquely suited to bend something as threatening as a needle, I was plenty able to handle other significant challenges.

Later, I used a potentially frightening situation to help my son develop a sense of pride in his own special attributes. At age two, my son leaned in toward a hot griddle and sizzled his arm on an inch-wide stretch of hot metal. Fortunately, my training in Ericksonian hypnosis had me well prepared for this type of crisis. After quickly applying ice to the wound, I commented that he was unbelievable, that almost any other child would be crying uncontrollably. I had moved so rapidly with the ice that he had not yet had time to decide how his arm felt. While he was deciding what to make of the situation, I suggested that the only possible reason for him not crying was that he must have figured out some way to turn off his pain. After he had sat for a few minutes, calmly and quietly, with ice on his arm, I indicated that we would soon remove the ice to see if he would be lucky enough to have a pirate scar. This was a verification of a future possibility. If he did develop a scar, I wanted him to feel good about it. As he eagerly looked, I suggested he would have a scar on his wrist, just as tough as any pirate ever had. I then showed him the scar on my wrists from when I was a boy. Throughout the ordeal, Trevor did not show any signs of fear or pain. Eight years later, you can see the scar on his wrist, but it has never bothered him nor does he shy away from making pancakes on a griddle.

Redefine Weaknesses as Useful Attributes

As a general rule, children love to hear parents describe the positive qualities that make them unique from others: "Only you have this special feature!" Similarly, adult clients respond well to the type of encouragement that communicates the idea that they are unique. Self-efficacy is greatly enhanced when clients start to think, "There is probably no other who can do this like me." Any attribute for which there is convincing evidence can be used.

For example, I recently commented on an elderly widow's ability to stand up to others with the ferocity of a tiger when an injustice has occurred. The stories she had just finished telling me were evidence of it. The comment, which was directed at her core self, helped her feel greater emotional strength as she dealt with the loss of a husband who had always helped her feel safe. The effect is even more profound when that unique attribute is connected to important accomplishments that have been achieved: "Because of you your willingness to confront that administrator, new policies have been put in place, and others are going to benefit because of it."

It is more powerful yet if the client's individual symptomatic behavior is used as the means by which the clinical problem is resolved. This is a matter of transforming fear and weakness into strength.

As an example, I met with an 89-year-old woman who was fearful that she was loosing her mind and even more fearful that her two adult children were in great danger from members of the extended family. Her husband accused her of being crazy when she insisted that certain members of the family were attempting to control her mind through hypnosis. Whenever she was around these individuals, she became exceedingly agitated and hysterical. Her behavior did not seem to be the result of brain deterioration, since it first appeared at age 55, when she got the idea that her supervisors at work were trying to make her accept a position of responsibility that she did not want to take. After thirty years, her beliefs about this event (i.e., that hypnosis had been used to control her mind) had remained consistent. Outside of this specific concern, none of her other thoughts seemed delusional or schizophrenic. What did seem apparent was that her fear and panic were following a pattern of avoidance that is common with pathological anxiety. Her daughter had attempted to take her to medical doctors and a psychologist, but my client had refused to return, complaining that the doctors were too young or not experienced enough. My client wanted help, but did not know how anyone other than an expert in hypnosis could help her. Thus, she found her way to my office.

I listened carefully to her story, which included details of how distressed her body felt when someone was seeking to "take over [her] mind using hypnosis." My first remark to the woman and her daughter was that although I am an expert in hypnosis, I would never use it without her permission. I also insisted that the hypnosis I would use with her would not create the same awful feelings in her body, and if it did, she would tell me so that we could bring her out of trance immediately. Then I asked for her permission to test her hypnotic susceptibility, which she readily agreed.

Reaching forward, I took her hand, which was already lifting toward mine, and placed it out in front of her in a catatonic pose. As she sat staring at her floating hand, I marveled over her amazing responsiveness to hypnosis and began to list all the ways this could help her should she ever need medical intervention, such as hypnotic pain relief or therapeutic help. I told her she had a gift that after today could no longer be used against her. I then gave the woman the post-hypnotic suggestion that she could no longer be hypnotized by family members or anyone other than a doctor or a therapist, such as myself, who had her best interests in mind. I added that even with someone such as myself, she would not go into a trance unless the timing and the setting suited her.

At that point, her eyes popped open. I suggested we test the post-hypnotic suggestion with her daughter's help. Both agreed, so I took out a large crystal that dangled from the end of a gold cord and taught both mother and daughter a simple susceptibility test that usually produces evidence of automatic movements. However, after several attempts, the daughter was unable to get her mother to respond to suggestions of automatic movement. As the "expert," I took over the task of suggestion to show how it would work. However, the client blocked my attempts as well. This seemed to verify her new immunity to hypnotic suggestion.

After her success had been validated, the client shared with me her intense desire to protect her son and daughter from hypnosis. With tears filling her eyes, she insisted, "I am not doing this for myself. It is my daughter and my son. I want to protect them from those who would use hypnosis against them!"

As a gentle probe, I commented, "Most of us are first exposed to hypnosis as children. There are a lot of childhood games that involve hypnosis." As I expected, the elderly woman began to tell me about her frightening experience as a small girl. Growing up in the Mexican countryside, during the 1930s, she had walked into the room where her mother was lying in bed, terribly ill. A healer trained in alternative medicine was chanting and holding his hands over her stomach. He was attempting to use hypnosis to heal her gallstones. My client said that she cried and begged for her mother to go to a doctor for surgery. However, her mother told her that this man would heal her with hypnosis and that she should leave the room. Unfortunately, the gallbladder later burst, and her mother died. So early in her life, hypnosis became strongly associated with loss of control and loss of life. It was no wonder that a common neurotic idea—"Others might make me do something I don't want to do"—acquired seemingly psychotic dimensions. She had come to my office exceedingly anxious over the idea that she was as susceptible to hypnosis as her mother, and she left feeling affirmed and proud of her status as a *good hypnotic subject* with *rare abilities*.

Following this one session, there were no further complaints from my client or her family.[653] In this case, the woman had identified herself as "weak" and unusually susceptible to hypnosis. That is why her responsiveness to therapeutic hypnosis was the perfect target for praise and encouragement. This praise extended her positive inner labeling to include behaviors that she had previously viewed as negative.

In some cases, behavior that has been framed as a failure (and attached to a negative identity) can be reframed as an act of courage or love, thereby transforming the attributional effect. For example, at the beginning of my private practice, I met with a 65-year-old woman who was exceedingly phobic of medical doctors. She knew that she had cancer, but would not go to meet with the oncologist because of severe panic attacks. She recalled that the panic attacks began at age five, when she would run through the house screaming, "I'm dying! I'm dying!" As an adult, her shaking, heart palpitations, dizziness, and sense that she was dying were so severe that even after taking double her prescribed Xanex, she still could not come closer than one city block of the doctor's office.

At the start of the session, she expressed her needs very clearly. "I am in today because I will not go to doctors, [and] I know why." She explained that during childhood, both of her parents had engaged in horrible acts of violence against her, and even worse, her mother routinely made her visit a pediatrician who sexually abused her on his examining table. In an emotionless voice, she gave some details. "He was trying to teach me 'sexual expertise.'" Although some might argue that these sort of childhood memories could be the product of fantasy, she exhibited clear evidence of emotional disturbance, the nature of which seemed indicative of extraordinary traumatization in childhood.

As an essentially nonfunctioning adult, she was absolutely dependent on psychiatric care. She described her current psychiatrist as a decent man. However, she complained that the medication he prescribed did not stop the panic attacks and only made her feel "more stressed out." As she put it, "I am absolutely supersensitive to medication." She had recently visited another psychologist who trained her in biofeedback, but it did not bring the relief she sought. Fortunately, with a strong determination to get better and a willingness to experiment with the use of role-play and imagery, fol-

---

[653] Two years later, I met with the woman and her son for a different problem. When I asked about the outcome following her first visit, both assured me that after that visit she had had no further difficulty enjoying her time with her family members. Her fear of hypnosis had vanished.

lowing the fourth visit to my office she was able to overcome the panic and receive urgently needed medical attention.

However, the more important therapy seemed to revolve around a completely different matter, which she revealed during the second visit with me. This woman had suffered so greatly as a child that the thought of her children suffering any abuse or neglect was absolutely unbearable. There was nothing she wanted more than to be a loving mother. Yet her opinion of herself as a mother was that she had been a miserable failure. Twenty years before, when her son got in a serious automobile accident that left him paraplegic, she found herself unable to go to him at the hospital. Because of her own emotional paralysis, she could not explain to her husband or friends why she could not visit her severely injured son. Even worse, a psychologist she was meeting with at the time commented that she was emotionally unavailable to her son. She interpreted the remark as a damning rebuke from an expert and thereafter bore tremendous shame.

Having finished her story, she told me that she was the most "cold-blooded" and "uncaring" mother that ever walked the planet. She clearly needed a different idea about herself, so I responded, emphatically, "That's impossible."

After some hesitation and nervous movement she asked, "What do you mean it's impossible?"

I explained, "If you were truly as cold-blooded and uncaring as you just said, then you would not still be so concerned about your failure to visit his hospital room, 20 years after the fact. You just would not show so much distress over the idea. You would instead feel perfectly at ease with your behavior." Giving her a few moments to take that in, I continued, "Without even asking, I bet I can predict that you made more than one secret attempt to get inside that hospital."

Stunned, the woman responded, "Yes. I went inside the back entrance of the hospital and got to the elevator, but could not go inside. How did you know?"

Warmly I replied, "Because that is what a loving and caring mother would do." I then asked her to contrast the amount of care she had given her paraplegic son during his rehabilitation with the actions of others who had been critical of her.

The psychological reorganization that took place was both immediate and profound. A lifetime of chronic depression and self-hatred suddenly gave way to an optimistic embracing of self. "You are right! If I had not loved him, I would not have worked so hard to help him learn to walk with those canes. After the hospital, he moved back into our home, and I worked night and day, helping him learn how to walk again and how to feed himself. I hardly got any help from his father, who had told me I was so awful for not visiting him in the hospital."

A week later, on her third visit, she expressed how much she appreciated me telling her that she was a compassionate mother. Following that session, she had gone home and told her husband that he did not have the right to tell her that she was not a good mother. She explained to me that this was really new behavior for her. "In the past, I would feel completely helpless and overwhelmed with feelings of guilt." The one thing she wanted more than any other was to feel that she had succeeded in being a good mother to her son. With a brief reframe, she was able to recognize her sacrifices and her accomplishments as a mother. And following this intervention, she became more capable in many other areas of her life.[654]

Provide Skills Needed for Meeting Immediate Challenges

Based on extensive research, Bandura (1977) observed that exposing clients to credible models who achieve success in relevant areas helps augment both the clients' performance and self-efficacy. I experienced similar outcomes early in my career when I took a position as a group counselor for men attending a domestic-violence program. The existing format was a closed group of 10 or 12 men who be exposed to psychoeducational programming for a period of 12 weeks. Although this was common practice at the time, I decided to switch the format to an open group that had psychoeducational components, but also a flexible structure such that each meeting was individualized to fit the men's immediate challenges at home. Then I added a trained "peer counselor"—someone who had successfully altered problematic behaviors and learned new ways of relating to his partner.

The modifications to the group format produced dramatic results. The amount of resistance in the group all but disappeared, and the rate at which the group members demonstrated new skills increased. The men seemed more motivated to use the new strategies. Outcome data collected from the men's female partners indicated an unparalleled level of success.[655] I believe these outcomes were due in large part to the amount of positive encourage-

---

[654] As argued by Bandura (1986), mastery experiences that augment domain-specific self-efficacy can have ripple effects that extend over numerous life domains: "once established, enhanced self-efficacy tends to generalize to other situations" (p. 399).

[655] The data was collected by a female volunteer who functioned as a woman's advocate and who made certain to call when the men were not at home to monitor the conversation. Therefore, the bias was more likely to be in a negative rather than positive direction. Still, the success rates (with a six-month follow up) were much higher than what was reported in the literature.

ment[656] that was used in combination with strong role models, role-playing how to handle difficult situations, and systematic self-monitoring.[657]

Failure alone is painful, but when combined with the destruction of trust in the person who encouraged you to act with confidence, the result is cancerous. That is why it is imperative for the care provider to make certain that a client is not set up for failure. Positive self-perceptions created within the therapy office should have some grounding in the outside world. In other words, clients should not be set up for failure by being persuaded that they possess capabilities that are, in fact, lacking. This is one of the principles that separates self-esteem building from efforts to increase self-efficacy.[658] It is here that the process of guidance and encouragement intermingle in such a way that the therapy is designed to instill behavior needed for success in meeting immediate challenges and to encourage the implementation of that behavior.

The words "You can do it" should not be uttered until there is some type of evidence that the client can, in fact, succeed. However, even with this level of care, there is still risk involved in simply describing how a situation might be handled. I have had the unhappy experience of looking into the hurt and angry eyes of a child who used a strategy I described to attempt to stand up to a bully. Unfortunately, she was mocked by the bully for the failed attempt to stand up for herself. All it takes is one such experience to destroy the therapeutic bond.[659] This is one of many reasons why it is important to encourage clients to trust their own judgment and use new skills only when they feel ready or when it is clear that a possible failure will not be overwhelming.

Because failure is a part of the learning process, my preference is to have failure occur under controlled circumstances, so that the self-esteem is still protected. When teaching clients new skills that are needed for meeting immediate challenges, I often ask them to practice the skills in my office. In this way, I can offer encouragement as clients discover that something that seemed simple when described verbally may still be outside of

---

[656] The program did not use harsh confrontation or intimidation tactics because that was not the type of behavior that I wanted to model for use at home.

[657] Similarly, research on general self-efficacy has shown that it can be increased using a combination of modeling, role-play, and verbal encouragement (Eden & Aviram, 1993).

[658] While high self-esteem individuals are more likely to show persistence in the face of failure (Di Paula & Campbell, 2002; McFarlin, Baumeister, & Blascovich, 1984; Shrauger & Rosenberg, 1970), interventions designed to enhance self-efficacy have been associated with performance changes in over a thousand studies (Bandura, 1997).

[659] Research has shown that ruptures in the therapeutic relationship with children are more difficult to repair than ruptures in therapeutic relationships with adults (DiGiuseppe, Linscotte, & Jilton, 1996).

their range of ability.

For those who struggle with panic attacks, it is exceedingly beneficial to induce intentionally mini panic attacks so that the steps for dealing with a panic attack can be practiced.[660] Two skills often needed by families with chronic conflict include how to keep situations from escalating and how reconcile offenses once they have occurred. For teaching purposes, each of these skills are broken down into three brief steps.[661]

After the steps are described, most clients respond by saying that they already sort of do this and will have no problem doing it at home. But when asked to practice the steps in a brief role-play, the clients often falter at the first step and completely forget the last two. The role-play not only provides important opportunities to practice the new skill, but it also serves as a form of assessment, allowing the therapist to better determine what tasks are likely to result in success or failure. Once the new skills are acquired and positive results are obtained, the client's self-concept will improve in ways that would not have been possible otherwise.

Take Time to Celebrate the Client's Accomplishments

When the client starts to experience success, it is important to elicit concrete details about how this success occurred and then celebrate the accomplishment. This review and celebration is not only useful for future problem solving,[662] but also provides needed validation. To recognize the importance of this dynamic, think of children who eagerly scan the audience to see if their parents have come to see their piano recital or soccer game. Most likely, there will be some despair on the faces of the children if they find that there is no special person to witness their successes. Even if victory is achieved, it is robbed of its joy.[663] The same is true for adults, who seek to have their most important achievements, such as marriages, births,

---

[660] Inducing mini panic attacks produces a paradoxical effect because intentional attempts to do something that is entirely unintentional results in an increased sense of control, making the entire experience much less terrifying. The three steps I then teach include muscle relaxation; slow, deep breathing; and a deep focus on relaxing images.

[661] For example, when reconciliation is sought, the three steps are: (1) name in concrete terms the behavior you are apologizing for, (2) ask, and wait, for forgiveness, and (3) ask how you can make things better.

[662] Often individuals are aware of a positive outcome, but they fail to recognize how they contributed to it. So in an attempt to generalize useful behavior, the therapist will help identify what the client did well and how this skill can be applied to other settings.

[663] When alone, people show only small signs of happiness in response to happy situations; however, when socially interacting with others, their expression of joy is greatly increased. Even 10-month-old children show this tendency (Kraut & Johnston, 1979; Jones et al., 1991).

and graduations, shared with friends and family. It is in the sharing of good news that we maximize our joy.[664]

This important interpersonal process further demonstrates why the support received from a live caregiver cannot be replaced by self-help books or computer programs.[665] Even more than validating the occurrence of success, a skillful care provider also communicates the value placed on the accomplishment and the approval associated with it. When people enter into therapy, they are likely to end up sharing a great deal of information about themselves and their problems. If, during this process, they find that their therapist is equally interested in their accomplishments, then a greater self-confidence and joy develops along with a stronger relationship.[666] As one client phrased it, "I am doing so much better now. I think I can trace it back to that session when you told me that I do not have rid myself of the shame of what happened in the past, but instead I can outweigh it with awareness of my achievements." This woman had experienced a traumatic childhood filled with episodes of physical and sexual violence. She had been in and out of therapy for the past 20 years and expressed absolute disdain for the inevitable conversations about her past. So during her therapy with me, we did not discuss the past. Instead, I focused on her many here-and-now accomplishments, such as making it to therapy even when she did not feel like coming, her gentle assertiveness in the grocery store, her effort to decrease her obesity by improving her diet, and her brave response to the loss of a pet. During this long-term therapy, we discussed thousands of success experiences in detail, thus helping her connect with "normal" society.[667] The appraisal and valuing of her achievements produced a sense of pride that eventually outweighed the terrible shame from her past.[668]

When therapists seek to utilize the client's achievements, there are several approaches that can be taken. The first is to help clients recall and elaborate on positive events from the past. Even during intake assessment,

---

[664] It has been demonstrated that sharing good news or celebrating achievements produces higher positive affect and greater life satisfaction (Gable, et al., 2004; Langston, 1994).

[665] People prefer achievements that are validated, recognized, and valued by other people over solitary achievements (Baumeister & Leary, 1995).

[666] Approval is a prerequisite for forming and maintaining social bonds (Baumeister & Leary, 1995).\Pride seems to engender engagement and a sense of connection with others (Gable et al., 2004).

[667] Pride seems to engender engagement and a sense of connection with others (Gable et al., 2004).

[668] Symbolically speaking, this intervention fit her established coping mechanisms. The woman maintained excessive weight, which she felt protected her. Rather than attempting to outweigh the problem with food, I helped her outweigh it with success experiences. Subsequently, she slowly began to lose weight and quit drinking, which further reinforced her experience of success rather than shame.

it is important to have clients share information about good events as well as bad. Sharing good events affects the client's immediate coping abilities, in addition to setting the emotional tone for future visits. When one recalls information from the past, there is a psychological and physiological re-experiencing that takes place. This not only impacts the client's immediate affective experience, but it also strengthens the memory for the event,[669] causing its influence to stretch out like tentacles into the future. In other words, focused recall and elaboration leads to a reliving of events and an increased expectation for reoccurrence.[670] When the therapist intermittently guides the client into a discussion about positive events or happy memories, the increased saliency of the positive memory provides a sort of buffer against future negative events. By contrast, if the therapist were to spend every session focusing exclusively on painful or traumatic memories, then the total effect may be more dehabilitating than helpful. Even in therapy, it is important to help individuals focus on past events that make them feel good. As I like to tell my clients, when people spend some time thinking about positive events for which they feel blessed or grateful, their overall sense of well-being will increase.[671]

The fact that a person in distress needs to address his or her negative experiences is a point that should not be misunderstood. The Pollyannaish approach of only thinking positive thoughts is not only impossible, but also reduces the individual's readiness to learn and deal effectively with future threats.

However, in the same way that harmful physical substances should be stored in safe containers, during therapy, it is necessary to shield newly emerging joy or optimism from the pain and devastation of the past. One method of "containing" toxic experiences is to build associational bridges that bypass the worst aspects of the event. This new path of awareness may start with the reality of a negative event, but it quickly leads out and away to a new sense of mastery and positive expectancies for future events. In other words, rather than leaving the client to dwell on negative outcomes form the past, there is an attempt to reframe his or her understanding of the event so that it starts to feel inspirational rather than catastrophic. This reorganization of conditioned responses is what distinguishes therapeutic

---

[669] The act of communicating memories may involve rehearsal and elaboration, both of which seem likely to prolong and enhance the experience by increasing its salience and accessibility in memory (Gable et al., 2004).

[670] Tversky and Kahneman (1974) described the "availability heuristic" showing that people's assessments of the likelihood of events were related to the ease or "fluency" (Jacoby & Dallas, 1981), with which they could generate examples of those events.

[671] It has been found that reflecting on life's blessings, even just once a week, significantly increases happiness (Emmons & McCullough, 2003; Lyubomirsky, et. al., 2005).

reenactments from repetition compulsion and self-perpetuating spirals.[672]

I stumbled onto this technique early in my career when speaking with a client who was learning about relationships. Recalling his behavior from the past, he became distressed over the realization of how verbally and emotionally abusive he had been toward his high school girlfriend. As he began to elaborate on the memory, he explained, "She was probably the first person to come into my life who really showed me kindness and love. Then all I did was criticize and make fun of her."

Rather than leaving him in this spot, I lead him down a path of increased insight by asking what he had learned from the experience. He replied that obviously it is wrong to be so critical. He lamented over how he wished he could have at least apologized for what he did. Then he added, "It is too late to do anything about it now. I do not even know where she lives."

I then asked him to think more carefully about the lesson he learned from this relationship[673] and to think about the implications for his immediate circumstances. "Is there any way this learning might help you here and now?"

With a look of surprise and confusion, he slowly released his words. "Ohhhhh, you mean my wife that I am married to. I should apologize to her for how critical I have been?" Now that his negative memory served a function, it was possible to move to an achievement orientation. I said, "It is too late to apologize to your high school girlfriend, but it is not too late for your wife. She seems to be very hopeful for what you will achieve in therapy."

Healthy self-awareness includes reflection on distressing experiences, but in a way that reduces the spread of negative affect. The type of positive reframe illustrated here is based on the idea that mistakes are necessary for discovery and growth. When people are willing to both reflect on past mistakes and recognize accomplishments, then there is increased appreciation for their own strengths and weaknesses—something that is needed for decision making, self-governance, and the experience of mastery.[674]

A second way of uncovering the client's past achievements is to seek out evidence of small accomplishments. For instance, after listening to a woman criticize herself for having stayed in an abusive relationship for

---

[672] Accordingly, the reframing of distressing events in a positive light has been shown to increase long-term happiness (Lyubomirsky, et. al., 2005).

[673] Relationship-interaction events tend to be better remembered than other kinds of events (Berscheid, 1994).

[674] The client's experience of mastery in this case example was relational (to experience a positive connection with others for the first time), though in other instances, it may be visceral (to do something vital with they body that one has not been able to do before) or cognitive (to develop vital thoughts one has not allowed oneself to believe before).

many years, I might ask, "How did it eventually end?" A common response is, "Finally, I couldn't take it any more, so I left." This is something that can be treated as an accomplishment. "So you were able to get yourself out of an unhealthy situation. That is a fairly important accomplishment." If the client insists that it is not a very impressive accomplishment because it took her so long to get out, a positive focus is maintained without negating her perspective. "It may be just a small accomplishment, but if we get enough small accomplishments occurring at the same time, then they can lead to big life changes."

If individuals have a generally negative view of themselves, it will be difficult for them to associate large accomplishments with the self. However, accomplishments that are openly acknowledged as being small are sometimes more palatable. Because people often do not recognize gradual progress, it is helpful to watch for the smallest steps in the right direction. Rather than comparing clients to others, it is helpful to focus attention on where they were a year ago, or even last week, making certain to convey the message that every movement in the right direction is important.

A third method of counterbalancing negative experiences is to encourage clients to give full expression to any positive feelings they have located. It is not enough to reflect passively upon positive experiences from the past. In order to receive full benefit, the client will need to find words to describe the experience.[675] If a client is having difficulty identifying positive experiences from childhood, then more time needs to be spent exploring the adult personality of the individual. For some individuals, this domain of experiencing will be more accessible. After the caregiver discovers what activities the client enjoys most, duties that he or she performs at work, or private experiences that he or she does not expect others to understand, then these can be validated and studied until positive experiences begin to emerge. When offered this type of social support, clients will not only begin to feel better, but are also likely to experience improvements in health.[676]

The fourth and perhaps most important variable in this equation is the response of the care provider when positive experiences are communicated. When the client is recognizing the existence of personal achievement or personal joy, then the therapist should respond in a positive and energetic

---

[675] Labott, Ahleman, Wolever, and Martin (1990) found that when participants watched a happy video, their immune system showed increased activity, but only when they had been instructed to express their emotions.

[676] Positive cognitions and emotions have been found to reduce psychological despair (Thoits, 1983), result in greater motivation to care for oneself (e.g., Cohen, 1988), and result in suppressed neuroendocrine response and enhanced immune function (Cohen, 1988; Uchino et al., 1996).

manner. Individuals are more likely to feel understood, validated, and cared for when declaring positive, rather than negative, events to a responsive listener, making this activity important to relationship growth.[677] By contrast, if the therapist were to respond to the sharing of good news by pointing out the downside of a positive event or by minimizing its importance, then the response is likely to dampen or even reverse the positive affect produced by the good fortune, thus decreasing the client's desire to self-disclose.[678] So whenever a client is in a position to share good news, it is important for care providers to physically demonstrate their pleasure with a smile, a change in posture, a handshake, or, under certain circumstances, a hug. Rather than being a mechanism of avoidance, the celebration of positive events demonstrates that the therapist is not interested in focusing all of his or her energy on finding something wrong in the client's life.

Pressure to Perform Should Be Kept to a Minimum

This brings us to another important point—fear of failure. It is a powerful force that can produce seemingly irrational behavior and ironic results.

As a personal example, during my first year in high school, I tried out for the varsity tennis team and made it. However, the chances that I could make a significant contribution to the team were slim, since I had only started playing tennis in middle school and had minimal outside training. Most of the others on the team had been receiving private lessons since they were five or six years old. However, in the first statewide tournament of the year, I surprised everyone with some early wins. Then I went into a match against one of the better players from my own team. In my mind, he was unbeatable. So after defeating him four games in a row, I lost the next six. If I had reached five, I would have known that I could, in fact, beat him. However, just before reaching that point, something switched inside of me. I did not allow myself to win the set. Then in the second set, I came on strong and beat him again four games in a row. The wins were decisive. My serve was so powerful that many times he could not put his racket on the ball. However, having again hit some sort of psychological barrier, I lost the next six games in a row and thus lost the match.

---

[677] Researchers found that people with partners who tended to be energetically supportive of their achievements reported the highest level of relationship satisfaction, and positive-event support better predicted relationship satisfaction than did negative-event compassion (Gable et al, 2006).

[678] Accordingly, due to the affective rewards associated with positive-outcome disclosure to a responsive listener, the benefits of capitalization are likely to result in greater intimacy (Gable, et al., 2004).

Even though I had lost, many of the spectators came up to congratulate me. The long and hard-fought match had attracted a crowd. The coach had also been watching. Surprised by my performance, he expressed strong optimism for my future. However, after that day, I put my tennis racket away and never played again. I skipped out on tennis class for the rest of the semester. Although I received an *F* for the class and was kicked off the team, it was still better in my mind than risking the loss of what I had accomplished on that day. It was one of the few moments during a painful childhood that I had felt like a winner. This new and fragile sense of self was something that needed to be stored away in a place were it could not be challenged.[679]

The important point that should be taken from this illustration is that, for certain individuals, pressure to succeed should be kept to a minimum, especially during pivotal moments. The fact that achievement is sometimes sacrificed for the sake of self-esteem protection needs to be considered by any professional seeking to help clients achieve major life changes. If it seems that a given client is not adequately engaged in the therapy process, the natural tendency is to demand more involvement. However, when excessive demands are placed on a client who is experiencing a fear of failure, the probable outcome is withdrawal from therapy.

The behavior illustrated in my tennis story has been studied by researchers under the terminology of self-handicapping. While still a teenager, I joked about the behavior during a discussion of test-taking strategies with my best friend. In order to receive a passing grade in chemistry, he needed to score a grade of 75 or higher on the final exam. Up to that point, his exam scores had been much lower. His plan was to avoid studying for the exam. He seemed strangely confident in his strategy, so I asked him why he thought it was better not to prepare for the test. His explanation was simple and (in an adolescent way) made perfect sense. "If I put tons of effort into studying for this thing and fail anyway, then I have to consider myself an absolute failure. And if I study just a little and barely miss the mark, then I will be furious with myself for not having studied enough. But if I do not study at all and somehow luck out and get the grade I need, then I will know that I am a total bad-ass (i.e., a person who has achieved amazing success)!" Accordingly, researchers have found that self-handicapping does, in fact, protect low self-efficacy individuals from the experience of failure.[680]

---

[679] As has been demonstrated in research, an overarching need to protect the self-concept can result in absolute performance avoidance (Strube & Roemmle, 1985).

[680] In other words, by self-handicapping in this way, individuals have an excuse to help lessen the sense of failure. On the off chance that they do succeed, they will look even better for having succeeded despite the odds being against them (Baumgardner, Lake, & Arkin, 1985).

Because self-handicapping can be better managed once attention is drawn to it, I will sometimes explain the concept of self-esteem protection to clients who are at risk for self-handicapping.[681] In one such case, I described research in which the subjects who were fearful of failure choose to take a pill that would increase the probability of failure, rather than selecting the "success" pill.[682] The client I was speaking to had been placed on probation at work for alcohol-related problems. After listening to my mini lecture on social psychology, the client responded by defiantly asking, "What does this have to do with me? What is the failure pill that I am taking?" After a brief pause (to add effect), I replied, "It is alcohol." He immediately sank back into his chair and became momentarily lost in his thoughts. Then he responded, "You are right. I never thought of it that way. I did not think I had a choice, but maybe that is not true."

Within the context of therapy, a stalemate is likely to develop between the client and therapist if the latter misunderstands or discounts the function of these self-protective behaviors. When the therapist is able to recognize and take into account the client's self-esteem needs, then a path toward progress is more easily negotiated.

First, it is important to recognize that the reason for self-handicapping will vary depending on the self-esteem level of the client. When the client has high explicit self-esteem, then the handicapping behaviors are often intended to enhance the client's successes. For example, a client might boast, "No offense, but I have my own way of handling my anger and do not really need outside advice." The result is that the client shuts off outside resources while continuing to struggle with self-regulation. By contrast, individuals with low self-esteem tend to use self-handicapping to protect themselves from the threat of failure, which would be all the more devastating should they put great effort into a task and fail anyway.[683] A client might explain, "There is no point in me doing things differently. Nothing is going to improve her opinion of me." These individuals can seem unwilling to give therapy a chance to succeed. Low self-esteem clients might withhold important information from their therapists, knowing the therapy will fail, but still retaining the feeling that there is potential for future success. As one adolescent recently confessed to me, "I am not ready to tell you all

---

[681] Accordingly, researchers have found that people who are certain of their self-esteem, whether it is high or low, are less likely to self-handicap (Harris & Snyder, 1986).

[682] In the classic test of self-handicapping, researchers offered participants a "performance-enhancing" or "performance-debilitating" drug. As predicted, participants who expected to fail were more likely to choose the drug that would clinch their failure (Berglas & Jones, 1978).

[683] Thus, different people use the same (self-handicapping) strategy for different reasons (Baumeister, Tice, & Hutton, 1989; Tice, 1991).

that you need to know in order to help me, but maybe later." When I asked how much later, she casually responded, "Three to four years."

The point to be recognized is that therapists capable of meeting the client's self-esteem needs will not elicit as much defensive maneuvering from the client as they might if they aren't capable of meeting the client's needs. In other words, the critical task that the client is struggling to achieve (i.e., certainty of the core self) is made easier when the therapist is protective of the client's ego. If, as a teenager, I could have had a therapist convince me that my self-concept could remain high regardless of the outcome of the tennis tournament, and that I could possibly be surprised by yet unrecognized potential, I probably would have won the tennis match 6–0, 6–0.

Interestingly, I did have this sort of encouragement at the very start of my professional career. After getting a job in the field of domestic violence, I went to a more seasoned therapist, Betty Alice Erickson, for consultation. Looking back, I assume that she could sense some of my anxiety about being able to handle my new responsibilities. Her comment to me was, "You know, it is not going to be possible to help every client that comes your way. In our profession, you win some and you lose some. But I know that *you* have a lot of ability and that you will win far more than you lose. So you do not need to worry about those few occasions when the person just will not allow you to help him." This comment stuck in my mind and helped me feel better equipped to face the possibility of failure.

Of all the different ways in which a person can self-handicap, self-defamation is one that has great relevance to therapy. Self-defamation is the practice of presenting oneself to others in an excessively critical manner, constantly belittling and discounting the self, or using excessive modesty. While it may seem difficult to recognize the advantage created by self-defamation, it can serve some important self-esteem needs. If the therapist is too quick to rush in with a technique to correct the self-critical behavior (i.e., prescribing new, more positive self-talk), damage might be done to the client's sense of self. Statements by the client that sound self-defeating, such as, "I'm sure I am wrong for thinking this, but . . ." or "I just hate myself for the things I do," may be intended to protect the client from critical remarks that he or she automatically expects from others. If the therapist responds to this behavior by correcting the client (e.g., telling her that her thinking should not be so self-critical), then the client's fears of failure are realized on an even grander scale. Now it is not just a single comment that she failed to state correctly, but instead the entirety of her thinking processes are faulty! This is not to say that care providers would intend for their comments to be interpreted that way; however, people often hear what they are prepared to hear without stopping to consider what others might have wished to communicate.

As an extension of this type of self-handicapping, the client might strategically fail to perform what seems like a simple task. Using the example from above, the client who has been instructed to use more positive self-talk might get the prescribed statements mixed up or absentmindedly forget what words she is supposed to use. Or a new client may even fail to remember why he came to see a therapist. These strategic failures are intended to lower the therapist's expectations and, hopefully, eliminate the pressure on the client to perform.[684] Whenever self-defamation or strategic failure does occur, the therapist should remember the importance of verification both for the relationship and the client's sense of self. This means taking people at their word when they declare their shortcomings.

Disidentification is another means of self-handicapping that should be recognized by the therapist. In these cases, clients protect themselves from failure by disavowing any interest in success. Examples of disidentification include the husband in marriage counseling who declares he has no real interest in saving the marriage, or the teenager who responds to poor academic achievement by expressing a lack of concern over her grades. Whenever the threat of failure in a given situation becomes chronic, it can result in a reconceptualization of the self so that one's values shift away from the area of failure. As Steele (1997) pointed out, disidentification offers the retreat of not caring about something that might otherwise damage the sense of self; however, it can also undermine motivation to succeed. When disidentification occurs with clients, it is helpful to reconceptualize the task as being less self-relevant or inconsequential. In the case of marriage counseling, such a statement might be, "Whether or not your wife chooses to stay married to you is not really the major issue. Right or wrong, she is going to do what she thinks is right for her. What you need to focus on is the question of how you are going to feel good about yourself. If you try to do the right thing then regardless of the outcome, you will still have good reason to believe in yourself." Although it seems somewhat paradoxical to convince clients that a task does not matter so much in order to motivate them to apply more effort, this action will help increase the clients' interest in success.[685]

Another important self-handicapping behavior to understand is rationalization. While rationalization can help protect individuals from re-

---

[684] When a person fails rudimentary tasks, the natural consequence is a curtailing of performance demands (Baumgardner & Brownlee, 1987).

[685] Accordingly, research has shown that characterizing a task as unimportant or less self-relevant, versus highly consequential, will decrease the probability that self-handicapping will occur (DeGree & Snyder, 1985; Pyszczynski & Greenberg, 1983; Shepperd & Arkin, 1989).

gret, it can also have the unfortunate effect of decreasing learning. While regret threatens the self-esteem by causing people to question the goodness of their decisions, rationalization provides reassurance by justifying one's actions.[686] What this means for therapy is that the care provider should stand ready to defend the self-esteem of the client when mistakes are evident. Just as importantly, therapists should avoid the use of critical feedback when rationalization is used as a protective measure.[687] My experience has been that clients are aware, on a gut level, when they use rationalization to cover their mistakes, and they can sense when the therapist knows a mistake has been made. If clients are treated with kindness and care for their self-esteem, they will respond with gratitude and increased readiness to cooperate with future therapeutic requests. As I heard one experienced therapist say, "You always allow the client to save face."

The last self-handicapping behavior mentioned here is risk avoidance. If therapy is viewed as a change process, and change requires risk acceptance, then factors that compound risk avoidance should be well understood by those practicing in the field. Turning again to social psychology, researchers have found that under conditions in which the outcome of making a risky decision can result in threat to self-esteem, individuals low in self-esteem take fewer risks than individuals high in self-esteem.[688] In other words, such individuals will not be open to new experiences if they do not trust their ability to succeed. There must be some expectation that good things can come from one's self before the courage is found to strive for achievement.

This is the type of situation in which proper support from the therapist is of paramount importance. When therapists seek to motivate clients to attempt a change in behavior, they need to pay careful attention to the risks client are being asked to take. One useful strategy is to reduce the pressure to succeed with qualifying statements, such as, "You do not need to succeed at this task perfectly. Just the fact that you are willing to give it a try is enough." Often, I reassure low self-esteem clients with remarks such as, "It is not necessary for you to make a really big breakthrough in your therapy today. The fact that you got yourself here for the appointment is

---

[686] Accordingly, researchers have found that when people are protected from regret by being reminded of something good about themselves, they respond with less rationalization than those unprotected from regret (Sugden, 1985; Steele, 1988).

[687] For those with high self-esteem, this is not as much of an issue, since individuals with high self-esteem use less rationalization than those with low self-esteem (Insko & Gilmore, 1984).

[688] These researchers conclude that for those who are low in self-esteem, the anticipation of regret and the desire to maintain self-esteem underlies their risk aversion (Josephs et al., 1991).

good therapy in and of itself."[689] These clients tend to breathe a sigh of relief when told they do not have to accomplish major insights or a stunning breakthrough. If this permission is not given, they might leave the session apologizing for not having done enough.

By contrast, high self-esteem clients might respond with disappointment or even feel offended if the therapist were to make such a statement. For high self-esteem clients, it is more helpful to comment, "Not many have the courage to examine their lives and make these types of changes. And today you seem to have accomplished three weeks' worth of therapy all in one session!" As mentioned earlier, this type of statement enhances the value of the successes by increasing the clients' sense of joy and their readiness to take on further risks.

Having said all of this, I know from my experience that despite one's skill in dealing with resistance, it is practically impossible to help clients who insist on *absolute* security. Such individuals doggedly cling to illusory security, refusing to budge from rigid behaviors and inflexible values used to define themselves. What comes to mind is the adage "You can lead a horse to water, but you cannot make him drink." However, for those who are willing, the path toward greater self-esteem begins with encouragement to take small risks.

Regardless of the type of therapy, the client must agree to explore new thoughts, new behaviors, or new interactions with others, or at least new possibilities, all of which come with some degree risk. The importance of this first step is seen in individuals who suddenly begin to seek out greater challenges in their life after having come for a single session of therapy, or after having shared some piece of information they never before dared tell anyone. These are examples of small risks that lead to increased confidence.[690] Rather than seeking to convince my clients that therapy is a risk-free endeavor, I instead inform them of the most probable risks, and I promise to help them avoid unnecessary failure experiences. In addition to the ethics of informed consent, there are other reasons why the challenges of therapy should not be minimized. The greater the risk, the greater the satisfaction that will be produced when there is evidence of success.[691]

---

[689] These are the type of clients who respond to my post-session evaluation question, "What was most difficult about therapy today?" with the response, "Just getting here."

[690] The act of risk taking alone has been shown to increase self-confidence, increase one's sense of power over circumstances, increase one's ability to manage anxiety, and to improve one's decision-making capability (Ilardo, 1992; Neihart, 1999).

[691] In other words, when the probability of success is high, its attainment provides very little satisfaction, but when the probability of success is low, people feel a great deal of satisfaction from having the skill to overcome the odds and achieve success (Atkinson, 1983).

Improvements in Self-Concept Can Be Focused on Different Levels of Self

As has been argued throughout this chapter, it is important to have a positive self-concept.[692] Given the collective consensus that a positive attitude toward one's self is linked to general well-being, as well as dynamics that influence achievement in response to therapy, there should be some consideration of what is included in "self."[693]

Long ago, William James (1890) observed that "in its widest possible sense . . . a man's Me is the sum total of all that he can call his, not only his body and his psychic powers, but his clothes and his house, his wife and children, his ancestors and friends, his reputation and works, his lands and horses, and yacht and bank-account" (p. 291).[694] However, even within the same culture, the emphasis may sometimes shift between different levels of self.

Recognizing the fluidity of self, Sedikides and Brewer (2001) provide a conceptual framework, outlining three levels: the individual self, the relational self, and the collective self. The individual self is defined by personal characteristics, such as traits and beliefs, that make a person unique or set him or her apart from others as he or she works toward the achievement of personal goals. This self can be characterized as "I versus thou." The relational self involves connection in the form of interdependent, support-oriented relationships with specific others. This self is often characterized as "family." Finally, the collective self derives from membership with larger social networks in which the goals and needs of the group are considered primary. This self can be characterized as "us versus them."[695]

So within the context of therapy, there are many different forms of self that the relationship may benefit. Regardless of which level of self is being addressed, it must always be remembered that what the therapist comes to know about clients is not as important as what the clients learn about themselves. Within the context of a transformational relationship, clients are equipped with new, more positive understandings of themselves and their situation. This strategic outcome is a key characteristic that defines this type of helping relationship.

---

[692] Research has shown that a positive self-concept is strongly associated with happiness and satisfaction with life (Baumeister, Campbell, Krueger, & Vohs, 2003).

[693] According to Stein and Marcus (1994), "self" is a key psychological structure and a core determinant of emotional well-being.

[694] James's (1890) two-volume work was the first college textbook on the subject of psychology.

[695] In this model, each successive conceptualization of the self represents a greater level of inclusiveness (Brewer & Gardner, 1996; Markus & Kitayama, 1991; Sedikides & Brewer, 2001).

Attitudes About the Body Are Closely Tied Attitudes About the Individual Self

It should be apparent that the physical body is an important identity marker—one that starts at the level of the individual self. For those who are uncertain of what to think about the self, a focused conversation on the goodness of their physical body can produce surprising results. This is especially important for children, as they develop attitudes that will define them for a lifetime.

For example, an adult client (who had married a woman who really did not like him and who constantly pushed himself to do more than he was actually capable) one day came to the realization that he carried tremendous shame. When asked to trace the feelings of shame back to their point of origin, he recalled being mocked by his first-grade teacher. He had been asked to draw a picture of his body, and while passing by his desk, the teacher commented, "That looks like a monster." Even as a grown adult, he was still defensive, explaining to me that he had to use yellow to color in his figure's face because he did not have as many crayons as the other children. He also happened to be shorter than the other boys in the classroom, which only added to his feelings of inferiority.

Using a simple imagery exercise, I asked him to imagine me standing next to him in the classroom. Then I commented on the picture in positive ways, discussing how he had made good use of the colors available to him. I commented that it looked like a good strong body that contained secret potential, which the teacher and other students would not be able to see. I then invited him to develop new ideas about his own worth and the goodness of his future.

After this exercise, the man opened his eyes and sat motionless for some time. Then he commented, "That was good—really good." Following that session, he was better able to assert his needs and to consider himself worthy of opportunities that had previously been ignored. Because this drawing was a symbolic representation of his self, the way in which the picture was evaluated by those in authority strongly influenced his past and immediate self-concept.

Because attitudes about the body are closely tied to the individual self, others' willingness to affirm the goodness of the body can serve as a vital experience. When attempting to do this in therapy, it is important to direct positive comments at the care of the physical body—comments appropriate for a therapist to make to a client—rather than commenting on the sexual attractiveness of the body, which is better left to those with romantic ambitions. Thus, an attempt is made to emphasize the goodness of the client's anatomical and biological systems in such a way that the client becomes deeply interested in the goodness of this vital resource.

For those who have not learned to care for their body, proper encouragement might also require some counseling on sleep, nutrition, exercise, and boundaries that help protect one from sexual exploitation. The discussion might include exploration of different ways of getting exercise and determining what activity the client would most enjoy, or perhaps recommending a class in self-defense. If the client is persuaded to engage in these activities, then the client's increased care of the body will start to serve as evidence of his or her importance and worth.

Of course, the way in which other people treat one's body will also have a powerful influence on the overall self-concept. Sex, in particular, can serve as a self-defining experience. Positive boosts to the self-concept often occur within the context of a new romance. Perhaps this is part of the reason why falling in love is such a cherished experience within our society. Many clients have reported tremendous gains in their sense of personal value after developing a sexual relationship with someone who adored their body. As one client explained, "I just needed someone to validate the goodness of my body as I laid there fully naked."

The opportunity to come in and speak with a therapist about the new, more positive view of self following a positive sexual encounter can be affirming, while also creating some tricky dynamics. In the case of the woman mentioned above, she sought additional validation by flirtatiously asking, "What do you think? Am I sexy and gorgeous?" In an attempt to clarify the boundaries governing the therapeutic relationship, I replied, "I will leave it to your lover to give you feedback on that area of your life. My job is to pay attention to your mind and your emotional well-being. And I am very pleased to see that your overall feelings about yourself have improved."[696] Because lovers sometimes abandon those they once adored, it is essential that therapy offer the client new ideas about the goodness of the general self that have greater permanence than the fickleness of modern romance.

---

[696] While therapists and clients are discussing the psychological contingencies associated with the client's sexual experiences, it is important that the therapist create an environment that puts more emphasis on privacy than voyeurism. Just as in medicine, the ethical therapist does not request to be exposed to any more information than is necessary for the task at hand.

Encourage Clients to Feel Good About Symbols of the Self

As demonstrated in the case with the man who had his drawing from childhood affirmed in therapy, when negative attitudes toward the body do not yield to immediate forms of encouragement, then the focus of attention can be shifted toward symbolic or material identity markers outside the body. This may seem like a more superficial approach; however, it provides a useful alternative to no progress at all.

In fact, some material identity markers, such as a person's name, carry great emotional meaning. Where one's name is written and how it is used can impact one's sense of importance and value. That is why so many hospitals and university buildings bear the names of those who provided the endowment. Within the context of psychological care, clients certainly derive some sense of importance from having their name remembered. In more than one instance, I have listened to clients complain bitterly because the referring physician did not remember their name while discussing their medical status. The manner in which a care provider speaks the client's name can have either an encouraging or discouraging effect. For instance, does the tone of voice suggest that this is an important name? Does the care provider smile when speaking the client's name? Attention to the details of how a person is received or the manner in which discussions begin set the emotional tone for all the communication that follows.

Similarly, items such as trophies and medals, report cards, a wedding ring, or a house can be used to mark the psychological territory in which the self resides. This sense of self can be both coherent and stable as long as the identity marker is not lost or destroyed.[697] So in therapy, when speaking to someone who uses a wedding ring to define the self, it can be very helpful to admire the ring or to comment on its beauty. While still in training as a counselor intern, I conducted an interview with a woman who had left her marriage because of domestic violence. She was in the process of filing for divorce, but still wore her wedding ring. She told me that her mother had criticized her, telling her to stop wearing the ring. After sharing this, she stared down at her ring with a look of shame. She then asked if it was wrong of her to want to wear her ring.

My comment was that it was a beautiful ring that belonged to her so she could do as she pleased. The cumulative effect of numerous small comments such as this can be highly beneficial.[698] After hearing this, she looked

---

[697] The loss of such significant items as a wedding ring or baby pictures can be emotionally devastating in large part because a valued part of the self is gone (Burris & Rempel, 2004).

[698] Accordingly, research has shown that affirmation of the client is closely related to successful outcomes (Orlinsky, Grave & Parks, 1994).

less distressed and did not stare down as she had before. In this case, even as she sought to separate her identity from the person she had married, some of her sense of self (including her dreams for the future) was still tied up in the ring.

In another case, while I was working with a person who defined himself in great part as an artist, an emotional crisis occurred after a business decided to paint over the mural he had created in their lobby. He was especially wounded by the act because the mural contained images he considered to be a unique expression of self. After working through some of the murderous rage he felt toward the building's management, we developed a plan for how he might resurrect this part of himself in another form and in a new location. He responded well to this approach, and we were able to circumvent a depressive episode, which historically had proven to be violent and intense. A major part of his therapy was recognition from someone else of the importance of his sense of self and the worthiness of his effort to reconstruct it.

Encourage Clients to Make Positive Self-comparisons to Others

Another important factor to recognize about the individual self is that comparison to others will have a significant bearing on the self-concept. One way people discover who they are is by noticing how similar or different they are from those around them. People who have learned to focus their attention on those with a greater supply of positive attributes, such as beauty or intelligence, will always feel that they are lacking.[699] By contrast, those who have learned how to find and make favorable comparisons are more likely to feel good about their own identity.[700] Of course, while working with individuals who have a poor self-concept, it is more common to hear clients make unfavorable social comparisons. Therefore, the care provider should be prepared to disrupt this tendency with occasional positive comparisons. For example, "I am really surprised by how much we have been able to cover today! For most clients, this would be three or four sessions worth of work."[701] If the client responds with blushing and an embar-

---

[699] Research indicates that unfavorable social comparisons negatively impact self-esteem (Gruder, 1977; Tesser, 1988; Wills, 1981).

[700] In one study, those who compared themselves to people who are worse off more readily endorsed the idea that they are, in fact, above average (Wood, Taylor, & Lichtman, 1985). In another study, when women who were seeking support for cancer were asked how well they were coping compared with other cancer patients, 93% indicated that they were coping better than others (Taylor et al., 1986).

[701] For reasons of integrity, the details or content of the comparison should be true and spoken with absolute sincerity.

rassed smile, then it can be assumed that this seemingly casual remark had a meaningful impact.

Another problematic type of social comparison that seems to perpetuate feelings of inferiority is when the depressed clients compare themselves to others who seem to have more difficult circumstances and then feel guilty that they are not feeling good about their own lives. As one client explained, "Dr. Short, I feel so terrible when I think of this other person who is dying of cancer or about to become divorced. And then I realize I have absolutely no excuse for feeling as bad as I do. It makes me feel so guilty, and then I just end up beating myself up all day long."

Under these circumstances problems of depression are compounded with feelings of guilt. Ironically, moral-minded clients start to feel increasingly inferior as they learn of others' misfortune. My response has been to reframe the experience of sadness so that it serves as proof of the client's moral goodness: "Because you are an empathetic and caring person, it only makes sense that you will feel sad whenever you hear that something bad has happened to someone else. It is painful for people such as you and me to learn of other people's misery. However, this can be a little confusing, because your experience of sadness may be followed by a brief moment of gratitude that you are not having to suffer in the same way as this other individual. Both of these are appropriate emotional responses. And it is also appropriate that they are only momentary experiences. You do not need to feel bad forever because someone suffered an unfortunate event, and similarly, you do not need to feel perpetually grateful because it did not happen to you." Paradoxically, the general message is that clients have a right to feel good about themselves as a person, even when they are depressed.

My experience has been that, after providing permission for a reevaluation of the self, clients slowly learn to make social comparisons that are less incriminating. Even humorous remarks can have important implications for the sense of self. For example, the comment, "Well, I am certain that you have some clients who are crazier than I am," is one that should be affirmed and perhaps even elaborated on. "You are right about that. And, I might add, that none of my other clients are as quick witted as you." Comments that follow this type of interaction can contribute significantly to the overall sense of self.[702]

In general, any interpersonal exchange that results in the client evaluating the self in more positive and less negative terms than he or she ap-

---

[702] Repeated studies have found that healthy individuals have a pronounced bias such that desirable personality attributes are seen as more descriptive of the self than of others, while undesirable attributes are seen as less descriptive of the self than of others (Alicke, 1985; Brown, 1986; Rosenberg, 1979).

praises others is going to have a positive impact on the individual self.

The Relational Self Evolves in Response to Close Relationships and Is Two Dimensional

Unlike the individual self, the relational self is two-dimensional. It contains both you and me. And the more you like me, as I like you, then the stronger the sense of self that is produced.[703] One's identity, in terms of the relational self, is affected by the value judgment placed on others with whom there is a close relation.

When salient others, such as a parent or spouse, are viewed in a positive light, there is an increase in self-esteem. However, when close associations are established with those for whom there is low regard, the sense of self is compromised. This might explain the identity crisis that occurs when familiarity increases and romantic partners discover they had an overidealized view of the other.[704] Or similarly, a crisis can occur when a child who has idolized a parent grows old enough to recognize the parent's faults and limitations.

Given a feeling of choice, individuals will attempt to align themselves with successful others, while distancing from unsuccessful others.[705] Generally speaking, it only seems natural to seek a close connection with someone who is adored and highly admired.[706] The new "us" produces a higher status self.[707] But many who come to therapy may not feel deserving of such a partner. Sometimes, formal permission from an external authority figure is required. Thus, it can be helpful to encourage such clients to cultivate friendships with people whom they admire and who give them a feeling of importance.

---

[703] This is because individuals base their feelings of worth and value in part on the degree of acceptance they perceive from others (Baldwin & Sinclair, 1996; Cooley, 1902; Felson, 1989; Leary, Tambor, Terdal, & Downs, 1995; Mead, 1934).

[704] As mentioned earlier, the development of self-concept is a phenomenon that changes in response to other people and social relationships (Anderson & Chen, 2002; Baldwin, 1992; Banaji & Prentice, 1994; Hinkley & Anderson, 1996; James, 1890; Markus & Wurf, 1987; McGuire, 1983).

[705] This is known in social psychology as "basking in reflected glory," which has been described as an indirect form of self-enhancement, because the individual did not directly contribute to the outcome (Brown, Collins, & Schmidt, 1988; Cialdini et al., 1976; Tesser & Campbell, 1982).

[706] Under normal circumstances, individuals will seek out relationships with people whom they believe to be better than them, resulting in an "upward" comparison that presumably serves to boost self-esteem (Wheeler, 1966).

[707] When there is a perceived connection to a significant other, then there is an assimilation effect that can influence the self-concept (Blanton, 2001; Wood, 1989). If the significant other is seen in a relatively positive light, then the relationship can be used to promote feelings of personal worth (Tesser & Campbell, 1982).

Perhaps even more relevant, it should be recognized that a close association with a heroic figure, such as a care provider, could result in self-esteem enhancement.[708] Thus, when the client glorifies the therapist, imagining the many positive accomplishments the therapist has achieved, and then comments that it is great to have you as "my therapist," there is an expansion and enhancement of the client's sense of self. A useful response when this occurs is to acknowledge what "we" have accomplished and then elaborate on the goodness of the therapeutic alliance. My experience has been that under these conditions, the client might take some of the statements made by the therapist and own them as "my insights." When the therapist responds using inclusive pronouns such as "we" and "our," strength is added to the client's position so that it is not the merits of the individual self on which future action must depend. For example, the comment, "Our goal for today is . . . ," allows clients to be more optimistic about what might be achieved because they no longer have to rely solely on their individual strength.

While some might argue that client reliance upon the therapist's assumed capabilities is unhealthy, it should be recognized that the emergence of the relational self is as normal as the emergence of an individual self. Furthermore, progress towards a more positive self-concept sometimes needs to occur in a series of small steps. While it is not healthy for a person to lose his or her individual identity within the context of a close relationship, it is unlikely that this would happen under circumstances of normal ethical practice. As discussed in the chapter on attachment, the optimal conditions for a healthy and effective self is a state of equilibrium between the individual and relational parts of self.[709]

In the early 1940s, Harry Stack Sullivan[710] hypothesized that a child will develop a different sense of self in each of his or her primary relationships. Thus, there is a self-in-relation-to-mother, a self-in-relation-to-sister, to brother, and so on, and the salience of each self depends on who was most important to the young child. Sullivan believed that these self-representations are used later in life to relate to others.[711] Following years of study, it has become apparent that the relational self continues to develop so that self-representations are also derived from adult relationships and

---

[708] The assimilation effect occurs within the context of the relational self, when two or more persons share a common identity or are psychologically close (Aron et al., 1991; Brewer, 1991; Brewer & Weber, 1994; Brown et al., 1992; Pelham & Wachsmuth, 1995).

[709] It has been argued that a fully developed sense of self is good at both differentiation and relatedness, at stability and change, at internal awareness and external sensitivity (Lopez & Brennan, 2000).

[710] Sullivan is the founder of the interpersonal school of American psychoanalysis.

[711] This, of course, is what many psychotherapists would recognize as the phenomena of transference (Rioch, 1988).

then used as a starting point for various interpersonal transactions.[712] Once activated, the working self-concept helps organize and maintain the predictability of existing relationships while serving as a blueprint for the construction of new ones.[713] The greater the diversity in an individual's social relationships, the more self-information there is to consider, thus accounting for the increasing complexity of identity formation.[714] Of course, the more narrowly defined a person's sense of self, the less room there is for imperfection and less opportunity for success in a variety of fields.

A major implication for the therapy relationship is the importance of flexible and fluid relating. If the therapeutic relationship rigidly symbolizes only one type of relationship—for instance, a mother-child relationship—then the self-concept derived from that relationship will be the sole target of therapy. In contrast, when a therapist is able to represent many different individuals by cueing memories from a variety of contexts, then more of the client's personal identity is reached. Some of these cues are difficult to control, such as one's gender or facial features; however, there are numerous behavioral cues, including dominance or submission and affective tone that can be altered during therapy in order to access different working self-concepts.

For example, a therapist working with a woman who feels generally good about herself, except when she is in the presence of domineering men, will not have as much of an impact on the client's self in relation to dominant others if the therapist insists on an egalitarian or even slightly submissive posture with the client. These roles would only cue the client's self-concept that does not need therapy.

Of course, there are other methods for activating a problematic self-concept that do not rely on transference. Both psychodrama and gestalt therapy offer techniques for visualizing the presence of a significant other who has had some type of major impact on one's sense of self. My experience is that inviting, say, a hallucinated mother into the therapy room can produce results that are just as profound as the feeling that the therapist is

---

[712] For example, Hinkley and Anderson (1996) found that when participants were exposed to someone who reminded them of a significant other, their self-concepts shifted to resemble their perceptions of themselves in their relationship with the significant other. Similarly, Fitzsimons and Bargh (2003) found that participants who thought of a friend characterized themselves as more helpful than participants who thought of a coworker, presumably because friendships are more so characterized by mutual helpfulness.

[713] The working self-concept suggests that not all self-representations or identities that are part of the complete self-concept will be accessible at any one time (Kihlstrom & Cantor, 1984; Markus & Wurf, 1987).

[714] Modern travel and communication further decrease the likelihood that any single conception of self will develop and be maintained (Gergen, 1991).

like one's mother. And of course, family therapy provides a third option, which is to bring the actual person into the therapy room. Each of these methods helps increase the richness of the interpersonal transactions. The commonality across all of these methodologies is the activation of a problematic relationally defined self-concept, thereby making it available for care and encouragement.

Another highly relevant implication is the importance of generalization. If the therapist is successful in creating a stronger, more positive sense of self within the client, then it would be important for this particular self to be easily accessed in other social settings. If the therapy relationship is rigidly defined as "client-therapist" and the rituals conducted in the therapy office are unlike any found in normal society, then there is less likelihood of that self-concept having any real salience during the client's interactions with family, friends, and coworkers. Under these narrowly defined conditions, the self-esteem work done in therapy is not likely to resurface until the next therapy visit, or with luck, it might generalize to the next therapist the client sees, unless the new therapist has different rituals and interpersonal style. So, for the sake of generalization, it is often helpful to include some chit-chat at the end of a productive session—the type of talk that might occur between friends. Or the conversation might be more personal, but focused on topics that would come up in a conversation with a close sibling or a spouse. A discussion about the client's hobbies or personal interests takes on new meaning when the therapist is intent on connecting the positive self-concept created within therapy to the many selves experienced in the outside world.[715]

A Positive Collective Identity Is Especially Important for Those With Low Self-esteem

In groundbreaking research on social prejudice, Gordin Allport (1954) observed that as early as infancy, people categorize others into groups of familiar and unfamiliar classes. This process continues as children, adolescents, and adults categorize social groups in a way that defines "us" versus "them." This ability to belong to a group, and to derive a sense of identity from it, requires some level of discrimination or distinction. For example, an individual who feels good about his or her social affiliation might reflect, "I am glad I belong to this group because we have this important quality, while they are lacking the same quality." This need for comparison seems to

---

[715] Similarly, researchers argue that new personality development will only become manifest when there is some discernable change in how the person defines self in the context of his or her ongoing relationships with others (Lopez & Brennan, 2000).

serve as the basic mechanism by which we establish a collective identity.[716]

Although the concept of prejudice tends to carry negative connotations, human survival has long depended on close affiliation with social groups in which one can find food and shelter and avoidance of groups that represent a mortal threat.[717] From a psychological perspective, group membership continues to serve as an important source of self-esteem, especially for those with a compromised sense of the individual self. Perhaps this is because when operating from the position of the collective self, there is less need to stand on individual merits; rather, the merits of the group are available for ownership.

For those seeking to keep the topic of conversation as far as possible from discussions about the individual self, a focus on the collective self provides a nice alternative.[718] This behavior can be observed across seemingly divergent populations, such as the socialite who establishes her value by talking about the elite country club to which she belongs, or the gang member who claims he is nothing without his gang affiliation, or the sports fanatic who insists on wearing the team colors and logo and refers to the franchise as "his team," as if it were something he owned. Interestingly, people with low self-esteem are more likely to use group affiliation as a form of self-enhancement.[719] When used excessively, the collective identity acts as a shield to defend the more fragile individual self.[720]

The more dependent the individual is on the group for a positive identity, the more important it becomes to defend the group's value, often at the expense of the comparison group.[721] The tendency to view out-group mem-

---

[716] Allport identified this dichotomy as in-group versus out-group. It has sense been established that identity is jointly established by one's similarity to some and differences from others on socially important dimensions. The definition of who "we" are is based on differences from some other social grouping (LeVine & Campbell, 1971; Tajfel, 1982).

[717] The idea that negative reactions to out-groups can serve a self-protective function social is described in identity theory (Tajfel & Turner, 1986).

[718] In other words, a self-concept can also include broad social identities and collective relationships (Aron et al., 2004; Brewer & Gardner, 1996).

[719] For example, in one study researchers found that those with low self-esteem showed little favoritism when evaluating a product they had created. But the same individuals favored products from their group, which they had not helped create, and did so primarily by derogating the other group's product. The researchers concluded that although low self-esteem individuals are reluctant to engage in direct self-promotion, they are interested in enhancing self-worth through indirect means (Brown, Collins, & Schmidt, 1988).

[720] Chronically anxious individuals and those with low self-esteem are especially likely to exaggerate similarities and interdependencies with others. When threatened, they seek to avoid being compared as an individual with others and, when possible, seek refuge in the collective self (Gibbons & McCoy, 1991; Mikulincer, Orbach, & Iavnieli, 1998).

[721] As soon as a collective "us" is formed, those with defensive self-esteem will search for intergroup differences and even distort the impressions of others in an out-group to make themselves look good by contrast (Crocker, Thompson, McGraw, & Ingerman, 1987; Dunning, 2003).

bers as inferior to in-group members is most likely when the individual self is threatened by some type of negative feedback.[722] In therapy, this sort of self-protection should be recognized and treated with tolerance and care. For people who secretly despise themselves as individuals, it is too overwhelming to confront their discriminatory attitudes as an individual. Rather, these clients need opportunities to explore some of the ways that they feel joined to members in one group and distinct or separate from members of another group. As therapy progresses, it eventually becomes possible to probe deeper and learn how a stronger individual self might emerge.

Another defensive maneuver that may occur in therapy is when someone suddenly seeks to disidentify with a given group because it has appeared in a negative light.[723] When the client sadly says how miserable it is to see other depressed people "and realize that I am one of them," it can be helpful to offer an opportunity for disidentification: "Oh no! You are not like that. Most of my depressed clients are not able to come in and laugh during therapy the way you do. You belong to a whole different category of depressed individuals—the type that I really enjoy working with." Although this statement might at first seem dismissive, it does verify the client's subjective experience of being a depressed person, while simultaneously offering a way out for someone who has indicated that he or she wishes to have a more positive group affiliation. This type of external encouragement can be extremely important, especially when it communicates an expectation that positive outcomes will be achieved.[724]

In contrast, I have had some clients come to my office feeling doomed by a diagnosis from a previous care provider. Unfortunately, it is easy to damage a client's sense of self following a careless use of clinical labels. When this occurs, the client struggles under the burden of a clinically induced negative self-concept: "I guess I am a hopeless neurotic." Because it is often counterproductive to criticize established beliefs, another option is to build up the group to which the individual has developed a sense of belonging: "I think there is no better diagnosis than the one you have. Neurotics are often very conscientious people who are wonderful companions and employees. They tend to be kind, respectful, and work harder than others.

---

[722] For example, researchers have found that when participants are given the opportunity to affirm their individual identity, they are less likely to react negatively toward out-groups (Fein & Spencer, 1997).

[723] The devaluation of the group may be caused by external sources the individual's own reassessment (Mussweiler, Gabriel, & Bodenhausen, 2000).

[724] One study found that 70% of successful clients rated their therapist's confidence that they would improve, along with their therapist's encouragement and reassurance, as very or extremely important (Garfield, 1981).

In fact, it is normal neurotics that make our society function as well as it does! This is much better than being psychotic or character disordered."

After such a lecture, my clients often show visible improvement in posture and facial expression. I had a female client return the week after hearing similar comments to report that she had been bragging to her employer and colleagues about her status as a neurotic and that when they showed some concern, she confidently corrected them, saying, "No, it's wonderful to be neurotic. This is much better than what I thought my problem was!" Even her sister noticed the enhanced self-esteem. In a family session, she commented, "My sister has really changed. She is much more confident than before." Not only had my client's demeanor altered, but she also found a new romantic partner who treated her better than those in the past, and she took on more powerful roles at her company. Although her therapy consisted of more than this single interaction, on the whole, her progress came from encouragement aimed at enhancing her self-concept.

To achieve these types of outcomes, efforts at providing encouragement should be subtle and perpetual. Every word spoken by the therapist will be assigned meaning by the client. The implication of these comments is extremely important, even when the therapist is speaking about seemingly unrelated matters, such as the progress of other clients. While engaging in small talk, I will sometimes create a virtual collective, such as "people who strive for improvement" or "those who are unbelievably resilient" and then associate the client with the given collective. For example, "You remind me a lot of these people I have seen who have less-than-perfect childhoods, but still emerge to be strong and kind individuals. I am always amazed by people who can do this." In addition to the possibility of a self-fulfilling prophecy, this sort of comment also boosts the self-concept through association with an elite group. If the comments are placed within the context of causal conversation, then the client is under less pressure to formerly accept or deny the claim. Often, this type of comment will not receive an immediate reply, but then three weeks later, clients might comment on the resiliency of certain people and how they like to think of themselves that way. This would be an example of self-concept enhancement that started at the collective level and then slowly sifted down to the level of the individual self.

If this type of communication seems contrived, then one should consider what commonly occurs during the course of normal discussion, when there is little thought to identity formation. By definition, it is not unusual for those in dysfunctional families to have their sense of self damaged through association with a negative collective. A scornful parent might comment, "You look and act just like your aunt Mildred. She was absolutely crazy!" Actually, this statement represents a simultaneous attack on the individual self and the collective self, because individual behavior is targeted as well as the behavior of others in the collective. Of course, it is destructive to the self-esteem to learn as a child that you belong to a group of individuals whom everyone else views as fundamentally flawed. As would be expected, this is the type of experience and expectation that many bring to therapy. But a more insidious problem emerges when the therapist also inadvertently attacks the group to which the client feels closely affiliated. "I am sorry to say this, but your mother's comments were abusive. She should never have compared you to your aunt. You come from a very dysfunctional family." As accurate as the comments may be, they further damage the collective self-concept.

In order to maintain a happy marriage, a useful rule is never talk bad about your spouse's parents, even when he or she has vocalized tremendous anger or disappointment about them. In therapy, the same rule applies. So when a 20-year-old client recently commented, "My dad is a real jerk! He is telling me that I am fat and need a boob job!" my neutral reply was, "What is his reasoning?" The client explained that, like her, her father had a history of depression and believed from his experience the depression would go away once his daughter's physical appearance improved. Although I was privately horrified when she went on to explain that her father also wanted her stomach "stapled," I decided to test an idea I assumed was important to her. "It sounds like you have a dad who loves you, in the only way he knows." My response left space for her to defend her father, which she did. "Yeah, he just does not know much about women," she said.

Switching back to work on her individual self-concept, I acknowledged the potential pain that comes from having one's body criticized by a parent and then I made reference to her strength. The client bragged that she was tough enough to handle her father's comments, though with time it became apparent that his toxic influence was destroying her.[725]

Once again, as a general rule, the therapist should avoid criticizing the client's family or circle of close friends. In addition to damaging the client's sense of self, these types of remarks may severely compromise the therapeutic alliance.

---

[725] Two months later, this young woman decided that she could no longer live with her father. So she moved in with her mother and stepfather. Although the girl no longer came to therapy, the stepfather did! With me coaching him, positive boundaries and support were instituted for her in the new home. The stepfather's support helped end the girl's self-mutilation and suicide attempts.

It May Be Necessary to Target the Implicit Self-Concept

The case examples listed thus far have highlighted the use of conscious persuasion and explicit reasoning. However, with several of these clients, other, more far-reaching forms of communication were also incorporated. Such communication is sometimes needed because the use of reason and logic does not benefit clients who already think of themselves as valuable and capable, but still feel insecure and inferior.[726] In these cases, there tends to be problematic attitudes residing beneath conscious awareness.[727] These implicit attitudes are often less rational and deliberative and more closely related to affective experiences.[728] Because these types of negative attitudes are formed without the benefit of conscious deliberation, they tend to be more responsive to experiential exercises rather than cognitive strategies.[729]

What this means for therapy is that the stimulation of spontaneous processes, such as often occurs in psychodrama, gestalt, or other experiential techniques, may be instrumental in the proliferation of positive attitudes already established at a conscious level of awareness.[730] As one client said, "I know what I should believe up here" (pointing to his head). "Now I just need to figure out how to feel it down here" (pointing to his heart).

In its simplest form, the experiential exercise may be nothing more than a request for clients to spend two to three minutes imagining themselves in the future, acting under a new set of positive ideas and self-beliefs. In more complex cases, I have helped highly traumatized clients use mental imagery to create pseudoexperiences that are located back in time, during some crucial moment of development. My experience has been that while the conscious, deliberative parts of the mind are able to track what is happening and

---

[726] Research suggests that less conscious or denied self-associations can conflict with the more consciously endorsed ones (Bosson et al., 2000; Dijksterhuis, 2004; Greenwald et al., 2002).

[727] Theorists have proposed that people can hold two distinct attitudes toward the same attitude object at explicit and implicit levels (Epstein & Morling, 1995; Wilson, Lindsey, & Schooler, 2000).

[728] People are likely to experience implicit attitudes about the self as intuition or gut feelings (Jordan, Whitfield, & Zeigler-Hill, 2007).

[729] Implicit attitudes are formed primarily through the automatic processing and acceptance of feedback occurring outside of conscious awareness; therefore, these attitudes seem to be relatively insensitive to conscious correction (Gawronski & Bodenhausen, 2006; Hetts & Pelham, 2001).

[730] There is now research suggesting that the protective function of positive implicit self-esteem may be more important to overall psychological well-being than that of explicit self-esteem (Bosson et al., 2003; Hetts & Pelham, 2001; Spalding & Hardin, 1999; Spencer et al., 2005; Zeigler-Hill & Terry, 2007).

distinguish reality from fantasy, the affective components process it as if the exercise were a true memory. In other words, the client may have a real memory of sitting on the stairs, watching her father beat her mother, while the client feels terror and guilt because it seems that it was her misbehavior that started the conflict. This type of experience would certainly impact the child's self-evaluative processes at deep, hard-to-reach levels.

I asked the client who recalled this exact experience to reconstruct the event using imagery. However, during the moment of fear, a caring adult was introduced; that adult made the parents stop fighting and eventually had them apologize to their little girl and then explain that it was not her fault. In this new storyline, which she helped construct, the little girl was then hugged and told about her value to the family.

Immediately following this imagery exercise, the client opened her eyes and smiled broadly. She then released a deep breath and thanked me, saying that she felt much better. Even to me, an outside observer, it was clear something had shifted inside her. Afterward, she held her head a little higher, and she smiled more frequently. Her imagined reconstruction was not a "real" event, but it certainly was an affectively charged experience that carried implications for her immediate sense of self.[731] Throughout the entire exercise, I encouraged her to trust herself and the goodness of whatever outcome she constructed.[732] In this way, I viewed my approach to her more as an interpersonal event than an intrapsychic technique. Following this exercise, the positive benefits of the supportive relationship broadened, extending far back into her past.[733]

If, after you have read this chapter, it is not clear which level of identity needs to be addressed with a given client, then consider using the shotgun strategy. When seeking to enhance others' self-concept, I always aim for the core. However, I also use a wide spread of encouragement.

---

[731] Accordingly, researchers have found that mental imagery can have a powerful influence on implicit attitudes and automatic processes (Blair, Ma, & Lenton, 2001).

[732] Research has shown that when people are induced to trust their intuition, their implicit and explicit attitudes become more closely related to each other (Jordan, Whitfield, & Zeigler-Hill, 2007).

[733] It has been argued that the experience of the present moment can change the phenomenology of the past (Stern, 2004).

Chapter 8

Transformational Relationships Foster Autonomy
Rather Than Dependence

To the question of your life, you are the only answer.
To the problem of your life, you are the only solution.
—Jo Coudert, 1965

One last defining characteristic of any transformational relationship is its transience. In order to be transformational, the relationship must produce some moment at which the care receiver no longer needs supportive services from the care provider. This key factor makes a transformational relationship different from a supportive relationship that may have no anticipated end, such as marriage, parenthood, or residential care. And while there may be intermittent periods during which the client returns for additional services, it is difficult to argue that some type of transformation has occurred unless there is some moment of individuation, some moment at which clients are able to "do it on their own."

Therapy Should Be framed in a Way That Encourages
a Strong Sense of Personal Agency

Because it has been argued that Western society overemphasizes individualism (to the point of devaluing environmental and social contexts), it is fair to question whether individuation is indeed a universal need with global application.[734] While striving to promote individual empowerment and increased personal agency, care providers should have an informed view of why these qualities are considered to be so important.

Fortunately, much of this information can be found in the science underlying the theory of locus of control. Formulated within the framework of Julian Rotter's (1954) social-learning theory of personality, locus of con-

---

[734] While Western cultures tend to view the self as an independent biological entity with dispositional attributes detached from the environmental and social contexts, members of Eastern cultures tend to draw more of their identity from the social collective (Markus & Kitayama, 1991).

trol[735] is the extent to which individuals believe their life circumstances are a function of their own actions (internal locus of control) or external factors beyond their control (external locus of control). When comparing and contrasting these two groups, there is clear evidence that individuals who internally locate the power to shape future outcomes not only feel better about themselves,[736] but also perform better when problem solving.[737] By contrast, those who feel that they have less power over their fate are more likely to suffer both physically and psychologically.[738] The less personal agency individuals experience, the worse off they seem to be.[739] And while a perception of external control is certainly not the cause of all mental illness, it does seem to aggravate or intensify existing mental health problems.[740]

Transformational relationships encourage autonomy rather than dependence on other people or drugs. This does not mean that the therapy relationship is the only type of relationship that encourages personal agency;[741] however, the transience of the therapy relationship contributes to the profoundness of its impact. And while beliefs about personal agency can change as a result of experiences encountered in general society,[742] it is the unique responsibility of the care provider to ensure that the client leaves the relationship in better shape than when he or she entered.

While ethical care providers do not intentionally disempower their clients, the fact is that the provision of treatment is more readily associated

---

[735] Locus of control is one of the most studied variables in psychology (Rotter, 1990).

[736] An internal orientation for locus of control is closely linked to high self-esteem and high self-efficacy (Flowers, Milner, & Moore 2003; Lightsey et al., 2006; Wu, Tang, & Kwok 2004).

[737] Individuals with an internally oriented locus of control seek out more information during problem solving and learn more from their experiences than do those with an externally located locus of control (Pines & Julian, 1972; Seeman & Evans, 1962; Wolk & DuCette, 1974).

[738] Research has shown that those with an external locus of control have higher levels of psychological distress, more frequent illnesses, and a greater tendency toward clinical depression (Benassi, Sweeney & Dufour, 1988; Muhonen & Torkelson 2004; Wu, Tang, & Kwok, 2004).

[739] Studies show that the greater the person's sense of external control, the greater the debilitating effects (Butterfield, 1964; Strassberg, 1973).

[740] Those with an external locus of control show more severe psychiatric symptoms and a greater willingness to contemplate suicide. Schizophrenics are most dramatically affected by the perception of external control (Crepeau, 1978; Cromwell et al., 1961; Goodman et al., 1994; Lefcourt, 1976).

[741] The style of parenting under which children are raised also affects their orientation toward personal control (Marsiglia et al., 2007; McClun & Merrill 1998).

[742] Acquiring a college education has been found to shift locus of control to an internal orientation (Wolfle & List, 2004), while experiencing the divorce of one's parents during one's childhood has been found to negatively impact perceptions of personal control and ability to effect outcomes (Kalter et al., 1984).

with the provider's personal power than the agency of the recipient. If the treatment that is being used is highly invasive, and if successful outcomes are attributed to the actions of the therapist, then it is even more likely that the client's sense of dependency will increase as feelings of personal agency decrease.[743] Therapists who are eagerly seeking to increase treatment compliance are at greater risk of thoughtlessly responding with pleasure to statements that externalize the client's power (e.g., "Doctor, please tell me what I should do!"), while expressing displeasure with statements that internalize power (e.g., "Doctor, I do not mean to be disrespectful, but I just do not agree with your assessment of my situation!"). When therapists are unaware of how they might be conditioning clients, the influence becomes more difficult for clients to defend themselves against (because it is so subtle). While it is unlikely that one or two statements by a care professional will forever alter the client's locus of control, it is important to recognize that verbal suggestions can occur any time the therapist speaks. Clients enter therapy in a vulnerable state, often questioning their own personal power; therefore, they do not have to go into a hypnotic trance in order for the therapist's words to impact their self-concept.[744]

Because interpersonal factors obviously have an impact on thinking and doing, it is beneficial for the therapist to encourage clients to do their own independent exploration during problem-solving endeavors (e.g., "There are many things you can do. This is a workable situation, and it would not surprise me if you surprised yourself with what you discover that you can do").[745] In other words, attempts to encourage client autonomy (e.g., "I am going to let you do this; you are capable") coupled with balanced responsibility for therapy outcomes (e.g., "Your actions are important and will influence the outcome") will have some degree of influence on the client's immediate problem-solving perspective, perhaps even altering the client's long-standing attitudes about control over his or her life experience.[746]

Encourage Clients to Explore Their Own Ideas, Preferences and Opinions

Before there is a readiness for anyone to act, it is typically necessary to think about what one wishes to accomplish. Because novel human behavior

---

[743] Research has shown that invasive medical procedures can lead to a shift in locus of control to a more external direction (Balsmeyer, 1984).

[744] Accordingly, it has been demonstrated that externally oriented individuals are more susceptible to verbal conditioning (Alegre & Murray, 1974).

[745] Research has shown that invasive medical procedures can lead to a shift in locus of control to a more external direction (Balsmeyer, 1984).

[746] Accordingly, it has been demonstrated that externally oriented individuals are more susceptible to verbal conditioning (Alegre & Murray, 1974).

is guided mostly by means of reason, rather than animal instinct, decisions and choices become pivotal to the implementation of action. Accordingly, autonomous individuals who have an internal power orientation tend to regard life as a series of decisions. In this way, it is their own freedom of thought that produces a sense of capacity to influence external realities—"Cogito, ergo sum!"[747]

In order for the therapy relationship to support this idea, there needs to be a formal recognition that valuable resources, such time, money, and mental energy, have been brought into the interaction by both the client and the therapist. Thus, the relationship is framed as collaborators working together on effortful tasks toward an intrinsically rewarding experience.[748] In this way, the client is able to experience a stronger sense of personal agency[749] than would occur if the therapist merely began to apply standard therapy techniques, which may or may not be in line with the client's wishes.[750]

Of course, for this type of mutual consent to occur, the processes of therapy must be made explicit. The client will need to be informed of his or her options.[751] In addition to discussing treatment goals and answering general questions, the therapist should also obtain consent before probing into highly sensitive areas.[752] It is also important to discuss the client's expectations for treatment duration. I have found it helpful to ask, "How long do you think this should take?" and "How often do you feel that you need to come in?" The authoritative answer to these questions cannot be found in a treatment manual because it ignores the mediating effect of client choice.[753] Rather, the answers come from a combination of the client's self-

---

[747] This is René Descartes' famous argument, "I think, therefore I am." This very important idea has served as a foundational element of Western philosophy and the primary argument for empirical science.

[748] Patients who put more effort into fulfilling their role experienced therapy as more effective than those who expend less effort (Martin, Martin, Meyer, & Slemon, 1986).

[749] Providing clients with a selection of intervention alternatives has been found to decrease drop out and resistance, while increasing compliance and overall effectiveness of the treatment program (Costello, 1975; Parker, Winstead, & Willi, 1979).

[750] For example, often clients report that they do not want a silent therapist or a therapist who dwells exclusively on childhood (Glass, Arnkoff, & Shapiro, 2001).

[751] It has been argued that the intake process should include a negotiation of treatment variables (Van Audenhove & Vertommen, 2000). Success in therapy seems to be related to an agreement on methods, where therapists adjust to clients and vice versa (Schonfield et al., 1969).

[752] Each of these is considered to be a necessary component of a respectful working alliance (Erskine, Moursund, & Trautmann, 2003).

[753] Treatment acceptance and overall success rates have been found to increase with the number of treatment choices offered, whereas patient characteristics were poor predictors of compliance and outcome (Kissin, Platz & Su, 1971).

understanding and the care provider's experience with similar circumstances. As with most social endeavors, when both members of the therapy dyad are treated as valuable resources, then the probability of achievement is greatly enhanced.[754]

Here it is important to note that any input received from the client should be treated as valuable information. By contrast, I had the unpleasant experience of briefly being a patient to a medical doctor who sent me home with a pamphlet describing over a dozen different drugs. He told me, "These are drugs used to treat your condition. Take it home and study it. Then next week we will discuss your treatment options." Having made the mistake of studying this single piece of information, I returned a week later and let the doctor know which drug I felt most comfortable using. Casually dismissing my comments, he replied, "Well, that is an outdated list. There is a new drug on the market that I want to start you on." While he might have convinced himself he was using a collaborative approach, his narcissism got in the way of any real alliance building. Rather than developing a positive feeling about the doctor and myself, I left feeling foolish for having trusted him and angry over the time I wasted reading his ridiculous pamphlet.

If a care provider cannot seek input in full sincerity, then it is better not to seek input at all. After all, if the therapist enjoys client sincerity and respect, then he or she should be careful to initiate this type of reciprocal activity. Otherwise, the relationship, if it survives, is likely to spiral in a negative direction. When we decide that another person is not telling the truth, then we stop cooperating, and the practical benefits of language break down. Why listen if you cannot believe what you are being told? When we decide that another person is not likely to keep promises, then the practical benefit of negotiation breaks down. Why make a deal with someone who is not likely to follow through? This is why a genuine appreciation for what the client has to offer is so vital to the therapy process. The client's trust must be earned because without it, very little will be accomplished.

In order to help individuals who struggle against overwhelming problems, it is important to provide explicit permission to construct and verbalize one's own ideas, preferences, and opinions. For example, "What would you like to see happen? Forget about what others have said you must do. You have a right to your own opinion." For those who are sufficiently persuaded by these types of remarks, a very interesting phenomenon begins to

---

[754] Researchers have repeatedly found that client involvement and therapist involvement are correlated with therapy outcome (Gomes-Schwartz, 1978; Luborsky et al., 1983, 1985; Moras & Strupp, 1982; O'Malley, Suh, & Strupp, 1983; Strupp & Hadley, 1979).

occur. As the client begins to recognize that choices and options are available, energy is shifted from defending an overidealized image of others to a greater awareness of personal preferences. In the light of choice, a more clearly defined individual identity begins to emerge.[755] When this newly emerged identity is affirmed by the care provider, the client's relief is clearly visible and instantaneous.[756] Also, when therapists allow clients to engage their own use of reason to communicate what they need from therapy and how they wish to proceed, then the process of transformation is directly facilitated.[757]

When therapists offer clients explicit permission to construct their own line of thought, it is absolutely essential for the therapists to open up the interpersonal space in which the ideas are to grow. Although there may be moments when the therapist needs to act as a knowledgeable advisor, there are other times when the therapist can help clients shift from an external power orientation to an internal orientation by encouraging clients to develop their own insights and formulate their own conclusions.

A simple device for achieving this shift is the use of silence. Yvonne Dolan (2000) humorously told me that one of her most useful techniques was to bite her lip. Shortly after my conversation with her, I began using this technique. I discovered that when I was asked a question by a client, if I remained silent for a moment or two, often the client would comment, "Well, I guess now that I think about it, I already know the answer to that question." With just a little encouragement, clients will begin to elaborate on their own thinking, thereby gaining a stronger sense of what they can do about a given situation.

Another helpful tactic is to speak at a slower pace than is typical for normal social conversation. This gives the client more time to process what is being said and to develop his or her own perspective. If the client's eyes suddenly dart off in another direction, it is helpful to sit and wait until the client finishes the internal processing and renews eye contact. This can take a matter of seconds or minutes. I have patiently watched some clients spend as much as ten minutes silently processing their thoughts before they reorient to the conversation. Rather than being controlled by external demands for fluid conversation, they are allowed to set the pace of the dia-

---

[755] It has been argued that the therapist and client should be involved throughout therapy in a process of shared decision making, where goals are frequently discussed and agreed upon (Shick & Greta, 2001).

[756] When clients and therapists agree on goals requested during intake, clients are less distressed at the end of the interview (MacKay, Cox, Burrows, & Lazzerini, 1978).

[757] This type of reasoning provides clients with increased skill and confidence for future problem solving (Sloan & Schommer, 1982).

logue in accord with their internal needs.

In other cases, the extra space between the therapist's comments is used by the client to formulate and give a rebuttal. For example, a client may say, "I think I know where you are going with this, but I am not able to do X, Y, or Z." If the therapist does not rush in with a counterargument or different suggestions, some clients stop themselves and then apologize. "My last therapist hated it when I did this. I know that I am not supposed to use 'yes-but' statements."

Upon hearing this, I often seek to shift the locus of control in an internal direction. "Thank you for being so considerate, but it is not necessary to apologize for thinking and becoming actively engaged in the problem-solving process. We will not achieve as good of an outcome if you have me do all of the thinking. You know yourself best, and how you work. That is why it is so important for us to explore your concerns and for you to tell me what ideas you think will work." As the client is encouraged to believe in his or her problem-solving capabilities, the probability of psychological distress is decreased.[758]

One of the procedural cornerstones of the therapy developed by Carl Rogers (1951) involved the therapist's attempts to reflect back to clients their thoughts and feelings by responding with a summary of the clients' statements. Similarly, I have found it helpful to commit to memory certain statements made by the client and then quote him or her later in the session—or better yet, two to three weeks later. While leading therapy groups, I take note any time a group member makes a good point and then quote that person sometime later. As a result, individuals will often sit with a taller posture or reemphasize their point with greater conviction. Although there is something extra special about being quoted in front of a crowd of others, positive effects are achieved anytime clients hear their words quoted or incorporated into the dialogue. Doing so really shows that you were listening and that what they had to say was important. When the thought that is quoted is treated as a vital clue for future progress, then the clients' capacity to construct and implement their own ideas, preferences, and opinions is reinforced.

I have even had positive results when I was confused about who I was quoting. For example, while trying to explain a therapeutic concept, I shared with my client a story someone had told me about the bankruptcy of her business and her parent's failure to comfort her or even acknowledge

---

[758] By contrast, people who consider themselves to be ineffective problem solvers report that they are more interpersonally sensitive, less trusting of other people, more socially anxious, and less interpersonally assertive and engage in less social support (Heppner & Lee, 2002).

what had happened. After I described the strength of this person who was able to move beyond her parent's shortcomings, my client enthusiastically responded, "That was me who told you that!" A week later, she commented on the significance of my remarks. "It made me feel so good to hear you describing something I had said because then I knew I have important things to say!"

While you are encouraging clients to develop their own insights and to arrive at their own conclusions, it is helpful to provide mental scaffolding. This means taking steps to facilitate client understanding when problems seem overwhelming and then backing off when the clients are succeeding on their own. As progress continues, the skillful therapist is more likely to introduce thought-provoking questions rather than giving lots of advice or direction. Such questions help elicit the client's knowledge of possible alternatives. By allowing clients to piece together their own understandings and to proceed independently when fairing well, therapists can encourage the type of self-reliance essential for autonomous self-governance and ownership of positive therapy outcomes.

Secure a Commitment to Change from the Client

It is not enough to know what the client *wants* to do. The therapist must determine what the client is *willing* to do. It is necessary to determine how much energy a person is willing to invest in the process of transformation.

Unfortunately, some clients are not willing to make the required effort. For instance, I have had individuals come to therapy requesting hypnosis to help with weight loss, but when I talk about a program of exercise or eating healthy food, they inform me, "Well, that is going to be too difficult for me." Similarly, I asked one individual who insisted that he would be willing to do anything in order to quit smoking to go five days without smoking in order to test his resolve. His response was indignant. "I did not call you in order to go five days without smoking, all on my own! I called you for hypnosis to make me quit smoking." What this individual did not realize was that I could not help him unless he was willing to commit to some sort of effortful involvement.[759]

Responsibility for change most appropriately lies with the client. Therefore, treatment methods must not only compliment a client's personal preferences, but also activate the will for change. It is only after individuals

---

[759] As Kosidlack (1980) said, "Health cannot be given to people, it demands their active participation."

begin to accept responsibility for the circumstances in their lives that they can also experience a sense of self-determination. So another distinguishing factor in therapy relationships is that, from the start of the relationship, the care provider is trying to discover if the client is willing to commit to having a problem and willing to do something about it.

Goal setting and problem identification are two important beginning points in this process. Goals encourage an internal search for skills that allow the client to master environmental challenges. Establishing goals can lead to more ambitious thinking and doing.[760] This sense of direction keeps individuals from helplessly drifting along waiting for some outside force to push them in a new direction. When clients are able to identify what they perceive to be a problem, then the foundation for therapist's involvement is established. When a client comes to a therapist and says, "This is what is wrong in my life, and this is what I need to achieve," then a clear commitment has been made. Under these circumstances, the therapist should not interfere with the goals that the client has set for him- or herself.

However, there are those instances when clients are earnestly seeking information and want to learn from the therapist what they "should" correct in themselves. From a relational perspective, it is not difficult to see how the therapy relationship might develop as an extension of early attempts to win acceptance and approval from powerful authority figures. However, a person should not live under the shadow of someone else's agenda, whether that someone be a parent, spouse, or a therapist. While clients may be content to have the therapist diagnose the problem and prescribe how their life circumstances should be improved, this does not lead to an activation of the clients' own will. Under these circumstances, clients lose their status as a vital contributor, instead becoming a passive receiver of treatment. When the roles are assigned this way, the clients' failures in therapy become the sole responsibility of the therapist. What is needed instead is a strategy that makes it possible for clients to realize their own capacity for self-governance.

Because it is the client's formal declaration of choice, either by words or action, that tends to guide future behavior, the process of soliciting a formal commitment can determine the course of the relationship. In therapy, commitment is used to activate the power of will toward purposeful, goal-oriented behavior. This type of dialogue helps develop the client's capacity for responsibility, something that is prerequisite for personal agency.

---

[760] The use of goal setting combined with verbal persuasion has been shown to increase not only expectations, but performance as well (Garland & Adkinson, 1985). Goal setting seems to help increase the client's determination to initiate and tenaciously stay with a meaningful task, even in the face of adversity.

Of course, there are many methods of acquiring a formal commitment. Therapeutic contracting is probably one of the most common and straight-forward procedures for determining what a person is willing to do. A good contract provides both structure and flexibility by asking nuanced questions about goal setting—questions that address such topics as aspirations (e.g., "What would you wish for in a best case scenario?"), acceptable outcomes (e.g., "What would you be willing to live with?"), expectations (e.g., "How much progress do you think is possible?"), reservations (e.g., "What do you wish to avoid during therapy?"), and contextual information (e.g., "What are your long-term goals versus your intermediate or short-term goals?"). Problem identification is another important part of the contract, because it ensures that both the client and therapist are starting from a position of understanding and working toward a common end. Once clients sign the contract, their responsibility for cooperative participation is made explicit.

One thing that surprised me early in my career was the power of a signature. While working with court-ordered clients, I often found myself caught in debates about whether clients had previously agreed that there were things about themselves that they needed to work on. Each week, it felt like the therapy was having to start all over. Then I developed a written contract that clients signed (on the first appointment). After that, it was rare to hear clients argue that I was forcing unwanted services on them. On the few occasions when such arguments did occur, I only had to make reference to the contract, and the debate would suddenly end.

Another more subtle method of obtaining a commitment is to offer a limited array of options from which the client makes a choice. Those who have an external power orientation sometimes need to take small steps toward self-agency. Such a client may declare, "I know there is something wrong with me, but I just do not know what I *should* do!" Rather than telling this type of client what to do, the client's capacity for choice can be exposed by simply substituting the word *could* in place of *should.* For example, the therapist might respond, "You have described the things that you think are wrong with you. And it seems from what you have said that it is a lack of assertiveness that bothers you most. So this is something we *could* seek to change through therapy, or you *could* leave it alone and simply work around the problem." While this may seem like a forced choice,[761] it still places the origin of the overall therapy goals with the client. When

---

[761] Clients are told that they can do something to change the problem behavior or they can choose not to change it. Without any other obvious options, it seems like a forced choice. However, the choice is not so terrible because the therapist has already indicated that either option can result in positive outcomes.

necessary, I will more directly test the client's resolve by telling the client something that needs to be done and then asking if the client is willing to do it. For example, "Marriage counseling is going to require a careful look at some of your own flaws. Are you willing to do that?" After getting a yes response, my next statement would be, "So tell me about some of those flaws." This level of accountability can enable people to do things that they would otherwise dismiss as being too difficult. More importantly, the effortful response provides proof to the client that he or she is truly committed to the therapy process.[762]

Redirect Problem-Solving Efforts to Domains in Which the Client Can Exercise Some Control

Many individuals come to therapy having been demoralized by an extended struggle against seemingly insurmountable odds. These individuals may still be desperately trying to make things right, but their experience-based expectations of external control act as a barrier, obscuring their view of options for exercising personal power. A psychological blind spot is created, one that makes progress seem impossible.

This point was illustrated by a client who had recently lost her husband to heart disease (after previously losing her mother to cancer following nine years of bedside care, on top of the loss of her father, who died from alcoholism while she was young). After convincing herself that she must stop crying over her husband's death and get out of the house, she went to buy a greeting card, only to find herself outside the store, locked out of her car in the pouring rain. She had the keys in her hand and was pushing the button to open the car's automatic locks, but the transmitter in the key was wet and no longer functioning. Brought to tears, she stood there crying as she repeatedly pressed the unlock button. Finally, she went into the shop and asked the cashier if she could call her son and have him leave work to come and pick her up. Fortunately, the cashier had the presence of mind to ask if maybe she could help. She accompanied the grieving widow into the rain and simply used the manual key to open the door. My client had become so wrapped up in her efforts to make the push button work, and she was so oriented toward the impossibility of her entire situation, that it never occurred to her to use the key.

This same failure to recognize options for personal agency often occurs in regard to larger issues, such as one's marriage or the relationship with

---

[762] Patients who rated themselves as more committed to their role experienced greater symptom reduction at termination than patients who rated themselves as less committed (Gaston et al., 1991).

one's children. And it is these conditions that require a therapeutic environment that redirects attempts at problem solving to domains in which some success is possible.

When the therapy relationship is able to act as a catalyst for the reallocation of problem-solving energy, the outcomes can be extraordinary, even if the moment of contact was very brief. For example, I received an unexpected phone call from a woman I had seen three years prior. Initially, I did not recognize her name, but my memory was jarred by her description of events.

"I came for couples counseling with the man I was living with at the time," she said. "I do not know if you remember the session, Dr. Short, but shortly after we started, you told him to leave the office. Then [while he sat in the waiting room] you told me that I was in a dangerous relationship and that this person would undoubtedly hurt me and my children."

Because her tone was stern and serious, I experienced a brief moment of intense self-doubt. As she paused for a breath, I thought to myself, "I said all of that? Oh no! What was I thinking?"

Then she continued, "The reason I am calling today is because we are now going to court to press charges against [him] for molesting my son. It was shortly after my visit with you that I realized I had to get me and my son out of that house. Once we were safe, my son told me that this man had been molesting him and had threatened serious harm if he told anyone about it. I am just so thankful to you for what you did. It helped open my eyes, and now my son has me and the legal system working to defend him."[763]

After the call, I checked my notes. The therapy had consisted of only one visit, which lasted half an hour. She had scheduled couples counseling because she desperately wanted to find a way to make this man love her. She had already tried everything she knew to do, and still he treated her with contempt. As he sat in my office, I could see him exploiting her emotional vulnerabilities and retaliating in a way that reflected his unyielding determination to intimidate and punish her.[764] I did not know at the time that he was a sexual predator, but I could see that she was powerless in the domain in which she was trying to exercise control (i.e., she could not make him love her). So I demonstrated for her that he could be sent away, and after he was expelled from the office, I offered a shocking statement that I was certain was correct.[765] This single statement was the catalyst

---

[763] The boy was eight years of age during the time of the abuse.

[764] Before sending the couple away, I called the man back into the office and explained the reasons why I did not believe couples counseling would be productive. He did not resist the idea, but instead said that counseling seemed like an absolute waste of time.

[765] The statement was open ended enough to encompass any of a number of destructive behaviors, some of which he was demonstrating before my eyes.

that helped her find a new approach to her troubles.

While the therapy described above may seem too limited in scope to really address this woman's damaged self-concept, this brief contact resulted in an undeniable movement toward greater internalization of control. Not only that, it was the woman who decided to leave the abusive man. It was she who engaged the legal system and took him to court. Therefore, the credit for all of these accomplishments belonged entirely to her. The cumulative effect of these events is likely to have had a profound and lasting impact on her sense of self-agency.

As another example, while working with a 78-year-old male who felt utterly demoralized by the injustices of life, I found myself searching for some way to shift his frustrated problem-solving energies to a domain where he could achieve some success. Each morning he spent his time furiously writing letters to local officials while loudly and bitterly complaining (to an invisible audience) about accessibility issues that made it difficult to get his wife's wheelchair in an out of their apartment complex. These angry tirades were followed by excessive alcohol consumption that led to a drunken stupor.

His feeling that he could not control the events occurring in his life went as far back as his teenage years in Europe, when he spent three years in hiding because of Nazi occupation. As an adult, he had fallen in love and gotten married, but then lost his wife after a long, grueling battle with cancer. He described tremendous agony in watching his wife "turn into a vegetable on morphine." He had since remarried, but after being taken advantage of in business dealings, he had no money left other than a monthly social security check. Furthermore, his second wife had developed a severely dehabilitating condition that the doctors could not explain.

During the first therapy session, he said, in an upfront way, that he did not believe I could help his situation. He indicated that the only reason he came to counseling was because his wife had begged him. He also let me know that he doubted he would return unless I could convince him otherwise. As the session progressed, this fiercely self-sufficient individual surprised himself by thanking me for a statement I made during our conversation. Because I had been of some small help, he agreed to return for one more visit.

In order to understand why the second visit had such a dramatic impact on this client, it is necessary to appreciate the absolute sincerity of his love for his wife, coupled with the blinding effect created by an external locus of control. He truly saw no other alternative than to rage against a completely uncaring bureaucracy and then to sedate himself with alcohol in order to bring himself to a calmer state. His need to complain was so intense that it hardly left room for anyone else to speak. So it was a full 40 minutes into the session before I was able to secure his attention.

"Isolation is the most terrible form of torture known," I told him. "And the worst death imaginable is to die alone, with no one caring." This got him into a state of agreement and reflection. I continued, "For me to help you, I need you to recognize the value and importance of your relationship with your wife. She cares very deeply for you; therefore, the calmer and more okay you are, the less stress she will suffer."

He agreed, saying, "This is true. When the fence went up, I went completely berserk and probably aggravated her condition. I spent all my time thrashing about, so at two in the afternoon I got drunk and stayed drunk until I fell asleep."

Aiming for an explicit attitudinal shift, I explained, "That is probably very sad for her, because it would be like you watching your first wife die on morphine."

His response was immediate, "You are exactly right. And this is the second time I thank you."

Next, I explained how he was to internalize his power. "Your thrashing about comes from feelings of powerlessness, but you have a great deal of power to make your wife's life good and to promote justice. You must realize that you being *not* angry and *not* drunk is important to her well-being. It is not fair for your wife to lose you at two o'clock every afternoon and watch you become a vegetable. It is not just for your wife to hear that you want to kill yourself. That is not fair! And the person in control of this justice is you. You create [justice] through compassion and love."

The man sat quietly for a moment, and then spoke up. "I did not see that because I've been drunk." He followed this confession by pointing his finger at me and smiling warmly, "That is the third one! [Thank you]."

This was a proud man who stood by his word. To the best of my knowledge, our conversation ended his rumination, rage, and problem drinking.[766] No further therapy was needed. Although the outcome may seem somewhat spectacular, the dynamics are fairly common. When we start to believe that at least one other significant person is on our side, then the world suddenly seems like a less threatening place.[767]

---

[766] It is important to note that this client was 78 and had not had problems with drinking prior to the immediate problem situation. Although he was currently binge drinking, it is unlikely that he was a typical alcoholic.

[767] More specifically, researchers found that affirmation of important self-defining values and priorities, successes, and consensual convictions decreases rumination about threats (Shrira & Martin, 2005).

Attribute Successes to Personal Agency

The idea that a skillful therapist will attribute positive outcomes to the personal agency of the client is the final and most important point to be made about transformational relationships. However, this task may not be as straightforward as it at first seems. While it is generally empowering for individuals to view themselves as the agents of their own fate,[768] clients who are struggling to feel good about themselves need help selectively focusing on successes rather than failures.[769] When a person is highly affected by failure,[770] then the idea of accepting responsibly for outcomes can seem threatening or instantly disempowering. Therefore, it is important to recognize the need for clients' internal attributions of success to outweigh internal attributions of failure. In therapy, it would be important for the therapist to actively search for opportunities to help clients attribute meaningful successes to themselves.

For instance, a client who returns to college and starts attending classes may make a discounting statement such as, "The only reason I got in was because of luck. Once they figure-out how dumb I am, they are certain to kick me out." With the right type of questioning, the client can be persuaded to attribute the success to such internal factors as his or her timely completion of the application process, a willingness to attend the classes once they began, and a willingness to study between classes. My experience has been that it is obvious when the power orientation shifts inward, because the character of the comments change as clients become more proactive. Clients spontaneously begin to discuss additional accomplishments they would like to achieve (e.g., "Next, I need to figure out what my major is going to be and how it is going to help me get the job I want"). After entering into a supportive environment, clients will often surprise themselves with the successes they can achieve, even if they experience some small failures along the way.

One such client, who was horribly frightened of therapy, would come

---

[768] Research on locus of control has indicated that internally oriented individuals tend to attribute success and failure in task performances to themselves (Sosis, 1974; Lefcourt et al., 1975).

[769] Low self-esteem individuals explain negative events using internal causes. By contrast, high self-esteem individuals are more likely to make internal attributions for success and external attributions for failure (Greenwald, 1980; Lau & Russell, 1980; Miller & Ross, 1975; Peterson & Seligman, 1984; Whitley & Frieze, 1985).

[770] Those with low self-esteem tend to be more upset and more defeated by failure and less able to defend their overall self-image from failure than those with high self-esteem (Kernis, Brockner, & Frankel, 1989; Sweeney & Wells, 1990).

to her appointments 30 to 45 minutes late. The first time she entered the room, she sat in a cowered position as if she were expecting a strong rebuke. My response was, "You have told me a little bit about your past. You were treated so horribly by authority figures. As a child, you were not allowed any freedom. I am impressed that you are willing to come into therapy and work on yourself. There are so many people who need therapy but do not have the courage to come. We still have ten minutes left, and you would be surprised at how much therapy we can do in ten minutes." I felt that it was more therapeutic for her to arrive late and be met with kindness and approval than for her to perform perfectly in order to receive conditional acceptance. Although this client continued to arrive at least 25 minutes late, for the subsequent 60 appointments, she never missed a single session. In the end, she was able to stop drinking, put away fantasies of killing herself, develop new rewarding friendships with other females, and discontinue disability-support payments after starting a home-based business. Indeed, her failure to arrive on time did not prevent her from making remarkable progress, and it was this progress that she learned to focus on.

While it is almost always helpful to attribute successes that occur outside the office to the client's internal resources, it is equally important to recognize successes that occur within the therapy room and attribute these to the client. Unfortunately, it is often easier for clients to believe in the therapist's abilities rather than their own.[771] It is also common for clients to make obvious progress in response to talk therapy and then assign all the credit to psychotropic medication: "Without my medication, I would still be a disaster." When there is a failure to attribute any success to internal mechanisms, it is necessary to help the client start to claim responsibility even for the smallest of achievements. For example, this type of client should have his or her participation acknowledged by the therapist. When the therapist encourages the client with comments such as, "You are doing a very nice job of telling me the things that you need to say," a connection starts to form between the client's contribution and therapeutic accomplishments. For some, just the fact that they showed up for the appointment is a personal victory that is worth recognizing. When the therapist is able to make a clear connection between the client's actions and verifiable progress, then new expectations for the future start to emerge.[772]

---

[771] It is not uncommon for clients to attribute positive therapy outcomes to the personal attributes of their therapist (Lazarus, 1971; Sloane, Staples, Cristol, Yorkston, & Whipple, 1975).

[772] Wilkins (1971) attributed a large part of therapy effectiveness to the skill of the therapist in developing an "expectancy of therapeutic gain," as well as providing praise for improvement.

What this means is that it is not enough to help the client make progress; rather, there should also be some means of tracking the progress that is made.[773] Because forward movement is impossible to recognize without some sort of reference point, the documentation of goals at the start of therapy can serve as an essential tool for tracking progress. For information on client progress to remain fluid throughout the therapy process, it is helpful to specify immediate, intermediate, and long-term goals. I will often ask clients, "What would you like to achieve within the next couple of weeks? And the next several months? And over the upcoming years?" Although therapy is not intended to last for years, it is helpful to understand a person's long-term objectives so that his or her broader needs are fully recognized. A single woman who does not want to have children is different from a single woman who is 40 and wants be a mother someday. When progress is interpreted as being the direct result of achieving set goals, then the client learns to become more comfortable with the idea of accepting responsibility for outcomes.

Regarding the importance of progress monitoring, it should be noted that, in some instances, it can be difficult for clients to recognize that progress has occurred. While still young and inexperienced, I would become discouraged after asking clients, "Do you feel like progress is being made?" A common response was, "Not really. I feel a little better, but I do not know if things have really changed." This answer confused me, because I could often see that these clients were talking and acting differently in the therapy office. It was difficult to imagine that there were not some sort of improvements occurring at home as well. Then I learned the importance of probing beyond the initial response.

As an example, while working at a high school in an affluent neighborhood, I had a mother and father approach me for help with their 16-year-old son. The mother complained that her son was failing most of his classes; spent all of his time at home, sitting in front of the TV; and had so little regard for her that she could not even get him to eat supper at the table with the rest of the family. The father interjected that his greatest disappointment was that his son refused to interact with his paternal grandfather, who also lived in the home. This man had admired his father as a boy and was embarrassed by his son's disregard for the family. The parents wanted me to tell them what was wrong with their son.

I had already met with the boy and determined that he did not suffer from emotional problems. So I told the parents I did not think that there

---

[773] There is a growing body of research suggesting that tracking client progress can improve therapy outcomes (for a review, see Lambert et al., 2003).

was a problem with their son as much as with their method of discipline.

The mother looked at me with a stunned expression. So I explained, "There is absolutely no reason to believe that you cannot get him to the dinner table to eat with the family. Simply make having a meal contingent on his participation in the family dinner." She asked for clarification, so I explained, "Do not feed him unless he sits at the table. And if it were my son, I would require that he help set the table as well." I then turned to the father and pointed out that the $50 a week he paid his son for allowance could be made contingent on his son's willingness to study for one hour a day. Because I knew their child was friendly and had not been oppositional toward school authority figures, I did not expect that they would have any trouble turning his behavior around.

However, four months later at our second meeting, when I asked how their son was doing, they sadly reported that he had not made any real progress. They seemed so convinced of his lack of progress that I momentarily lost confidence and turned to double-check the folder where I had a list of his grades. His lowest grade had been raised to a *C*, and there was evidence of improvement in every single class.[774]

After I remarked on the evidence of progress, the parents conceded, "Well, yeah, he has done better at school. Perhaps he is just not going to make the type of grades that we did in school."[775]

I inquired further. "What about his refusal to eat with the family?"

Hearing this question, the mother's face brightened up. "Oh, well, he eats with us every night now. As a matter of fact, last night he volunteered to help me wash the dishes."

I then looked at the father. "Are you certain that you have not seen any changes?"

His facial expression also altered, "Well, now that you ask it that way, he has spent the last week working outside with his grandfather. They are building a fence around the backyard." Turning to his wife, as if he had just had a great epiphany, the father exclaimed, "I guess he is doing much better!"

For a brief moment, these parents almost had me convinced that the intervention had been a complete failure. Even worse, they still had themselves convinced that, as parents, their actions did not matter. The intent of my interactions with them was to increase their sense of personal power.

Because therapists are human, it is natural to want to receive credit for some of the progress that clients make in therapy. In fact, all people should want to feel capable in their professional endeavors. However, the process

---

[774] The problem was that the parents had been secretly hoping for straight *A*'s.
[775] The parents were both attorneys who had graduated from prestigious law schools.

of transformation is better facilitated when care providers are able to attribute successful outcomes to the agency of the client rather than to their own talents. The difference between temporary relief from emotional distress and true transformation is evidenced in the fact that those who develop a stronger sense of personal agency are less likely to experience the same types of problems in the future.[776] When clients learn to see themselves as responsible for their changed behavior, the expectation of maintaining gains is more likely, and, thus, a helpful self-fulfilling prophecy is created.[777]

In summary, it should be noted that relational-based transformation depends in great part on a utilization of capacities preexisting within the individual. This matters more than the brief and fleeting influences of an external agent. Therefore, while therapists seek to build transformational relationships, the use of sophisticated techniques and the replication of academically endorsed protocols are of less importance than their attention to what the client is capable of accomplishing. Those who lack a sense of personal power believe that the events that occur in their lives have little to do with their own choices and decisions. When clients are encouraged to think about desired outcomes, long-term goals, and strategic possibilities, then the control orientation shifts to an internal locus of control. After clients achieve gains in therapy, it is important to help them attribute their progress to personal agency. In this way, there is a greater sense of control over one's own destiny, and more good is expected during future efforts at problem solving.

---

[776] Research has shown that clients who attribute positive outcomes to their actions, rather than to an external agent, such as the therapist, have lower rates of relapse, when using long-term outcome measures (Deci & Ryan, 1985; Harackiewicz et al., 1987; Weinberger 1995).

[777] Research has shown that post-treatment expectancies predict the stability of psychotherapeutic change (Bandura, 1989; Weinberger, 1995; Weinberger & Eig, 1999).

CONCLUSION

Psychotherapy Is Primarily a Relationship Between Two People

I began this book with a quote from Thomas Szasz and a description of a seemingly trivial event that took place in the London underground during a significant moment in my life. From these, it is possible to deduce everything that needs to be recognized within the remainder of the text. When the time is right, as it was for me, a single event can spark a life-changing process of transformation. Once I knew that I wanted to be better prepared to provide care to others, then the decision to become a psychologist easily followed.

More often than not, it is the experience of distress or dissatisfaction with one's self that precedes change; therefore, the client's subjective distress serves as a natural starting point in any discussion of transformation. As I traveled across Europe, separating myself from all that was familiar and safe, I experienced a heightened desire to understand the people of this world in all their diversity and distinctiveness. By contrast, a person who insists on standardized routines for relating to others severely limits the number of people he or she can comfortably engage and the depth of connection that will develop. Healthy relationships are characterized by an ongoing process of discovery. Those who are skillful at relating never stop the process of getting to know those with whom they interact.

Although I spent a significant amount of time on my own, my journey began and ended alongside a trusted companion, someone who had been my best friend since early childhood. Accordingly, it is through our relationships with others that we discover our value, stretch our limits, gain new abilities, and collaboratively create a meaning for our existence.

If you have read this book from front to back, then you have journeyed with me from my days as an uncertain adolescent to a rewarding career dedicated to the provision of expert psychological care. My study of individuals is ongoing, and with each person I encounter, I learn something new. Even more importantly, I have learned to absorb the reality of human suffering not as a helpless spectator, but instead as an enthusiastic problem solver who routinely celebrates the resiliency and progress of those with whom I have collaborated and come to know. As an added benefit, my professional skill has carried over into my personal life, increasing my capacity to connect more deeply with friends, family, and with myself. For these reasons, I am grateful for what I have received from my work, and it is my sincere wish that the information in this book serves others as well as it has served me. Before ending our time together, I would like to conclude with an overview of the core relational dynamics in Part I and their connection to the relational objectives described in Part II.

In the end, the primary goal of transformational relationships is not to change who the person is, but rather to work collaboratively with existing beliefs, behaviors, and emotions so that new avenues for self-expression are created. When individuals find acceptance for their shortcomings or respect for the experiences they have encountered, then they are better positioned to start the process of healing and growth. Therefore, the first relational dynamic described in this text is *verification* and the first relational objective is increased *self-awareness*. Social-science researchers have found that the verification of core beliefs is essential to relational sustainability. When people feel verified in their personal understandings on critical issues, then not only is the interaction less threatening, but it also makes sense to those involved. One reason people become so enthusiastic when they learn that they are speaking to someone who grew up in the same small town as they did, or someone who studied the same college major they did, is that similarity on critical issues produces automatic understanding and a shared sense of identity. In therapy, these core beliefs become relevant in any deep discussion of the self, others, the reasons for change, or the expectation of how change will occur. While working within the client's subjective reality, the entire therapy endeavor seeks to address what the client perceives to be the problem and a search for what the client will perceive as a meaningful resolution. When the client is treated as the final authority on his or her needs, the interdependent process of transformation and self-determination naturally follow.

Areas of Core Belief	Interpersonal Dynamics	Therapeutic Verification
Self	A client with low self-esteem will avoid therapists who use too much praise initially, while those with high explicit self-esteem will avoid therapists who are perceived as being overly critical.	For low self-esteem clients, accept what it is that they do not like about themselves while remaining optimistic about future opportunities for change. When seeking to affirm, pick an area of the self where the client's attitudes are more neutral. For high self-esteem clients, affirm the most highly valued aspects of self while questioning other areas of self that might still need improvement.
Others	Based on past relationships, clients may have come to the conclusion that no one could ever love them, that all people are selfish; or that, in the end, those whom they trust will abandon them. With these beliefs comes biased processing (i.e., people find what they are looking for) and a narrow range of interpersonal strategies aimed at defending against the behavior that is expected from others.	The more transference interpretations are used, the poorer the alliance between client and therapist is. Instead, the client's right to defend against these behaviors should be verified. You might say, for example, "If you notice me using any of these undesirable behaviors, please point it out so I can make immediate corrections." This verification helps clarify your positive intentions while drawing attention to subsequent behaviors that do not fit the client's rigid expectations.
Reasons for change	Most clients are motivated to continue therapy primarily by a desire to eliminate or reduce distress. Some clients are not experiencing intense distress, but rather are motivated by a desire to increase future rewards.	For those focused on distress, make certain to identify key areas of distress and address those areas quickly and directly. Also make certain that therapy does not become another cause of distress. For those focused on future rewards, make certain to identify high-priority objectives and begin monitoring progress towards those objectives.
Expectation for change	During any conversation about a problem situation, clients will give small clues that gradually illuminate the paradigm of change by which they operate. When there are similarities in client-therapist perspectives and expectations toward therapy, there is a greater probability of positive treatment outcomes.	The therapist may adopt the client's ideas as the treatment plan is formed or jump to other ideas, using the client's statements as a starting point. It is also helpful to incorporate into the plan the strategies or healing rituals that the client expects will produce positive results.

As can be seen, verification in therapy is essentially a matter of choosing the conceptual framework in which to present ideas. Less skillful practitioners will use their own intellectual understandings as the default strategy for communicating new ideas to clients. However, when one is able to build on existing foundations, then a lot less excavation is required. When the therapist is able to establish therapy goals that are derived from the client's personal interests and use interventions that fit the client's theory of change, then less resistance is encountered. The therapist's intellectual flexibility is not derived from academic theories of change but rather from a careful study of the client's internal experiences and needs.

One should recognize the importance of verifying the uniqueness and existence of an individual personality. If the therapist seems to understand and accept the client as he or she is, then greater hope is available to the struggling individual. This acceptance cannot be achieved if the primary purpose of the therapist is to change the thoughts and beliefs of the person with whom he or she is working. Therefore, the therapeutic relationship is used to foster an internally derived process of transformation in which the individuals that have come for help find that they are better off for what they have endured than if the problem had never occurred.[778]

The next core dynamic presented in this text is *affect attunement.* Because every interaction communicates some type of emotional tone, it is the task of the therapist to decide which emotion is most likely to resonate with a given client at any given moment. Because affective states change quickly, affect attunement requires immediacy and recognition of when shifts occur. This assessment relies on facial expression, voice tonality, posture, and other forms of nonverbal communication more so than verbal dialogue.

If the therapist is able to synchronize with the client's affective state, then the strategic use of this emotional communication will create a closer and more satisfying relational experience for the client. Positive emotional sentiment is almost always beneficial for those who need support. However, the expression of negative emotions facilitates connection if the client is experiencing strong negative feelings and is, therefore, intolerant of joyful, happy feelings. When the therapist is able to empathetically experience and sort through the feelings that reside within the client, then the therapist's care and the client's receptivity are greatly enhanced. Negative emo-

---

[778] This is referred to as "utilization" within the Ericksonian literature, which is defined by acceptance of the client in his current condition, with the existing set of beliefs and behaviors. For Erickson, the relationship with the patient was not predicated on a demand for change but instead on acceptance, establishing what is worthy and good about the person (Short, Erickson, Erickson-Klein, 2005).

Client's Emotional State	High Attunement	Low Attunement
Misery and Sadness	Palpable relief occurs when individuals learn that they do not have to carry their burdens alone (e.g., "I am so sorry that happened to you. As a child you did not deserve to be abused."). The attunement is achieved both verbally and through nonverbal behavior.	It is wrong to show a great deal of sadness in response to a sad tale if the client shared the story showing no affect. An emotional reaction could overwhelm the client. It is not the informational content, but the expressed emotion that is the object of affect attunement.
Anger and Resentment	When establishing relationships with hostile individuals, complementarity in hostile behavior is more beneficial to the development of therapeutic alliance than friendly behavior. However, anger should be directed away from the client. It is possible to be unhappy alongside the client without being hostile to the client.	Individuals who are angry or resentful are less likely to feel understood or listened to if the therapist responds to their outbursts with a calm, subdued demeanor. The expression of remorse or regret can also be problematic, in some instances leading to an escalation in tension or increased probability of retaliation.
Fear and Anxiety	It is appropriate to show concern for those who are worried or fearful. This concern does not need to be expressed as fear over external threats, which might make the client's anxiety worse. Instead, the therapist's worries are aimed at the client's subjective experience (e.g., "I'm worried that if you allow the fear to take over, you will not find out what you are capable of achieving.").	In some instances, efforts to encourage or embolden others can come across as dismissive or condescending (e.g., "Do not worry. I am confident you will be able to handle this."). Also, it does not work well to tell others not to worry. If no one else shows evidence of concern, individuals are likely to feel misunderstood or bad about themselves.
Joy	Joy is greatly increased when others share in the experience; even 10-month-old children show this tendency. When clients experience joy, it is helpful to have someone who will validate the accomplishment and share in their delight.	An unfortunate breakdown in the relationship occurs when therapists: a) respond to the client's joy with guarded optimism, b) if they express concern that the client is in denial about deeper issues, or c) if the therapist does not know what to say when there are no problems to discuss.

tions, such as sadness and anger or fear and anxiety, are particularly important to recognize because they allow the therapist to make sense of the client's emotional distress and, therefore, respond with greater empathy, kindness, and finely tuned helping behavior. Of course, it is also important to recognize positive emotions, such as joy, so that they can be reinforced and celebrated.

It is also important to note that in complementary relationships, the client's affect is not mimicked; rather, a shared emotional experience is used to generate greater understanding and increased opportunity for collaboration. This subtle distinction may seem insignificant; however, the implications impact the overall authenticity of the client therapist connection. If a given relationship is viewed as a living thing capable of growth, then shared experiences are equivalent to the sustenance by which that growth is fed. In the therapy room, a person's most important life experiences are communicated not only with words, but also with an emotional reliving of the event. When affect attunement is achieved, isolation is decreased and combined interpersonal strength is more readily generated.

Another task that is important for therapy is choosing how much or how little to do for others. This is addressed in the discussion on *reciprocity*, which is one of the most important means by which we calibrate the social-accounting system. This social accounting system helps ensure equanimity and, thus, protects individual resources and promotes mutual satisfaction. Rather than assuming that interpersonal exchanges are linear, with unilateral outcomes, reciprocity helps illuminate the circular exchanges that take place during the course of normal relating. In other words, every action is regulated by the expectation of matched behaviors: "I will not become hostile with you because I do not want you to become hostile with me" or "I will self-disclose something to you so that you will, in turn, self-disclose to me."

For the finer details of interpersonal behavior, where there are no laws guiding conduct, equanimity is maintained through comparison and contrast of one's actions up against the actions of another. This can occur in a negative form, "Do not do this to me unless you want me to do it to you," or in a positive form, "I am doing this for you because I want you to return the favor." When reciprocity occurs, then both individuals will be acting within the same code of conduct, even if there is not some outside force mandating compliance. Therefore, reciprocity is particularly important for intimate, day-to-day interactions that form the foundation of one's self-concept.

When circumstance has forced individuals to trust in the strength and

Activity	Cooperative Behaviors That Are Mutually Reinforcing	When One Partner Operates Under a Different Set of Rules
Participation	Active participation of clients in therapy is associated with increased empowerment. When therapists and clients both participate in treatment planning, and when therapists explain the rationale for the plan and how it works, clients are more satisfied with the initial session.	Apathy is created when the therapist puts a great deal of effort into treatment planning and thinking about the problem, and when the client puts less and less effort into the problem-solving process. Conversely, if the therapist just sits and listens (as the client does all of the talking, having to determine both what questions to ask and what the answers should be), then the client may leave feeling resentful.
Self-Disclosure	Not only do clients have a greater liking for therapists who offer reciprocal self-disclosure, but they also tend to have less symptom distress after treatment.	Inequity occurs when clients are required to self-disclose embarrassing or controversial details of their private life and the therapist refuses to self-disclose any information. On the flip side, if therapists are the only ones allowed to describe their ideas for therapy, then resentment could develop on the client's part.
Personal Growth	Clients who are able to help their therapist in some way experience an emotional boost and are more appreciative of the relationship. Accordingly, people prefer relationships in which both parties give and receive care.	If clients are left feeling that they are the only ones who have received benefit from the meetings, then a sense of shame could develop. If the therapist does not accept any supportive gestures and does not indicate a willingness to self-improve, then the client may feel more self-critical.

Exceptions	Dynamics	Solution
Anxious Attachment Style	The Anxious style is characterized by intense needs for intimacy and evidence of availability (both physical and emotional). These demands often exceed what others are able to provide resulting in high drama or exaggerated displays of distress. There is also a tendency to be highly self-critical, resulting in hypersensitivity to criticism.	When there is chronic anxiety about the availability of outside support, external permission for self-acceptance and self-approval is needed. The client is likely to feel comfortable with overt displays of support and emotional closeness, however, the therapist should avoid becoming the client's sole attachment figure.
Avoidant Attachment Style	Avoidants cope by suppressing emotions and remaining highly self-reliant. While anxiously attached individuals are likely to feel most understood and cared for when asked to self-disclose problems, avoidants may not return if too much self-disclosure is requested. Avoidants often do not know how to regulate the flow of emotion; thus, processing emotions can lead to an emotional crisis. These individuals are likely to feel extremely uncomfortable if hugged or touched.	With regard to emotional self-disclosure, move at a pace that is slightly behind rather than out in front of the client. Listen when clients express concern about crying; do not push forward with increased emotional arousal. When discussing the client's history, stop the conversation before the client is overwhelmed with emotion. Introduce moments of light-hearted conversation. Give the individual a wide perimeter of personal space. Do not initiate hugs or other forms of caring touch.
Fearful Ambivalent Attachment Style	This is a confusing relational style in which the individual is both overly dependant and clingy while also experiencing discomfort with personal vulnerability and tremendous resentment toward attachment figures. These individuals have difficulty communicating their emotional needs and often fail to establish clear boundaries. These individuals can be highly dramatic, intensely insecure, and quick to perceive rejection or abandonment from others.	Establish clear boundaries and define each person's role early in therapy. Stay away from neutral comments that could be easily misunderstood. Instead, state a clear commitment to working with the client. Help the client learn how to return to a relaxed state when feeling emotionally overwhelmed. Rather than using direct confrontation, have the client comment on his or her behavior. Expose the inner dialogue that is taking place.
Attachment System Has Deactivated/Exploratory System Is Active	There may be instances when the client has come for a therapy session, but is not currently experiencing distress. This state of personal security will produce a desire for increased autonomy.	*Do not* dig deeper for problems. Instead, have clients describe their progress, and congratulate and affirm their accomplishments. Rather than offering guidance, become curious about what the client wants to do next. Determine if further help is needed. It might be time to spread sessions out or to end the therapy.

flexibility of someone they hardly know, then it helps if even the most minor interaction is governed by some principle that seems both fair and just. Reciprocity regulates the give and take of relationships. In therapy, there are many difficult tasks that are made easier when cooperation is used as an added motivational force. Three general activities include participation in problem solving, self-disclosure, and personal growth. If stated out loud, the logic of reciprocity would sound something like this, "I am not going to work any harder on this problem than you are willing to work," or "I will tell a little bit about myself, and then it will be your turn to tell a little bit about yourself," or finally, "I am willing to experience some growth at my end if you will be willing to also experience some growth." As seen in the following table, the application of reciprocity leads to greater satisfaction for both partners in the relationship. But even more importantly, open acknowledgement of the mutual benefit derived from a transformational relationship benefits the self-concept of all who are involved. As noted in chapter 7, this is a core relational objective.

Another critical assessment in therapy is to determine whether to increase or decrease emotional proximity. This decision is better informed when one understands the dynamics of *attachment*. Attachment is a relational bond that forms during moments of intense need or insecurity. Attachment is responsible for feelings of love, care, and emotional connectedness. While it is reasonable to assume that all significant interpersonal relationships involve some amount of personal need and willingness to receive support, it is not a one-size-fits-all process. Although the therapist should always communicate some degree of concern for the client's welfare, there are some individuals who exhibit a need to avoid dependency on others, while others may simultaneously experience strong feelings of dependency and fearfulness of a strong attachment. As seen in the following table, the formation of an attachment relationship requires flexibility and discernment by the therapist.

Secure attachment results from a matching of need and support, resulting in greater emotional stability and social integration. In general, a good relational fit occurs when one person shows distress and another offers support in the form of availability and emotional closeness. A successful collaboration will not develop when pairing two helpers or when pairing two seekers of help. Thus, a client seeking help naturally fits with a therapist who has taken the role of emotional confidante and empathetic listener. This approach works well with those who have a secure or anxious attachment style. However when working with clients who have an avoidant or fearful attachment style, these dynamics will need to be ad-

Conclusion

Variable Attribute	Dominance	Submission
Timing	**Takes the Lead** **Moderate Dominance**: First to extend hand for handshake, first to sit, first to speak, picks the topic of discussion, sets the agenda for the interaction **Intense Dominance**: Seeks immediate compliance, makes others wait, insists on having the final word	**Tends to Follow** **Moderate Submission**: Waits for cue to shake hands, wants to be told where to sit, waits for statements to reply to, seeks clarification on what to discuss, more comfortable when following a set structure **Intense Submission**: Is uncertain of what to do, refuses to take the lead, waits to be told when to talk
Attention	**External Focus** **Moderate Dominance**: Visually studies others, speaks to be heard, questions and evaluates others' behavior (positive or negative) **Intense Dominance**: Prolonged stare, draws attention to others' area of weakness, demands others listen	**Internal Focus** **Moderate Submission**: Gaze shifts to one's own hands or feet, speech is hesitating and tentative, questions and corrects one's self **Intense Submission**: Does not visually engage others, consumed with attention to personal flaws, does not wish to speak
Size	**Expansion** **Moderate Dominance**: Consumes more physical space by leaning forward or stretching legs forward, expands rib cage, offers big ideas, speaks the longest **Intense Dominance**: Makes grand gestures, maintains wide visual field, "owns" everything in the room and seeks to manage it	**Contraction** **Moderate Submission**: Keeps limbs and possessions close to the body, shoulders rounded down, does not have a strong personal opinion, has little to say **Intense Submission**: Arms and legs drawn up into the torso, chin tucked down into the neck, does not wish to manage items outside a small personal space
Height and Strength	**Elevation** **Moderate Dominance**: Chin points upward, head held high, seeks to take on challenges, builds arguments **Intense Dominance**: Statements are self-aggrandizing, standing over the therapist, sets the standards	**Retreat** **Moderate Submission**: Chin pulled in, head is lowered to the shoulders, seeks help with challenges, seeks the correct answer **Intense Submission**: Statements are self-deprecating, body is sinking down, does not question the standards

justed so that a nonthreatening connection is established.

As a final point, all sustainable relationships require some degree of *structure*, so that shared resources are successfully managed and conflict is minimized. It is the dominant individual that provides the leadership necessary for productive encounters. Because the therapist is a highly educated expert, it is often assumed that he or she will exercise dominance by managing shared resources, such as the time, the topic of conversation, and the use of therapeutic techniques. Because those who are hurting, or in need, tend to seek help from someone higher in the dominance hierarchy, those who wish to function as providers of professional care should be prepared to engage in prosocial acts of dominance.

However, increased autonomy (the relational objective most closely associated with ongoing transformation) is difficult to achieve if the therapist refuses to surrender the dominant position occasionally. Skillful care providers switch from dominant to submissive postures when circumstances indicate that this shift is beneficial for the client. This is most likely to be the case when the client is needing to feel safe by exercising some control, or when he or she needs to have new attempts at self-assertion affirmed and validated.

Because individuals with equal displays of dominance or submission will repel rather than attract, therapists need to rapidly decide whether to respond to clients with dominance or submission. Even within the context of day-to-day encounters, untrained individuals quickly determine who is dominant and who is submissive. However, during therapy the intensity and duration of the dominance or submission are varied depending on the relationship stance of the individual client. A sense of satisfaction and harmony is better achieved when the intensity of the dominance and submission is matched. For well-matched pairs who are moderately dominant and submissive, the differences are so slight that most typically will not detect them. By contrast, intensely submissive individuals seek out a greater degree of guidance and structure, the type that intensely dominant individuals are comfortable providing. Even so, for the relationship to remain positive and transformational, the therapist should not interfere with client autonomy and never use aggression or intimidation when clients are not yielding to persuasive efforts.

That which tends to be the natural byproduct of strong healthy relationships also tends to be good therapy. Complementarity is fundamentally important to relationships because it is the dynamic that ensures sustainability and promotes receptivity to interpersonal experiences. The strategic formation of a transformational relationship is what differentiates therapy from other intense forms of interpersonal influence. At this time, all of the major schools of therapy recognize the importance of the quality of relationship between a client and his or her care provider. Likewise, research has produced incontrovertible evidence that people in secure relationships have better cardiovascular health, stronger immune systems, lower mortality rates from cancer, less depression, and less anxiety, and that they face psychological trauma with more emotional resilience.[779] Within the context of healthy relationships, individuals are able to gain the experience of identity, meaning, choice, and love. The combination of these produces hope and resiliency, which function as the driving forces behind survival and growth. Therefore, if, from time to time, each of us is willing stop and ask, "What can I do so that others are better off for having known me?" then it is not only the lives of others' that are improved, but also the meaning of one's own existence.

---

[779] The failure of physiological systems impacted by social support may contribute to the leading causes of death in the United States, including cardiovascular disorders, cancer, and respiratory illnesses (e.g., Sarason, Sarason, & Gurung, 1997; Uchino, Cacioppo, & Kiecolt-Glaser, 1996).

Appendix A

GENERAL FUNCTIONING

SAS-A₃
ASSESSMENT PROTOCOL

Name: _____ Date: _____

First, read a descriptor to identify different areas of personal distress. *Next*, Rate your sense of distress using the first number that comes to mind. *Mark* your answer by **circling** a number on the graph that best represents your high point and a number for your low point during the last **seven** days. For example, if your pain was as high as 10 but never less than 7, then the numbers "10" and "7" would be circled in the column marked "Pain."

DESCRIPTORS

Pain: How much pain, discomfort, tension, or physical distress are you experiencing in your body?

Behavior: How troubled are you by your words, actions, or past behavior?

Isolation: How much isolation, shyness, loneliness, or powerlessness are you experiencing?

Sadness: How much sadness, hopelessness, or worthlessness are you experiencing?

Anxiety: How much anxiety, nervousness, or panic are you experiencing?

Anger: How much anger, irritability, resentment, or violent urges are you experiencing?

Fear: How much fear, insecurity, or phobic avoidance are you experiencing?

Threats: How concerned are you about the intentions or threatening actions of others?

Thinking: How troubled are you by unwelcome thoughts or strange ideas?

Sexuality: How troubled are you by nudity, sexual desire, or other's sexual expectations?

GRAPH

Circle high scores for most severe distress over 7 days

Pain	Behavior	Isolation	Sadness	Anxiety	Anger	Fear	Threats	Thinking	Sexuality
10	10	10	10	10	10	10	10	10	10
9	9	9	9	9	9	9	9	9	9
8	8	8	8	8	8	8	8	8	8
7	7	7	7	7	7	7	7	7	7
6	6	6	6	6	6	6	6	6	6
5	5	5	5	5	5	5	5	5	5
4	4	4	4	4	4	4	4	4	4
3	3	3	3	3	3	3	3	3	3
2	2	2	2	2	2	2	2	2	2
1	1	1	1	1	1	1	1	1	1
0	0	0	0	0	0	0	0	0	0

And, circle low scores for least severe distress over 7 days

NOTES

List anything that is important for the therapist to know for today's session: (you may leave the space blank)

_____

_____

_____

Additional forms available by request
SAS@IamDrShort.com

Licensed for Professional Use Only

Appendix B

SESSION OUTCOMES

SAS-B
ASSESSMENT PROTOCOL

Name: _____ Date: _____

Please describe your experience in today's session by completing the sentence stems below. At the end of each sentence blank, circle the number that best describes how strongly you feel about this statement. Your honest feedback will help your clinician better respond to your needs.

Minimal Certainty → I do not feel that I can answer this = 1

Average Certainty → This answer seems to be accurate = 2

Great Certainty → I feel very strongly about my response = 3

The most difficult part of this session was	3	2	1
The most helpful part of this session was	3	2	1
After this session, I am more likely to	3	2	1
I am still probably not yet ready to	3	2	1
The thing most likely to help me is	3	2	1
I am just now starting to realize	3	2	1

How satisfied do you feel with this therapy session?

Low Satisfaction   1   2   3   4   5   6   7   8   9   10   High Satisfaction

Appendix C

TREATMENT CONTRACT

SAS-C₃
ASSESSMENT PROTOCOL

Name: _____ Date: _____

BEHAVIORS TO REDUCE	Behaviors that create more problems or cause the greatest distress	BEHAVIORS TO INCREASE	Behaviors that make the problem less likely, alternatives, solutions

LONG-TERM GOALS	What experiences would you like to have years from now?	SHORT-TERM GOALS	What experiences would you like to have within the next few months?	IMMEDIATE GOALS	What experiences would you like to have within the next several days?

Estimated number of sessions: ____ Key SAS-A Scale: ____ Aimline Start: ____ Finish: ____ CS: ____ TD: ____

AIMLINE & PROGRESS MONITORING

Visit	1	2	3	4	5	6	7	8	9	10	11	12	13	14	15	16	17	18	19	20	
10																					100
9																					90
8																					80
7																					70
6																					60
5																					50
4																					40
3																					30
2																					20
1																					10
0																					05

Treatment Plan: Rank the top three treatment elements that seem most likely to be helpful (#1-3). The therapist will recommend and explain any other methods that seem necessary for appropriate treatment planning.

___ Someone to listen ___ Emotional support ___ Safe Environment ___ Review my past ___ Insight into problems

___ Expert advice ___ Learn new skills ___ An unbiased opinion ___ Modify my behavior ___ Genuine acceptance

During therapy I wish to avoid:

Client's responsibility: I understand it is my responsibility to inform the therapist of any changes in my goals for treatment or questions or concerns I have about the treatment process. My commitment to treatment increases the probability of success.

Client Signature: _____

Date: _____

Therapist's responsibility As the therapist it is my responsibility to inform the client of any deviations from this mutually agreed upon treatment plan and any known risks such as strong emotional reactions or impact on social networks.

Therapist Signature: _____

Date: _____

List of Case Examples

A burned arm...245

An elderly woman with exceedingly low self-esteem..................................42

An overweight woman outweighs her shame from childhood..................253

The biology major..14

The boy who needed to have his natural talents valued............................237

The boy whose father was a suspected serial killer...................................79

The boy with impacted bowels...172

The client who cried on the floor...105

The client who suggested sex..90

The client who was 45 minutes late to her appointments........................295

The client who was quoted..287

The foster mom who claimed to be abused by her child..........................157

The girl who was loving only while physically ill....................................131

The graduate who lost his parents..191

The intellectually challenged student who would not give up.................193

The man who blamed his trouble on the white establishment...................36

The man who bought his wife handcream for Christmas..........................114

The man who cried for hours...122

The man who did not believe he would respond to therapy.......................82

The man who did not know his actions mattered.....................................113

The man who drove others off the road...59

The man who feared success...52

The man who hid his need for relationship advice....................................55

The man who liked to have accidents in public.......................................184

The man who needed to realize his wife was lying to him.......................218

The man who needed to tell his father to fuck-off....................................185

The man who raged at injustice..293

The man who raped his daughter...116

The man who remembered being told that his self-portrait
looked like a monster...265

The man who threatened to kill himself..101

The man who was afraid he would molest children...235

The man who was being chased by Jesus Christ
and an army of Martians...30

The man who was defiant and extremely susceptible to suggestion 199

The man who was looking for Erickson 46

The man who was too ashamed to admit to his problem...................................22

The man whose anger turned to tears...126

The misdiagnosed seizure disorder 71

The narcissist who bragged to his wife about his progress 44

The narcissist who took the role of therapist..43

The parents who could not see progress until questioned............................297

The pregnant college student who had to make a difficult choice..............219

The suicidal teen who talked his friend out of committing suicide............216

The teen who gave away his secrets...171

The teen who refused to speak..17

The teenage girl who was told by her father
that she needed cosmetic surgery...277

The teenager who self-mutilated...141

The teenager who was hiding something...12

The violent man who needed love...136

The woman who appreciated being interrupted 214

The woman who became suicidal after
being praised for her progress...52

The woman who did not know how to find home..210

The woman who did not want to be told she was muttering 194

The woman who had an unnecessary affair...109

The woman who lost all that she had to an iatrogenic illness.......................39

The woman who needed a way to stop criticizing herself 228

The woman who needed protection from hypnosis...246

The woman who needed quiet time..218

The woman who needed to be validated..266

The woman who needed to reject her mother 139

The woman who planned to kill herself
once her daughter went off to college...61
The woman who sent a list of problems 48
The woman who thought it was a sin to like herself.......................41
The woman who thought she would go crazy if her husband died...........111
The woman who wanted to solve problems her own way.....................210
The woman who wanted to wear her ring...267
The woman who was a good teacher...236
The woman who was ashamed of her smoky smell............................229
The woman who was in denial about her husband's poor prognosis.......222
The woman who was phobic of hospitals..248
The woman who was proud to be a neurotic.......................................276
The woman whose husband was preparing to kill her........................181
The woman whose son was being molested by her boyfriend.................292
The young misanthrope...68

References

Abelson, R. P., & Prentice, D. A. (1989). Beliefs as possessions: A functional perspective. In A. R. Pratkanis, S. J. Breckler, & A. Greenwald (Eds.), Attitude structure and function (pp. 361–381). Hillsdale, NJ: Erlbaum.

Abramson, L. Y., Seligman, M. E. P., & Teasdale, J. D. (1978). Learned helplessness in humans: Critique and reformulation. Journal of Abnormal Psychology, 87, 49–74.

Ackerman, S. J., Benjamin, L. S., Beutler, L. E., Gelso, C. J., Goldfried, M. R., Hill, C., ... Rainer, J. (2001). Empirically supported therapy relationships: Conclusions and recommendations of the Division 29 Task Force. Psychotherapy: Theory, Research, Practice, Training, 38, 495–497.

Adler, A. (1927). The practice and theory of individual psychology. New York: Harcourt, Brace & World.

Alegre, C., & Murray, E. (1974). Locus of control, behavioral intention, and verbal conditioning. Journal of Personality, 42, 668–681.

Alexander, F. (1963). The dynamics of psychotherapy in the light of learning theory American Journal of Psychiatry, 120, 440–448.

Alicke, M. D. (1985). Global self-evaluation as determined by the desirability and controllability of trait adjectives. Journal of Personality and Social Psychology, 49, 1621–1630.

Allport, G. W. (1954). The nature of prejudice. Reading, MA: Addison-Wesley.

Allyn, D. (2004). I can't believe I just did that. New York: Tarcher/Penguin.

American Psychological Association (2002). Ethical principles of psychologists and code of conduct. American Psychologist, 57, 1060–1073.

American Psychological Association (2007). Record keeping guidelines. American Psychologist, 62, 993–1004.

Anderson, S. M., & Chen, S. (2002). The relational self: An interpersonal social cognitive theory. Psychological Review, 109, 619–645.

Andreas, S. (2002). Transforming Your Self: Becoming who you want to be. Moab, UT: Real People Press.

Andrews, J. D. W. (1990). Interpersonal self-confirmation and challenge in psychotherapy. Psychotherapy, 27, 485–504.

Andrews, J. D. W. (1993). The active self model: A paradigm for psychotherapy integration. In G. Stricker & J. R. Gold (Eds.), Comprehensive handbook of psychotherapy integration (pp. 165–183). New York: Plenum Press.

Antill, J. K. (1983). Sex role complementarity versus similarity in married couples. Journal of Personality and Social Psychology, 45, 145–155.

Appelbaum, A. (1972). A critical re-examination of the concept of "motivation for change" in psychoanalytic treatment. International Journal of Psychoanalysis, 53, 51–59.

Argyle, M. (1988). Bodily communication (2nd ed.). London: Methuen.

Armstrong, J. G., & Roth, D. M. (1989). Attachment and separation in eating disorders: A preliminary investigation. International Journal of Eating Disorders, 8, 141–155.

Aron, A., McLaughlin-Volpe, T., Mashek, D., Lewandowski, G., Wright, S. C., & Aron, E. N. (2004). Including others in the self. In W. Stroebe & M. Hewstone (Eds.), European review of social psychology (Vol. 15, pp. 101–132). Hove, United Kingdom: Psychology Press.

Atkinson, J. W. (1957). Motivational determinants of risk-taking behavior. Psychological Review, 64, 359–372.

Atkinson, J. W. (1983). Old and new conceptions of how expected consequences influence actions. In N. T. Feather (Ed.), Expectations and actions: Expectancy–value models in psychology (pp. 17–52). Hillsdale, NJ: Erlbaum.

Bachelor, A., & Horvath, A. (1999). The therapeutic relationship. In M. A. Hubble, B. L. Duncan, & S. D. Miller (Eds.), The heart and soul of change: What works in therapy (pp. 133–178). Washington, DC: American Psychological Association.

Baldwin, J. M. (1902). Social and ethical interpretations in mental development. New York: Macmillan.

Baldwin, M. W. (1992). Relational schemas and the processing of social information. Psychological Bulletin, 112, 461–484.

Baldwin, M. W. (1997). Relational schemas as a source of if–then self-inference procedures. Review of General Psychology, 1, 326–335.

Baldwin, M. W., & Sinclair, L. (1996). Self-esteem and "if . . . then" contingencies of interpersonal acceptance. Journal of Personality and Social Psychology, 71, 1130–1141.

Balsmeyer, B. (1984). Locus of control and the use of strategies to promote self-care. Journal of Community Health Nursing, 1, 171-179.

Banaji, M. R., & Prentice, D. A. (1994). The self in social context. Annual Review of Psychology, 45, 297–332.

Bandura, A. (1977). Self-efficacy: Toward a unifying concept of behavior change. Psychological Review, 84, 191–215.

Bandura, A. (1986). Social foundations of thought and action: A social cognitive view. Englewood Cliffs, NJ: Prentice Hall.

Bandura, A. (1989). Human agency in social cognitive theory. American Psychologist, 44, 1175–1184.

Bandura, A. (1997). Self-efficacy: The exercise of control. New York: W. H. Freeman.

Barbee, A. P. (1990). Interactive coping: The cheering-up process in close relationships. In S. Duck (Ed.), Social support in relationships (pp. 47–65). Newbury Park, CA: Sage.

Bargh, J. A. (1994). The four horsemen of automaticity: Awareness, intention, efficiency, and control in social cognition. In R. S. Wyer & T. K. Srull (Eds.), Handbook of social cognition (2nd ed., pp. 1–40). Hillsdale, NJ: Erlbaum.

Bargh, J. A., Chaiken, S., Govender, R., & Pratto, F. (1992). The generality of the automatic attitude activation effect. Journal of Personality and Social Psychology, 62, 893–912.

Barrett, L. F., Robin, L., Pietromonaco, P. R., & Eyssell, K. M. (1998). Are women the "more emotional" sex? Evidence from emotional experience in social context. Cognition & Emotion, 12, 555–578.

Barrett, M. S., & Berman, J. S. (2001). Is psychotherapy more effective when therapists disclose information about themselves? Journal of Consulting and Clinical Psychology, 69, 597–609.

Barsade S. G. (2002). The ripple effect: Emotional contagion and its influence on group behavior. Administrative Science Quarterly; 47, 644–675

Bartholomew, K., & Horowitz, L. M. (1991). Attachment styles among young adults: A test of a four category model. Journal of Personality and Social Psychology, 61, 226–244.

Bateman, A. W., & Fonagy, P. (2000). Effectiveness of psychotherapeutic treatment of personality disorder. British Journal of Psychiatry, 177, 138.

Bateson, G. (1936/1958). Naven. Cambridge, England: Cambridge University Press.

Baumeister, R. F. (1998). The self. In D. T. Gilbert, S. T. Fiske, & G. Lindzey (Eds.), The handbook of social psychology (4th ed., pp. 680–740). Boston: McGraw-Hill.

Baumeister, R. F., & Jones, E. E. (1978). When self-presentation is constrained by the target's prior knowledge: Consistency and compensation. Journal of Personality and Social Psychology, 36, 608–618.

Baumeister, R. F., & Leary, M. R. (1995). The need to belong: Desire for interpersonal attachments as a fundamental human motivation. Psychological Bulletin, 117, 497–529.

Baumeister, R. F., & Tice, D. M. (1984). Role of self-presentation and choice in cognitive dissonance under forced compliance: Necessary or sufficient causes? Journal of Personality and Social Psychology, 46, 5–13.

Baumeister, R. F., & Wotman, S. R. (1992). Breaking hearts: The two sides of unrequited love. New York: Guilford Press.

Baumeister, R. F., Campbell, J. D., Krueger, J. I., & Vohs, K. D. (2003). Does high self-esteem cause better performance, interpersonal success, happiness, or healthier lifestyles? Psychological Science in the Public Interest, 4, 1–44.

Baumeister, R. F., Tice, D. M., & Hutton, D. G. (1989). Self-presentational motivations and personality differences in self-esteem. Journal of Personality, 57, 547–579.

Baumeister, R. F., Wotman, S. R., & Stillwell, A. M. (1993). Unrequited love: On heartbreak, anger, guilt, scriptlessness, and humiliation. Journal of Personality and Social Psychology, 64, 377–394.

Baumgardner, A. H., & Brownlee, E. A. (1987). Strategic failure in social interaction: Evidence for expectancy disconfirmation processes. Journal of Personality and Social Psychology, 52, 525–535.

Baumgardner, A. H., Lake, E. A., & Arkin, R. M. (1985). Claiming mood as a self-handicap: The influence of spoiled and unspoiled public identities. Personality and Social Psychology Bulletin, 11, 349–357.

Bavelas, J. B., Black, A., Lemery, C. R., & Mullett, J. (1986). "I show how you feel": Motor mimicry as a communicative act. Journal of Personality and Social Psychology, 50, 322–329.

Beck, J. S. (1995). Cognitive therapy: Basics and beyond. New York: Guilford.

Becker, E. (1968). The structure of evil. New York: Braziller.

Bem, D. J. (1967). Self-Perception: An alternative interpretation of cognitive dissonance phenomena. Psychological Review, 74, 183–200.

Benassi V. A., Sweeney P. D., & Dufour C. L. (1988). Is there a relation between locus of control orientation and depression? Journal of Abnormal Psychology, 97, 357–67.

Berenbaum, H., & James, T. (1994). Correlates and retrospectively reported antecedents of alexithymia. Psychosomatic Medicine, 56, 353–359.

Bergin, A., & Lambert, M. (1978). The evaluation of therapeutic outcomes. In S. Garfield & A. Bergin (Eds.), Handbook of psychotherapy and behavior change (2nd ed., pp. 139–189). New York: Wiley.

Berglas, S., & Jones, E. E. (1978). Drug choice as a self-handicapping strategy in response to noncontingent success. Journal of Personality and Social Psychology, 36, 405–417.

Berk, M. S., & Anderson, S. M. (2000). The impact of past relationships on interpersonal behavior: Behavioral confirmation in the social-cognitive process of transference. Journal of Personality and Social Psychology, 79, 546–562.

Berman, J. S., & Norton, N. C. (1985). Does professional training make a therapist more effective? Psychological Bulletin, 98, 401–407.

Bernieri, F. J., & Rosenthal, R. (1991). Interpersonal coordination: Behavior matching and interactional synchrony. In R. S. Feldman & B. Rime (Eds.), Fundamentals of nonverbal behavior (pp. 401–432). Cambridge, England: Cambridge University Press.

Berscheid, E. (1994). Interpersonal relationships. Annual Review of Psychology, 45, 79–129.

Berscheid, E. (1999). The greening of relationship science. American Psychologist, 54, 260–266.

Berscheid, E., & Reis, H. T. (1998). Attraction and close relationships. In D. T. Gilbert, S. T. Fiske, & G. Lindzey (Eds.), The handbook of social psychology (Vol. 2, 4th ed., pp. 193–281). New York: McGraw-Hill.

Beutler, L. E., & Malik, M. (2002). Rethinking the DSM-IV: Psychological perspectives. Washington, DC: American Psychological Association.

Blair, I. V., Ma, J. E., & Lenton, A. P. (2001). Imagining stereotypes away: The moderation of implicit stereotypes through mental imagery. Journal of Personality & Social Psychology, 81, 828–841.

Blanton, H. (2001). Evaluating the self in the context of another: The three-selves model of social comparison assimilation and contrast. In G. B. Moskowitz (Ed.), Cognitive social psychology: The Princeton Symposium on the Legacy and Future of Social Cognition (pp. 75–87). Mahwah, NJ: Erlbaum.

Blau, P. M. (1956). Bureaucracy in modern society. New York: Random House.

Bloom, M. V. (2005). Origins of healing: An evolutionary perspective of the healing process. Families, Systems, & Health, 23, 251–260.

Bordin, E. S. (1979). The generalizability of the psychoanalytic concept of the working alliance. Psychotherapy: Theory, Research and Practice, 16, 252–260.

Bordin, E. S. (1994). Theory and research on the therapeutic working alliance: New directions. In A. O. Horvath & L. S. Greenberg (Eds.), The working alliance: Theory, research and practice (pp. 13–37). New York: Wiley.

Bosson, J. K., Brown, R. P., Zeigler-Hill, V., & Swann, W. B., Jr. (2003). Self-enhancement tendencies among people with high explicit self-esteem: The moderating role of implicit self-esteem. Self and Identity, 2, 169–187.

Bosson, J. K., Swann, W. B., Jr., & Pennebaker, J. W. (2000). Stalking the perfect measure of implicit self-esteem: The blind men and the elephant revisited. Journal of Personality and Social Psychology, 79, 631–643.

Bowlby, J. (1973). Attachment and loss, Vol. 2: Separation. New York: Basic Books.

Bowlby, J. (1988). A secure base: Parent-child attachment and healthy human development. New York: Basic Books.

Bradley, E. J., & Peters, R. D. (1991). Physically abusive and non-abusive mothers' perceptions of parenting and child behavior. American Journal of Orthopsychiatry, 61, 455–460.

Brehm, J. W. (1966). A theory of psychological reactance. San Diego, CA: Academic Press.

Brehm, S. S. (1987). Social support and clinical practice. In J. E. Maddux, C. D. Stoltenberg, & R. Rosenwein (Eds.), Social processes in clinical and counseling psychology (pp. 26–38). New York: Springer-Verlag.

Brennan, K. A., & Bosson, J. K. (1998). Attachment-style differences in attitudes toward and reactions to feedback from romantic partners: An exploration of the relational bases of self-esteem. Personality and Social Psychology Bulletin, 24, 699–714.

Brennan, K. A., & Morris, K. A. (1997). Attachment styles, self-esteem, and patterns of seeking feedback from romantic partners.. Personality and Social Psychology Bulletin, 23, 23–31.

Brennan, K. A., & Shaver, P. R. (1995). Dimensions of adult attachment, affect regulation, and romantic relationship functioning. Personality and Social Psychology Bulletin, 21, 267–283.

Brennan, K. A., & Shaver, P. R. (1998). Attachment styles and personality disorders: Their connections to each other and to parental divorce, parental death, and perceptions of parental caregiving. Journal of Personality, 66, 835–878.

Brennan, K. A., Clark, C. L., & Shaver, P. R. (1998). Self-report measurement of adult attachment: An integrative overview. In J. A. Simpson & W. S. Rholes (Eds.), Attachment theory and close relationships (pp. 46–76). New York: Guilford Press.

Brewer, M. B. (1991). The social self: On being the same and different at the same time. Personality and Social Psychology Bulletin, 17, 475–482.

Brewer, M. B., & Weber, J. G. (1994). Self-evaluation effects of interpersonal versus intergroup social comparison. Journal of Personality and Social Psychology, 66, 268–275.

Brewer, M.B., & Gardner, W.L. (1996). Who is this "we"? Levels of collective identity and self representations. Journal of Personality and Social Psychology, 71, 83–93.

Briñol P & Petty RE (2003). Overt head movements and persuasion: A self-validation analysis. Journal of Personality and Social Psychology, 84, 1123–1139.

Brock, T. C. (1967). Communication discrepancy and intent to persuade as determinants of counterargument production. Journal of Experimental Social Psychology, 3, 296–309.

Brokaw, D. W., & McLemore, C. W. (1983). Toward a more rigorous definition of social reinforcement: Some interpersonal clarifications. Journal of Personality and Social Psychology, 44, 1014–1020.

Brown, J. D. (1986). Evaluations of self and others: Self-enhancement biases in social judgments. Social Cognition, 4, 353–376.

Brown, J. D., & Dutton, K. A. (1995). The thrill of victory, the complexity of defeat: Self-esteem and people's emotional reactions to success and failure. Journal of Personality and Social Psychology, 68, 712–722.

Brown, J. D., & Smart, S. A. (1991). The self and social conduct: Linking self-representations to prosocial conduct. Journal of Personality and Social Psychology, 60, 368–375.

Brown, J. D., Collins, R. L., & Schmidt, G. W. (1988). Self-esteem and direct versus indirect forms of self-enhancement. Journal of Personality and Social Psychology, 55, 445–453.

Brown, J. D., Novick, N. J., Lord, K. A., & Richards, J. A. (1992). When Gulliver travels: Social context, psychological closeness, and self-appraisals. Journal of Personality and Social Psychology, 62, 712–727.

Buchheim, A., & Mergenthaler, E. (2000). The relationship among attachment representation, emotion-abstraction patterns, and narrative style: A computer-based text analysis of the Adult Attachment Interview. Psychotherapy Research, 10, 390–407.

Bugental, D. B. (2000). Acquisition of the algorithms of social life: A domain-based approach. Psychological Bulletin, 126, 187–219.

Bugental, D. B., Blue, J. B., & Cruzcosa, M. (1989). Perceived control over caregiving outcomes: Implications for child abuse. Developmental Psychology, 25, 532–539.

Bugental, D. B., Blue, J., & Lewis, J. (1990). Caregiver cognitions as moderators of affective reactions to "difficult" children. Developmental Psychology, 26, 631–638.

Bugental, D. B., Blue, J., Cortez, V., Fleck, K., Kopeikin, H., Lewis, J. C., & Lyon, J. (1993). Social cognitions as organizers of autonomic and affective responses to social challenge. Journal of Personality and Social Psychology, 64, 94–103.

Bugental, D. B., Brown, M., & Reiss, C. (1996). Cognitive representations of power in caregiving relationships: Biasing effects on interpersonal interaction and information processing. Journal of Family Psychology, 10, 397–407.

Burnum, J. F. (1974). Outlook for treating patients with self-destructive habits. Annals of Internal Medicine, 81, 387–393.

Burris, C. T., & Rempel, J. K. (2004). "It's the End of the World as We Know It": Threat and the Spatial–Symbolic Self. Journal of Personality and Social Psychology, 86, 19–42.

Butterfield, E. C. (1964). Locus of control, test anxiety, reactions to frustration and achievement attitudes. Journal of Personality, 32, 298–311.

Butzel, J. S., & Ryan, R. M. (1997). The dynamics of volitional reliance: A motivational perspective on dependence, independence, and social support. In G. R. Pierce, B. Lakey, I. G. Sarason, & B. R. Sarason (Eds.), Sourcebook of social support and personality (pp. 49–67). New York: Plenum.

Byrne, D. (1971). The attraction paradigm. New York: Academic Press.

Byrne, D., & Griffitt, W. (1969). Similarity and awareness of similarity of personality characteristic determinants of attraction. Journal of Experimental Research in Personality, 3, 179–186.

Calder, B. J. (1978). Cognitive response, imagery, and scripts: What is the cognitive basis of attitude. Advances in Consumer Research, 5, 630–634.

Calder, B. J., Insko, C. A., & Yandell, B. (1974). The relation of cognitive and memorial processes to persuasion in a simulated jury trial. Journal of Applied Social Psychology, 4, 62–93.

Campbell, J. D. (1986). Similarity and uniqueness: The effects of attribute type, relevance, and individual differences in self-esteem and depression. Journal of Personality and Social Psychology, 50, 281–294.

Campbell, J. D. (1990). Self-esteem and clarity of the self-concept. Journal of Personality and Social Psychology, 59, 1–12.

Campbell, J. D., Trapnell, P. D., Heine, S. J., Katz, I. M., Lavallee, L. F., & Lehman, D. R. (1996). Self-concept clarity: Measurement, personality correlates, and cultural boundaries. Journal of Personality and Social Psychology, 70, 141–156.

Cappella, J. N., & Palmer, M. T. (1990). Attitude similarity, relational history, and attraction: The mediating effects of kinesic and vocal behaviors. Communication Monographs, 57, 161–183.

Carnelley, K. B., Pietromonaco, P. R., & Jaffe, K. (1994). Depression, working models of others, and relationship functioning. Journal of Personality and Social Psychology, 66, 127–140.

Carnelley, K. B., Pietromonaco, P. R., & Jaffe, K. (1996). Attachment, caregiving, and relationship functioning in couples: Effects of self and partner. Personal Relationships, 3, 257–278.

Carson, R. C. (1969). Interaction concepts of personality. Chicago: Aldine.

Cassel, J. C. (1976). The contribution of the social environment to host resistance. American Journal of Epidemiology, 104, 107–123.

Cassidy, J., & Kobak, R. R. (1988). Avoidance and its relation to other defensive processes. In J. Belsky & T. Nezworski (Eds.), Clinical implications of attachment (pp. 300–323). Hillsdale, NJ: Erlbaum.

Chaiken, S. (1980). Heuristic versus systematic information processing and the use of source versus message cues in persuasion. Journal of Personality and Social Psychology, 39, 752–756.

Chang, P. (1994). Effects of interview questions and response type on compliance: An analogue study. Journal of Counseling Psychology, 41, 74–82.

Charny, E. J. (1966). Psychosomatic manifestations of rapport in psychotherapy. Psychosomatic Medicine, 28, 305–315.

Chartrand, T. L., & Bargh, J. A. (1999). The chameleon effect: The perception behavior link and social interaction. Journal of Personality and Social Psychology, 76, 893-910.

Cheney, D. L., & Seyfarth, R. M. (1985). Social and nonsocial knowledge in vervet monkeys. Philosophical Transactions of the Royal Society of London, 308, 187–201.

Cheng, H., & Furnham, A. (2004). Perceived parental rearing style, self-esteem and self-criticism ad predictors of happiness. Journal of Happiness Studies, 5, 1–21.

Cheung, S. K., & Sun, S. Y. K. (2000). Effects of self-efficacy and social support on the mental health conditions of mutual-aid organization members. Social Behavior and Personality, 28, 413-422.

Chiao, J. Y. (2006). Building blocks to human social hierarchy: Psychological and neural investigations of social dominance perception. Dissertation Abstracts International: Section B: The Sciences and Engineering, 67, 2851.

Christensen, A. & Heavey, C. L. (1990). Gender and social structure in the demand/withdraw pattern of marital conflict. Journal of Personality and Social Psychology, 59, 73–81.

Cialdini, R. B., & Mirels, H. L. (1976). Sense of personal control and attributions about yielding and resisting persuasion targets. Journal of Personality and Social Psychology, 33, 395-402.

Cialdini, R. B., Borden, R. J., Thorne, A., Walker, M. R., Freeman, S., & Sloan, L. R. (1976). Basking in reflected glory: Three (football) field studies. Journal of Personality and Social Psychology, 34, 366-375.

Cialdini, R. B., Braver, S. L., & Lewis, S. K. (1974). Attributional bias and the easily persuaded other. Journal of Personality and Social Psychology, 30, 631-637.

Claiborn, C. D., Goodyear, R. K., Horner, P. A. (2001). Feedback. Psychotherapy: Theory, Research, Practice, Training, 38, 401-405.

Clark, L. A., & Watson, D. (1988). Mood and the mundane: Relations between daily life events and self-reported mood. Journal of Personality and Social Psychology, 54, 296-308.

Clark, M. S., Pataki, S. P., & Carver, V. (1996). Some thoughts and findings on self-presentation of emotions in relationships. In G. J. O. Fletcher & J. Fitness (Eds.), Knowledge structures in close relationships: A social psychological approach (pp. 247-274). Mahwah, NJ: Erlbaum.

Clore, G. L., & Byrne, D. (1974). A reinforcement-affect model of attraction. In T. L. Huston (Ed.), Foundations of interpersonal attraction (pp. 143-170). New York: Academic Press.

Cohen, L. H., Towbes, L. C., & Flocco, R. (1998). Effects of induced mood on self-reported life events and perceived and received social support. Journal of Personality and Social Psychology, 55, 669-674.

Cohen, S. (1988). Psychosocial models of social support in the etiology of physical disease. Health Psychology, 7, 269.

Cohen, S. (2004). Social relationships and health. American Psychologist, 59, 676-684.

Cohen, S., & Willis, T. A. (1985). Stress, social support, and the buffering hypothesis. Psychological Bulletin, 98, 310-357.

Collins, N. L. (1996). Working models of attachment: Implications for explanation, emotion, and behavior. Journal of Personality and Social Psychology, 71, 810-832.

Collins, N. L., & Feeney, B. C. (2000). A safe haven: An attachment theory perspective on support seeking and caregiving in intimate relationships. Journal of Personality and Social Psychology, 78, 1053-1073.

Collins, N. L., & Feeney, B. C. (2004). Working models of attachment shape perceptions of social support: Evidence from experimental and observational studies. Journal of Personality and Social Psychology, 87, 363-383.

Collins, N. L., & Miller, L. C. (1994). Self-disclosure and liking: A meta-analytic review. Psychological Bulletin, 116, 457-475.

Collins, N. L., & Read, S. J. (1990). Adult attachment, working models and relationship quality in dating couples. Journal of Personality and Social Psychology, 58, 644-663.

Collins, N. L., & Read, S. J. (1994). Cognitive representations of attachment: The structure and function of working models. In K. Bartholomew & D. Perlman (Eds.), Attachment processes in adulthood (pp. 53-92). London: Jessica Kingsley.

Collins, N. L., Dunkel-Schetter, C., Lobel, M., & Scrimshaw, S. C. M., (1993). Social support in pregnancy: Psychosocial correlates of birth outcomes and postpartum depression. Journal of Personality and Social Psychology, 65, 1243-1258.

Collins, R. L., & DiPaula, A. (1997). Personality and the provision of support: Emotions felt and signaled. In G. R. Pierce, B. Lakey, I. G. Sarason, & B. R. Sarason (Eds.), Sourcebook of social support and personality (pp. 429-443). New York: Plenum.

Constantino, M. J., & Castonguay, L. G. (2003). Learning from the basics: Clinical implications of social, developmental, and cross-cultural study of the self. Journal of Psychotherapy Integration, 13, 3–8

Constantino, M. J., Castonguay, L. G., & Schut, A. J. (2002). The working alliance: A flagship for the "scientist–practitioner" model in psychotherapy. In G. S. Tryon (Ed.), Counseling based on process research: Applying what we know (pp. 81–131). Boston: Allyn & Bacon.

Cook, K. (1987). Social exchange theory. Beverly Hills, CA: Sage.

Cook, W. L. (2000). Understanding attachment security in family context. Journal of Personality and Social Psychology, 78, 285–294.

Cooley, C. H. (1902). Human nature and the social order. New York: Schocken.

Coons, S. J., McGhan, W. F., Bootman, J. L., & Larson, L. N. (1989). The effect of self-care information on health-related attitudes and beliefs of college. Journal of American College Health, 38, 121–124.

Cooper, M. L., Shaver, P. R., & Collins, N. L. (1998). Attachment styles, emotion regulation, and adjustment in adolescence. Journal of Personality and Social Psychology, 74, 1380–1397.

Costello, R. M. (1975). Alcoholism treatment and evaluation: In search of methods. International Journal of the Addictions, 10, 251–275.

Coudert, J. (1965). Advice from a Failure. New York, Stein & Day.

Crepeau, J. J. (1978). The effects of stressful life events and locus of control on suicidal ideation. Unpublished research, University of Massachusetts. Cited in S. R. Maddi (1989). Personality theories: A comparative analysis. Chicago: Dorsey Press.

Crocker, J., Thompson, L. L., McGraw, K. M., & Ingerman, C. (1987). Downward comparison, prejudice, and evaluations of others: Effects of self-esteem and threat. Journal of Personality and Social Psychology, 52, 907–917.

Cromwell, R., Rosenthal, D., Shakow, D., & Kahn, T. (1961). Reaction time, locus of control, choice behavior and descriptions of parental behavior in schizophrenic and normal subjects. Journal of Personality, 29, 363–380.

Crowell, J. A., Treboux, D., Gao, Y., Fyffe, C., Pan, H., & Waters, E. (2002). Assessing secure base behavior in adulthood: Development of a measure, links to adult attachment representations, and relations to couples' communication and reports of relationships. Developmental Psychology, 38, 679–693.

Cummings, N. (2002). An interview with Nicholas Cummings, Ph.D., Sc.D., by Dan Short, Milton H. Erickson Foundation Newsletter, 22, 3, http://www.erickson-foundation.org/ipages/newsletterpdfs/Vol%2022%20No%203.pdf.

Cunningham, M. R., & Barbee, A. P. (2000). Social support. In C. Hendrick & S. S. Hendrick (Eds.), Close relationships: A sourcebook (pp. 273–285). Thousand Oaks, CA: Sage.

Cutrona, C. E. (1982). Transition to college: Loneliness and the process of social adjustment. In L. A. Peplau & D. Perlman (Eds.), Loneliness: A sourcebook of current theory, research, and therapy (pp. 291–309). New York: Wiley.

Cutrona, C. E. (1990). Stress and social support: In search of optimal matching. Journal of Social and Clinical Psychology, 9, 3–14.

Cutrona, C. E. (1996). Social support in couples: Marriage as a resource in times of stress. Thousand Oaks, CA: Sage.

Dakof, G. A. & Taylor, S. E. (1990). Victims' perceptions of social support: What is helpful from whom? Journal of Personality and Social Psychology, 58, 80–89.

Darby, B. W., & Schlenker, B. R. (1982). Children's reactions to apologies. Journal of Personality and Social Psychology, 43, 742–753.

Darwin, C. (1899). The expression of the emotions in man and animals. New York: Appleton.

Davis, C. (1997). Normal and neurotic perfectionism in eating disorders: An interactive model. International Journal of Eating Disorders, 22, 421–426.

Dawes, R. M. (1989). Experience and validity of clinical judgment: The illusory correlation. Behavioral Sciences and the Law, 1, 457–467.

De La Ronde, C., & Swann, W. B. (1993). Caught in the crossfire: Positivity and self-verification strivings among people with low self-esteem. In R. F. Baumeister (Ed.), Self-esteem: The puzzle of low self-regard (pp. 147–165). New York: Plenum Press.

de Waal, F. (1982). Chimpanzee politics: Sex and power among apes. Baltimore: Johns Hopkins University Press.

de Waal, F. (2001). The ape and the sushi master: cultural reflections by a primatologist. New York: Basic Books.

Deci, E. L., & Ryan, R. M. (1985). Intrinsic motivation and self-determination in human behavior. New York: Plenum Press.

Deci, E. L., & Ryan, R. M. (2000). The "what" and "why" of goal pursuits: Human needs and the self-determination of behavior. Psychological Inquiry, 11, 227–268.

DeGree, C. E., & Snyder, C. R. (1985). Adler's psychology (of use) today: Personal history of traumatic life events as a self-handicapping strategy. Journal of Personality and Social Psychology, 48, 1512–1519.

DeMarree, K. G., Petty, R. E., & Brinol, P. (2007). Self-certainty: Parallels to attitude certainty. International Journal of Psychology and Psychological Therapy, 7, 159–188.

DeNeve, K., & Cooper, H. (1998). The happy personality: A meta-analysis of 137 personality traits and subjective well-being. Psychological Bulletin, 124, 197–229.

DePaulo, B. M., & Friedman, H. S. (1998). Nonverbal communication. In S. T. Fiske, D. Gilbert, & G. Lindzey (Eds.), The handbook of social psychology (3rd ed., Vol. 2, pp. 3–40). Boston: McGraw-Hill.

Derlega, V. J., Wilson, M., & Chaikin, A. L. (1976). Friendship and disclosure reciprocity. Journal of Personality and Social Psychology, 34, 578–582.

Di Paula, A., & Campbell, J. D. (2002). Self-esteem and persistence in the face of failure. Journal of Personality and Social Psychology, 83, 711–723.

Diehl, M., Elnick, A. B., Bourbeau, L. S., & Labouvie-Vief, G. (1998). Adult attachment styles: Their relations to family context and personality. Journal of Personality and Social Psychology, 74, 1656–1669.

Diener, E., & Diener, M. (1995). Cross-cultural correlates of life satisfaction and self-esteem. Journal of Personality and Social Psychology, 68, 653–663.

Dienstbier, R. A., Hillman, D., Lehnhoff, J., Hillman, J., & Valkenaare (1975). An emotion attribute approach to moral behavior: Interfacing cognitive and avoidance theories of moral development. Psychological Review, 82, 299.

DiGiuseppe, R., Linscott, J., & Jilton, R. (1996). Developing the therapeutic alliance in child-adolescent psychotherapy. Applied and Preventive Psychology, 5, 85–100.

DiMatteo, M. R., Tarranta, A., Friedman, H. S., & Prince, L. M. (1980). Predicting Patient's Satisfaction from Physicians' Nonverbal Communication Skills. Medical Care, 18, 376–387

DiPaula, A., & Campbell, J. D. (2002). Self-esteem and persistence in the face of failure. Journal of Personality and Social Psychology, 83, 711–724.

Dolan, R. T., Arnkoff, D. B., & Glass, C. R. (1993). Client attachment style and the psychotherapist's interpersonal stance. Psychotherapy, 30, 408–412.

Dolan, Y. (2000). An interview with Yvonne Dolan, MSW, by Dan Short, Milton H. Erickson Foundation Newsletter, 20, 2, http://www.erickson-foundation.org/ipages/newsletterpdfs/Vol%2020%20No%202.pdf.

Downey, G., Freitas, A. L., Michaelis, B., & Khouri, H. (1998). The self-fulfilling prophecy in close relationships: Rejection sensitivity and rejection by romantic partners. Journal of Personality and Social Psychology, 75, 545–560.

Dozier, M. (1990). Attachment organization and treatment use for adults with serious psychopathological disorders. Development and Psychopathology, 2, 47–60.

Dozier, M., Cue, K., & Barnett, L. (1994). Clinicians as caregivers: Role of attachment organization in treatment. Journal of Consulting and Clinical Psychology, 62, 793–800.

Driscoll, D. M., Hamilton, D. L., & Sorrentino, R. M. (1991). Uncertainty orientation and recall of person-descriptive information. Journal of Personality and Social Psychology, 17, 494–500.

Dryer, D. C., & Horowitz, L. M. (1997). When do opposites attract?: Interpersonal complementarity versus similarity. Journal of Personality and Social Psychology, 72, 592–603.

Dubois, D. L., & Flay, B. R. (2004). The healthy pursuit of self-esteem: Comment on and alternative to the Crocker and Park (2004) formulation. Psychological Bulletin, 130, 415–420.

Duke, M. P., Lazarus, A., & Fivush, R. (2008). Knowledge of family history as a clinically useful index of psychological well-being and prognosis: A brief report. Psychotherapy: Theory, Research, Practice, Training, 45, 268–272.

Duncan, B. L. (2002). The legacy of Saul Rosenzweig: The profundity of the dodo bird. Journal of Psychotherapy Integration, 12, 32–57.

Dunkel-Schetter, C., Blasband, D. E., Feinstein, L. G., & Herbert, T. B. (1992). Elements of supportive interactions: When are attempts to help effective? In S. Spacapan & S. Oskamp (Eds.), Helping and being helped: Naturalistic studies. The Claremont Symposium on applied psychology (pp. 83–114). Newbury Park, CA: Sage.

Dunkle, J. H., & Friedlander, M. L. (1996). Contribution of therapist experience and personal characteristics to the working alliance. Journal of Counseling Psychology, 43, 456–460.

Dunkley, D. M., Zuroff, D. C., & Blankstein, K. R. (2003). Self-critical perfectionism and daily affect: Dispositional and situational influences on stress and coping. Journal of Personality and Social Psychology, 84, 234–252.

Dunning, D. (2003). The zealous self-affirmer: How and why the self lurks so pervasively behind social judgment. In S. J. Spencer, S. Fein, & M. P. Zanna (Eds.), Motivated social perception: The Ontario Symposium Vol. 9: Ontario Symposium on personal and social psychology (pp. 45–72). Mahwah, NJ: Erlbaum.

Durana, C. (1998). The use of touch in psychotherapy: Ethical and clinical guidelines. Psychotherapy, 35, 269–280.

Dykman, B., Abramson, L. Y., Alloy, L. B., & Hartlage, S. (1989). Processing of ambiguous and unambiguous feedback by depressed and nondepressed college students: Schematic biases and their implications for depressive realism. Journal of Personality and Social Psychology, 56, 431–445.

Eagly, A. H., & Chaiken, S. (1993). Psychology of attitudes. Fort Worth, TX: Harcourt, Brace, Jovanovich.

Eames, V., & Roth, A. (2000). Patient attachment orientation and the early working alliance: A study of patient and therapist reports of alliance quality and ruptures. Psychotherapy Research, 10, 421–434.

Eaton, J., Struthers, C. W., & Santelli, A. G. (2006). The mediating role of perceptual validation in the repentance-forgiveness process. Personality and Social Psychology Bulletin, 32, 1389–1401.

Eden, D., & Aviram, A. (1993). Self-efficacy training to speed reemployment: Helping people to help themselves. Journal of Applied Psychology, 78, 352–360.

Eden, D., & Ravid, G. (1982). Pygmalion vs. self-expectancy effects of instructor- and self-expectancy on trainee performance. *Organizational Behavior and Human Performance, 30,* 351–364.

Edwards, C. E., & Murdock, N. L. (1994). Characteristics of therapist self-disclosure in the counseling process. *Journal of Counseling and Development, 72,* 384–389.

Edwards, G., Orford, J., Egert, S., Guthrie, S., Hawker, A., Hensman, C., . . . Taylor, C. (1977). Alcoholism: A controlled trial of "treatment" and "advice." *Journal of Studies on Alcohol, 38,* 1004–1031.

Eibl-Eibesfeldt, I. (1975). *Ethology: The biology of human behavior.* New York: Holt, Rinehart & Winston.

Eisenthal, S., Koopman, C., & Lazare, A. (1983). Process analysis of two dimensions of the negotiated approach in relation to satisfaction in the initial interview. *Journal of Nervous and Mental Disease, 171,* 49–54

Elkin, I., Shea, M. T., Watkins, J. T., Imber, S. D., Sotsky, S. M., Collins, J. F., . . . Parloff, M. B. (1989). National Institute of Mental Health Treatment of Depression Collaborative Research Program: General effectiveness of treatments. *Archives of General Psychiatry, 46,* 971–982.

Elliot, A. J., & Reis, H. T. (2003). Attachment and exploration in adulthood. *Journal of Personality and Social Psychology, 85,* 317–331.

Ellis, A. (2000). *How to control your anxiety before it controls you.* New York: Citadel Press

Emmons, R. A. & McCullough, M. E. (2003). Counting blessings versus burdens: An experimental investigation of gratitude and subjective well-being. *Journal of Personality and Social Psychology, 84,* 377–389.

Epstein, S., & Morling, B. (1995). Is the self motivated to do more than enhance and/or verify itself? In M. H. Kernis (Ed.), *Efficacy, agency, and self-esteem* (pp. 9–29). New York: Plenum.

Erickson, M. H. (1934). A brief survey of hypnotism. Reprinted in Rossi, E. L. (Ed.), *The collected papers of Milton H. Erickson,* Vol. III (1980, 3--12). New York: Irvington.

Erickson, M. H. (1944). Hypnosis in medicine. *Medical Clinics of North America.* Reprinted in Rossi, E. L. (Ed.), *The collected papers of Milton H. Erickson,* Vol. IV (1980, 14–27). New York: Irvington.

Erickson, M. H. (1959). A lecture by Milton H. Erickson, San Francisco, September 11, 1959. Cited in D. Short, B. A. Erickson, & R. Erickson-Klein (2005). *Hope and resiliency: The therapeutic strategies of Milton H. Erickson.* London: Crown House.

Erickson, M. H. (1964). The burden of responsibility in effective psychotherapy. *The American Journal of Clinical Hypnosis, 6,* 269–271.

Erskine, R., Moursund, J., & Trautmann R. (2003). Beyond empathy: A therapy of contact-in-relationship. *Journal of Psychotherapy Integration, 13,* 96–100.

Estroff, S. D., & Nowicki, S. (1992). Interpersonal complementarity, gender of interactants, and performance on puzzle and word tasks. *Personality and Social Psychology Bulletin, 18,* 351–356.

Eton, J., Struthers, C. W., Shomrony, A., & Santelli, A. G. (2007). When apologies fail: The moderating effect of implicit and explicit self-esteem on apology and forgiveness. *Self and Identity, 6,* 209–222.

Exline, J. J., & Baumeister, R. F. (2000). Expressing forgiveness and repentance: Benefits and barriers. In M. E. McCullough, K. I. Pargament, & C. E. Thoresen (Eds.), *The psychology of forgiveness* (pp. 133–155). New York: Guilford.

Exline, J. J., Baumeister, R. F., Bushman, B. J., Campbell, W. K., & Finkel, E. J. (2004). Too proud to let go: Narcissistic entitlement as a barrier to forgiveness. *Journal of Personality and Social Psychology, 87,* 894–912.

Eysenck, H. J., & Wakefield, J. A. (1981). Psychological factors as predictors of marital satisfaction. Advances in Behavior Research and Therapy, 3, 151–192.

Farber, B. A. (2003). Patient self-disclosure: A review of the research. Journal of Clinical Psychology, 59, 589–600.

Farber, B. A., Berano, K. C., Capobianco, J. A. (2004). Clients' perceptions of the process and consequences of self-disclosure in psychotherapy. Journal of Counseling Psychology, 51, 340–346.

Farber, B. A., Lippert, R. A., & Nevas, D. B (1995). The therapist as attachment figure. Psychotherapy: Theory, Research, Practice, Training, 32, 204–212.

Fazio, R. H. (1989). On the power and functionality of attitudes: The role of attitude accessibility. In A. R. Pratkanis, S. J. Breckler, & A. G. Greenwald (Eds.), Attitude structure and function (pp. 153–180). Mahwah, NJ: Erlbaum.

Fazio, R. H. (2001). On the automatic activation of associated evaluations: An overview. Cognition and Emotion, 14, 1–27.

Fazio, R. H., Effrein, E. A., & Falender, V. J. (1981). Self-perceptions following social interactions. Journal of Personality and Social Psychology, 41, 232–242.

Feeney, B. C. (2004). A secure base: Responsive support of goal strivings and exploration in adult intimate relationships. Journal of Personality and Social Psychology, 87, 631–648.

Feeney, B. C., & Collins, N. L. (2001). Predictors of caregiving in adult intimate relationships: An attachment theoretical perspective. Journal of Personality and Social Psychology, 80, 972–994.

Feeney, J. A. (1998). Adult attachment and relationship-centered anxiety. In J. A. Simpson & W. A. Rholes (Eds.), Attachment theory and close relationships (pp. 189–218). New York: Guilford Press.

Feeney, J. A. (1999). Adult attachment, emotional control, and marital satisfaction. Personal Relationships, 6, 169-185.

Feeney, J. A., & Noller, P. (1990). Attachment style as a predictor of adult romantic relationships. Journal of Personality and Social Psychology, 58, 281–291.

Feeney, J. A., & Ryan, S. M. (1994). Attachment style and affect regulation: Relationships with health behavior and family experiences of illness in a student sample. Health Psychology, 13, 334–345.

Feeney, J. A., Noller, P., & Callan, V. J. (1994). Attachment style, communication and satisfaction in the early years of marriage. In K. Bartholomew & D. Perlman (Eds.), Attachment processes in adulthood: Vol. 5. Advances in personal relationships (pp. 269–308). London: Jessica Kingsley.

Fein, S., & Spencer, S. J. (1997). Prejudice as self-image maintenance: Affirming the self through derogating others. Journal of Personality and Social Psychology, 73, 31–44.

Felson, R. B. (1989). Parents and the reflected appraisal process: A longitudinal analysis. Journal of Personality and Social Psychology, 56, 965–971.

Ferguson, M. J., & Bargh, J. A. (2004). Liking is for doing: The effects of goal pursuit on automatic evaluation. Journal of Personality and Social Psychology, 87, 557–572.

Fisher, J. D., Nadler, A., & Whitcher-Alagna, S. (1982). Recipient reactions to aid. Psychological Bulletin, 91, 2–54.

Fiske, A. P., Haslam, N., & Fiske, S. T. (1991). Confusing one person with another: What errors reveal about the elementary forms of social relations. Journal of Personality and Social Psychology, 60, 656–674.

Fiske, S. T. (1993). Controlling other people: The impact of power on stereotyping. American Psychologist, 48, 621–628.

Fiske, S. T. (1998). Stereotyping, prejudice, and discrimination. In D. Gilbert, S. Fiske, & G. Lindzey (Eds.), The handbook of social psychology (4th ed., Vol. 2, pp. 357–411). New York: McGraw-Hill.

Fiske, S. T., & Neuberg, S. L. (1990). A continuum model of impression formation, from category-based to individuating processes: Influence of information and motivation on attention and interpretation. In M. P. Zanna (Ed.), Advances in experimental social psychology (Vol. 23, pp. 1–74). San Diego, CA: Academic Press.

Fiske, S. T., & Taylor, S. E. (1984). Social cognition. Reading, MA: Addison-Wesley.

Florian, V., Milulincer, M., & Bucholtz, I. (1995). Effects of adult attachment style on the perception and search for social support. Journal of Psychology, 129, 665–676.

Flowers, L. A., Milner, H. R., & Moore, J. L. (2003). Effects of locus of control on African-American high school seniors' educational aspirations: implications for preservice and inservice high school teachers and counselors. High School Journal, 87, 39–50.

Fonagy, P., Gergely, G., Jurist, E. L., & Target, M. (2002). Affect regulation, metallization, and the development of the self. New York: Other Press.

Foreman, S. A., & Marmar, C. R. (1985). Therapist actions that address initially poor therapeutic alliances in psychotherapy. American Journal of Psychiatry, 142, 922–926.

Fraley, R. C., & Shaver, P. R. (1997). Adult attachment and the suppression of unwanted thoughts. Journal of Personality and Social Psychology, 73, 1080–1091.

Fraley, R. C., & Shaver, P. R. (1998). Airport separations: A naturalistic study of adult attachment dynamics in separating couples. Journal of Personality and Social Psychology, 75, 1198–1212.

Fraley, R. C., Davis, K. E., & Shaver, P. R. (1998). Dismissing-avoidance and the defensive organization of emotion, cognition, and behavior. In J. A. Simpson & W. S. Rholes (Eds.), Attachment theory and close relationships (pp. 249–279). New York: Guilford Press.

Fraley, R. C., Garner, J. P., & Shaver, P. R. (2000). Adult attachment and the defensive regulation of attention and memory: Examining the role of preemptive and postemptive defensive processes. Journal of Personality and Social Psychology, 79, 816–826.

Frank, J. D. (1971). Therapeutic factors in psychotherapy. American Journal of Psychotherapy, 25, 350–361.

Frank, J. D. (1974). Persuasion and healing (rev. ed.). New York: Schocken.

Frank, J. D., & Frank, J. B. (1991). Persuasion and healing: A comparative study of psychotherapy (3rd ed.). Baltimore: Johns Hopkins University Press.

Frankl, V. E. (1996). An interview with Viktor Frankl, MD, by Dan Short. Milton H. Erickson Foundation Newsletter, 16, 3 (Phoenix, AZ: Milton H. Erickson Foundation Archives).

Fredrickson, B. L., & Losada, M. (2005). Positive emotions and the complex dynamics of human flourishing. American Psychologist, 60, 678–686.

Freud, S. (1901–1905). Fragment of an analysis of a case of hysteria. In J. Strachey (Ed. and Trans.), The standard edition of the complete psychological works of Sigmund Freud (Vol. 7, pp. 3–122). London: Hogarth.

Freud, S. (1913). On the beginning of treatment: Further recommendations on the technique of psychoanalysis. In J. Strachey (Ed.), The standard edition of the complete psychological works of Sigmund Freud (Vol. 12, pp. 122–144). London: Hogarth.

Freud, S. (1914). On narcissism: An introduction. In J. Strachey (Ed.), The standard edition of the complete psychological works of Sigmund Freud (Vol. 14, pp. 76-104). London: Hogarth.

Freud, S. (1924). Further remarks on the defense neuropsychoses. In J. Strachey (Ed.), The standard edition of the complete psychological works of Sigmund Freud (Vol. 1). London: Hogarth.

Freud, S. (1940/1953). Abriss der psychoanalyse [An outline of psychoanalysis]. Frankfurt am Main, Germany: Fischer Bucherei.

Frey, S., Jorns, U., & Daw, W. (1980). A systematic description and analysis of nonverbal interaction between doctors and patients in a psychiatric interview. In S. A. Corson, E. O. Corson, & J. A. Alexander (Eds.), Ethology and nonverbal communication in mental health (pp. 231–258). New York: Pergamon.

Fuller, F., & Hill, C. E. (1985). Counselor and helpee perceptions of counselor intentions in relation to outcome in a single counseling session. Journal of Counseling Psychology, 32, 329–338.

Gable, S. L., Gonzaga, G. C., & Strachman, A. (2006) Will you be there for me when things go right? Supportive responses to positive event disclosures. Journal of Personality and Social Psychology, 91, 904–917.

Gable, S. L., Reis, H. T., Impett, E. A., & Asher, E. R. (2004). What do you do when things go right? The intrapersonal and interpersonal benefits of sharing positive events. Journal of Personality and Social Psychology, 87, 2004, 228–245.

Garb, H. B., & Schramke, C. J. (1996). Judgment research and neuropsychological assessment: A narrative review and meta-analysis. Psychological Bulletin, 120, 140–153.

Garfield, S. L. (1981). Critical issues in the effectiveness of psychotherapy. In C. E. Walker (Ed.), Clinical practice of psychology (pp. 161–188). Elmsford, NY: Pergamon.

Garland, H., & Adkinson, J. H. (1985). Standards, persuasion, and performance: A test of cognitive mediation theory. Group & Organization Studies, 12, 208–220.

Gaston, L. (1990). The concept of the alliance and its role in psychotherapy: Theoretical and empirical considerations. Psychotherapy, 27, 143–153.

Gaston, L., Marmar, C. R., Gallagher, D. & Thompson, L. W. (1991). Alliance prediction of outcome beyond intreatment symptomatic change as psychotherapy process. Psychotherapy Research, 1, 104–113.

Gawronski, B., & Bodenhausen, G. V. (2006). Associative and propositional processes in evaluation: An integrative review of implicit and explicit attitude change. Psychological Bulletin, 132, 692–731.

Gelso, C. J., & Carter, J. A. (1985). The relationship in counseling and psychotherapy: Components, consequences, and theoretical antecedents. The Counseling Psychologist, 13, 155–243.

Gelso, C. J., & Hayes, J. A. (2001). Countertransference management. Psychotherapy: Theory, Research, Practice, Training, 38, 418–422.

George, C., & Solomon, J. (1999). Attachment and caregiving: The caregiving behavioral system. In J. Cassidy & P. R. Shaver (Eds.), Handbook of attachment: Theory, research, and clinical applications (pp. 649–670). New York: Guilford Press.

Gergen, K. J. (1991). The saturated self: Dilemmas of identity in contemporary life. New York: Basic Books.

Gibbons, F. X., & McCoy, S. B. (1991). Self-esteem, similarity, and reactions to active versus passive downward comparison. Journal of Personality and Social Psychology, 60, 414–424.

Gilbert, D. T., & Osborne, R. E. (1989). Thinking backward: Some curable and incurable consequences of cognitive busyness. Journal of Personality and Social Psychology, 57, 940–949.

Glass, C. R., Arnkoff, D., & Shapiro, S. J. (2001). Expectations and preferences. Psychotherapy: Theory, Research, Practice, Training, 38, 455–461.

Goffman, E. (1971). Relations in public: Microstudies of the public order. New York: Basic.

Gold, G. J., & Weiner, B. (2000). Remorse, confession, group identity, and expectancies about repeating a transgression. Basic and Applied Social Psychology, 22, 291–300.

Goldberg, S. (1997). Attachment and childhood behavior problems in normal, at risk, and clinical samples. In L. Atkinson & K. J. Zucker (Eds.), Attachment and Psychopathology (pp. 171–195). New York: Guilford.

Goldfried, M. R. (1980). Toward the delineation of therapeutic change principles. American Psychologist, 35, 991–999.

Goldfried, M. R. (1999). A participant-observer's perspective on psychotherapy integration. Journal of Psychotherapy Integration, 9, 235–242.

Goldfried, M. R. (2004). Integrating Integratively Oriented Brief Psychotherapy. Journal of Psychotherapy Integration, 14, 93–105.

Goldstein, A. P. (1962). Therapist-patient expectancies in psychotherapy. Oxford, UK: Pergamon.

Goldstein, J. M., Cohen, P., Lewis, S. A., & Struening, E. L. (1988). Community treatment environments: Patient vs. staff evaluations. Journal of Nervous and Mental Disease, 176, 227–233.

Gomes-Schwartz, B. (1978). Effective ingredients in psychotherapy: Prediction of outcome from process variables. Journal of Consulting and Clinical Psychology, 46, 1023–1035.

Goodall, J. (1986). The chimpanzees of Gombe: Patterns of behavior. Cambridge, MA: Belknap Press of Harvard University Press.

Goodman S. H., Cooley E. L., Sewell D. R., & Leavitt N. (1994). Locus of control and self-esteem in depressed, low-income African-American women. Community Mental Health Journal, 30, 259–269.

Gottman, J. M. (1979). Marital interaction: Experimental investigations. New York: Academic Press.

Gottman, J. M. (1994). What Predicts Divorce? The Relationship Between Marital Processes and Marital Outcomes. Hillsdale, New Jersey, Lawrence Erlbaum Associates, Inc.

Gouaux, C. (1971). Induced affective states and interpersonal attraction. Journal of Personality and Social Psychology, 20, 37–43.

Grau, I., & Doll, J. (2003). Effects of Attachment Styles on the Experience of Equity in Heterosexual Couples Relationships. Experimental Psychology, 50, 298–310.

Greenberg, J., & Pyszczynski, T. (1985). Compensatory self-inflation: A response to the threat to self-regard of public failure. Journal of Experimental Social Psychology, 49, 351–372.

Greenberg, J., Solomon, S., & Pyszczynski, T. (1997). Terror-management theory of self-esteem and cultural worldviews: Empirical assessments and conceptual refinements. In M. P. Zanna (Ed.), Advances in experimental social psychology (Vol. 29, pp. 61–139). New York: Academic Press.

Greenberg, J., Solomon, S., Pyszczynski, T., Rosenblatt, A., Burling, J., & Lyon, D. (1992). Why do people need self-esteem? Converging evidence that self-esteem serves an anxiety-buffering function. Journal of Personality and Social Psychology, 63, 913–922.

Greenberg, L. S. & Pascual-Leone, J. (1995). A dialectical constructivist approach to experiential change. In R. A. Neimeyer & M. J. Mahoney (Eds.), Constructivism in psychotherapy (pp. 169–191). Washington, DC: American Psychological Association.

Greenberg, L. S. & Safran, J. D. (1987). Emotion in psychotherapy: Affect, cognition, and the process of change. New York: Guilford Press.

Greenberg, L. S. (2002). Emotion-focused therapy: Coaching clients to work with their feelings. Washington, DC: American Psychological Association.

Greenberg, L. S., Elliott, R., Watson, J. C., & Bohart, A. C. (2001). Empathy. Psychotherapy: Theory, Research, Practice, Training, 38, 380–384.

Greenberg, L. S., Rice, L. N. & Elliott, R. (1993). Facilitating emotional change: The moment-by-moment process. New York: Guilford Press.

Greenson, R. R. (1965). The working alliance and the transference neurosis. The Psychoanalytic Quarterly, 34, 151–181.

Greenwald, A. G. (1980). The totalitarian ego: Fabrication and revision of personal history. American Psychologist, 35, 603–618.

Greenwald, A. G., Banaji, M. R., Rudman, L. A., Farnham, S. D., Nosek, B. A., & Mellott, D. S. (2002). A unified theory of implicit attitudes, stereotypes, self-esteem, and self-concept. Psychological Review, 109, 3–25.

Greenwald, A. G., McGhee, D. E., & Schwarz, J. L. K. (1998). Measuring individual differences in implicit cognition: The Implicit Association Test. Journal of Personality and Social Psychology, 74, 1464–1480.

Gruder, C. L. (1977). Choice of comparison persons in evaluating oneself. In J. M. Suls & R. L. Miller (Eds.), Social comparison processes: Theoretical and empirical perspectives (pp. 21–41). Washington, DC: Hemisphere.

Grusec, J. E., & Mammone, N. (1995). Features and sources of parents' attributions about themselves and their children. In N. Eisenberg (Ed.), Review of personality and social psychology (Vol. 15, pp. 49–73). Thousand Oaks, CA: Sage.

Grzegorek, J. L., Slaney, R. B., Franze, S., & Rice, K. G. (2004). Self-criticism, dependency, self-esteem, and grade point average satisfaction among clusters of perfectionists and nonperfectionists. Journal of Counseling Psychology, 51, 192–200.

Gurman, A. S. (1977). The patient's perceptions of the therapeutic relationship. In A. S. Gurman & A. M. Razin (Eds.), Effective psychotherapy (pp. 503–545). New York: Pergamon.

Hadley, J. A., Holloway, E. L., & Mallinckrodt, B. (1993). Common aspects of object relations and self representations in offspring from disparate dysfunctional families. Journal of Counseling Psychology, 40, 348–356.

Haggbloom, S. J. (2002). The 100 most eminent psychologists of the 20th century. Review of General Psychology, 6, 139–152.

Haley, J. (1986). The power tactics of Jesus Christ and other essays. Rockville: MD: Triangle Press.

Hammer, M. (1981). "Core" and "extended" social networks in relation to health and illness. Social Science and Medicine, 17, 405–411.

Harackiewicz, J. M., Sansone, C., Blair, L. W., & Epstein, J. A., (1987). Attributional processes in behavior change and maintenance: Smoking cessation and continued abstinence. Journal of Consulting and Clinical Psychology, 55, 372–378.

Harris, R. N., & Snyder, C. R. (1986). The role of uncertain self-esteem in self-handicapping. Journal of Personality and Social Psychology, 51, 451–458.

Harvey, S. and Kelly, E. (1993). Evaluations of the quality of parent-child relationships: A longitudinal case study. Arts in Psychotherapy, 20, 71–82.

Hass, R. G., & Grady, K. (1975). Temporal delay, type of forewarning, and resistance to influence. Journal of Experimental Social Psychology, 11, 459–469.

Hatcher, R. L. (1999). Therapists' views of treatment alliance and collaboration in therapy. Psychotherapy Research, 9, 405–423.

Hatcher, R. L., & Barends, A. W. (1996). Patients' views of the alliance in psychotherapy: Exploratory factor analysis of three alliance measures. Journal of Consulting and Clinical Psychology, 64, 1326–1336.

Hatfield, E., Cacioppo, J. T., & Rapson, R. L. (1994). Emotional contagion. New York: Cambridge University Press.

Hawley, P. H. (1999). The ontogenesis of social dominance: A strategy-based evolutionary perspective. Developmental Review, 19, 97–132.

Hawley, P. H. (2002). Social dominance and prosocial and coercive strategies of resource control in preschoolers. International Journal of Behavioral Development, 26, 167–176.

Hawley, P. H., & Little, T. D. (1999). On winning some and losing some: A social relations approach to social Dominance in toddlers. Merrill-Palmer Quarterly, 45, 185–214.

Hawley, P. H., Little, T. D., & Pasupathi, M. (2002). Winning friends and influencing peers: Strategies of peer influence in late childhood. International Journal of Behavioral Development, 26, 466–474.

Hays, R. B. (1985). A longitudinal study of friendship development. Journal of Personality and Social Psychology, 48, 909–924.

Hazan, C., & Shaver, P. (1987). Romantic love conceptualized as an attachment process. Journal of Personality and Social Psychology, 52, 511–524.

Hazan, C., & Shaver, P. R. (1990). Love and work: An attachment-theoretical perspective. Journal of Personality and Social Psychology, 59, 270–280.

Heatherington, L., & Friedlander, M. L. (1990). Complementarity and symmetry in family therapy communication. Journal of Counseling Psychology, 37, 261–268.

Henry, W. P. (1998). Science, politics, and the politics of science: The use and misuse of empirically validated treatment research. Psychotherapy Research, 8, 126–140.

Henry, W. P., & Strupp, H. H. (1994). The therapeutic alliance as interpersonal process. In A. O. Horvath & L. S. Greenberg (Eds.), The working alliance: Theory, research and practice (pp. 51–84). New York: Wiley.

Heppner, P. P., & Lee, D. (2002). Problem-solving appraisal and psychological adjustment. In C. R. Snyder & S. J. Lopez (Eds.), Handbook of positive psychology (pp. 288–298). New York: Oxford University Press.

Herman, J. L. (1992). Trauma and recovery. New York: Basic Books.

Hersen, M., Kazdin, A. E., & Bellack, A. S. (1991). The clinical psychology handbook. New York: Pergamon Press.

Hesse, E. (1999). The Adult Attachment Interview: Historical and current perspectives. In J. Cassidy & P. R. Shaver (Eds.), Handbook of attachment: Theory, research, and clinical applications (pp. 395–433). New York: Guilford Press.

Hetts, J. J., & Pelham, B. W. (2001). A case for the nonconscious self-concept. In G. B. Moskowitz (Ed.), Cognitive social psychology: The Princeton Symposium on the legacy and future of social cognition (pp. 105–123). Mahwah, NJ: Erlbaum.

Higgins, E. T. (1998). Promotion and prevention: Regulatory focus as a motivational principle. In P. M. Zanna (Ed.), Advances in experimental social psychology (Vol. 30, pp. 1–46). New York: Academic Press.

Higgins, E. T., Shah, J., & Friedman, R. (1997). Emotional responses to goal attainment: Strength of regulatory focus as a moderator. Journal of Personality and Social Psychology, 72, 515–525.

Hill, C. E., & Knox, S. (2001). Self-Disclosure. Psychotherapy: Theory, Research, Practice, Training, 38, 413–417.

Hill, C. E., Helms, J. E., Tichenor, V., Spiegel, S. B., O'Grady, K. E., & Perry, E. S. (1988). The effects of therapist response modes in brief psychotherapy. Journal of Counseling Psychology, 35, 222–233.

Hill, C. E., Mahalik, J. R., & Thompson, B. J. (1989). Therapist self-disclosure. Psychotherapy, 26, 290–295.

Hill, C. E., Nutt-Williams, E., Heaton, K. J., Thompson, B. J., & Rhodes, R. H. (1996). Therapist retrospective recall impasses in long-term psychotherapy: A qualitative analysis. Journal of Counseling Psychology, 43, 207–217.

Hill, C. E., Thompson, B. J., Cogar, M. C., & Denman, D. W. (1993). Beneath the surface of long-term therapy: Therapist and client report of their own and each other's covert processes. Journal of Counseling Psychology, 40, 278–287.

Hinkley, K., & Anderson, S. M. (1996). The working self-concept in transference: Significant-other activation and self-change. Journal of Personality and Social Psychology, 71, 1279–1295.

Hixon, J. G., & Swann, W. B. (1993). When does introspection bear fruit? Self-reflection, self-insight, and interpersonal choices. Journal of Personality and Social Psychology, 64, 35–43.

Hobbs, N. (1962). Sources of gain in psychotherapy. American Psychologist, 17, 741–747.

Hokanson, J. E., Rubert, M. P., Welker R. A., Hollander, G. R., & Hedeen, C. (1989). Interpersonal concomitants and antecedents of depression among college students. Journal of Abnormal Psychology, 98, 209–217.

Holmes, J. G. (2002). Interpersonal expectations as the building blocks of social cognition: An interdependence theory perspective. Personal Relationships, 9, 1–26.

Homans P. (1995). Jung in context: Modernity and the making of a psychology. Chicago: University of Chicago Press.

Horowitz, L. M., Dryer, D. C., & Krasnoperova, E. N. (1997). The circumplex structure of interpersonal problems. In R. Plutchik & H. R. Conte (Eds.), Circumplex models of personality and emotions. Washington, DC: American Psychological Association.

Horowitz, L. M., Locke, K. D., Morse, M. B., Waikar, S. V., Dryer, D. C., Tarnow, E., & Ghannam, J. (1991). Self-derogations and the interpersonal theory. Journal of Personality and Social Psychology, 61, 68–79.

Horowitz, L. M., Rosenberg, S. E., & Bartholomew, K. (1993). Interpersonal problems, attachment styles, and outcome in brief dynamic psychotherapy. Journal of Consulting and Clinical Psychology, 61, 549–560.

Horvath, A. O. (2001). The alliance. Psychotherapy: Theory, Research, Practice, Training, 38, 365–372.

Horvath, A. O., & Greenberg, L. S. (1986). The development of the working alliance inventory. In L. S. Greenberg & W. M. Pinsoff (Eds.), The psychotherapeutic process: A research handbook (pp. 529–556). New York: Guilford Press.

Horvath, A. O., & Greenberg, L. S. (1994). The working alliance: Theory, research, and practice. New York: Wiley.

Horvath, A. O., & Luborsky, L. (1993). The role of the therapeutic alliance in psychotherapy. Journal of Consulting and Clinical Psychology, 61, 561–573.

Horvath, A. O., & Symonds, D. B. (1991). Relationship between working alliance and outcome in psychotherapy: A meta-analysis. Journal of Counseling Psychology, 38, 139–149.

Horvath, A. O., Marx, R. W., & Kamann, A. M. (1990). Thinking about thinking in therapy: An examination of clients' understanding of their therapists' intentions. Journal of Consulting and Clinical Psychology, 58, 614–621.

Hoyt, M., Xenakis, S., Marmar, C., & Horowitz, M. J. (1983). Therapists' actions that influence their perceptions of "good" psychotherapy sessions. Journal of Nervous and Mental Disease, 171, 400–404.

Hrynchak, D., & Fouts, G. (1998). Perception of affect attunement by adolescents. Journal of Adolescence, 21, 43–48.

Ickes, W. (1997). Introduction. In W. Ickes (Ed.), Empathic accuracy (pp. 1–16). New York: Guilford Press.

Ilardo, J. (1992) Risk-taking for personal growth. Oakland, CA: Harbinger.

Insko, C. A., & Gilmore, R. F. (1984). Self-esteem and the evaluation of chosen and unchosen alternatives. Representative Research in Social Psychology, 14, 12–29.

Iwakabe, S., Rogan, K., & Stalikas, A. (2000). The relationship between client emotional expressions, therapist interventions, and the working alliance: An exploration of eight emotional expression events. Journal of Psychotherapy Integration, 10, 375–401.

Jacobs, A. (1974). The use of feedback in groups. In A. Jacobs & W. E. Spradlin (Eds.), The group as an agent of change (pp. 408–448). New York: Behavioral Publications.

Jacobson, N. S. (1989). The politics of intimacy. Behavior Therapist, 12, 29–32.

Jacobson, N. S., & Gottman, J. M. (1998). When men batter women: New insights into ending abusive relationships. New York: Simon & Schuster.

Jacoby, L. L., & Dallas, M. (1981). On the relationship between autobiographical memory and perceptual learning. Journal of Experimental Psychology: General, 3, 306–340.

James, W. (1890). Principles of psychology (Vols. I–II). New York: Henry Holt & Company.

James, W. (1892/1985). Psychology: The briefer course. Notre Dame, IN: University of Notre Dame Press.

Jeson, A. M., & Moore, S. G. (1977). The effect of attribution statements on cooperativeness and competitiveness in school age boys. Child Development, 48, 305–307.

Johnson, E. A., Vincent, N., & Ross, L. (1997). Self-deception versus self-esteem in buffering the negative effects of failure. Journal of Research in Personality, 31, 385–405.

Johnson, S. M. (2002). Emotionally Focused Couple Therapy with Trauma Survivors. New York, Guilford.

Johnson, S. M., & Whiffen, V. E. (1999). Made to measure: Adapting emotionally focused couples therapy to couples attachment styles. Clinical Psychology: Science and Practice, 6, 366-381.

Jones, B. (1983). Healing factors of psychiatry in light of attachment theory. American Journal of Psychotherapy, 35, 235–244.

Jones, E. E., Rhodewalt, F., Berglas, S. C., & Skelton, A. (1981). Effects of strategic self-presentation on subsequent self-esteem. Journal of Personality and Social Psychology, 41, 407–421.

Jones, S. S., Collins, K., & Hong, H. W. (1991). An audience effect on smile production in 10-month-old infants. Psychological Science, 2, 45–49.

Jones, W. H. (1981). Loneliness and social contact. Journal of Social Psychology, 113, 295–296.

Jones, W. H., Freemon, J. E., & Goswick, R. A. (1981). The persistence of loneliness: Self and other determinants. Journal of Personality, 49, 27–48.

Jordan, C. H., Whitfield, M., & Zeigler-Hill, V. (2007). Intuition and the correspondence between implicit and explicit self-esteem. Journal of Personality and Social Psychology, 93, 1067–1079.

Josephs, R. A., Larrick, R. P., Steele, C. M., & Nisbett, R. E. (1991). Protecting the self from the negative consequences of risky decisions. Journal of Personality and Social Psychology, 62, 26–37.

Judge, T. A., Erez, A., & Bono, J. E. (1998). The power of being positive: The relation between positive self-concept and job performance. Human Performance, 11, 167–187.

Judge, T. A., Erez, A., Bono, J. E., & Thoresen, C. J. (2002). Are measures of self-esteem, neuroticism, locus of control, and generalized self-efficacy indicators of a common core construct? Journal of Personality and Social Psychology, 83, 693–710.

Kalter, N., Alpern, D., Spence, R., & Plunkett, J. W. (1984). Locus of control in children of divorce. Journal of Personality Assessment, 48, 410–414.

Kanninen, K., Salo, J., & Punamäki, R. L. (2000). Attachment patterns and working alliance in trauma therapy for victims of political violence. Psychotherapy Research, 10, 435–449.

Karen, R. (1994). Becoming attached: Unfolding the mystery of the infant-mother bond and its impact on later life. New York: Warner.

Keating, C. (1985). Human dominance signals: The primate in us. In S. L. Ellyson & J. F. Dovidio (Eds.), Power, dominance, and nonverbal behavior (pp. 89–108). New York: Springer-Verlag.

Kemp, M. A., & Neimeyer, G. J. (1999). Interpersonal attachment: Experiencing, expressing, and coping with stress. Journal of Counseling Psychology, 46, 388–394.

Kendall, P. C., Kipnis, D., & Otto-Salaj, L. (1992). When clients don't progress: Influences on and explanations for lack of therapeutic progress. Cognitive Therapy and Research, 16, 269 –281.

Kernis, M. H., Brockner, J., & Frankel, B. S. (1989). Self-esteem and reactions to failure: The mediating role of overgeneralization. Journal of Personality and Social Psychology, 57, 707–714.

Kiesler, D. J. (1966). Some myths of psychotherapy research and the search for a paradigm. Psychological Bulletin, 65, 110–136.

Kiesler, D. J. (1983). The 1982 interpersonal circle: A taxonomy for complementarity in human transactions. Psychological Review, 90, 185–214.

Kiesler, D. J. (1996). Contemporary interpersonal theory and research: Personality, psychopathology and psychotherapy. New York: Wiley.

Kiesler, D. J., & Watkins, L. M. (1989). Interpersonal complementarity and the therapeutic alliance: A study of relationship in psychotherapy. Psychotherapy, 26, 183–194.

Kihlstrom, J. F., & Cantor, N. (1984). Mental representations of the self. In L. Berkowitz (Ed.), Advances in Experimental Social Psychology (Vol. 17, pp. 1–47). New York: Academic Press.

Kim, H. S., Sherman, D. K., & Taylor, S. E. (2008). Culture and social support. American Psychologist, 63, 518–526.

Kipnis, D. (1976). The power holders. Chicago: University of Chicago Press.

Kirsch, I. (1990). Changing expectations: A key to effective psychotherapy. Pacific Grove, CA: Brooks/Cole.

Kissin, B., Platz, A., & Su, W. H. (1971). Selective factors in treatment choice and outcome in alcoholics. In N. K. Mello & J. H. Mendelson (Eds.), Recent advances in studies of alcoholism (pp. 781–802). Washington, DC: U.S. Government Printing Office.

Kitchener, K. S. (1985). Ethical principles and decisions in student affairs. In J. H. Cannon and R. D. Brown (Eds.), New Directions in Student Services: Applied ethics in student services (No. 30, pp. 17–29). San Francisco: Jossey Bass.

Kivlighan, D. M. (1985). Feedback in group psychotherapy: Review and implications. Small Group Behavior, 16, 373–385.

Klohnen, E. C., Luo, S. (2003). Interpersonal attraction and personality: What is attractive—self similarity, ideal similarity, complementarity, or attachment security? Journal of Personality and Social Psychology, 85, 709–722.

Knox, S., Hess, S., Petersen, D., & Hill, C. E. (1997). A qualitative analysis of client perceptions of the effects of helpful therapist self-disclosure in long-term therapy. Journal of Counseling Psychology, 44, 274–283.

Kobak, R. (1994). Adult attachment: A personality or relationship construct? Psychological Inquiry, 5, 42–44.

Kobak, R. R., & Hazan, C. (1991). Attachment in marriage: Effects of security and accuracy of working models. Journal of Personality and Social Psychology, 60, 861–869.

Kobak, R. R., & Sceery, A. (1988). Attachment in late adolescence: Working models, affect regulation, and perception of self and others. Child Development, 59, 135–146.

Kobak, R. R., Cole, H. E., Ferenz, G. R., & Fleming, W. S. (1993). Attachment and emotion regulation during mother-teen problem solving: A control theory analysis. Child Development, 64, 231–245.

Kohut, H. (1971). The analysis of the self. New York: International Universities Press.

Kohut, H. (1984). How does analysis cure? (A. Goldberg & P. Stepanksy, Eds.) Chicago: University of Chicago Press.

Kokotovic, A. M., & Tracey, T. J. (1987). Premature termination at a university counseling center. Journal of Counseling Psychology, 34, 80–82.

Kosidlack, J. (1980). Self-help for senior citizens. Journal of Gerontological Nursing, 6, 663–668.

Krampen, G. (1989). Perceived child rearing practices and the development of locus of control in early adolescence. International Journal of Behavioral Development, 12, 177–193.

Kraut, R. E., & Johnston, R. (1979). Social and emotional messages of smiling: An ethological approach. Journal of Personality and Social Psychology, 37, 1539–1553.

Krosnick, J. A., & Petty, R. E. (1995). Attitude strength: An overview. In R.E. Petty & J.A. Krosnick (Eds.), Attitude strength: Antecedents and consequences. (pp. 1–24). Mahwah, NJ: Erlbaum.

Kunce, L. J., & Shaver, P. R. (1994). An attachment-theoretical approach to caregiving in romantic relationships. In K. Bartholomew & D. Perlman (Eds.), Advances in personal relationships (Vol. 5, pp. 205–237). London: Jessica Kingsley.

Labott, S. M., Ahleman, S., Wolever, M. E., & Martin, R. B. (1990). The physiological and psychological effects of the expression and inhibition of emotion. Behavioral Medicine, 16, 182–189.

LaGuardia, J. G., Ryan, R. M., Couchman, C. E., & Deci, E. L. (2000). Within-person variation in security of attachment: A self-determination theory perspective on attachment, need fulfillment, and well-being. Journal of Personality and Social Psychology, 79, 367–384.

Lakey, B., & Cassady, P. B. (1990). Cognitive processes in perceived social support. Journal of Personality and Social Psychology, 59, 337–343.

Lakey, B., McCabe, K. M., Fisicaro, S. A., & Drew, J. B. (1996). Environmental and personal determinants of support perceptions: Three generalizability studies. Journal of Personality and Social Psychology, 70, 1270–1280.

Lakoff, G., & Johnson, M. (1999). Philosophy in the flesh: The embodied mind and its challenges to Western thought. New York: Basic Books.

Lambert, M. J., & Barely, D. E. (2001). Research summary on the therapeutic relationship and psychotherapy outcome. Psychotherapy: Theory, Research, Practice, Training, 38, 357–361.

Lambert, M. J., & Bergin, A. E. (1994). The effectiveness of psychotherapy. In A. E. Bergin & S. L. Garfield (Eds.), Handbook of psychotherapy and behavior change (4th ed., pp. 143–189). New York: Wiley.

Lambert, M. J., & Ogles, B. M. (2004). The efficacy and effectiveness of psychotherapy. In M. J. Lambert (Ed.), Bergin and Garfield's handbook of psychotherapy and behavior change (5th ed., pp. 139–193). New York: Wiley.

Lambert, M. J., & Okiishi, J. C. (1997). The effects of the individual psychotherapist and implications for future research. Clinical Psychology: Science and Practice, 4, 66–75.

Lambert, M. J., Shapiro, D. A., & Bergin, A. E. (1986). The effectiveness of psychotherapy. In S. L. Garfield & A. E. Bergin (Eds.), Handbook of psychotherapy and behavior change (3rd ed., pp. 157–211). New York: Wiley.

Lambert, M. J., Whipple, J. L., Hawkins, E. J., Vermeersch, D., Nielsen, S. L., & Smart, D. W. (2003). Is it time to track patient outcome on a routine basis? Clinical Psychology: Science and Practice, 10, 288–301.

Langston, C. A. (1994). Capitalizing on and coping with daily-life events: Expressive responses to positive events. Journal of Personality and Social Psychology, 67, 1112–1125.

Lansford, E. (1986). Weakenings and repairs of the working alliance in short-term psychotherapy. Professional Psychology: Research and Practice, 17, 364–366.

Lanzetta, J. T., & Englis, B. G. (1989). Expectations of cooperation and competition and their effects on observers' vicarious emotional responses. Journal of Personality and Social Psychology, 33, 354–370.

Larrick, R. P. (1993). Motivational factors in decision theories: The role of self-protection. Psychological Bulletin, 113, 440–450

Larsen, D. L., Attkisson, C. C., Hargreaves, W. A., & Nguyen, T. D. (1979). Assessment of client/patient satisfaction: Development of a general scale. Evaluation and Program Planning, 2, 197–207.

Latty-Mann, H., & Davis, K. E. (1996). Attachment theory and partner choice: Preferences and actuality. Journal of Social and Personal Relationships, 13, 5–23.

Lau, R. R., & Russell, D. (1980). Attributions in the sports pages: A field test of some current hypotheses about attribution research. Journal of Personality and Social Psychology, 39, 29–38.

Laurenceau, J. P., Barrett, L. F., & Pietromonaco, P. (1998). Intimacy as an interpersonal process: The importance of self-disclosure, partner disclosure, and perceived partner responsiveness in interpersonal exchanges. Journal of Personality and Social Psychology, 74, 1238–1251.

Laursen, B., & Bukowski, W. M. (1997). A developmental guide to the organization of close relationships. International Journal of Behavioral Development, 21, 747–770.

Lazarus, A. A. (1971). Behavior therapy and beyond. New York: McGraw-Hill.

Lazarus, A. A. (1977). Has behavior therapy outlived its usefulness? American Psychologist, 32, 550–554.

Leary, M. R., & Baumeister, R. F. (2000). The nature and function of self-esteem: Sociometer theory. In M. P. Zanna (Ed.), Advances in experimental social psychology (Vol. 32, pp. 1–62). New York: Academic Press.

Leary, M. R., Tambor, E. S., Terdal, S. K., & Downs, D. L. (1995). Self-esteem as an interpersonal monitor: The sociometer hypothesis. Journal of Personality and Social Psychology, 68, 518–530.

Leary, T. (1957). Interpersonal diagnosis of personality. New York: Ronald Press.

Lecky, P. (1945). Self-consistency: A theory of personality. New York: Island Press.

Lefcourt, H. J. (1976). Locus of Control: Current Trends in Theory and Research. Hillsdale, NJ: Earlbaum.

Lefcourt, H. J., Hogg, E., Struthers, S., & Holmes, C. (1975). Causal attributions as a function of locus of control, initial confidence, and performance outcomes. Journal of Personality and Social Psychology, 32, 391–397.

Lehman, D. R., & Hemphill, K. J. (1990). Recipients' perceptions of support attempts and attributions for support attempts that fail. Journal of Social and Personal Relationships, 7, 563–574.

Levenson, R. W., & Gottman, J. M. (1985). Physiological and affective predictors of change in relationship satisfaction. Journal of Personality and Social Psychology, 49, 85–94.

LeVine, R. A., & Campbell, D. T. (1971). Ethnocentrism: Theories of conflict, ethnic attitudes, and group behavior. New York: Wiley.

Levy, K. N., Blatt, S. J., & Shaver, P. R. (1998). Attachment styles and parental representations. Journal of Personality and Social Psychology, 74, 407–419.

Lewan, P. C., & Stotland, E. (1961). The effects of prior information on susceptibility to an emotional appeal. Journal of Abnormal and Social Psychology, 62, 450–453.

Lewis, M. (1994). Does attachment imply a relationship or multiple relationships? Psychological Inquiry, 5, 47–51.

Lichenberg, J. W., Wettersten, K. B., Mull, H., Moberly, R. L., Merkey, K. B., & Corey, A. T. (1988). Relationship and control as correlates of psychotherapy quality and outcome. Journal of Clinical and Consulting Psychology, 45, 322–337.

Lieberman, M. D., Eisengerger, N. I., Crockett, M. J., Tom, S. M., Pfeifer, J. H., & Way, B. M. (2007). Putting feelings into words: Affect labeling disrupts amygdala activity to affective stimuli. Psychological Science, 18, 421–428.

Lightsey, O. R., Burke, M., Ervin, A., Henderson, D., & Yee, C. (2006). Generalized self-efficacy, self-esteem, and negative affect. Canadian Journal of Behavioural Science, 38, 72–80.

Lipsey, M. W., & Wilson, D. B. (1993). The efficacy of psychological, educational, and behavioral treatment: Confirmation from meta-analysis. American Psychologist, 48, 1181–1209.

Liu, T. J., & Steele, C. M. (1986). Attributional analysis as self-affirmation. Journal of Personality and Social Psychology, 51, 531–540.

Locke, E. A., Shaw, K. N., Saari, L. M., & Latham, G. P. (1981). Goal setting and task performance: 1969–1980. Psychological Bulletin, 90, 125–152.

Locke, K. D., & Horowitz, L. M. (1990). Satisfaction in interpersonal interactions as a function of similarity in level of dysphoria. Journal of Personality and Social Psychology, 58, 823–831.

Loeb, R. C. (1975). Concomitants of boys' locus of control examined in parent-child interactions. Developmental Psychology, 11, 353–358.

Lopez, F. G. (1996). Attachment-related predictors of constructive thinking among college students. Journal of Counseling and Development, 75, 58–63.

Lopez, F. G., & Brennan, K. A. (2000). Dynamic processes underlying adult attachment organization: Toward an attachment theoretical perspective on the healthy and effective self. Journal of Counseling Psychology, 47, 283–300.

Lopez, F. G., Fuendeling, J., Thomas, K., & Sagula, D. (1997). An attachment-theoretical perspective on the use of splitting defenses. Counseling Psychology Quarterly, 10, 461–472.

Lopez, F. G., Gover, M. R., Leskela, J., Sauer, E. M., Schirmer, L., & Wyssmann, J. (1997). Attachment styles, shame, guilt, and collaborative problem-solving orientations. Personal Relationships, 4, 187–199.

Lopez, F. G., Mauricio, A. M., Gormley, B., Simko, T., & Berger, E. (2001). Adult attachment orientations and college student distress: The mediating role of problem coping styles. Journal of Counseling & Development, 79, 459–464.

Lopez, F. G., Melendez, M., Sauer, E. M., Berger, E., & Wyssmann, J. (1998). Internal working models, self-reported problems, and help-seeking attitudes among college students. Journal of Counseling Psychology, 45, 79–83.

Lorenz, K. (1952). King Solomon's Ring. New York. Thomas Y. Crowell.

Luborsky, L., Crits-Christoph, P., Alexander, L., Margolis, M., & Cohen, M. (1983). Two helping alliance methods for predicting outcomes of psychotherapy. Journal of Nervous and Mental Disorders, 171, 480–491.

Lussier, Y., Sabourin, S., & Turgeon, C. (1997). Coping strategies as moderators of the relationship between attachment and marital adjustment. Journal of Social and Personal Relationships, 14, 777–791.

Lydon, J., Zanna, M. P., & Ross, M. (1988). Bolstering attitudes by autobiographical recall: Attitude persistence and selective memory. Personality and Social Psychology Bulletin, 14, 78–86.

Lyubomirsky, S., Sheldon, K. M., & Schkade, D. (2005). Pursuing happiness: The architecture of sustainable change. Review of General Psychology, 9, 111–131.

MacKay, C., Cox, T., Burrows, G. & Lazzerini, T. (1978). An inventory for the measurement of self-reported stress and arousal. British Journal of Social and Clinical Psychology, 17, 283–284.

Maddux, J. E, & Rogers, R. W. (1980). Effects of source expertness, physical attractiveness, and supporting arguments on persuasion: A case of brains over beauty. Journal of Personality and Social Psychology, 39, 235–244.

Mahoney, M. J. (1991). Human change processes: The scientific foundations of psychotherapy. New York: Basic Books.

Main, M., Kaplan, N., & Cassidy, J. (1985). Security in infancy, childhood, and adulthood: A move to the level of representation. Monographs of the Society for Research in Child Development, 50, 66–104.

Major, B., Spencer, S., Schmader, T., Wolfe, C., & Crocker, J. (1998). Coping with negative stereotypes about intellectual performance: The role of psychological disengagement. Personality and Social Psychology Bulletin, 24, 34–50.

Mallinckrodt, B. (1996). Change in working alliance, social support, and psychological symptoms in brief therapy. Journal of Counseling Psychology, 43, 448–455.

Mallinckrodt, B., & Wei, M. (2003). Attachment, social competencies, interpersonal problems, and psychological distress. In B. Mallinckrodt (Chair), Expanding applications of adult attachment theory: Coping assets and deficits. Symposium presented at the 111th Annual Convention of the American Psychological Association, Toronto, Ontario, Canada.

Mallinckrodt, B., Coble, H. M., & Gantt, D. L. (1995). Toward differentiating client attachment from working alliance and transference: Reply to Robbins. Journal of Counseling Psychology, 42, 320–322.

Mallinckrodt, B., Gantt, D. L., & Coble, H. M. (1995). Attachment patterns in the psychotherapy relationship: Development of the client attachment to therapist scale. Journal of Counseling Psychology, 42, 307–317.

Mallinckrodt, B., King, J. L., & Coble, H. M. (1998). Family dysfunction, alexithymia, and client attachment to therapist. Journal of Counseling Psychology, 45, 497–504.

Mallinckrodt, B., McCreary, B. A., & Robertson, A. K. (1995). Co-occurrence of eating disorders and incest: The role of attachment, family environment, and social competencies. Journal of Counseling Psychology, 42, 178–186.

Mallinckrodt, B., Porter, M. J., & Kivlighan, D. M. (2005). Client attachment to therapist, depth of in-session exploration, and object relations in brief psychotherapy. Psychotherapy: Theory, Research, Practice, Training, 42, 85–100.

Mann, L. (1980). Cross-cultural studies of small groups. In H. Triandis & R. Brislin (Eds.), Handbook of cross-cultural psychology: Social psychology (Vol. 5, pp. 155–209). Boston: Allyn & Bacon.

Mann, M. (1950). Primer on alcoholism. New York: Rinehart.

Markey, P. M., Funder, D. C., & Ozer, D. J. (2003). Complementarity of interpersonal behaviors in dyadic interactions. Personality and Social Psychology Bulletin, 29, 1082–1090.

Markus, H. M., & Kitayama, S. (1991). Culture and the self: Implications for cognition, emotion, and motivation. Psychological Review, 98, 224–253.

Markus, H. R., & Wurf, E. (1987). The dynamic self-concept: A social psychological perspective. Annual Review of Psychology, 38, 299–337.

Markus, H., & Kunda, Z. (1986). Stability and malleability of the self-concept. Journal of Personality and Social Psychology, 51, 858–866.

Markus, H., & Zajonc, R. B. (1985). The cognitive perspective in social psychology. In G. Lindzey & E. Aronson (Eds.), Handbook of social psychology (Vol. 1, pp. 137–230). New York: Random House.

Markus, H., Smith, J., & Moreland, R. L. (1985). Role of the self-concept in the perception of others. Journal of Personality and Social Psychology, 49, 1494–1512.

Marsiglia, C. S., Walczyk, J. J., Buboltz, W. C., & Griffith-Ross, D. A. (2007). Impact of parenting styles and locus of control on emerging adults' psychosocial success. Journal of

Educational and Human Development, 1. Retrieved from http://www.scientificjournals.org/journals2007/articles/1031.htm.

Martin, D. J., Garske, J. P., & Davis, M. K. (2000). Relation of the therapeutic alliance with outcome and other variables: A meta-analytic review. Journal of Consulting and Clinical Psychology, 68, 438–450.

Martin, J., Martin, W., Meyer, M., & Slemon, A. (1986). Empirical investigation of the cognitive meditational paradigm for research on counseling. Journal of Counseling Psychology, 33, 115–123.

Martin, J., Martin, W., Meyer, M., & Slemon, A. G. (1987). Cognitive mediation in person-centered and rational-emotive therapy. Journal of Counseling Psychology, 34, 251–260.

Martorell, G. A., & Bugental, D. B. (2006). Maternal variations in stress reactivity: Implications for harsh parenting practices with very young children. Journal of Family Psychology, 20, 641–647.

May, J. L., & Hamilton, P. A. (1980). Effects of musically evoked affect on women's interpersonal attraction and perceptual judgments of physical attractiveness of men. Motivation and Emotion, 4, 217–228.

McAdams, D. P. & Bryant, F. B. (1987). Intimacy motivation and subjective mental health in a nationwide sample. Journal of Personality, 55, 395–413.

McClun, L. A., & Merrell, K. W. (1998). Relationship of perceived parenting styles, locus of control, and self-concept among junior high age students. Psychology in the Schools, 35, 381–392.

McCluskey, U., Roger, D., & Nash, P. (1997). A preliminary study of the role of attunement in adult psychotherapy. Human Relations, 50, 1261–1273.

McCullough, M. E., Rachal, K. C., Sandage, S. J., Worthington, E. L., Jr., Brown, S. W., & Hight, T. L. (1998). Interpersonal forgiving in close relationships: II. Theoretical elaboration and measurement. Journal of Personality and Social Psychology, 76, 1586–1603.

McCullough, M. E., Worthington, E. L. Jr., & Rachal, K. C. (1997). Interpersonal forgiving in close relationships. Journal of Personality and Social Psychology, 73, 321–336.

McFarlin, D. B., Baumeister, R. F., & Blascovich, J. (1984). On knowing when to quit: Task failure, self-esteem, advice, and nonproductive persistence. Journal of Personality, 52, 138–155.

McGregor, I., Nail, P. R., Marigold, D. C., & Kang, S. (2005). Defensive pride and consensus: Strength in imaginary numbers. Journal of Personality and Social Psychology, 89, 978–996.

McGuire, W. J. (1983). A contextualist theory of knowledge: Its implications for innovations and reform in psychological research. In L. Berkowtiz (Ed.), Advances in experimental social psychology (Vol. 16, pp. 1–47). New York: Academic Press.

McGuire, W. J., & McGuire, C.V. (1988). Content and process in the experience of the self. In L. Berkowitz (Ed.), Advances in experimental social psychology (Vol. 21, pp. 97–144). San Diego, CA: Academic Press.

McHugo, G., Lanzetta, J. T., & Bush, L. K. (1991). The effect of attitudes on emotional reaction to expressive displays of political leaders. Journal of Nonverbal Behavior, 15, 19–41.

Mead, G. H. (1934). Mind, self and society. Chicago: University of Chicago Press.

Meyer, B., & Pilkonis, P. A. (2001). Attachment style. Psychotherapy: Theory, Research, Practice, Training, 38, 466–472.

Mickelson, K. D., Kessler, R. C., & Shaver, P. R. (1997). Adult attachment in a nationally representative sample. Journal of Personality and Social Psychology, 73, 1092–1106.

Miczek, K. A., & Tornatzky, W. (1996). Ethnopharmacology of aggression: Impact on autonomic and mesocorticolimbic activity. In C. F. Ferris & T. Grisso (Eds.), Understanding aggressive behavior in children (pp. 60–77). New York: New York Academy of Sciences.

Mikulincer, M. (1995). Attachment style and the mental representation of the self. Journal of Personality and Social Psychology, 69, 1203–1215.

Mikulincer, M. (1997). Adult attachment style and information processing: Individual differences in curiosity and cognitive closure. Journal of Personality and Social Psychology, 72, 1217–1230.

Mikulincer, M. (1998a). Adult attachment style and affect regulation: Strategic variations in self-appraisals. Journal of Personality and Social Psychology, 75, 420–435.

Mikulincer, M. (1998b). Attachment working models and the sense of trust: An exploration of interaction goals and affect regulation. Journal of Personality and Social Psychology, 74, 1209–1224.

Mikulincer, M., & Arad, D. (1999). Attachment working models and cognitive openness in close relationships: A test of chronic and temporary accessibility effects. Journal of Personality and Social Psychology, 77, 710–725.

Mikulincer, M., & Florian, V. (1998). The relationship between adult attachment styles and emotional and cognitive reactions to stressful events. In J. A. Simpson & W. S. Rholes (Eds.), Attachment theory and close relationships (pp. 143–165). New York: Guilford.

Mikulincer, M., & Florian, V. (2000). Exploring individual differences in reactions to mortality salience: Does attachment style regulate terror management mechanisms? Journal of Personality and Social Psychology, 79, 260–273.

Mikulincer, M., & Florian, V. (2001). Attachment style and affect regulation: Implications for coping with stress and mental health. In G. Fletcher & M. Clark (Eds.), Blackwell handbook of social psychology: Interpersonal processes (pp. 537–557). Oxford, England: Blackwell.

Mikulincer, M., & Horesh, N. (1999). Adult attachment style and the perception of others: The role of projective mechanisms. Journal of Personality and Social Psychology, 76, 1022–1034.

Mikulincer, M., & Nachshon, O. (1991). Attachment styles and patterns of self-disclosure. Journal of Personality and Social Psychology, 61, 321–331.

Mikulincer, M., & Orbach, I. (1995). Attachment styles and repressive defensiveness: The accessibility and architecture of affective memories. Journal of Personality and Social Psychology, 68, 917–925.

Mikulincer, M., & Shaver, P. R. (2001). Attachment theory and intergroup bias: Evidence that priming the secure base schema attenuates negative reactions to out-groups. Journal of Personality and Social Psychology, 81, 97–115.

Mikulincer, M., & Shaver, P. R. (2003). The attachment behavioral system in adulthood: Activation, psychodynamics, and interpersonal processes. In M. P. Zanna (Ed.), Advances in experimental social psychology (Vol. 35, pp. 53–152). San Diego, CA: Academic Press.

Mikulincer, M., Dolev, T., & Shaver, P. R. (2004). Attachment-related strategies during thought suppression: Ironic rebounds and vulnerable self-representations. Journal of Personality and Social Psychology, 87, 940–956.

Mikulincer, M., Florian, V., & Tolmacz, R. (1990). Attachment styles and fear of personal death: A case study of affect regulation. Journal of Personality and Social Psychology, 58, 273–280.

Mikulincer, M., Florian, V., & Weller, A. (1993). Attachment styles, coping strategies, and posttraumatic psychological distress: The impact of the Gulf War in Israel. Journal of Personality and Social Psychology, 64, 817–826.

Mikulincer, M., Gillath, O., Halevy, V., Avihou, N., Avidan, S., & Eshkoli, N. (2001a). Attachment theory and reactions to others' needs: Evidence that activation of the sense of attachment security promotes empathic responses. Journal of Journal of Personality and Social Psychology, 81, 1205–1224.

Mikulincer, M., Hirschberger, G., Nachmias, O., & Gillath, O. (2001b). The affective component of the secure base schema: Affective priming with representations of attachment security. Journal of Personality and Social Psychology, 81, 305–321.

Mikulincer, M., Horesh, N., Eilati, I., & Kotler, M. (1999). The association between adult attachment style and mental health in extreme life-endangering conditions. Personality and Individual Differences, 27, 831–842.

Mikulincer, M., Shaver, P. R., Gillath, O., & Nitzberg, R. A. (2005). Attachment, caregiving, and altruism: Boosting attachment security increases compassion and helping. Journal of Personality and Social Psychology, 89, 817–839.

Miller, D. T., & Norman, S. A. (1975). Actor-observer differences in perceptions of effective control. Journal of Personality and Social Psychology, 31, 503–515.

Miller, D. T., & Ross, M. (1975). Self-serving biases in the attribution of causality: Fact or fiction? Psychological Bulletin, 82, 213–225.

Miller, J. F. (1983). Coping with chronic illness. Philadelphia: F. A. Davis.

Miller, P. C., Lefcourt, H. M., Holmes, J. G., Ware, E. E., & Saleh, W. E. (1986). Marital locus of control and marital problem solving. Journal of Personality and Social Psychology, 51, 161–169

Miller, S. D., Duncan, B. L., & Hubble, M. A. (1997). Escape from Babel. New York: Norton.

Miller, S. D., Duncan, B. L., & Hubble, M. A. (2004). Beyond integration: The triumph of outcome over process in clinical practice. Psychotherapy in Australia, 10, 32–43.

Miller, W. R., & Hester, R. K. (1980). Treating the problem drinker: Modern approaches. In W. R. Miller (Ed.), The addictive behaviors: Treatment of alcoholism, drug abuse, smoking, and obesity (pp. 11–141). Oxford, England: Pergamon.

Miller, W. R., & Rollnick, S. (2002). Motivational interviewing: Preparing people for change (2nd ed.). New York: NY. Guilford Press.

Missirlian, T. M., Toukmanian, S. G., Warwar, S. H., & Greenberg, L. S. (2005). Emotional arousal, client perceptual processing, and the working alliance in experiential psychotherapy for depression. Journal of Consulting and Clinical Psychology, 73, 861–871.

Mitchell, S. A., & Aron, L. (1999). Relational Psychoanalysis. New York: Analytic.

Mohl, P. C., Martinez, D., Ticknor, C., Huang, M., & Cordell, L. (1991). Early dropouts from psychotherapy. Journal of Nervous and Mental Disease, 179, 478–481.

Moradi, B., Fischer, A. R., Hill, M. S., Jome, L. M., & Blum, S. A. (2000). Does "feminist" plus "therapist" equal "feminist therapist"? Psychology of Women Quarterly, 30, 6–43.

Moras, C., & Strupp, H. H. (1982). Pretherapy interpersonal relations, patients' alliance, and outcome in brief therapy. Archives of General Psychiatry, 39, 405–409.

Moreland, R. L. (1987). The formation of small groups. In C. Hendrick (Ed.), Group processes: Review of personality and social psychology (Vol. 8, pp. 80–110). Newbury Park, CA: Sage.

Moreland, R. L., & Sweeney, P. (1984). Self-expectancies and reactions to evaluations of personal performance. Journal of Personality, 52, 156–176.

Morf, C. C., & Rhodewalt, F. (2001). Unraveling the paradoxes of narcissism: A dynamic self-regulatory processing model. Psychological Inquiry, 12, 177–196.

Moskowitz, D. S. (1993). Dominance and friendliness: On the interaction of gender and situation. Journal of Personality, 61, 387–409.

Moskowitz, D. S. (1993). Dominance and friendliness: On the interaction of gender and situation. Journal of Personality, 61, 387–409.

Mother Teresa (1995). A simple path (compiled by Lucinda Vardey). New York, Random House.

Mueller, T. (2008, December). King Herod revealed: The Holy Land's visionary builder. National Geographic, 214, 34–59.

Muhonen, T., & Torkelson, E. (2004). Work locus of control and its relationship to health and job satisfaction from a gender perspective. Stress and Health, 20, 21–28.

Muran, J. C., Gorman, B., Safran, J. D., Twining, L., Samstag, L. W., & Winston, A. (1995). Linking in-session change to overall outcome in short-term cognitive therapy. Journal of Consulting and Clinical Psychology, 63, 651–657.

Murphy, B., & Bates, G. W. (1997). Adult attachment style and vulnerability to depression. Personality and Individual Differences, 22, 835–844.

Murray, S. L., Holmes, J. G., Bellavia, G., Griffin, D. W., & Dolderman, D. (2002). Kindred spirits? The benefits of egocentrism in close relationships. Journal of Personality and Social Psychology, 82, 563–581.

Murray, S. L., Rose, P., Bellavia, G. M., Holmes, J. G., & Garrett K., A. (2002). When rejection stings: How self-esteem constrains relationship-enhancement processes. Journal of Personality and Social Psychology, 83, 556–573.

Mussweiler, T., Gabriel, S., & Bodenhausen, G. V. (2000). Shifting social identities as a strategy for deflecting threatening social comparisons. Journal of Personality and Social Psychology, 79, 398–409.

Neihart, M. (1999). Systematic risk-taking. Roeper Review 21, 289–291.

Newby-Clark, I. R., McGregor, I., & Zanna, M. P. (2002). Thinking and caring about cognitive inconsistency: When and for whom does attitudinal ambivalence feel uncomfortable? Journal of Personality and Social Psychology, 82, 157–166.

Noë, R. (1990). A veto game played by baboons: a challenge to the use of the Prisoner's Dilemma as a paradigm for reciprocity and cooperation. Animal Behavior, 39, 78–90.

Noller, P., & Ruzzene, M. (1991). Communication in marriage: The influence of affect and cognition. In G. J. O. Fletcher & F. D. Fincham (Eds.), Cognition and close relationships (pp. 203–234). Hillsdale, NJ: Erlbaum.

Norcross, J. C. (2001). Purposes, processes, and products of the task force on empirically supported therapy relationships. Psychotherapy: Theory, Research, Practice, Training, 38, 345–356.

Norcross, J. C. (2002). Psychotherapy relationships that work: Therapist contributions and responsiveness to patients. New York: Oxford University Press.

Norman, D. A., & Shallice, T. (2000). Attention to action: Willed and automatic control of behaviour. In M. S. Gazzaniga, Cognitive neuroscience: A reader (pp. 376-390). Oxford, England: Blackwell.

Norman, R. (1976). When what is said is important: A comparison of expert and attractive sources. Journal of Experimental Social Psychology, 12, 294–300.

O'Leary, A. (1985). Self-efficacy and health. Behavior Research and Therapy, 23, 437–451.

O'Connor, B. P., & Dyce, J. (1997). Interpersonal rigidity, hostility, and complementarity in musical bands. Journal of Personality and Social Psychology, 72, 362–372.

Ogilvie, D. M., & Ashmore, R. (1991). Self-with-other representation as a unit of analysis in self-concept research. In R. C. Curtis (Ed.), The Relational Self (pp. 282–314). New York: Guilford.

Okiishi, J. C., Lambert, M. J., Eggett, D., Nielsen, S. L., & Dayton, D. D. (2006). An analysis of therapist treatment effects: Toward providing feedback to individual therapists on their clients' psychotherapy outcome. Journal of Clinical Psychology, 62, 1157–1172.

Okiishi, J., Lambert, M. J., Nielsen, S. L., & Ogles, B. M. (2003). Waiting for super shrink: An empirical analysis of therapist effects. Clinical Psychology and Psychotherapy, 10, 361–373.

Olson, J. M., Roese, N. J., & Zanna, M. P. (1996). Expectancies. In E. T. Higgins & A. W. Kruglanski (Eds.), Social psychology: Handbook of basic principles (pp. 211–238). New York: Guilford Press.

O'Malley, S. S., Suh, C. S., & Strupp, H. H. (1983). The Vanderbilt psychotherapy process scale: A report on the scale development and process-outcome study. Journal of Consulting and Clinical Psychology, 51, 581–586.

Orlinsky, D. E., & Howard, K. I. (1980). Gender and psychotherapeutic outcome. In A. M. Brodksy & R. T. Hare-Mustin (Eds.), Women in psychotherapy (pp. 3–34). New York: Guilford.

Orlinsky, D. E., & Howard, K. I. (1986). Process and outcome in psychotherapy. In S. L. Garfield & A. E. Bergin (Eds.), Handbook of psychotherapy and behavior change (3rd ed., pp. 311–381). New York: Wiley.

Orlinsky, D. E., Grave, K., & Parks, B. K. (1994). Process and outcome in psychotherapy—noch einmal. In A. E. Bergin & S. L. Garfield (Eds.), Handbook of psychotherapy and behavior change (4th ed., pp. 257–310). New York: Wiley.

Owens, G., Crowell, J., Pan, H., Treboux, D., O'Connor, E., & Waters, E. (1995). The prototype hypothesis and the origins of attachment working models: Adult relationships with parents and romantic partners. In E. Waters, B. Vaughn, G. Posada, & K. Kondo-Ikemura (Eds.), Caregiving, cultural, and cognitive perspectives on secure-base behavior and working models: New growing points of attachment theory and research. Monographs of the Society for Research in Child Development, 60, 216–233.

Papageorgis, D. (1968). Warning and persuasion. Psychological Bulletin, 70, 271–282.

Parish, T. S. (1988). Helping college students take control of their lives. College Student Journal, 22, 64–69.

Parker, M. W., Winstead, D. K., & Willi, F. J. P. (1979). Patient autonomy in alcohol rehabilitation: I. Literature review. International Journal of the Addictions, 14, 1015–1022.

Patterson, C. H. (1984). Empathy, warmth, and genuineness: A review of reviews. Psychotherapy, 21, 431–438.

Paulhus, D. L. (1982). Individual differences, self-presentation, and cognitive dissonance: Their concurrent operation in forced compliance. Journal of Personality and Social Psychology, 43, 838–852.

Paulhus, D. L. (1998). Interpersonal and intrapsychic adaptiveness of trait self-enhancement: A mixed blessing? Journal of Personality and Social Psychology, 74, 1197–1208.

Paulhus, D. L., & Martin, C. L. (1988). Functional flexibility: A new conception of interpersonal flexibility. Journal of Personality and Social Psychology, 55, 88–101.

Pearce, P. L. (1980). Strangers, travelers, and Greyhound terminals: A study of small-scale helping behaviors. Journal of Personality and Social Psychology, 38, 935–940.

Peck, M. S. (1978). The road less traveled: A new psychology of love, traditional values, and spiritual growth. New York: Simon and Schuster.

Pelham, B. W. (1991). On confidence and consequence: The certainty and importance of self-knowledge. Journal of Personality and Social Psychology, 50, 518–530.

Pelham, B. W., & Swann, W. B. (1989). From self conceptions to self-worth: On the sources and structure of global self-esteem. Journal of Personality and Social Psychology, 57, 672–680.

Pelham, B. W., & Wachsmuth, J. O. (1995). The waxing and waning of the social self: Assimilation and contrast in social comparison. Journal of Personality and Social Psychology, 69, 825–838.

Pennebaker, J. W. (1997). Opening up: The healing power of expressing emotions. New York: Guilford Press.

Peplau, L. A., & Perlman, D. (1982). Perspectives on loneliness. In L. A. Peplau & D. Perlman (Eds.), Loneliness: A sourcebook of current theory, research, and therapy (pp. 1–20). New York: Wiley.

Perls, F. (1970). Four lectures. In J. Fagan & I. Shepard (Eds.) Gestalt therapy now (pp. 14–24). New York: Harper & Row.

Peterson, C., & Seligman, M. E. (1984). Causal explanations as a risk factor for depression: Theory and evidence. Psychological Review, 91, 347–374.

Petty, R. E. , Ostrom, T.M., & Brock, T. C. (1981). Historical foundations of the cognitive response approach to attitudes and persuasion. In R. E. Petty, T. M. Ostrom, & T. C. Brock (Eds.), Cognitive responses in persuasion (pp. 5–29). Hillsdale, NJ: Erlbaum.

Petty, R. E., & Brinol, P. (2006). A metacognitive approach to "implicit" and "explicit" evaluations: Comment on Gawronski and Bodenhausen. Psychological Bulletin, 132, 740–744.

Petty, R. E., & Cacioppo, J. T. (1979). Effects of forewarning of persuasive intent and involvement on cognitive responses and persuasion. Personality and Social Psychology Bulletin, 5, 173–176.

Petty, R. E., & Krosnick, J. A. (1995). Attitude strength: Antecedents and consequences. Mahwah, NJ: Erlbaum.

Petty, R.E., & Cacioppo, J.T. (1981/1996). Attitudes and persuasion: Classic and contemporary approaches. Boulder, CO: Westview Press.

Petty, R.E., & Cacioppo, J.T. (1986). Communication and persuasion: Central and peripheral routes to attitude change. New York: Springer-Verlag.

Pfaff, D. W. (2007). The neuroscience of fair play: Why we (usually) follow the Golden Rule. New York: Dana Press.

Pietromonaco, P. R., & Barrett, F. L. (1997). Working models of attachment and daily social interactions. Journal of Personality and Social Psychology, 73, 1409–1423.

Pinel, E. C., & Constantino, M. J. (2003). Putting self-psychology to good use: When social and clinical psychologists unite. Journal of Psychotherapy Integration, 13, 9–32.

Pines, H. A., & Julian, J. W. (1972). Effects of task and social demands on locus of control differences in information processing. Journal of Personality, 40, 407–416.

Piper, W. E., Azim, H. F., Joyce, A. S., & McCallum, M. (1991). Transference interpretations, therapeutic alliance, and outcome in short-term individual psychotherapy. Archives of General Psychiatry, 48, 946–953.

Piper, W. E., DeCarufel, F. L., & Szkrumelak, N. (1985). Patient predictors of process and outcome in short-term individual psychotherapy. Journal of Nervous and Mental Disease, 173, 726–733.

Piper, W. E., Ogrodniczuk, J. S., Joyce, A. S., McCullum, M., Rosie, J. A., O'Kelly, J. G., & Steinberg, P. I. (1999). Prediction of dropping out in time-limited, interpretive individual psychotherapy. Psychotherapy, 36, 114–122.

Pistole, M. C. (1996). After love: Attachment styles and grief themes. The Family Journal, 4, 199–207.

Pope, K. S. (2001). Sex between therapist and client. In J. Worell (Ed.), Encyclopedia of sex and gender (pp. 955–962). New York: Academic Press.

Priebe, S., & Gruyters, T. (1993). The role of helping alliance in psychiatric community care: A prospective study. Journal of Nervous and Mental Disease, 181, 552–557.

Priester, J. R., & Petty, R. E. (2001). Extending the bases of subjective attitudinal ambivalence: Interpersonal and intrapersonal antecedents of evaluative tension. Journal of Personality and Social Psychology, 80, 19–34.

Pyszczynski, T., & Greenberg, J. (1983). Determinants of reduction in intended effort as a strategy for coping with anticipated failure. Journal of Research in Personality, 17, 412–422.

Pyszczynski, T., & Greenberg, J. (1987). Self-regulatory preservation and the depressive self-focusing style: A self-awareness theory of reactive depression. Psychological Bulletin, 102, 122–138.

Raine, A., Meloy, J. R., Bihrle, S., Stoddard, J., LaCasse, L., & Buchsbaum. M. S. (1998). Reduced prefrontal and increased subcortical brain functioning assessed using positron emission tomography in predatory and affective murderers. Behavioral Science and the Law, 16, 319–332.

Raleigh, M. J., McGuire, M. T., Brammer, G. L., Pollack, D. B., & Yuwiler, A. (1991). Serotonergic mechanisms promote dominance acquisition in adult make vervet monkeys. Brain Research, 559, 181–190.

Ramsdell, P. S., & Ramsdell, E. R. (1993). Dual relationships: Client perceptions of the effect of client-counselor relationship on the therapeutic process. Clinical Social Work Journal, 21, 195–212.

Reandeau, S. G., & Wampold, B. E. (1991). Relationship of power and involvement to working alliance : A multiple-case sequential analysis of brief therapy. Journal of Counseling Psychology, 38, 107–114.

Reik, T. (1944). A psychologist looks at love. New York: Farrar, Strauss & Co.

Reis, B. F., & Brown, L. G. (1999). Reducing psychotherapy dropouts: Maximizing perspective convergence in the psychotherapy dyad. Psychotherapy, 36, 123–136.

Reis, H. T. (1990). The role of intimacy in interpersonal relations. Journal of Social and Clinical Psychology, 9, 15–30.

Reis, H. T., & Shaver, P. (1988). Intimacy as an interpersonal process. In S. W. Duck (Ed.), Handbook of personal relationships (pp. 367–389). New York: Wiley.

Reis, H. T., Collins, W. A., & Berscheid, E. (2000). The relationship context of human behavior and development. Psychological Bulletin, 126, 844–872.

Reis, H. T., Wheeler, L., Kernis, M. H., Spiegel, N., & Nezlek, J. (1985). On specificity in the impact of social participation on physical and psychological health. Journal of Personality and Social Psychology, 48, 456–471.

Rhodes, R. H., Hill, C. E., Thompson, B. J., & Elliott, R. (1994). Client retrospective recall of resolved and unresolved misunderstanding events. Journal of Counseling Psychology, 41, 473–483.

Rhodewalt, F. (2001). The social mind of the narcissist: Cognitive and motivational aspects of interpersonal self-construction. In J. P. Forgas, K. Williams, & L. Wheeler (Eds.), The social mind: Cognitive and motivational aspects of interpersonal behavior (pp. 177–198). New York: Cambridge University Press.

Rhodewalt, F., & Morf, C. C. (1998). On self-aggrandizement and anger: A temporal analysis of narcissism and affective reactions to success and failure. Journal of Personality and Social Psychology, 74, 672–685.

Rholes, W. S., Simpson, J. A., & Orina, M. M. (1999). Attachment and anger in an anxiety-provoking situation. Journal of Personality and Social Psychology, 76, 940–957.

Rice, K. G., FitzGerald, D. P., Whaley, T. J., & Gibbs, C. L. (1995). Cross-sectional and longitudinal examination of attachment, separation-individuation and college student adjustment. Journal of Counseling & Development, 73, 463–474.

Rioch, J. (1988). The transference phenomenon in psychoanalytic therapy. In B. Wolstein (Ed.), Essential papers on countertransference. New York: University Press. (Reprinted from Psychiatry [1943], 6, 147–156.)

Ritts, V., & Stein, J. R. (1995). Verification and commitment in marital relationships: An exploration of self-verification theory in community college students. Psychological Reports, 76, 383–386.

Rizvi, S. L., Reynolds, S. K., Comtois, K. A., & Linehan, M. M. (2000, November). Therapeutic alliance in the treatment of borderline personality disorder. Paper presented at the Association for Advancement of Behavior Therapy, New Orleans. Cited in C. R. Glass, D.

Arnkoff, & S. J. Shapiro (2001). Expectations and preferences. Psychotherapy: Theory, Research, Practice, Training, 38, 455–461.

Roberts, J. E., Gotlib, I. H., & Kassel, J. D. (1996). Adult attachment security and symptoms of depression: The mediating roles of dysfunctional attitudes and low self-esteem. Journal of Personality and Social Psychology, 70, 310–320.

Roberts, N., & Noller, P. (1998). The associations between adult attachment and couple violence: The role of communication patterns and relationship satisfaction. In J. A. Simpson & W. A. Rholes (Eds.), Attachment theory and close relationships (pp. 317–350). New York: Guilford Press.

Robins, R. W., Hendin, H. M., & Trzesniewski, K. H. (2001). Measuring global self-esteem: Construct validation of a single item measure and the Rosenberg Self-Esteem Scale. Personality and Social Psychology Bulletin, 27, 151–161.

Rodewalt, F., & Tragakis, M. W. (2003). Self-esteem and self-regulation: Toward optimal studies of self-esteem. Psychological Inquiry, 14, 66–70.

Rogers, C. R. (1942). Counseling and psychotherapy. Boston: Houghton Mifflin.

Rogers, C. R. (1951). Client-centered therapy. Boston: Houghton Mifflin.

Rosen, S., Mickler, S. E., & Collins, J. E. (1987). Reactions of would-be helpers whose offer of help is spurned. Journal of Personality and Social Psychology, 53, 288–297.

Rosenberg, M. (1965). Society and the adolescent self-image. Princeton, NJ: Princeton University Press.

Rosenberg, M. (1979). Conceiving the self. New York: Basic Books.

Rosenzweig, S. (1936). Some implicit common factors in diverse methods of psychotherapy. American Journal of Orthopsychiatry, 6, 412–415.

Roskos-Ewoldsen, D. R., & Fazio, R. H. (1992). On the orienting value of attitudes: Attitude accessibility as a determinant of an object's attraction of visual attention. Journal of Personality and Social Psychology, 63, 198–211.

Ross, L. (1977). The intuitive psychologist and his shortcomings: Distortions in the attribution process. In L. Berkowitz (Ed.), Advances in experimental social psychology (Vol. 10, pp. 173–220). New York: Academic Press.

Rotter, J. B. (1954). Social learning and clinical psychology. New York: Prentice-Hall.

Rotter, J. B. (1990). Internal versus external control of reinforcement: a case variable. American Psychologist, 45, 489–493.

Rounsaville, B. J., Chevron, E. S., Prusoff, B. A., Elkin, I., Imber, S., Sotsky, S., & Watkins, J. (1987). The relation between specific and general dimensions of the psychotherapy process in interpersonal psychotherapy of depression. Journal of Consulting and Clinical Psychology, 55, 379–384.

Rubino, G., Barker, C., Roth, T., & Fearon, P. (2000). Therapist empathy and depth of interpretation in response to potential alliance ruptures: The role of therapist and patient attachment styles. Psychotherapy Research, 10, 408–420.

Rucker, D. D., & Petty, R. E. (2004). When resistance is futile: Consequences of failed counterarguing for attitude certainty. Journal of Personality and Social Psychology, 86, 219–235.

Rutte, C., & Taborsky, M. (2007). Generalized reciprocity in rats. PloS Biology, 5. Retrieved from http://www.plosbiology.org/article/info:doi/10.1371/journal.pbio.0050196.

Sable, P. (1997). Disorders of adult attachment. Psychotherapy: Theory, Research, Practice, Training, 34, 286–296.

Sadler, P., Woody, E. (2003). Is who you are who you're talking to? Interpersonal style and complementarity in mixed-sex interactions. Journal of Personality and Social Psychology, 84, 80–96.

Safran, J. D. (1993). Breaches in the therapeutic alliance: An arena for negotiating authentic relatedness. Psychotherapy, 30, 11–24.

Safran, J. D., & Wallner, L. K. (1991). The relative predictive validity of two therapeutic alliance measures in cognitive therapy. Psychological Assessment: A Journal of Consulting and Clinical Psychology, 3, 188–195.

Safran, J. D., Muran, J. C., & Wallner-Samstag, L. (1994). Resolving therapeutic alliance ruptures: A task analytic investigation. In A. O. Horvath & L. S. Greenberg (Eds.), The working alliance: Theory, research and practice (pp. 225–258). New York: Wiley.

Safran, J. D., Muran, J. C., Samstag, L. W., & Stevens, C. (2001). Repairing Alliance Ruptures. Psychotherapy: Theory, Research, Practice, Training, 38, 406–412.

Samstag, L. W., Batchelder, S., Muran, J. C., Safran, J. D., & Winston, A. (1998). Predicting treatment failure from in-session interpersonal variables. Journal of Psychotherapy Practice & Research, 5, 126–143.

Sapolsky, R. M. (1991). Testicular function, social rank, and personality among wild baboons. Psychoneuroendocrinology, 16, 281–293.

Sarason, I. G., & Sarason, B. R. (1986). Experimentally provided social support. Journal of Personality and Social Psychology, 50, 1222.

Sarason, B. R., Sarason, I. G., & Gurung, R. A. R. (1997). Close personal relationships and health outcomes: A key to the role of social support. In S. Duck (Ed.), Handbook of personal relationships: Theory, research, and interventions (2nd ed., pp. 547–573). New York: Wiley.

Saunders, S. M., Howard, K. I., & Orlinsky, D. E. (1989). The Therapeutic Bond Scales: Psychometric characteristics and relationship to treatment effectiveness. Psychological Assessment, 1, 323–330.

Schacht, T. E. (1991). Can psychotherapy education advance psychotherapy integration? A view from the cognitive psychology of expertise. Journal of Psychotherapy Integration, 1, 305–320.

Scharfe, E., & Bartholomew, K. (1995). Accommodation and attachment representations in young couples. Journal of Social and Personal Relationships, 12, 389–401.

Schlenker, B. R. (1985). Identity and self-identification. In B. R. Schlenker (Ed.), The self and social life (pp. 65–99). New York: McGraw-Hill.

Schlenker, B. R., Dlugolecki, D. W., & Doherty, K. (1994). The impact of self presentations on self-appraisals and behavior: The roles of commitment and biased scanning. Personality and Social Psychology Bulletin, 20, 20–33.

Schoenrade, P. A., Batson, C. D., Brandt, J. R., & Loud, R. E. (1986). Attachment, accountability, and motivation to benefit another not in distress. Journal of Personality and Social Psychology, 51, 557–563.

Schonfield, J., Stone, A. R., Hoehn-Saric, R., Imber, S. D., & Pande, S. K. (1969). Patient-therapist convergence and measures of improvement in short-term psychotherapy. Psychotherapy: Theory, Research and Practice, 6, 267–272.

Schulman, B. (1979). Active patient orientation and outcomes in hypertension treatment. Medical Care, 17, 267–280.

Scott, C. K., Fuhrman, R. W., & Wyer, R. S. (1991). Information processing in close relationships. In G. J. O. Fletcher & F. D. Fincham (Eds.), Cognition and close relationships (pp. 37–68). Hillsdale, NJ: Erlbaum.

Sedikides, C., & Brewer, M. B. (2001). Individual self, relational self, collective self. Philadelphia: Psychology Press.

Sedikides, C., Campbell, W. K., Reeder, G., Elliot, A. J., & Gregg, A. P. (2002). Do others bring out the worst in narcissists? The "others exist for me" illusion. In Y. Kashima, M. Foddy, & M. Platow (Eds.), Self and identity: Personal, social, and symbolic (pp. 103–123). Mahwah, NJ: Erlbaum.

Sedikides, C., Rudich, E. A., Gregg, A. P., Kumashiro, M., & Rusbult, C. (2004). Are normal narcissists psychologically healthy?: Self-esteem matters. Journal of Personality and Social Psychology, 87, 400–416.

Seeman, M., & Evans, J. (1962). Alienation and learning in a hospital setting. American Psychological Review, 27, 772–782.

Selzer, M. L. (1957). Hostility as a barrier to therapy in alcoholism. Psychiatric Quarterly, 31, 301–305.

Senior, C., Barnes, J., Jenkins, R., Landau, S., Phillips, M., L., & David, A. S. (1999). Attribution of social dominance and maleness to schematic faces. Social Behavior and Personality, 27, 331–338.

Shaver, P. R., & Hazan, C. (1993). Adult romantic attachment: Theory and evidence. Advances in Personal Relationships, 4, 29–70.

Shepperd, J. A., & Arkin, R. M. (1989). Determinants of self-handicapping: Task importance and the effects of preexisting handicaps on self-generated handicaps. Personality and Social Psychology Bulletin, 15, 101–112.

Sherman, S. J., Presson, C. C., Chassin, L., Corty, E. & Olshavsky, R. (1983). The false consensus effect in estimates of smoking prevalence: Underlying mechanisms. Personality and Social Psychology Bulletin, 9, 197–207.

Shick, T., & Greta, W. (2001). Goal consensus and collaboration. Psychotherapy: Theory, Research, Practice, Training, 38, 385–389.

Short, D. (1999). Hypnosis and children: An analysis of theory and research. In B. Matthews and J. Edgette (Eds.), Current thinking and practices in brief therapy (pp. 285–335), Philadelphia: Taylor and Francis.

Short, D., Erickson, B. A., & Erickson-Klein, R. (2005). Hope and resiliency: The therapeutic strategies of Milton H. Erickson. London: Crown House.

Shrauger, J. S. (1975). Responses to evaluation as a function of initial self-perceptions. Psychological Bulletin, 82, 581–596.

Shrauger, J. S., & Lund, A. (1975). Self-evaluation and reactions to evaluations from others. Journal of Personality, 43, 94–108.

Shrauger, J. S., & Rosenberg, S. E. (1970). Self-esteem and the effects of success and failure on performance. Journal of Personality, 38, 404–417.

Shrira, I., & Martin, L. L. (2005). Stereotyping, self-affirmation, and the cerebral hemispheres. Personality and Social Psychology Bulletin, 31, 846–856.

Siegel, D. J. (2010). Mindsight: The New Science of Personal Transformation. New York. Bantam Books.

Siegel, D. J., & Hartzell, M. (2003). Parenting from the Inside Out. New York. Tarcher/Penguin.

Siegler, R. S. (2005). Children's learning. American Psychologist, 60, 769–778.

Simon, J. C. (1990). Criteria for therapist self-disclosure. In G. Stricker & M. Fisher (Eds.), Self-disclosure in the therapeutic relationship (pp. 207–225). New York: Plenum.

Simpson, J. A. (1990). Influence of attachment styles on romantic relationships. Journal of Personality and Social Psychology, 59, 971–980.

Simpson, J. A., Rholes, W. A., & Phillips, D. (1996). Conflict in close relationships: An attachment perspective. Journal of Personality and Social Psychology, 71, 899–914.

Simpson, J. A., Rholes, W. S., & Nelligan, J. S. (1992). Support seeking and support giving within couples in an anxiety-provoking situation: The role of attachment styles. Journal of Personality and Social Psychology, 62, 434–446.

Simpson, J. A., Rholes, W. S., Campbell, L., Tran, S., & Wilson, C. L. (2003). Adult attachment, the transition to parenthood, and depressive symptoms. Journal of Personality and Social Psychology, 84, 1172–1187.

Simpson, J. A., Rholes, W. S., Orina, M. M., & Grich, J. (2002). Working models of attachment, support giving, and support seeking in a stressful situation. Personality and Social Psychology Bulletin, 28, 598–608.

Slaney, R. B., Rice, K. G., & Ashby, J. S. (2002). A programmatic approach to measuring perfectionism: The Almost Perfect Scales. In G. L. Flett & P. L. Hewitt (Eds.), Perfectionism: Theory, research, and treatment (pp. 63–88). Washington, DC: American Psychological Association.

Sloan, M., & Schommer, B. (1982). What to get your patient involved in his care? Use a contract. Nursing, 82, 48–49.

Sloane, R. B., Staples, F. R., Cristol, A. H., Yorkston, N. J. I., & Whipple, K. (1975). Short-term analytically oriented psychotherapy vs. behavior therapy. Cambridge, MA: Harvard University Press.

Smith, E. R., Murphy, J., & Coats, S. (1999). Attachment to groups: Theory and measurement. Journal of Personality and Social Psychology, 77, 94–110.

Smith, M. L., Glass, G. V., & Miller, T. I. (1980). The benefits of psychotherapy. Baltimore: Johns Hopkins University Press.

Snyder, M., & Stukas, A. A. (1999). Interpersonal processes: The interplay of cognitive, motivational, and behavioral activities in social interaction. Annual Review of Psychology, 50, 273–303.

Sorrentino, R. M., & Roney, C. J. R. (1990). Uncertainty orientation: Individual differences in the self-inference process. In J. M. Olson, & M. P. Zanna (Eds.), Self-inference processes: The Ontario Symposium (Vol. 6, pp. 239-258). Hillsdale, NJ: Erlbaum.

Sorrentino, R. M., & Short, J. C. (1986). Uncertainty orientation, motivation and cognition. In R. M. Sorrentino & E. T. Higgins (Eds.), The handbook of motivation and cognition: Foundations of social behaviour (pp. 379–403). New York: Guilford Press.

Sorrentino, R. M., Hewitt, E. C., & Raso-Knott, P. A. (1992). Risk-taking in games of chance and skill: Informational and affective influences on choice behavior. Journal of Personality and Social Psychology, 62, 522–533.

Sorrentino, R. M., Holmes, J. G., Hanna, S. E., & Sharp, A. (1995). Uncertainty orientation and trust in close relationships: Individual differences in cognitive styles. Journal of Personality and Social Psychology, 68, 314–327.

Sosis, R. H. (1974). Internal-external control and the perception of responsibility of another for an accident. Journal of Personality and Social Psychology, 30, 1031–1034.

Sours, J. A. (1974). The anorexia nervosa syndrome. International Journal of Psychoanalysis, 55, 567–576.

Spalding, L. R., & Hardin, C. D. (1999). Unconscious unease and self-handicapping: Behavioral consequences of individual differences in implicit and explicit self-esteem. Psychological Science, 10, 535–539.

Spencer, S. J., Jordan, C. H., Logel, C. E. R., & Zanna, M. P. (2005). Nagging doubts and a glimmer of hope: The role of implicit self-esteem in self-image maintenance. In A. Tesser, J. V. Wood, & D. A. Stapel (Eds.), On building, defending and regulating the self: A psychological perspective (pp. 153–170). New York: Psychology Press.

Sroufe, L. A., & Fleeson, J. (1986). Attachment and the construction of relationships. In W. W. Hartup & Z. Rubin (Eds.), Relationships and development (pp. 51–71). Hillsdale, NJ: Erlbaum.

Stansfield, S. A., & Marmot, M. G. (1992). Social class and minor psychiatric disorder in British civil servants: A validated screening survey using the General Health Questionnaire. Psychological Medicine, 22, 739–749.

Staub, E. (1974). Helping a distressed person: Social, personality, and stimulus determinants. In L. Berkowitz (Ed.), Advances in experimental social psychology, (Vol. 7, pp. 294–339). New York: Academic Press.

Steele, C. M. (1975). Name-calling and compliance. Journal of Personality and Social Psychology, 31, 361–369.

Steele, C. M. (1988). The psychology of self-affirmation: Sustaining the integrity of the self. In L. Berkowitz (Ed.), Advances in experimental social psychology (Vol. 21, pp. 261–302). New York: Academic Press.

Steele, C. M. (1997). A threat in the air: How stereotypes shape intellectual identity and performance. American Psychologist, 52, 613–629.

Steele, C. M., Spencer, S. J., & Lynch, M. (1993). Self-image resilience and dissonance: The role of affirmational resources. Journal of Personality and Social Psychology, 64, 885–896.

Stein, K. F., & Markus, H. R. (1994). The organization of the self: An alternative focus for psychopathology and behavior change. Journal of Psychotherapy Integration, 4, 317–353.

Stern, D. N. (1974). Mother and infant at play: The didactic interaction involving facial, vocal, and gaze behaviors. In M. Lewis & L. Rosenbaum (Eds.), The effect of the infant on its caregiver (pp. 187–231). New York. Wiley.

Stern, D. N. (1985). The interpersonal world of the infant: View from psychoanalysis and developmental psychology. New York. Basic Books.

Stern, D. N. (2004). The present moment in psychotherapy and everyday life. New York: Norton.

Stern, D. N., Sander, L. W., Nahum, J. P., Harrison, A. M., Lyons-Ruth, K., Morgan, A. C., . . . & Tronick, E. Z. (1998). Non-interpretive mechanisms in psychoanalytic therapy: The "something more" than interpretation. International Journal of Psycho-Analysis, 79, 903–921.

Stiles, W. B., Glick, M. J., Osatuke, K., Hardy, G. E., Shapiro, D. A., Agnew-Davies, R., . . . & Barkham, M. (2004). Patterns of alliance development and the rupture-repair hypothesis: Are productive relationships U-shaped or V-shaped? Journal of Counseling Psychology, 51, 81-91.

Stiles, W. B., Shapiro, D. A., & Elliott, R. (1986). Are all psychotherapies equivalent? American Psychologist, 41, 165–180.

Stockton, R. & Morran, D. K. (1981). Feedback exchange in personal growth groups: Receiver acceptance as a function of valence, session, and order of delivery. Journal of Counseling Psychology, 28, 490–497.

Strassberg, D. S. (1973). Relationships among locus of control, anxiety, and valued goal expectations. Journal of Consulting and Clinical Psychology, 2, 319.

Strkker, G., & Fisher, M. (1991). Self-disclosure in the therapeutic relationship. New York: Plenum.

Strong, S. R., & Claiborn, C. D. (1982). Change through interaction: Social psychological processes of counseling and psychotherapy. New York: Wiley.

Strong, S. R., Hills, H. I., Kilmartin, C. T., DeVries, H., Lanier, K., & Nelson, B. N. (1988). The dynamic relations among interpersonal behaviors: A test of complementarity and anticomplementarity. Journal of Personality and Social Psychology, 54, 798–810.

Strube, M. J., & Roemmle, L. A. (1985). Self-enhancement, self-assessment, and self-evaluative task choice. Journal of Personality and Social Psychology, 49, 981–993.

Strupp, H. H. (1993). The Vanderbilt Psychotherapy Studies: Synopsis. Journal of Consulting and Clinical Psychology, 61, 431–433.

Strupp, H. H., & Hadley, S. W. (1979). Specific vs. nonspecific factors in psychotherapy: A controlled study of outcome. Archives of General Psychiatry, 36, 1125–1136.

Suddarth, B. H., & Slaney, R. B. (2001). An investigation of the dimensions of perfectionism in college students. Measurement and Evaluation in Counseling and Development, 34, 157–165.

Sugden, R. (1985). Regret, recrimination, and rationality. Theory and Decision, 19, 77–99.

Sullivan, H. S. (1953). The interpersonal theory of psychiatry. New York: W. W. Norton.

Suls, J., & Wan, C. K. (1987). In search of the false uniqueness phenomenon: Fear and estimates of social consensus. Journal of Personality and Social Psychology, 52, 211–217.

Swann, W. B. (1983). Self-verification: Bringing social reality into harmony with the self. In J. Suls and A. G. Greenwald (Eds.), Psychological perspectives on the self (Vol. 2, pp. 33–66). Hillsdale, NJ: Erlbaum.

Swann, W. B. (1987). Identity negotiation: Where two roads meet. Journal of Personality and Social Psychology, 53, 1038–1051.

Swann, W. B., & Hill, C. A. (1982). When our identities are mistaken: Reaffirming self-conceptions through social interaction. Journal of Personality and Social Psychology, 43, 59–66.

Swann, W. B., & Predmore, S. C. (1985). Intimates as agents of social support: Sources of consolation or despair? Journal of Personality and Social Psychology, 49, 1609–1617.

Swann, W. B., & Read, S. J. (1981a). Self-verification processes: How we sustain our self-conceptions. Journal of Experimental Social Psychology, 17, 351–372.

Swann, W. B., & Read, S. J. (1981b). Acquiring self-knowledge: The search for feedback that fits. Journal of Personality and Social Psychology, 41, 1119–1128.

Swann, W. B., De La Ronde, C., & Hixon, J. G. (1994). Authenticity and positivity strivings in marriage and courtship. Journal of Personality and Social Psychology, 66, 857–869.

Swann, W. B., Wenzlaff, R. M., & Tafarodi, R. W. (1992). Depression and the search for negative evaluations: More evidence of the role of self-verification strivings. Journal of Abnormal Psychology, 101, 314–371.

Swann, W. B., Wenzlaff, R. M., Krull, D. S., & Pelham, B. W. (1992). Allure of negative feedback: Self-verification strivings among depressed persons. Journal of Abnormal Psychology, 101, 293–306.

Swann, W.B., & Ely, R.J. (1984). A battle of wills: Self-verification versus behavioral confirmation. Journal of Personality and Social Psychology, 46, 1287–1302.

Sweeney, P. D., & Wells, L. E. (1990). Reactions to feedback about performance: A test of three competing models. Journal of Applied Social Psychology, 20, 818–834.

Szasz, T. (2005). The History of psychotherapy. A topical panel discussion at the 2005 Evolution of Psychotherapy Conference, Anaheim, California (recording). Retrieved from http://www.ericksonfoundationstore.com.

Tajfel, H. (1982). Social psychology of intergroup relations. Annual Review of Psychology, 33, 1–39.

Tajfel, H., & Turner, J. C. (1986). The social identity theory of intergroup behavior. In S. Worchel & W. Austin (Eds.), Psychology of intergroup relations (pp. 7–24). Chicago: Nelson.

Tallman, K., & Bohart, A. (1999). The client as a common factor: Clients as self-healers. In M. Hubble, B. Duncan, & S. Miller (Eds.), The heart and soul of change: What works in therapy (pp. 91–131). Washington, DC: American Psychological Association.

Tannenbaum, P. H., Macauley, J. R., & Norris, E. L. (1966). Principle of congruity and reduction of persuasion. Journal of Personality and Social Psychology, 3, 233–238.

Tarlow, E. M., & Haaga, D. A. F. (1996). Negative self-concept: Specificity to depressive symptoms and relation to positive and negative affectivity. Journal of Research in Personality, 30, 120–127.

Taylor, S. E. (1998). The social being in social psychology. In D. Gilbert, S. Fiske, & G. Lindzey (Eds.), The handbook of social psychology (Vol. 2, 4th ed., pp. 58–95). New York: McGraw-Hill.

Taylor, S. E., & Brown, J. D. (1988). Illusion and well-being: A social psychological perspective on mental health. Psychological Bulletin, 103, 193–226.

Taylor, S. E., Falke, R. L., Shoptaw, S. J., & Lichtman, R. R. (1986). Social support, support groups, and the cancer patient. Journal of Consulting and Clinical Psychology, 54, 608–615.

Taylor, S. E., Welch, W., Kim, H. S., & Sherman, D. K. (2007). Cultural differences in the impact of social support on psychological and biological stress responses. Psychological Science, 18, 831–837.

Teevan, R. C., & McGhee, P. E. (1972). Childhood development of fear of failure motivation. Journal of Personality & Social Psychology, 21, 345–348.

Tennen, H., & Herzberger, S. (1987). Depression, self-esteem, and the absence of self-protective attributional biases. Journal of Personality and Social Psychology, 52, 72–80.

Tesser, A. (1988). Toward a self-evaluation maintenance model of social behavior. Advances in Experimental Social Psychology, 21, 181–227.

Tesser, A. (1991). Emotion in social comparison and reflection processes. In J. Suls & T. A. Wills (Eds.), Social comparison: Contemporary theory and research (pp. 117–148). Hillsdale, NJ: Erlbaum.

Tesser, A. (2000). On the confluence of self-esteem maintenance mechanisms. Personality and Social Psychology Review, 4, 290–299.

Tesser, A. (2001). Self-Esteem. In A. Tesser & N. Schwarz (Eds.), Blackwell handbook of social psychology: Intraindividual processes (pp. 479–498). Oxford, England: Blackwell.

Tesser, A., & Campbell, J. (1982). Self-evaluation maintenance and the perception of friends and strangers. Journal of Personality, 50, 261–279.

Tesser, A., & Cornell, D. P. (1991). On the confluence of self processes. Journal of Experimental Social Psychology, 27, 501–526.

Tesser, A., & Smith, J. (1980). Some effects of task relevance and friendship on helping: You don't always help the one you like. Journal of Experimental Social Psychology, 16, 582–590.

Tessler, R. C., & Schwartz, S. H. (1972). Help seeking, self-esteem, and achievement motivation: An attributional analysis. Journal of Personality and Social Psychology, 21, 318–326.

Teyber, E. (2000). Interpersonal process in psychotherapy: A relational approach (4th ed.). Stanford, CA: Thomson Learning.

Thoits, P. A. (1983). Multiple identities and psychological well-being: A reformulation and test of the social isolation hypothesis. American Sociological Review, 48, 174–187.

Thomas, E., Polansky, N., & Kounin, J. (1955). The expected behavior of a potentially helpful person. Human Relations, 8, 165–174.

Tice, D. M. (1991). Esteem protection or enhancement? Self-handicapping motives differ by trait self-esteem. Journal of Personality and Social Psychology, 60, 711–725.

Tice, D. M. (1992). Self-presentation and self-concept change: The looking glass self as magnifying glass. Journal of Personality and Social Psychology, 63, 435–451.

Tidwell, M. O., Reis, H. T., & Shaver, P. R. (1996). Attachment, attractiveness, and social interaction: A diary study. Journal of Personality and Social Psychology, 71, 729–745.

Tiedens, L. Z. (2001). Anger and advancement versus sadness and subjugation: The effect of negative emotion expressions on social status conferral. Journal of Personality and Social Psychology, 80, 86–94.

Tiedens, L. Z., & Fragale, A. R. (2003). Power moves: Complementarity in dominant and submissive nonverbal behavior. Journal of Personality and Social Psychology, 84, 558–568.

Tiedens, L. Z., Jimenez, M. C. (2003). Assimilation for affiliation and contrast for control: Complementary self-construals. Journal of Personality and Social Psychology, 85, 1049–1061.

Tolaas, J. (1991). Notes on the origin of some spatialization metaphors. Metaphor and Symbolic Activity, 6, 203–218.

Toner, I. J., Moore, L. P., & Emmons, B. A. (1980). The effect of being labeled on subsequent self-control in children. Child Development, 51, 618–621.

Tormala, Z. L., & Petty, R. E. (2002). What doesn't kill me makes me stronger: The effects of resisting persuasion on attitude certainty. Journal of Personality and Social Psychology, 83, 1298–1313.

Torrey, W. C., Mueser, K. T., McHugo, G. H., & Drake, R. E. (2000). Self-esteem as an outcome measure in studies of vocational rehabilitation for adults with severe mental illness. Psychiatric Services, 51, 229–233.

Tracey, T. J. (1986). Interactional correlates of premature termination. Journal of Consulting and Clinical Psychology, 54, 784–788.

Tracey, T. J. (1993). An interpersonal stage model of the therapeutic process. Journal of Counseling Psychology, 40, 396–409.

Tracey, T. J. (1994). An examination of the complementarity of interpersonal behavior. Journal of Personality and Social Psychology, 67, 864–878.

Tracey, T. J. (2002). Stages of counseling and therapy: An examination of complementarity and the working alliance. In G. S. Tryon (Ed.), Counseling based on process research: Applying what we know (pp. 265–297). Boston: Allyn & Bacon.

Tracey, T. J., Ryan, J. M., & Jaschik-Herman, B. (2001). Complementarity of interpersonal circumplex traits. Personality and Social Psychology Bulletin, 27, 786–797.

Tracey, T. J., Sherry, P., Albright, J. M. (1999). The interpersonal process of cognitive-behavioral therapy: An examination of complementarity over the course of treatment. Journal of Counseling Psychology, 46, 80–91.

Truax, C. B., & Carkhuff, R. R. (1965). Client and therapist transparency in the psychotherapeutic encounter. Journal of Counseling Psychology, 12, 3–10.

Truax, C. B., Tomlinson, T., & van der Veen, F. Symposium: a program in psychotherapy and psychotherapy research (Chair: C. R. Rogers), American Psychological Association, September, 1961. Cited in Truax, C. B., & Carkhuff, R. R. (1965). Client and therapist transparency in the psychotherapeutic encounter. Journal of Counseling Psychology, 12, 3–10.

Tversky, A., & Kahneman, D. (1974). Judgment under uncertainty: Heuristics and biases. Science, 185, 1124–1131.

Tyron, G. S., & Kane, A. S. (1990). The helping alliance and premature termination. Counseling Psychology Quarterly, 3, 233–238.

Tyron, G. S., & Kane, A. S. (1993). Relationship of working alliance to mutual and unilateral termination. Journal of Counseling Psychology, 40, 33–36.

Tyron, G. S., & Kane, A. S. (1995). Client involvement, working alliance and type of therapy termination. Psychotherapy Research, 5, 189–198.

Tyrrell, C. L., Dozier, M., Teauge, G. B., & Fallot, R. D. (1999). Effective treatment relationships for persons with serious psychiatric disorders: The importance of attachment states of mind. Journal of Clinical and Consulting Psychology, 67, 725–733.

Uchino, B. N., Cacioppo, J. T. & Kiecolt-Glaser, J. K. (1996). The relationship between social support and physiological processes: A review with emphasis on underlying mechanisms and implications for health. Psychological Bulletin, 119, 488–531.

Urry, H. L., Nitschke, J. B., Dolski, I., Jackson, D. C., Dalton, K. M., & Mueller, C. J. (2004). Making a life worth living: Neural correlates of well-being. Psychological Science, 15, 367–372.

Van Audenhove, C., & Vertommen, H. (2000). A negotiation approach to intake and treatment choice. Journal of Psychotherapy Integration, 10, 287–299.

van Ijzendoorn, M. H. (1995). Adult attachment representations, parental responsiveness, and infant attachment: A meta-analysis on the predictive validity of the adult attachment interview. Psychological Bulletin, 117, 387–403.

Veitch, R., & Griffitt, W. (1976). Good news, bad news: Affective and interpersonal effects. Journal of Applied Social Psychology, 6, 69–75.

Vinokur, A. D., & van Ryn, M. (1993). Social support and undermining in close relationships: Their independent effects on mental health of unemployed persons. Journal of Personality and Social Psychology, 65, 350–359.

Wallace, J. L., & Vaux, A. (1993). Social support network orientation: The role of adult attachment style. Journal of Social and Clinical Psychology, 12, 354–365.

Wampold, B. E. (1997). Methodological problems in identifying efficacious psychotherapies. Psychotherapy Research, 7, 21–44.

Wampold, B. E. (2001). The great psychotherapy debate: Models, methods, and findings. Mahwah, NJ: Erlbaum.

Wampold, B. E., Mondin, G. W., Moody, M., Stich, F., Benson, K., & Ahn, H. (1997). A meta-analysis of outcome studies comparing bona fide psychotherapies: Empirically "all must have prizes." Psychological Bulletin, 122, 203–215.

Warneken, F., & Tomasello, M. (2007). Helping and cooperation at 14 months of age. Infancy, 11, 271–294.

Warneken, F., Chen, F., & Tomasello, M. (2006). Cooperative activities in young children and chimpanzees. Child Development, 77, 640–663.

Watkins, C. E. (1990). The effects of counselor self-disclosure: A research review. The Counseling Psychologist, 18, 477–500.

Watson, D., & Clark, L. A. (1984). Negative affectivity: The disposition to experience aversive emotional states. Psychological Bulletin, 96, 465–490.

Watson, D., Suls, J., & Haig, J. (2002). Global self-esteem in relation to structural models of personality and affectivity. Journal of Personality and Social Psychology, 83, 185–197.

Wayment, H. A., & Vierthaler, J. (2002). Attachment style and bereavement reactions. Journal of Loss & Trauma, 7, 129–149.

Wegner, D. M. (1992). You can't always think what you want: Problems in the suppression of unwanted thoughts. In M. P. Zanna (Ed.), Advances in experimental social psychology (Vol. 25, pp. 193–225). San Diego, CA: Academic Press.

Wei, M., Heppner, P. P., & Mallinckrodt, B. (2003). Perceived c as a mediator between attachment and psychological distress: A structural equation modeling approach. Journal of Counseling Psychology, 50, 438–447.

Wei, M., Mallinckrodt, B., Larson, L. M., & Zakalik, R. A. (2005). Adult attachment, depressive symptoms, and validation from self versus others. Journal of Counseling Psychology, 52, 368–377.

Wei, M., Mallinckrodt, B., Russell, D. W., & Abraham, W. T. (2004). Maladaptive perfectionism as a mediator and moderator between adult attachment and depressive mood. Journal of Counseling Psychology, 51, 201–212.

Weinberger, J. (1995). Common factors aren't so common: The common factors dilemma. Clinical Psychology: Science and Practice, 2, 45–69.

Weinberger, J., & Eig, A. (1999). Expectancies: The ignored common factor in psychotherapy. In I. Kirsch (Ed.), How expectancies shape experience (pp. 357–382). Washington, DC: American Psychological Association.

Weiner, B., Graham, S., Peter, O., & Zmuidinas, M. (1991). Public confession and forgiveness. Journal of Personality, 59, 281–312.

Weisfeld, G. E., & Beresford, J. M. (1982). Erectness of posture as an indicator of dominance or success in humans. Motivation and Emotion, 6, 113–129.

Weisz, C., & Wood, L. F. (2005). Social identity support and friendship outcomes: A longitudinal study predicting who will be friends and best friends four years later. Journal of Social and Personal Relationships, 22, 416–432.

Werner-Wilson, R., Price, S., Zimmerman, T.S., & Murphy, M. (1997). Client gender as a process variable in marriage and family therapy: Are women clients interrupted more than men clients? Journal of Family Psychology, 11, 373–377.

Westmaas, J. L., & Silver, R. C. (2001). The role of attachment in responses to victims of life crises. Journal of Personality and Social Psychology, 80, 425–438.

Wheeler, L. (1966). Motivation as a determinant of upward comparison. Journal of Experimental Social Psychology,1, 27-31.

Wheeler, L., Reis, H. T., & Nezlek, J. (1983). Loneliness, social interaction, and sex roles. Journal of Personality and Social Psychology, 45, 943–953.

Whipple, J. L., Lambert, M. J., Vermeersch, D. A., Smart, D. W. Nielsen, S. L., & Hawkins, E. J. (2003). Improving the effects of psychotherapy: The use of early identification of treatment and problem-solving strategies in routine practice. Journal of Counseling Psychology, 50, 59–68.

Whitley, B. E., & Frieze, I. H. (1985). Children's causal attributions for success and failure in achievement settings: A meta-analysis. Journal of Educational Psychology, 77, 608–616.

Wicklund, R. A. (1982). How society uses self-awareness. In J. Suls (Ed.), Psychological perspectives on the self (Vol. 1, pp. 209–230). Hillsdale, NJ: Erlbaum.

Wiggins, J. S. (1982). Circumplex models of interpersonal behavior in clinical psychology. In P. C. Kendall & J. N. Butcher (Eds.), Handbook of research methods in clinical psychology (pp. 183–221). New York: Wiley.

Wilder, D. A., & Thompson, J. E. (1980). Intergroup contact with independent manipulations of in-group and out-group interaction. Journal of Personality and Social Psychology, 38, 589–603.

Wilkins, W. (1971). Desensitization: Social and cognitive factors underlying the effectiveness of Wolpe's procedure. Psychological Bulletin, 76, 311–317.

Wills, T. A. (1981). Downward comparison principles in social psychology. Psychological Bulletin, 90, 245–271.

Wills, T. A. (1985). Supportive functions of interpersonal relationships. In S. Cohen & S. L. Syme (Eds.), Social support and health (pp. 61–82). New York: Academic Press.

Wilson, T. D., Lindsey, S., & Schooler, T. Y. (2000). A model of dual attitudes. Psychological Review, 107, 101–126.

Wolfe, B. E. (2003). Knowing the self: Building a bridge from basic research to clinical practice. Journal of Psychotherapy Integration, 13, 83-95.

Wolfle, L. M., & List, J. H. (2004). Temporal stability in the effects of college attendance on locus of control. Structural Equation Modeling, 11, 244–260.

Wolk, S., & DuCette, J. (1974). Intentional performance and incidental learning as a function of personality and task dimensions. Journal of Personality and Social Psychology, 29, 91–101.

Wood, J. V. (1989). Theory and research concerning social comparisons of personal attributes. Psychological Bulletin, 106, 231–248.

Wood, J. V., Taylor, S. E., & Lichtman, R. R. (1985). Social comparison in adjustment to breast cancer. Journal of Personality and Social Psychology, 49, 1169–1183.

Worell, J. (2001). Feminist interventions: Accountability beyond symptom reduction. Psychology of Women Quarterly, 25, 335–343.

Wright, R. (2001). Self-certainty and self-esteem. In T. J. Owens, S. Stryker, & N. Goodman (Eds.), Extending self-esteem theory and research: Sociological and psychological currents. (pp. 101–134). New York: Cambridge University Press.

Wu, A. M. S., Tang, C. S. K., & Kwok, T. C. Y. (2004). Self-efficacy, health locus of control, and psychological distress in elderly Chinese women with chronic illness. Aging and Mental Health, 8, 21–28.

Yapko, M. D. (2003). Trancework: In Introduction to the Practice of Clinical Hypnosis. New York. Brunner-Routledge.

Zajonc, R. B. (1998). Emotions. In D. T. Gilbert, S. T. Fiske, & G. Lindzey (Eds.), The handbook of social psychology (Vol. 2, 4th ed., pp. 591–632). New York: McGraw-Hill.

Zajonc, R. B., Adelmann, P. K., Murphy, S. T., & Niedenthal, P. M. (1987). Convergence in the physical appearance of spouses. Motivation and Emotion, 11, 335–346.

Zeig, J. K. (1983). Ericksonian Psychotherapy: Structures. New York: Brunner Mazel.

Zeigler-Hill, V., & Terry, C. (2007). Perfectionism and explicit self-esteem: The moderating role of implicit self-esteem. Self and Identity, 6, 137–153.

Zuroff, D. C., & Fitzpatrick, D. K. (1995). Depressive personality styles: Implications for adult attachment. Personality and Individual Differences, 18, 253–265.

Index

Abandonment, 23, 103-104, 109-112, 116, 119, 131, 140, 185, 217, 228
Abortion, 220-221, 229
Abuse
  alcohol, 53n, 186,
  drug, 23
  emotional, 149, 151, 193, 228, 232n
  physical, 50-51, 186, 249,
  sexual, 20n, 53n, 74, 127, 156, 194, 228, 232n, 248, 292n
Achievement orientation, 58n, 255
AD/HD, 71-72
Addiction, 22-23, 28, 31, 46, 48n, 78, 229
Adler, Alfred, 4, 225
Affect attunement, 26, 65-67, 70-71, 74-77, 82-83, 204, 304, 306
Alexithymia, 66n
Alliance
  bonding, 66n, 97, 106, 114
  ruptures, 176, 177, 177n, 189n, 217n, 251n
Allport, Gordin, 273, 274n
Altruism, 2, 116, 199
Ambiguity, 134n
American Psychological Association, 178n
Anger, 21-22, 60, 67, 69, 70n, 71, 73-74, 76n, 78-79, 86, 99n, 107, 113, 114, 118-120, 127, 130, 154, 156, 158, 173, 177n, 181n, 216, 218, 259, 277, 306
Antony, Mark, 183
Anxiety, 32, 38-40, 50, 67, 81, 99n, 103-106, 107n, 108, 110-112, 113n,

116n, 118, 123, 124n, 128n, 130, 132, 139-140, 141n, 143-144, 155, 157-158, 193, 199-200, 225n, 229n, 237, 246, 260, 263n, 306, 312
Anxious attachment, 104-105, 108, 113-116, 127, 134n, 309
Assessment, 11-18, 28, 31, 43, 48, 158, 217, 228n, 252-253, 283, 304, 309
Assimilation effect, 159n, 270n, 271n
Attachment avoidance, 103, 118, 124n, 130, 143
Authority figures, 12, 39, 55, 76n, 77, 131, 171, 173, 186, 192-194, 265, 270, 289, 296, 298
Automatic processing, 278n
Autonomy, 103, 175, 207, 213n, 281-299, 311
Availability heuristic, 254n
Avoidant attachment, 118, 120n, 123, 127n, 143, 216

Bandura, Albert, 240n, 241, 242n, 250, 251n, 299n
Bateson, Gregory, 18
Becker, Ernest, 225
Berscheid, Ellen, 7, 15n, 66n, 99n, 175n, 203n, 255n
Bias, ix, 25n, 169, 228n, 250n, 269n
Blame, 15, 46n, 47, 48n, 56, 60, 112, 115, 125, 127, 132, 176, 181, 230
Bohr, Niels, 209
Borderline Personality Disorder, 127n, 190
Boundaries, 74, 90-91, 103, 106, 116-

117, 129, 140, 147, 154n, 159, 163, 178n, 193, 266, 277n
Bowlby, John, 97, 148

Cancer, 109n, 217, 248, 251, 268n, 269, 291, 293, 312
Causal attribution, 175n
Certainty-oriented, 45n, 160n
Caesar Augustus, 183
Childbirth, 135, 229, 252
Circumplex model, 24n, 26n
Client satisfaction, 18n, 28-29, 40, 57, 62, 70n, 176, 198, 309
Clinical judgment, 12n, 15n
Cognitive overload, 23n, 122n
Cognitive-behavioral, 3, 17n, 22n, 189
Collaborative approach, 3, 7, 11, 16, 44, 86, 88, 139, 198-200, 285, 302
Complementary interactions, 16-17
Compulsive behavior, 32, 106, 115
Compulsory clientele, 34
Confirmatory bias, 25n
Conflict avoidance, 124
Confrontation, 30, 59-62, 74, 107, 154, 165n, 181, 233, 251n
Confucius, 85
Conscious deliberation, 18n, 25, 278
Consent, 88-89, 200n, 263, 284
Cooperation, 86, 88, 141, 309
Core components of therapy, 8, 175, 206, 207n
Corrective emotional experience, 81n
Coudert, Jo, 281
Critical thinking, 121n

Darwin, Charles, 66n
Death, 58, 85n, 102n, 111, 116, 118, 120, 135, 180, 188, 222, 223n, 291, 294,
312n
Deductive reasoning, 12, 14
Delacroix, Eugène, 203n
Demand–withdraw pattern, 140n
Denial, 35, 47, 99, 117, 124n, 222, 231n
Dependency, 82, 104-105, 108, 110, 113, 131, 199n, 200, 283, 309
Depression, 48-49, 52-54, 99n, 104n, 107n, 108n, 111, 123, 192, 211, 219-220, 225n, 226n, 241n, 244, 249, 269, 277, 282n, 312
Diagnostic labeling, 12, 13, 127n, 129,
Directive therapies, 58
Disarming strategy, 187
Disclosure, 92, 216, 217n, 218, 224n, 257
Disidentification, 261, 275
Disintegration anxiety, 81
Divorce, 36, 48, 78, 97, 108, 116, 129, 167, 182, 228, 267, 282n
Dodo verdict, 5, 6n
Dominance, 24-26, 40, 147-169, 172-176, 180-189, 193, 196-198, 272, 311
    coercive, 39, 148n, 153-154, 157, 161, 163-164, 166-169, 172, 174, 184-185, 199
    posturing, 150, 158n
    prosocial, 153-154, 157-158, 166, 187, 311
    protherapeutic, 154, 157, 160
Double-bind, 233

Effortful cognitive processing, 23, 214, 218, 284, 288, 291
Ego-strengthening, 18
EMDR, 46
Emotional
    attachment, 97, 101, 129, 143-144

attunement, 222
bleed, 105
communication, 66, 73n, 304
contagion, 66n, 78n, 80n
energy, 37n, 48, 66, 74, 78
Empathy, 3, 73n, 121n, 126, 134, 140,
    156, 189n, 205n, 216n, 231, 241n,
    306
Enabling, 123, 132, 291
Enlightenment, xii
Environmental illness, 39
Equality, 4, 25, 86-87, 149
Erickson, Milton, 3, 32, 46-48, 52n,
    196n, 213, 234, 304n
Ethics, 70, 74, 175, 263
External validation, 4, 111, 140n, 165
Externalize the problem, 125, 283

False consensus effect, 211n
Family history, 129n
Fear of
    failure, 51-52, 257-258
    rejection54, 107, 128
    success, 52
Fearful attachment, 127-129
Feedback, 5n, 11, 12n, 19, 28, 38, 40-
    43, 59, 87-93n, 132n, 140n, 144,
    165n, 171, 176n, 195, 209n, 214,
    218-219, 229n, 231, 232n, 262,
    266, 275, 278n
Fiduciary relationship, 206n
Frankl, Viktor, 239
Freedom of will, 88
Freud, Sigmund, 2, 8, 31, 189, 197,
    209n
Gandhi, Mahatma, 152
Gastrointestinal distress, 38, 199,
    237
Generalization, 243, 273
Goal, 8, 39, 49, 97n, 115, 139n, 171,

175, 271, 302
attainment, 48n, 95n,
consensus, 48n, 82
directed, 59n, 204
setting, 49, 81, 289-290
God, 42, 63, 139, 223, 231n
Goodall, Jane, 147
Great Depression, 42

Haley, Jay, 183
Herod, 183
Hippocratic Oath, 175
Hostility, 14, 24, 73-78, 114, 156,
    230n, 231n
Humor, 75, 80, 113, 190, 200, 235
Hyper vigilance, 110
Hypothesis-testing, 58n

Idealized self, 30-32
Imagery, 222, 248, 265, 278-279
Immune system, 256n, 312
Implicit social support, 223
Incest, 53, 105
Indoctrination, 213
Inductive reasoning, 12, 14
Inferiority complex, 225
Inferiority, feelings of, 189, 265, 269
Insight, xii, 2, 5, 8, 12n, 23, 53, 78,
    93n, 148, 168, 218, 223, 244, 255,
    263, 271, 286, 288
Intake interview, 18n, 117, 156, 173,
    253, 284n, 286n
Interdependence, 90, 125, 199
Intimacy, 29, 64, 81, 92, 94, 95n, 108,
    109n, 114, 121, 124, 125, 128, 133n,
    149, 161n, 215, 257n
Introspection, 23, 136

James, William, 65, 77, 226, 264
Jealousy, 110

Jesus Christ, 31, 47, 63, 85, 180

King, Martin Luther, 37, 152
Kohut, Heinz, 81, 225

Learned helplessness, 244
Locus of control, 226n, 227, 281-283, 287, 293, 295n, 299n
Loneliness, 58, 92n, 99n, 104n, 110, 116, 119, 122, 124, 127, 145, 203, 204n, 210, 225n, 226n
Lorenz, Konrad, 179, 180
Love withdrawal, 106n

Manipulation, 19, 118, 214, 219
Marital infidelity, 109, 153n
Marriage counseling, 31, 261, 291
Matching hypothesis, 210n
Mental scaffolding, 288
Minimalization, 124n
Mortality, 35n, 312
Mother Teresa, 144
Motivation, 3, 25, 47-52, 55-62, 70n, 82, 193, 199, 207n, 213n, 215n, 216n, 240n, 241n, 256n, 261, 309
Motor mimicry, 82, 83n
Muhammad, 85

Narcissism, 230n, 285
Negative affect reciprocity, 74n
Negotiation, 17, 20, 26, 88n, 284n, 285
Neuroticism, 226n
Non-directive approach, 57, 186
Non-orthodox, 5

Obsessive-compulsive, 32
Oppositional Defiant Disorder, 12

Pain relief, 22-23, 45-46, 50, 56, 86n, 104-105, 109, 114, 118-119, 122, 127 -128, 135, 162, 179n, 230, 245, 247, 254, 277
Panic, 31, 39, 48, 54, 157, 246, 248-249, 252
Panic attack, 39, 252
Paradigm of change, 44-47
Paranoia, 99n
Peck, Scott, 26
Perfectionism, 106-107
Perls, Fritz, 8
Persuasion, 22, 160n, 170, 171n, 172n, 185n, 227n, 236, 278, 289n
Pfaff's theory, 86n
Placebo effect, 53n
Positive feedback, 42-43, 92n, 229n, 231-232, 232n
Positive reciprocal interaction spiral, 81, 89
Positive reinforcement, 52
Positive treatment outcomes, 3n, 44n
Postural expansion, 150n
Preconscious knowledge, 12n
Prefrontal cortex, 154n
Premature termination, 19n, 99
Problem identification, 81, 289-290
Problem solving, 57n, 116-117, 134n, 143, 162, 166, 176n, 191, 207, 209, 218-219, 223, 252, 282, 283, 286n, 187, 291-293, 299, 309
Productivity, 17n
Prognosis, 129n
Projection, 99, 121n, 125, 230
Promotion motivation, 56n
Psychoanalysis, x, 47, 271n
Psychotic symptoms, 31, 45-46, 98, 111, 247, 276
Psychotropic medication, 101, 296

Rationalization, 261-262

Reflexive awareness, 19n

Relational model, 17n, 19, 26n, 87, 213n

Relational schema, 21-23

Resentment, 61, 99n, 107, 114n, 127, 193, 200

Resilience, 102n, 139n, 312

Right hemisphere processing, 181n

Risk avoidance, 262

Rogers, Carl, 2-3, 6, 192, 197, 2, 205n, 227n, 287

Role-play, 5, 192, 248, 251n, 252

Rosenzweig, Saul, 5, 212

Rotter, Julian, 282n

Rumination, 36n, 105, 294

Safe haven, 31, 97-98, 142, 223

Schizophrenia, 32

Secure attachment, 98-99, 114, 132-136, 140-141, 144, 309

Secure relationships, 97, 312

Security priming, 138n

Self-care, 58

Self-confirming feedback, 41n

Self-defamation, 260-261

Self-determination, 185, 212-213, 237, 289, 302

Self-determination theory, 213n

Self-disclosure, 24, 29, 53, 55, 92-95, 99, 122-125, 130n, 212n, 223, 309

Self-efficacy, 139n, 226n, 227, 240n, 241-242, 245, 250, 251n, 258, 282n

Self-enhancement, 270n, 274

Self-esteem, 40-43, 53, 56-57, 62n, 91, 99n, 104n, 106n, 113, 120, 139n, 144n, 190, 203, 214, 225-238, 240-242, 251, 258-263, 268, 270, 278, 282n, 295

Self-fulfilling prophecy, 299

Self-governance, 218, 221, 255, 289

Self-handicapping, 258-262

Self-monitoring, 45, 228, 251

Self-mutilation, 53n, 142

Self-referential processing, 215, 228

Self-reinforcement, 120

Self-reinforcing feedback loop, 132n, 140n

Self-verification, 19n

Separation anxiety, 110

Sex, 29, 90, 108-109, 112, 115, 134n, 138n, 220, 266

Shame, 22, 52, 74, 90, 99n, 105, 109-110, 216, 230, 236, 249, 253, 265, 267

Short, Trevor, 245

Similarity-attraction hypothesis, 29

Social

    attraction, 29

    comparison, 269

    environment, 15-16, 41, 175

    hierarchies, 66n, 147

    support, 67n, 74n, 97n, 99n, 100, 102n, 140, 204n, 210n, 214, 223, 256, 287n, 312n

Somatic symptoms, 38, 88n

Somatization, 38n

Stereotyping, 12

Stress, x, 1, 38, 48, 50, 97, 99n, 102, 119-122, 225n, 236, 294

Subjective

    desires, 48

    reaction, 70

    reality, 38, 302

Submission, 25, 148-153, 159, 180-184, 187-188, 193, 194-197, 272, 311

Suicidal ideation, 61-62, 178, 220

Suicide, 17, 107, 217, 277n, 282n

Sullivan, Harry Stack, 271
Support
    emotional, 97n, 126n, 191, 206
    informational, 206,
    instrumental, 206n
Suppression, 99, 119, 122, 123n, 216
Symmetrical interactions, 16,

Tailored relationship, 3, 7, 11n, 22, 44, 93, 95, 100, 204, 237
Tao Te Ching, xii, 197
Testosterone, 153, 193n
Theoretical models, 99n
Therapeutic alliance, 2n, 3n, 11n, 19, 25, 34, 39, 44n, 68n, 99, 139, 152, 175, 177n, 212n, 271, 277
Therapeutic goals, 139, 204
Touch, 2, 6, 72, 102, 105
Tracking, 81, 297
Transference, 2, 128n, 186n, 189, 195n, 271n, 272
Transformational
    experiences, 209
    insights xii
    moment, 106, 142
    process, 2
    reasoning, 15
    relationship, x, 1, 8, 10, 74, 91, 129, 136, 152, 175, 198, 204, 206n, 207, 209-210, 242, 264, 281-282, 295, 299, 302, 309, 311
Transparency, 93n, 94, 231
Trauma, xi, 243, 312
Treatment manual, 48, 205, 284
Trust, 3n, 19, 22, 35, 36, 39-41, 45, 47, 52, 59-62, 71, 77, 92, 94, 97n, 102n, 103n, 110, 116, 156, 161, 169, 206n, 207, 218-219, 241n, 251, 262, 279, 285, 306
Tunnel vision, 4

Uncertainty-oriented, 45n
Unconscious, 3n, 13, 19, 75, 127, 138n, 174
Unilateral approach, 3n, 87-88, 149
Utilization, 62, 213, 299, 304n

Victimization, 131, 183
Virgin Mary, 138-139
Vulnerability, 21, 29, 114, 123, 125n, 128, 188-189, 206n, 245

Wisdom, xii, 19, 85, 141